Samuel Robinson Clarke

The magistrates' manual

Being annotations of the various acts relating to the rights, powers and duties of justices of the peace

Samuel Robinson Clarke

The magistrates' manual
Being annotations of the various acts relating to the rights, powers and duties of justices of the peace

ISBN/EAN: 9783337223595

Printed in Europe, USA, Canada, Australia, Japan

Cover: Foto ©Suzi / pixelio.de

More available books at **www.hansebooks.com**

THE

MAGISTRATES' MANUAL:

BEING

ANNOTATIONS OF THE VARIOUS ACTS RELATING TO THE RIGHTS, POWERS, AND DUTIES OF JUSTICES OF THE PEACE;

WITH A

SUMMARY OF THE CRIMINAL LAW.

BY

S. R. CLARKE,

OF OSGOODE HALL, BARRISTER-AT-LAW;

AUTHOR OF "THE CRIMINAL LAW OF CANADA," "THE INSOLVENT ACT OF 1875 AND AMENDING ACTS," ETC.

Labor omnia vincit.

TORONTO:

HART & RAWLINSON, 5 KING-STREET WEST.

1878.

PRINTED BY
HUNTER, ROSE & Co.,
TORONTO.

PREFACE.

No previous writer on magisterial law has cited the cases decided in Canada, either as to the practice or the law with which the magistracy have to deal. Besides, the ever active legislators have wrought considerable alteration in the statute law since the last publication on the subject.

The within work cites all the cases which have been decided in Canada, in any way relating to the rights, powers, and duties of Justices of the Peace. So far as applicable, the English cases, down to the first day of January, 1878, have also been given. Several Canadian cases, in advance of the regular reports, have been kindly furnished me by H. C. W. Wethey, Esquire, reporter to the Court of Queen's Bench in Ontario. My thanks are also due to Mr. Wethey for the care and labour bestowed on the preparation of the table of cases.

It is hoped that this work will meet with the approval of those for whom it has been written. No pains have been spared in its preparation, and the requirements of the magistracy have been kept constantly in view.

It has been my aim to make the work concise and to compress it within moderate compass. I have not thought it necessary to print the statute law in full, assuming that the magistrates are already supplied with the Acts relating to criminal law. But I have referred to the statutes so as to indicate the nature of their provisions, and have noted all the amending and repealing statutes.

It must be remembered that the work does not embrace the local laws of any Province, but only the laws of Canada.

The elaborate works on the same subject in England contain much that is wholly inapplicable in Canada. In reference to Canadian law, it is believed that this work deals with every matter of importance contained in the English works, whilst its moderate size will render the different subjects of easy reference. In the summary of the criminal law, the various offences have been alphabetically arranged, and the latest cases in England and Canada, more particularly such as elucidate any principle or are of general application, have been cited.

Should the work supply the want which I have reason to believe has been long felt by the magistracy, my aim and ambition will be abundantly satisfied.

S. R. C.

TORONTO,
22nd January, 1878.

TABLE OF CONTENTS.

TABLE OF ABBREVIATIONS.

Allen.	Allen's Reports, New Brunswick.
Berton	Berton's Reports, New Brunswick.
C. L. J. N. S.	Canada Law Journal, new series.
Cochran	Cochran's Reports, Nova Scotia.
C.P. (Ont.)............	Common Pleas Reports, Ontario.
Draper	Draper's Reports, Ontario.
Hannay	Hannay's Reports, New Brunswick.
James..................	James' Reports, Nova Scotia.
Kerr	Kerr's Reports, New Brunswick.
L. C. G....................	Local Courts Gazette, Ontario.
L. C. J.	Lower Canada Jurist.
L. C. L. J...............	Lower Canada Law Journal.
L. C. R..................	Lower Canada Reports.
Oldright................	Oldright's Reports, Nova Scotia.
O. S......................	Upper Canada Queen's Bench Reports, old series.
P. R. (Ont.)	Upper Canada Practice Reports.
Pugsley	Pugsley's Reports, New Brunswick.
Q. B. (Ont.)	Queen's Bench Reports, Ontario.
R. & J., Dig.............	Robinson & Joseph's Digest Reports, Ontario.
Russell & Chesley.........	Russell & Chesley's Reports, Nova Scotia.
Stephen's Dig..........	Stephen's Digest, New Brunswick Reports.
Stuart....................	Stuart's Reports, Quebec.
Stuart's V. A. Reps......	Stuart's Vice-Admiralty Reports, Quebec.
Taylor	Taylor's Reports, Ontario.
Thomson................	Thomson's Reports, Nova Scotia.
U. C. L. J.............	Upper Canada Law Journal.

TABLE OF CASES CITED.

MAGISTRATES' MANUAL.

INTRODUCTORY CHAPTER.

JUSTICES of the Peace may be divided into two classes, namely, those appointed by Commission, and those who are such for the time being merely by virtue of holding some other office. Thus, in Ontario, the head of every council, the police magistrate of every city and town, and the reeve of every town, township, and incorporated village, shall, *ex officio*, be Justices of the Peace for the whole county or union of counties in which their respective municipalities lie; and aldermen in cities shall be Justices of the Peace for such cities. Rev. Stat. (Ont.), chaps. 72, s. 4, and 174, s. 395; see also *R.* v. *Mosier*, 4 P.R. (Ont.) 64.

Every police magistrate shall also be *ex officio* a Justice of the Peace for the city or town for which he holds office. *Ib.* chap. 72, s. 4.

The power, office, and duty of a Justice of the Peace depend on his Commission, and on the several statutes which have created objects of his jurisdiction. His Commission first empowers him simply to conserve the peace, and thereby gives him all the power of ancient conservators at the common law in suppressing riots and affrays, in taking securities for the peace, to commit felons and other inferior criminals. It also empowers any two or more of them to hear and determine felonies and misdemeanors, which is the ground of their jurisdiction at sessions. When a statute enables two Justices to do an act, the Justices sitting in quarter sessions may do the same act; for they are not the less Justices of the Peace because they are sitting in court in that capacity. *Fraser* v. *Dickson*, 5 Q B. (Ont.), 233.

The mere appointment as Justice will not authorize the person appointed to act, until he has duly qualified. But if any person act as a Justice of the Peace without being qualified, his acts are not invalid; his name being in the Commission, and he being therefore a Justice of the Peace (*Margate, P.* v. *Hannan*, 3 B. & A., 266); but he is liable to a penalty of one hundred dollars. Rev. Stat. (Ont.), chap. 71, s. 12.

Under the Con. Stat. Can., chap. 100, s. 3; Rev. Stat. (Ont.), chap. 71, s. 7, a Justice must have an interest in land in his actual possession to the value of $1,200. But this statute does not require him to have a legal estate in the property; it is sufficient if the land, though mortgaged in fee, exceeds by $1,200 the amount of the mortgage money. *Fraser* q.t., v. *McKenzie*, 28 Q. B. (Ont.), 255.

The object of the statute, as to the qualification of Justices of the Peace, was twofold: first, that the Justices should be of the most sufficient persons; secondly, that they should be worth in unencumbered real estate to the value of $1,200, at least, to satisfy any one who should be wronged by their proceedings. In an action against defendant for acting as a Justice of the Peace without sufficient property qualification, where the evidence offered by the plaintiff as to the value of the land and premises on which defendant qualified, was vague, speculative, and inconclusive, one of the witnesses, in fact, having afterwards recalled his testimony as to the value of a portion of the premises, and placed a higher estimate upon it; while the evidence tendered by the defendant was positive, and based upon tangible data, it was held that the jury were rightly directed, "that they ought to be fully satisfied as to the value of the defendant's property before finding for the plaintiff, that they should not weigh the matter in scales too nicely balanced, and that any reasonable doubt should be in favour of the defendant." *Squier*, q.t. v. *Wilson*, 15 C. P. (Ont.), 284; 1 U. C. L. J., N.S., 152.

Prior to the passing of the 29 Vic. chap. 12, the oath of qualification by a Justice of the Peace had to be taken before some Justice of the Peace of the county for which he intended to act. It could not be administered by the Clerk of the Peace for such county under the Writ of *Dedimus Potestatem*, issued with the

Commission of the Peace. *Herbert*, q.t. v. *Dowswell*, 24 Q.B. (Ont.), 427.

The 29 Vic. chap. 12, recites that certain Justices had theretofore, in error, taken and subscribed the oath of qualification before a Clerk of the Peace of the district or county, or before a Commissioner authorized, by *Dedimus Potestatem*, to administer oaths and declarations, and it confirms such oaths so taken, and indemnifies the Justice from all penalties and forfeitures in respect thereof. The Act also prescribes before whom oaths shall hereafter be taken.

The oath of qualification is as follows:—

"I, A.B., do swear that I, truly and *bona fide*, have to and for my own proper use and benefit, such an estate as qualifies me to act as a Justice of the Peace for the county (*or as the case may be*) of , according to the true intent and meaning of the Act respecting the qualification and appointment of Justices of the Peace to wit (*nature of such estate, whether land, and if land designating*), and that the same is lying and being (*or* issuing out of lands, tenements, and hereditaments situate), within the Township (*or* in the several Townships, *or as the case may be*) of . So help me God."

A certificate of such oath is then to be deposited in the office of the Clerk of the Peace for the County. Rev. Stat. (Ont.), chap. 71, s. 9.

A certificate purporting to be under the hand and seal of the Clerk of the Peace, that he did not find in his office any qualification filed by the Magistrate, is not sufficient evidence that the Magistrate is not properly qualified to take a recognizance. *R.* v. *White*, 21 C. P. (Ont.) 354.

A person assuming to act as a Justice of the Peace, not under any commission as a Justice, but as an Alderman of a city, is not as such Alderman legally qualified to act as a Justice until he has taken the oath of qualification required by the Municipal Acts Rev. Stat. (Ont.) chap. 174 (*R.* v. *Boyle*, 4 C. L. J., N. S. 256; 4 P. R. (Ont.) 256).

But having taken such oath he is not required to have any additional property qualification or to take any further oath to enable him to act as a Justice of the Peace. Rev. Stat. (Ont.) chap. 174, s. 397. As to the qualification of Mayors, Reeves, Aldermen, &c., see Rev. Stat. (Ont.) chap. 174, s. 70.

No Attorney or Solicitor in any Court whatever shall be a Justice of the Peace during the time he continues to practise as an Attorney and Solicitor. Rev. Stat. (Ont.) chap. 71, s. 5. No person having, using or exercising the office of Sheriff or Coroner, shall be competent or qualified to be a Justice of the Peace. *Ib.* s. 6.

The Statute 1st Mary, sess. 2, chap. 8, s. 2, which provides that no person exercising the office of Sheriff of any county shall use or exercise the office of Justice of the Peace by force of any commission or otherwise in any county where he shall be Sheriff, during the time of his exercising the office of Sheriff, has not been affected by any subsequent addition to the duties of Justices of the Peace, and continues to disqualify a Justice from acting as such while he holds the office of Sheriff. *Ex parte Colville*, L. R. 1 Q. B. D. 133.

The acts of a Justice of the Peace are either *ministerial* or *judicial*. He acts ministerially in preserving the peace, receiving complaints against persons charged with indictable offences, issuing summonses or warrants thereon, examining the informant and his witnesses, binding over the parties to prosecute and give evidence, bailing the supposed offender, or committing him for trial. He acts judicially in all cases of summary jurisdiction. His conviction, drawn up in due form and unappealed against, is conclusive, and cannot be disputed by action, though if he act illegally, maliciously or corruptly, he is punishable by information or indictment as we shall hereafter see.

All offences cognizable by a Justice of the Peace, are divided into two general classes, namely, firstly, those which the law requires to be sent to a *higher tribunal* for trial, wherein he acts *ministerially*, and secondly, those over which the Justice has summary jurisdiction, wherein he acts *judicially*. (MacNabb, 4, 5.)

It is necessary that the number of Justices required by the Act or law on which the information or complaint is framed, should hear and decide the case, but in the absence of any provision in the Act or law on which the proceedings are founded, requiring two or more Justices, then one Justice may hear, try, and determine the case. 32 & 33 Vic., chap. 31, ss. 27 & 28.

In the case of a person charged with felony one Justice cannot admit to bail. 32 & 33 Vic., chap. 30, s. 52.

Under the Commission of the Peace, Justices have a general power for conservation of the peace and the apprehension and commitment of felons. The commission gives them jurisdiction in all indictable offences to discharge, admit to bail, or commit for trial. *Connors* v. *Darling*, 23 Q. B. (Ont.) 543.

The maxim *omnia præsumuntur rite esse actu* does not apply to give jurisdiction to Justices or other inferior tribunals. *R.* v. *Atkinson*, 17 C. P. (Ont.) 302. On this principle in a prosecution for a penalty under a by-law of a corporation, the by-law must be proved, for it must appear on the face of the proceeding that there is jurisdiction. *R.* v. *Wartman*, 4 Allen, 73 ; *R.* v. *All Saints*, 7 B. & C. 785.

Before proceeding in any matter the Justice should consider 1st, whether he has jurisdiction—this is given by his commission, or by the particular statute under which the proceedings are taken ; 2nd, If more than one, or any particular description of Justice is required. In indictable cases one Justice may do everything required to be done out of sessions, except admit to bail. (See section 52 of 32 & 33 Vic., chap. 30.) In summary proceedings one Justice may receive the information and issue the summons, or warrant and process for enforcing judgment, even when the statute requires the case to be heard by more than one Justice. (32 & 33, Vic., chap. 31, s. 85.) 3rd, Whether a time is limited for any of the proceedings. In indictable cases, with very few exceptions, there is none. In summary cases the information must be laid within three months (See 32 & 33 Vic., chap. 31, s. 26.)

In general the authority of Justices is limited to the district for which they are appointed, and they can only exercise their powers while they are themselves within that district, for their authority is local rather than personal, but it seems that acts purely ministerial, such as receiving informations, taking recognizances, &c., may be done elsewhere, though anything founding proceedings of a penal nature, and any coercive or judicial act is utterly void unless done within the district. Dalton, c. 25; see *New-hold* v. *Coltman*, 6 Exch. 189.

A Justice's jurisdiction is limited to the county or place for which he is appointed, and to give him jurisdiction the offence must be committed in that county or place, and the offender must reside there, or if not so committed the offender must reside or be in such county or place. (32 & 33 Vic., chap. 30, s. 1; *Ib.*, chap. 31, s. 1.

The Imperial Statute (28 Geo. 3, chap. 49, s. 4) enabling Justices of the Peace for counties at large to act as such within any city being a county of itself, situate therein or adjoining such county, is local in its character and is not in force in this Province. Therefore, in the case of a felony committed in a county, Justices of the Peace of that county have no jurisdiction to administer oaths or examine witnesses in a city within the county in relation to that felony so committed outside of the city limits. *R.* v. *Row*, 14 C. P. (Ont.) 307. See also *Hunt* v. *McArthur*, 24 Q. B. (Ont.), 254.

By the 32 & 33 Vic., chap. 29, s. 8, where a felony or misdemeanor is committed on the boundary of two or more districts, counties or places, or within the distance of one mile of any such boundary, or in any place with respect to which it may be uncertain within which of two or more districts, counties or places it is situate, or when any felony or misdemeanor is begun in one district, county or place, and completed in another, every such felony or misdemeanor may be dealt with, inquired of, tried, determined and punished in any one of the said districts, counties or places, in the same manner as if it had been actually and wholly committed therein. By section 9, when any felony or misdemeanor is committed on any person, or on or in respect of any property in or upon any coach, waggon, cart, or other carriage whatever, employed in any journey, or is committed on any person, or on or in respect of any property on board any vessel, boat or raft whatever, employed in any voyage or journey upon any navigable river, canal, or inland navigation, such felony or misdemeanor may be dealt with, inquired of, tried, determined, and punished in any district, county, or place, through any part whereof such coach, waggon, cart, carriage or raft passed in the course of the journey or voyage during which such felony or misdemeanor was committed, in the same manner as if it had been actually committed in such district, county or place.

And by section 10, in all cases where the side, centre, bank, or other part of any highway, or of any river, canal, or navigation, constitutes the boundary of any two districts, counties, or places, any felony or misdemeanor mentioned in the two last preceding sections may be dealt with, inquired of, tried, determined, and punished in either of such districts, counties, or places through or adjoining to or by the boundary of any part whereof such coach, waggon, cart, carriage, or vessel, boat, or raft, passed in the course of the journey or voyage during which such felony or misdemeanor was committed, in the same manner as if it had been actually committed in such district, county, or place.

Where any felony has been wholly committed within Canada, the offence of any person who is an accessory either before or after the fact to such felony, may be dealt with by any court which has jurisdiction to try the principal felony, or any felonies committed in any place in which the act, by reason whereof such person shall have become such accessory, has been committed; and in every other case the offence of any person who is an accessory, either before or after the fact, to any felony, may be dealt with by any court which has jurisdiction to try the principal felony, or any felonies committed in any place in which such person is apprehended or is in custody. 31 Vic., chap. 72, s. 8. The 32 & 33 Vic, chap. 17, s. 2, repealed so much of the above section as related to felonies not wholly committed in Canada, and to persons accessories to such felonies.

Under the 32 & 33 Vic., chap. 21, s. 121, persons having in their possession in any part of Canada, property stolen in another part, may be tried and dealt with where they have the property; and under s. 112, where a party has in his possession in Canada, property stolen in any other country, he may be tried and dealt with where he has the property. See *R.* v. *Hennessy*, 35 Q.B. (Ont.), 603; see also ss. 66, 72, 105, and 106 of the 32 & 33 Vic., chap. 21.

It is to be observed, also, that under sections 24 and 46 of the 32 & 33 Vic. chap. 30, a Justice has power to hear the case and discharge, commit, or admit to bail in cases where the offence is not committed in his jurisdiction, but the accused is within such jurisdiction. There is no doubt that a statute may empower a Justice to act beyond the limits of his jurisdiction as assigned by his commission. Thus under section 6 of the 31 Vic., chap. 15, to prevent the unlawful training of persons to the use of arms, all Justices of the Peace for any district, county, or place in Canada, have concurrent jurisdiction as Justices of the Peace with the Justices of any other district, county, or place, in all cases as to carrying into execution the provisions of the Act as fully and effectually as if each of such Justices was in the Commission of the Peace for such other district, county, or place.

The Act 32 & 33 Vic., chap. 20, s. 9, provides where a person feloniously stricken, poisoned, or hurt, upon the sea, or any place out of Canada, dies in Canada, or being hurt in Canada dies upon the sea, or at any place out of Canada, the offence may be dealt with in the district, county, or place in Canada in which such death, stroke, poisoning, or hurt happens, in the same manner in all respects as if the offence had been wholly committed in that district, county, or place.

As to the venue in cases of coinage offences, see 32 & 33 Vic., chap. 18, s. 29.

In forgery, the offender, whether principal or accessory, may be tried in the county or place where he is apprehended or is in custody. 32 & 33 Vic., chap. 19, s. 48. In the cases, also, of bigamy and perjury, the offender may be tried and punished in the county or place where he is apprehended or is in custody. 32 & 33 Vic., chap. 20, s. 58; 32 & 33 Vic., chap. 23, s. 8; 33 Vic., chap. 26, s. 3. As to kidnapping, see 32 & 33 Vic. chap. 20, s. 71.

See section 4 of the 31 Vic., chap. 14, as to the venue under the Act to protect the inhabitants of Canada against lawless aggressions. See section 83 of the 31 Vic., chap. 10, as to the venue in the case of offences against the Act for the regulation of the postal service. See section 100 of the 40 Vic., chap. 10, as to customs offences.

It is to be observed that under the Interpretation Act, 31 Vic., chap. 1, s. 7, twenty-fifthly, if anything is directed to be done by or before a magistrate or a Justice of the Peace, or other public functionary or officer, it shall be done by or before one whose jurisdiction or powers extend to the place where such thing is to be done.

As the words, " dealt with, inquired of, tried, determined, and punished," frequently occur in the statutes, it may be observed that the words, " dealt with," apply to justices of the peace ; "inquired of," to the Grand Jury ; " tried," to the Petty Jury ; and " determined and punished," to the Court. *R.* v. *Ruck*, 1 Russell, 757, note *y*.

In all cases the first official step to be taken by the Justice is to receive an information or complaint in writing and upon oath generally, from a credible person, that an offence has been committed within his jurisdiction, such information or complaint stating as near as may be, the *name of the offender* (if known), the *nature of the offence,* the *person against whom*, and the *time when*, and the *place where* the said offence was perpetrated.

Although the statutory form of information given by the 32 & 33 Vic., chap. 30, schedule A, does not contain a prayer for the issue of a summons or warrant, it is usual after the statement of the offence to add, " and the said informant prays that a warrant may issue to apprehend the said A. B., and to cause him to be brought before the said Justice, or such other Justice as may then be there ; or that a summons may issue requiring the said A.B. to appear before the said Justice, or such other Justice as may then be there, that justice may be done in the premises."

Upon receiving this information, the Justice should refer to the statute or by-law creating the offence, as to the mode of procedure ; and if it is one over which he has summary jurisdiction, whether the complaint is made within the time prescribed by such statute or by-law ; and if no time is limited, must be guided by the 32 & 33 Vic., chap. 31, s. 26, which directs that the prosecution of offences shall be commenced *within three months* after the *commission* of the offence.

It is recommended that the Justice should on all occasions, when taking informations, carefully read over and explain them to the informants, so as to satisfy himself that they are perfectly understood; because it not unfrequently happens that ignorant persons undesignedly mis-state and confuse the facts, so as to mis-lead the Justice, and cause the information to be incorrectly prepared.

If it appear to the Justice, that the offence was committed within his jurisdiction, or that the person charged is within such jurisdiction, and that the application is made in due time, he should at once issue his summons or warrant to bring the accused before him, describing the offence in such summons or warrant, from the information or complaint sworn to. If a summons be issued, reasonable time should be given the defendant to appear; if a warrant be issued, it must be executed forthwith. A summons should be issued in all cases over which the law gives a Justice summary jurisdiction, in the first place, unless some good and sufficient reason should exist for issuing a warrant. In all cases of felony and in most indictable misdemeanors, a warrant, and not a summons, should be granted in the first instance. Warrants for felony, or breach of the peace, and search warrants, may be granted and executed on Sunday, or any other day or night. 32 & 33 Vic. chap. 30, s. 8.

We will now suppose the complainant and defendant to be in attendance with their witnesses on the day when, and at the place where, it was appointed to hold the Court. If the offence complained of be one over which the Justice or Justices has or have summary jurisdiction, the Court is an open one, to which the public have the right of access. 32 & 33 Vic., chap. 31, s. 29.

The Court having been opened by the constable announcing such opening, and calling for order, the names of the parties should then be called, and the information or complaint read to the accused by the Justice, and in cases of summary jurisdiction, the question asked, if he admit the truth of the complaint, or, if he have any cause to shew why he should not be convicted, or why an order should not be made against him, *as the case may be.* 32 & 33 Vic. chap. 31, s. 37.

If he voluntarily admit it, and offer no defence, the Court has only to consider the amount of punishment to be inflicted. *Ib.* s. 38. As to cases arising under the Act respecting the prompt and summary administration of criminal justice in certain cases, see 32 & 33 Vic., chap. 32, ss. 3 & 4.

It is always desirable to take the defendant's admission in writing, and signed by him if he will. If the offence be not admitted, the Justice must proceed to take the evidence of the complainant and his witnesses, and afterwards that of the witnesses for the defendant. In cases of indictable offences there is no right to examine witnesses for the accused, though the statement of the accused himself is taken. See 32 & 33 Vic., chap. 30, s. 31. In the case of summary convictions the defendant has a right to give evidence both of himself and witnesses. 32 & 33 Vic., chap. 31, s. 39.

The evidence should be taken down in writing, (see *R.* v. *Flannigan* 32 Q. B. (Ont.) 593, 599,) as near as may be in the words of the witnesses; the evidence of each to be signed by him, as also by the Justice or presiding Justice. Before the witness signs the evidence he has given, it should be read over to him, to ascertain whether it has been correctly taken down, or that his right meaning has been expressed: any mistake should be corrected before he signs it. If the Justice should see any good cause for so doing, he may adjourn the hearing of the case to some future day, and in the meantime commit the defendant to the common gaol, or may discharge him, upon his entering into a recognizance, with or without sureties, for his appearance at the time appointed. 32 & 33 Vic., chap. 31, ss. 22 & 46. Persons charged with indictable offences may be remanded by warrant from time to time for any period not exceeding eight days at any one time, or may be verbally remanded for any time not exceeding three clear days. 32 & 33 Vic., chap. 30, ss. 41 & 42.

In many cases, particularly in indictable offences, it is desirable for the Justice to order the witnesses on both sides to leave the Court; but it is important to observe, that if any witness should remain in Court, notwithstanding any such order, his evidence cannot be safely refused.

In the case of indictable offences after the first examination of witnesses, they may be cross-examined by the prisoner; and when their evidence is completed, their depositions are to be read by the Justice to the accused: and then any statement he may make, after being duly cautioned, as directed in the 32 & 33 Vic., chap. 30. ss. 31 & 32. is to be taken down in writing as nearly as possible in his own words, signed by him, if he will, as well as by the acting Justice or Justices.

The Justice or Justices having heard the evidence on both sides, the first question to determine is, whether the charge is sustained by the evidence; or, in indictable offences, although the offence may not be clearly proved, whether there is sufficient doubt to send the case to another tribunal; or the case may be adjourned for further hearing. If the case can be disposed of summarily, the Justice or Justices will adjudge the amount of the penalty to be imposed. under the limitations of the statutes creating the offence, together with the costs, which should be recorded on the proceedings, together with the period of imprisonment, with or without hard labour, to be awarded in case of non-payment of fine and costs: a minute of which should be served on the defendant, if he have to pay money, for which no fee should be paid: before which service no warrant of distress or commitment shall be issued. 32 & 33 Vic., chap. 31, s. 52.

If more than one Justice be acting, the judgment should be according to the opinion of the majority, and when two or more Justices are required they must be present and acting together during the whole of the hearing and determination of the case. 32 & 33 Vic., chap. 31, s. 88.

Though all Justices who choose to attend at petty sessions may act and take part in the business, if one comes into Court in the middle of a case and takes part, the proceedings should be commenced *de novo* unless the parties choose to waive the objection. *Re Jefferys*, 34 J. P. 727. The chairman or presiding Justice may vote, but he is not entitled to a double or casting vote. If the Justices are equally divided in opinion, there should be no adjudication, but the Justices should adjourn the case to a future day, and then entirely rehear the case, when other magistrates may be present, or further evidence adduced. If no adjudication be made, nor the case postponed, the information may be laid again, if the time for doing so has not expired, and the proceedings be wholly recommenced. If the judgment be given, it may be altered during the same sitting, but not afterwards. Two or more Justices may lawfully do whatever any one Justice may do alone.

With respect to indictable offences, where the Justice or Justices intend to commit the prisoner for trial, *he should not be specially committed for trial to any particular court, but to the next court of competent criminal jurisdiction.* In every case, where a person is committed for trial, or bailed to answer to a criminal charge, the Justice of the Peace so committing or bailing shall deliver, or cause to be delivered, the informations, depositions, examinations, recognizances and papers connected with the charge, to the proper officer of the Court in which the trial is to be had, before or at the opening of the Court, on the first day of the sitting thereof. 32 & 33 Vic., chap. 30, s. 38.

When a Justice commits a prisoner to gaol, or holds him to bail to take his trial, the Justice should at once, and before the parties leave his presence, or the proceedings be considered as concluded, bind over the prosecutor and the witnesses to prosecute and give evidence at the next court of competent criminal jurisdiction at which the accused is to be tried; in which case the Justice must at the same time give a notice of such binding, signed by him, to the several persons bound. 32 & 33 Vic., chap. 30, ss. 36 & 37.

It is not unusual for persons, on conviction, to request the Justices to allow time for payment of the fine, at the same time offering to pay down part immediately. Such applications cannot be safely granted, as it is conceived that after part payment the right of commitment would be gone, the Justice having no power to apportion the period of imprisonment. The law does not intend or provide for a man to suffer two modes of punishment, *i. e.*, by purse and person, for the same offence; and on this principle, when the goods of an offender are not sufficient to satisfy a distress, they ought not to be taken, *but the ulterior punishment resorted to.*

Justices are sometimes requested to re-hear a case after the decision has been pronounced, on the ground of the parties having been taken by surprise by the evidence, or of having, subsequently to the hearing, discovered testimony which might have affected the judgment. Justices have, however, no power to re-open the investigation after they have once given judgment, and after the Court is closed. The only way, then, of impeaching their judgment is by appeal or by *certiorari.*

Justices are not obliged to fix the fine or imprisonment at the time of conviction, but may take time either for the purpose of informing themselves as to the legal penalty, or of taking advice as to the law applicable to the case.

The parties are not entitled to copies of depositions in cases of summary conviction, and their only mode of compelling the production of the original is by *certiorari.* Neither is a person committed for default of sureties, and discharged at the sessions, entitled to a copy of the depositions on which his commitment proceeded; but they should be furnished by the Justice if paid therefor.

In indictable cases, however, at any time after the examinations have been completed, and before the first sitting of the Court at which any person is to be tried, such person may require, and shall be entitled to have, copies of the depositions on paying a reasonable sum for the same, not exceeding five cents for one hundred words. 32 & 33 Vic., chap. 30, s. 58.

But this section only gives the right to such copies after all the examinations have been completed, and only in the event of the prisoner being committed for trial, or released on bail to appear for trial. *R.* v. *Fletcher*, 13 L. J. (N.S.), M. C. 67.

Justices of the Peace should refrain from taking part in any matters in which they individually have a personal interest, however small. *R.* v. *Hammond*, 27 J.P. 793.

If any one of the Justices be interested, it will invalidate the decision of all, even although there have been a majority for the decision without counting the vote of the interested party, and where such Justice took part in the discussion, but retired from the bench before the other Justices came to the vote, the Court held that it invalidated the decision. *R.* v. *Hertfordshire*, 6 Q.B. 753. But where the Magistrate did not know, and from the nature of the proceedings could not know that he was interested in the matter, this rule has been holden not to apply. *R.* v. *Surrey*, 21 L. J. M. C. 195.

If the Justice is interested, it is immaterial that he takes no part in the matter. If there is a disqualifying interest, the Justice should not sit in the case, and the Court will not enter into the question as to whether his interest affected the decision. A disqualifying interest is not confined to pecuniary interest, but the interest if not pecuniary must be substantial. Pecuniary interest, however small, disqualifies the Justice, so does real bias in favour of one of the parties; but the mere possibility of bias does not *ipso facto* avoid the Justice's decision. *R.* v. *Meyer*, L. R., 1 Q. B. D. 173; *R.* v. *Rand*, L. R. 1 Q. B. 230–3.

If the Justice is interested in the prosecution, as where he is a member of a Division of the Sons of Temperance, by which a prosecution for selling liquor is carried on, he is incompetent to try the case, and a conviction before him is bad. *R.* v. *Simmons*, 1 Pugsley, 159.

An attachment has been granted against Commissioners of a Court of Requests, for trying causes in which they were interested, though the interest was remote. *R.* v. *McIntyre*, Taylor, 22.

On application for a *certiorari* to quash an order or conviction for interest in the Justices, it should clearly appear that the applicant did not know of such interest, and did not acquiesce in the jurisdiction. *Ex parte Ilchester*, 25 J. P., 56, *Wakefield* v. *West Riding*, 35, L. J., M. C., 69.

If any person assault a Justice, the latter might, at the time of the assault, order him into custody, but when the act is over, and time intervenes, so that there is no present disturbance, it becomes, like any other offence, a matter to be dealt with upon proper complaint upon oath to some other Justice, who might issue his warrant, for a magistrate is not allowed to act officially in his own case, except *flagrante delicto*, while there is otherwise danger of escape, or to suppress an actual disturbance, and enforce the law while it is in the act of being resisted. *Powell* v. *Williamson*, 1 Q. B. (Ont.), 156.

Where a Justice acts in his office with a partial, malicious, or corrupt motive, he is guilty of a misdemeanor, and may be proceeded against by indictment or information.

The Court will in general grant a criminal information against Justices for any gross act of oppression committed by them in the exercise or pretended exercise of their duties as Justices, and whenever there can be shown any vindictive or corrupt motive. (See *R.* v. *Cozens*, 2, Doug. 426; *R.* v. *Somersetshire*, 1 D. & R. 442. The misconduct must have arisen in connection with his public duties. *R.* v. *Arrowsmith*, 2 Dowl., N. S. 704. And where a criminal information is applied for against a magistrate for improperly convicting a person of an offence the Court will not entertain the motion, however bad the conduct of the magistrate may appear, unless the party applying make oath that he is not really guilty of the offence of which he was convicted. *R.* v. *Webster*, 3 T. R., 388. And indeed in all cases of an application for a criminal information against a magistrate for anything done by him in the exercise of the duties of his office, the question has always been not whether the act done might, upon a full and mature investigation, be found strictly right, but from what motive it had proceeded, whether from a dishonest, oppressive or corrupt motive, or from mistake or error, in the former case alone they have become the objects of punishment. *R.* v. *Brown*, 3 B. & Ald., 432-4.

It is to be observed that the 32 & 33 Vic., chap. 31, s. 82, does not prevent the prosecution by indictment of a Justice of the Peace for any offence, the commission of which would subject him to indictment at the time of the coming into force of this Act.

No application can be made against a Justice for anything done in the execution of his office without previous notice. *R.* v. *Heming*, 5 B. & A. 666. The Justice is entitled to six days' notice of motion for a criminal information. *R.* v. *Heustis*, 1 James 101; *Re Bustard* v. *Schofield*, 4 O. S. 11. The affidavit in support of the motion should not be entitled in a suit pending (*ib*).

Where the notice is to answer the application within four days after the service of the notice, it will not suffice, though the motion is not actually made until the six days have expired. The application must not (when the misconduct occurs before the term) be made so late in the term that the magistrate cannot answer it the same term, because the pendency of such a motion might affect his influence as magistrate in the meantime. *R.* v. *Heustis*, 1 James, 101.

Justices of the Peace acting judicially, in a proceeding in which they have power to fine and imprison, are Judges of Record, and have power to commit to prison orally without warrant for contempt committed in the face of the Court. *Armstrong* v. *McCaffrey*, 1 Hannay, 517 ; *Ovens* v. *Taylor*, 19 C.P. (Ont.), 53. Thus if the Justice be called "a rascal and a dirty mean dog," "a damned lousy scoundrel," "a confounded dog," &c., the Justice has a right to imprison as often as the offence is committed. *R.* v. *Scott*, 2 U. C. L. J., N.S., 323. The Justice, while discharging his duty, has power to protect himself from insult and to repress disorder, by committing for contempt any person who shall violently or indirectly interrupt his proceedings, and the Justice may, upon view and without any formal proceedings, order at once into custody any person obstructing the course of justice, or he may commit him until he find sureties for the peace. But the Justice has no power at the time of the misconduct, much less on the next day, to make out a warrant to a constable, and to commit the party to gaol for any certain time by way of punishment without adjudging him formally after a summons to appear for hearing to such punishment on account of his contempt, and a hearing of his defence and making a minute of the sentence. *Re Clarke*, 7 Q.B. (Ont.), 223 ; See also, *Jones* v. *Glasford*, R. & J. Dig. 1974.

A prisoner was convicted three several times the same day for insolent conduct to a magistrate on the bench, and detained in prison under three several warrants, all dated the same day, the periods of imprisonment in the two last commencing from the expiration of the one preceding it, but the first to be computed "from the time of his arrival and delivery (by the bailiff) into your (the gaoler's) custody, thence forward." It was held that the Magistrate had the right to convict for the contempt, and to sentence for continuing periods, but that the periods of imprisonment depending on the will of the officer who was to deliver him to the gaoler were uncertain, and the prisoner was therefore entitled to his discharge. *R.* v. *Scott*, 2 U. C. L. J., N.S., 323.

It has been doubted whether a Justice of the Peace executing his duty in his own house, and not presiding in any court, can legally punish for a contempt committed there. *McKenzie* v. *Mewburn*, 6 O.S., 486.

The 32 & 33 Vic., chap. 31, s. 92, expressly gives to any Judge of Sessions of the Peace, Police District, or Stipendiary Magistrate, sitting at any police court or other place, such and the like powers and authority to preserve order in said courts; and by the like ways and means as now by law are or may be exercised and used in like cases and for the like purposes by any court of law in Canada, or by the Judges thereof respectively during the sittings thereof; and by section 93 in all cases where any resistance is offered to the execution of any summons, warrant of execution, or other process, the due execution thereof may be enforced by the means provided by the law for enforcing the execution of the process of other courts in like cases.

Justices should be careful not to abuse their position; and by either knowing their powers or in ignorance of them inflict a wrong upon a party or witness, or maliciously punish him by the use of insulting and improper language. Where language of this character is used without any legal justification, exemplary damages will be given against the Justice. *Clissold* v. *Machell*, 25 Q. B. (Ont.), 80, affirmed in appeal, 26 Q. B. (Ont.), 422.

A magistrate charged with the preservation of the peace in a city, who causes the military to fire upon a person, whereby the latter is wounded, is not liable in an action of damages at the suit of the injured party, if it be made to appear that though there was no necessity for the firing, yet the circumstances were such that a person might have been reasonably mistaken in his judgment as to the necessity for such firing. *Stevenson* v. *Wilson*, 2 L. C. J., 254. In this case the Riot Act was read before the firing.

An action for damages will lie against any person who in the presence of the magistrate, and while the Court is sitting, assaults any of the parties concerned, or accuses such party of crime in the face of the Court. See *Belanger* v. *Gravel*, 1 L. C. L. J., 98; *Gravel* v. *Belanger*, 3 L. C. L. J., 69.

An action will not lie against a Judge for anything done by him in his judicial capacity, and within his jurisdiction, although there may be an improper exercise of jurisdiction. (See *Dickerson* v. *Fletcher*, Stuart, 276; *Gugy* v. *Kerr*, Stuart, 292; *Garner* v. *Coleman*, 19 C.P. (Ont.), 106; *Agnew* v. *Stewart*, 21 Q.B. (Ont.), 306. And from the opinion of the Court in *Garner* v. *Coleman*, supra, and *Scott* v. *Stansfield*, L. R. 3 *Ex.*, 320; 18 L. T. N. S., 572; it would seem that no action at law can be maintained against a Judge of a Court of Record for anything done in his judicial capacity though there is malice and a want of reasonable and probable cause. The Court do not say that the Judge is not amenable to punishment by impeachment in Parliament, but seem disposed to protect him from an action before a Jury. The general rule is that a Justice like other Judges is not liable for any mistake or error of judgment, or for anything he does judicially when acting within his jurisdiction, though he may be wrong. *Garnett* v. *Farrand*, 6 B. & C., 611; *Mills* v. *Collett*, 6 Bing., 85.

Where a Justice of the Peace acts judicially in a matter in which by law he has jurisdiction, and his proceedings appear to be good upon the face of them, no action will lie against him or if an action be brought the proceedings themselves will be a sufficient justification. See *Brittain* v. *Kinnaird*, 1 Brod. & B., 432; *Fawcett* v. *Fowles*, 7 B. & C., 394. If, therefore, an action of trespass be brought against magistrates for convicting a person and causing him to be imprisoned in a case where the magistrate had jurisdiction, the plaintiff must be non-suited if a valid and subsisting conviction be adduced and proved. *Stamp* v. *Sweetland*, 14 L. J. M. C., 184; *Mould* v. *Williams*, 5 Q.B., 469; or, if the conviction has been quashed, then case, not trespass, is the form of action that ought to be adopted. *Baylis* v. *Strickland*, 1 Man & Gr., 59. All this is now fully declared in Ontario, by the Rev. Stat. chap. 73, s. 1, *et seq.*, see notes to this Statute, *post.*

What we have hitherto been considering have been actions

against Justices for something done by them in their judicial character. For what they do in their ministerial character without reference to their judicial authority, their power of justifying will depend in a great measure upon the legality of the proceedings upon which these acts are founded, see *Weaver* v. *Price,* 3 B. & Ad., 409. Thus, if the Justice exceeds the authority the law gives him in his ministerial acts, he thereby subjects himself to an action as if he commit a prisoner for re-examination for an unreasonable time, although he do so from no improper motive, he is liable to an action for false imprisonment. *Davis* v. *Capper,* 10 B. & C., 28. So if he commit a man for a supposed crime where there has in fact been no accusation against him, he is liable to an action of trespass for false imprisonment (*Morgan* v. *Hughes,* 2 T. R., 225); but if he commit him for a reasonable time, although the statute under which he is acting gives him no authority to do so, he is not liable to an action, for authority so to commit is given to Justices. 32 & 33 Vic., chap. 30, s. 47; *Gelan* v. *Hall,* 27 L. J. M.C., 78; *Haylock* v. *Sparke,* 4 E. & B., 471; *Linford* v. *Fitzroy,* 13 Q.B., 240.

When property or title is in question, the jurisdiction of Justices of the Peace to hear and determine in a summary manner is ousted, and when a *bona fide* claim is made the Justices have no jurisdiction and ought not to convict. *R.* v. *Cridland,* 7 E. & B., 853. It is not sufficient to take away their jurisdiction that the defendant *bona fide* believed that he had a right, it is for the Justices to decide, if the claim of right is fair and reasonable, and if they hold that it is not, they are bound to go on and decide the case (*R* v. *Mussett,* 26 L. T., N. S., 429), but if the matter is doubtful, it will be enough to stop their proceedings, and they cannot give themselves jurisdiction by a false decision. *R.* v. *Nunnely,* E. B. & E., 852. But although as a rule Justices have no power to enquire into a case involving a title to real property yet, when the title is itself the question which they have to decide, their jurisdiction remains. *Williams* v. *Adams,* 2 B. & S., 312.

A *bona fide* claim of right which cannot exist in law will not oust the Justice's jurisdiction. *Hargreaves* v. *Diddams,* L. R.

10 Q. B., 582. *Hudson* v. *Macrae*, 4 B. & S., 585, followed. See also *Watkins* v. *Major*, L. R., 10 C. P., 662.

The jurisdiction of the Justice is not ousted by the mere *bona fide* belief of the person offending that his act was legal (*White* v. *Feast*, L. R., 7 Q. B., 351), but it is restricted to cases where the Justices are satisfied of the fairness and reasonableness of the claim of right. *R.* v. *Mussett*, 26 L. T., N. S., 429.

---

32 & 33 VIC., CHAP. XXX.

An Act respecting the duties of Justices of the Peace, out of Sessions, in relation to persons charged with Indictable Offences.

[*Assented to 22nd June*, 1869.]

WHEREAS it is expedient to assimilate, amend and consolidate the Statute Laws of the several Provinces of Quebec, Ontario, Nova Scotia and New Brunswick, respecting the duties of Justices of the Peace out of sessions in relation to persons charged with indictable offences, and to extend the same as so consolidated to all Canada : Therefore, Her Majesty, by and with the advice and consent of the Senate and House of Commons of Canada, enacts as follows :

It will be seen that the Act, as originally framed, applied only to the Provinces of Quebec, Ontario, Nova Scotia, and New Brunswick. It was extended to the Province of British Columbia by the 37 Vic., chap 42 ; to Manitoba by the 34 Vic., chap. 14 ; to Prince Edward Island, by the 40 Vic., chap. 4 ; to the District of Keewatin by the 39 Vic., chap. 21, so far as respects indictable offences committed in the said District, and triable in Manitoba, or committed in some Province in Canada, and the offender apprehended in the said District. The Act was also extended to the North-West Territories by 38 Vic., chap. 49, schedule B, so far as respects indictable offences committed in the North-West Territories and triable in Manitoba or committed in some Province of Canada, and the offender apprehended in the North-West Territories.

1. In all cases where a charge or complaint (A) is made before any one or more of Her Majesty's Justices of the Peace for any Territorial Division in Canada, that any person has committed, or is suspected to have committed, any treason or felony, or any indictable misdemeanor or offence within the limits of the jurisdiction of such Justice or Justices of the Peace, or that any person guilty or suspected to be guilty of having committed any such crime or offence elsewhere out of the jurisdiction of such Justice or Justices, is residing or being, or is suspected to reside or be within the limits of the jurisdiction of such Justice or Justices, then, and in every such case, if the

person so charged or complained against is not in custody, such Justice or Justices of the Peace may issue his or their warrant (B) to apprehend such person, and to cause him to be brought before such Justice or Justices, or any other Justice or Justices for the same Territorial Division.

Without an information properly laid, a Justice has no jurisdiction over the person of an offender; and if he issues a warrant without any information being laid, he is liable in trespass (*Appleton* v. *Lepper*, 20 C. P. (Ont.), 138); so if a Justice, after an offender is brought before him on a warrant, commits him for trial where there is no prosecutor, no examination of witnesses, and no confession of guilt under the statute, he is liable in trespass (*Ib.*, 138, citing *Connors* v. *Darling*, 23 Q.B. (Ont.), 541).

To give the magistrate jurisdiction there must either be an information for a criminal offence, or the information must be waived by the accused. *Crawford* v. *Beattie*, 39 Q. B. (Ont.), 26; *Caudle* v. *Seymour*, 1 Q.B., 889; *R.* v. *Shaw*, 12 L. T., N. S., 470–3; *R.* v. *Fletcher*, L. R., 1 C. C. R., 320.

Even where an information is properly laid, if the offence is not committed within the limits of the Justice's jurisdiction, the offender must reside or be within such limits (see sections 1 and 4). The commission of an offence within the Justice's jurisdiction gives him authority, on an information properly laid, to issue his summons or warrant, though the offender at the time the information is laid have departed from the county or place in which the Justice acts. In case of fresh pursuit the offender may be apprehended at any place in the next adjoining territorial division, and within seven miles of the border of the first-mentioned territorial division (see section 19). In other cases the warrant may be backed so as to authorize the apprehension of the offender at any place in Canada, out of the jurisdiction of the Justice issuing the warrant (see section 23).

The form of information given in the schedule to this Act does not contain any statement of the offence. The author has, therefore supplemented the Form A, with statements of offences in different cases. As we have already seen, the information should also contain a prayer for the issue of a summons or warrant. The information need not be written on parchment, nor does it require the statement of any venue in the body thereof, but the district, county, or place named in the margin thereof, shall be the venue for all the facts stated in the body of the information.

Where it is necessary to state the ownership of property belonging to partners in trade, joint tenants, parceners, or tenants in common, it is sufficient to name one of such persons, and to state the property to belong to the person so named and another or others, as the case may be. See *R.* v. *Cavanagh*, 27 C. P. (Ont.), 537; 32 & 33 Vic., chap. 29, ss. 13, 15, 17. As to the description of property in the information in different cases, and when it is unnecessary to lay it in any person, see 32 & 33 Vic., chap. 29, ss. 19–22.

The information is not to be held insufficient for want of the averment of any matter unnecessary to be proved, nor for the omission of the words, "as appears upon the record," or "as appears by the record;" or of the words, "with force and arms;" or of the words, "against the peace;" or for the insertion of the words, "against the form of the statute," instead of the words, "against the form of the statutes," or *vice versa*, or for the omission of such words, or for the want of an addition, or for an imperfect addition of any person mentioned in the information, or for that any person mentioned in the information is designated by a name of office or other descriptive appellation instead of his proper name; or for omitting to state the time at which the offence was committed, in any case where time is not of the essence of the offence, or for stating the time imperfectly, or for stating the offence to have been committed on a day subsequent to the laying of the information, or on an impossible day, or on a day that never happened, or for want of a proper or perfect venue, or for want of a proper or formal conclusion, or for want of or imperfection in the addition of any defendant, or for want of the statement of the value or price of any matter or thing or the amount of damage, injury, or spoil, in any case where the value or price, or the amount of damage, injury, or spoil is not of the essence of the offence. 32 & 33 V., chap. 29, s. 23. Section 24 provides:—

Whenever it is necessary to make an averment in an information as to any instrument, whether the same consists wholly or in part of writing, print or figures, it shall be sufficient to describe such instrument by any name or designation by which the same may be usually known, or by the purport thereof, without setting out any copy or fac-simile of the whole or of any part thereof. Section 25 provides: Whenever in any information it is necessary to make an averment as to any money or to any note of any bank, or Dominion or Provincial note, it shall be sufficient to describe such money or note simply as money, without any allegation (so far as regards the description of the property), specifying any particular coin or note, and such averment shall be sustained by proof of any amount of coin, or of any such note, although the particular species of coin of which such amount was composed, or the particular nature of the note be not proved. See *R.* v. *Cavanagh*, 27 C. P. (Ont.), 537; as to informations for offences committed after a previous conviction, see 32 & 33 Vic., chap. 29, s. 26.

Informations before Magistrates must be taken as nearly as possible in the language used by the party complaining. See *Cohen* v. *Morgan*, 6 D. & R., 8; *McNellis* v. *Garthshore*, 2 C. P. (Ont.), 464.

If by reasonable intendment the information can be read as disclosing a criminal offence, the rule is so to read it. See *Lawrenson* v. *Hill*, 10 Ir. C. L. R., 177.

An information charging the plaintiff with having unlawfully taken away a pair of shutters belonging to the plaintiff, and having converted the same to his own use against the form of the statute, does not charge a felony. *Tempest* v. *Chambers*, 1 Stark., 67.

An information charging that the plaintiff did "abstract from the table in the house of John Evans, a paper being a valuable security for money," does not charge a felony. *Smith* v. *Evans*, 13 C. P. (Ont.), 60.

An information that "the said Ellen Kennedy has the key of a house in her possession, the property of the complainant, and would not give it up" to the complainant's agent, contains nothing which by reasonable intendment can be construed as charging criminality. *Lawrenson* v. *Hill*, 10 Ir. C. L. R., 177.

An information which stated that A. B. had neglected to return a gun which had been lent to him, and for which he had been repeatedly asked, was not construed as charging criminality. *McDonald* v. *Bulwer*, 11 L. T., N. S., 27.

If the information discloses no offence in law, it will not authorize the issue of a warrant by a magistrate as there is nothing to found the magistrate's jurisdiction. *Stephens* v. *Stephens*, 24 C. P. (Ont.), 424.

The warrant mentioned in this section must be under the hand and seal of the Justice, and directed as in form B. It may be issued on a Sunday as well as on any other day. See section 8. The information must also be in writing and on oath when it is intended to issue a warrant in the first instance. *Friel* v. *Ferguson*, 15 C. P. (Ont.), 584. See sec. 9, as to the cases in which a warrant may issue in the first instance. See sec. 27.

The warrant of a magistrate is only *prima facie*, not conclusive, evidence of its contents, and though a warrant recites the laying of an information, and though in an action against the magistrate it is put in on behalf of the plaintiff, still the recital of the information is not conclusive, and evidence may be given to show that such information was not in fact laid. *Friel* v. *Ferguson*, 15 C. P. (Ont.), 584.

2. In all cases the Justice or Justices to whom the charge or complaint is preferred, instead of issuing in the first instance his or their warrant to apprehend the person charged or complained against, may, if he or they think fit, issue his or their summons (C) directed to such person, requiring him to appear before the Justice or Justices, at the time and place to be therein mentioned, or before such other Justice or Justices of the same Territorial Division as may then be there, and if, after being served with the summons in manner hereinafter mentioned, he fails to appear at such time and place, in obedience to such summons, the Justice or Justices, or any other Justice or Justices of the Peace for the same Territorial Division, may issue his or their warrant (D) to apprehend the person so charged or complained against, and cause such person to be brought before him or them, or before some other Justice or Justices of the Peace for the same Territorial Division to answer to the charge or complaint, and to be further dealt with according to law; but any Justice or Justices of the Peace may, if he or they see fit, issue the warrant hereinbefore first mentioned, at any time before or after the time mentioned in the summons for the appearance of the accused party.

Under this section it would appear that the power to finally dispose of the case does not belong exclusively to the Justice who issues the summons, though in this Act there is no provision similar to that contained in sections 85, 86 and 87 of the Act relating to summary convictions and orders, see *R.* v. *Milne*, 25 C. P. (Ont.), 94.

3. In all cases of indictable offences committed on the high seas, or in any creek, harbour, haven or other place, in which the Admiralty of England have or claim to have jurisdiction, and in all cases of offences committed on land beyond the seas for which an indictment may be preferred, or the offender may be arrested in Canada, any one or more Justice or Justices for any Territorial Division in which any person charged with having committed, or being suspected to have committed any such offence, shall be or be suspected to be, may issue his or their warrant (D 2) to apprehend such person, to be dealt with as therein and hereby directed.

The great inland lakes of Canada are within the Admiralty jurisdiction, and offences committed on them are as though committed on the high seas, and therefore any magistrate of this Province has authority to inquire into offences committed on said lakes, although in American waters. *R.* v. *Sharp*, 5 P. R (Ont.), 135.

As to the jurisdiction of the Admiralty, see *R.* v. *Keyn*, L. R., 2 Ex. D., 63.

See also on the above section, *R.* v. *Eyre*, L. R., 3 Q. B., 487.

The Statute 32 & 33 Vic., chap. 29, s. 136, enacts, when any felony punishable under the laws of Canada has been committed within the jurisdiction of any Court of Admiralty in Canada, the same may be dealt with, inquired of, tried, and determined in the same manner as any other felony committed within that jurisdiction.

4. In case an indictment be found by the Grand Jury in any Court of Criminal Jurisdiction, against any person then at large, and whether such person has been bound by any recognizance to appear to answer to any such charge, or not, and in case such person has not appeared and pleaded to the indictment, the person who acts as Clerk of the Crown or Chief Clerk of such Court, shall, at any time at the end of the term or sittings of the Court at which the indictment has been found, upon application of the prosecutor, or of any per-

son on his behalf, and on payment of a fee of twenty cents, grant to such prosecutor or person a certificate (F) of such indictment having been found; and upon production of such Certificate to any Justice or Justices of the Peace for the Territorial Division in which the offence is in the indictment alleged to have been committed, or in which the person indicted resides, or is supposed or suspected to reside or be, such Justice or Justices shall issue his or their warrant (G) to apprehend the person so indicted, and to cause him to be brought before such Justice or Justices, or any other Justice or Justices for the same Territorial Division, to be dealt with according to law.

This certificate can only be obtained after the assizes or sessions, for during the assizes or sessions the prosecutor may obtain a Bench warrant (see section 17). But it is not only in cases where the prosecutor has omitted to apply for a Bench warrant during the assizes or sessions, but also where he has applied and got it, that this mode of obtaining a Justice's warrant to apprehend a party indicted may be useful—for it may often happen that whilst the Bench warrant is in the possession of a constable in another county, or in a distant part of the same county, there may be an opportunity of apprehending the defendant in another part of the county or in another county.

An indictment may be preferred for any offence, at the Court having jurisdiction to try it, without any preliminary inquiry before Justices, except in cases provided by the 32 & 33 Vic., chap. 29, s. 28, as amended by the 40 Vic., chap. 26.

If the Justices before whom any person is charged with any of the offences named in these statutes refuse to commit, the prosecutor, if he desire it, may enter into a recognizance to prefer an indictment for the offence; and such recognizance, with the information and depositions, if any, shall be returned to the Court in which the indictment is to be preferred. 32 & 33 Vic., chap. 29, s. 29.

The finding of an indictment in the cases mentioned in the fourth section of this Act, gives the Justice jurisdiction to issue his warrant to apprehend the person against whom such indictment is found.

5. If the person be thereupon apprehended and brought before any such Justice or Justices, such Justice or Justices, upon its being proved upon oath

or affirmation before him or them that the person so apprehended is the person charged and named in the indictment, shall, without further inquiry or examination, commit (H) him for trial or admit him to bail in manner hereinafter mentioned.

6. If the person so indicted is confined in any gaol or prison for any other offence than that charged in the indictment at the time of such application and production of such certificate to the Justice or Justices, such Justice or Justices, upon its being proved before him or them upon oath or affirmation, that the person so indicted and the person so confined in prison are one and the same person, shall issue his or their warrant (I) directed to the gaoler or keeper of the gaol or prison in which the person so indicted is then confined, commanding him to detain such person in his custody until, by Her Majesty's Writ of Habeas Corpus, or by order of the proper Court, he be removed therefrom for the purpose of being tried upon the said indictment, or until he be otherwise removed or discharged out of his custody by due course of law.

7. Nothing in this Act contained shall prevent the issuing or execution of Bench Warrants, whenever any Court of competent jurisdiction thinks proper to order the issuing of any such warrant.

8. Any Justice or Justices of the Peace may grant or issue any Warrant as aforesaid, or any Search Warrant, on a Sunday as well as on any other day.

This section does not authorize the issue of a summons on a Sunday; but all persons guilty of indictable offences may be arrested on Sunday. *Rawlins* v. *Ellis*, 16 M. & W., 172; 29 Car. 2, chap. 7, s. 6.

9. In all cases when a charge or complaint for an indictable offence is made before any Justice or Justices, if it be intended to issue a warrant in the first instance against the party charged, an information and complaint thereof (A) in writing, on the oath or affirmation of the informant, or of some witness or witnesses in that behalf, shall be laid before such Justice or Justices.

10. When it is intended to issue a summons instead of a warrant in the first instance, the information and complaint shall also be in writing, and be sworn to or affirmed in manner aforesaid except only in cases where by some Act or law it is specially provided that the information and complaint may be by parole merely, and without any oath or affirmation to support or substantiate the same.

A summons issued under the 4 & 5 Vic., chap. 26, for malicious injuries to property, must be upon complaint under oath. *Ex parte Hook*, 3 L. C. R., 496.

11. **No objection shall be taken or allowed to any information and complaint for any alleged defect therein, in substance or in form, or for any variance between it and the evidence adduced on the part of the prosecution, before the Justice or Justices who take the examination of the witnesses in that behalf.**

A man accused of crime before a magistrate, who raises no objection to the form of the information, and is tried and convicted, is by the operation of this section much in the same position as a man indicted for crime who omits to demur to or quash the indictment, pleads not guilty, is tried and convicted. All defects apparent on the face of the information are waived. *Crawford* v. *Beattie*, 39 Q. B. (Ont.), 28; *R.* v. *Cavanagh*, 27 C.P. (Ont.), 537; 32 & 33 Vic., chap. 29, s. 32. In *R.* v. *Cavanagh*, *supra*, it was held that an information for an offence punishable on summary conviction, might be amended; and in *Crawford* v. *Beattie*, *supra*, it seemed to be assumed that the same course might be pursued in the case of an information for an indictable offence. On objection, therefore, taken to an information, the magistrate may allow it to be amended in the same manner as an indictment under 32 & 33 Vic., chap. 29, s. 32; see also *Re Conklin*, 31 Q. B. (Ont.), 160.

This section was framed not only to meet the case of a variance between the information and the evidence (see *Whittle* v. *Frankland*, 5 L. T., N. S., 639); but to cure defects in the information either in "substance or in form," where the evidence discloses an offence. But it does not enable the Justice to summon a person for one offence requiring a particular punishment, and without a fresh information, convict him of a different offence requiring a different punishment. *Martin* v. *Pridgeon*, 1 E. & E., 778; *R.* v. *Brickhall*, 10 L. T., N. S., 385. The plaintiff was brought before defendant and another magistrate on the 2nd of January, 1875, under a summons issued by defendant, on an information that he did on &c. "obtain, by false pretences, from complainant, the sum of five dollars contrary to law," omitting the words "with intent to defraud," which, by the Statute 32 & 33 Vic., chap. 21, s. 93, is made part of the offence. The plaintiff did not, when before the magistrate, pretend ignorance of the charge, or take any objection to the information, and it was held that the defendant had jurisdiction, for the information might, by intendment, be read, as charging the statutable offence, and if not, the plaintiff should have taken his objection before the magistrate, when the information might have been amended and re-sworn, and that he was precluded from raising it in this action. *Crawford* v. *Beattie*, 39 Q. B. (Ont.), 13.

12. If a credible witness proves upon oath (E 1) before a Justice of the Peace, that there is reasonable cause to suspect that any property whatsoever, on or with respect to which any larceny or felony has been committed, is in any dwelling house, outhouse, garden, yard, croft or other place or places, the Justice may grant a Warrant (E 2) to search such dwelling house, garden, yard, croft or other place or places, for such property, and if the same, or any part thereof be then found, to bring the same and the person or persons in whose possession such house or other place then is, before the Justice granting the Warrant, or some other Justice for the same Territorial Division.

By the Act respecting larceny and other similar offences, 32 & 33 Vic., chap. 21, s. 117, if any credible witness proves upon oath, before a Justice of the Peace, a reasonable cause to suspect that any person has in his possession, or in his premises, any property whatsoever, on or with respect to which any offence punishable, either upon indictment or upon summary conviction, by virtue of this Act has been committed, the Justice may grant a warrant to search for such property, as in the case of stolen goods.

In cases of forgery, express provision is also made for the issue of a search warrant, 32 & 33 Vic. chap., 19, s. 53. So in the case of larceny from mines, or of ores, minerals or quartz, a general search warrant may be issued by a Justice of the Peace as in the case of stolen goods, 32 & 33 Vic., chap. 21, s. 33. So in the case of making gunpowder, &c., to commit offences, 32 & 33 Vic., chap. 22, s. 63.

The party requiring a search warrant must go before a Justice of the Peace of the county or other jurisdiction where the premises intended to be searched are situate, and make oath of circumstances, showing a reasonable ground for suspecting that the goods are upon these premises. He must also shew, upon oath, either that the goods were stolen or that he has reason to suspect that they have been stolen, for a positive oath that a felony was committed, of goods, is not necessary to justify a magistrate in granting a search warrant for them. *Elsee* v. *Smith*, 1 Dowl. & Ry. 97. The warrant may be issued on a Sunday. 32 & 33 Vic., chap. 30, s. 8.

13. Upon information and complaint as aforesaid, the Justice or Justices receiving the same may, if he or they think fit, issue his or their summons or warrant as hereinbefore directed, to cause the person charged to be and appear as therein and thereby directed; and every summons (C) shall be directed to the party so charged by the information, and shall state shortly the matter of such information, and shall require the party to whom it is directed to be and appear at a certain time and place therein mentioned, before the Justice who issues the summons, or before such other Justice or Justices of the Peace for the same Territorial Division as may then be there, to answer to the charge, and to be further dealt with according to law.

The words in this section, "if he or they think fit," give the Justices a discretion in the issuing of the summons or warrant; but they are bound to exercise this discretion on the evidence of a criminal offence, which the information discloses, and if, on a consideration of something extraneous or extra judicial, they refuse the summons or warrant, the Court will order them to issue it. *R.* v. *Adamson*, L. R., 1 Q. B. D., 201.

14. Every such Summons shall be served by a Constable or other Peace Officer upon the person to whom it is directed, by delivering the same to the party personally, or if he cannot conveniently be met with, then by leaving the same for him with some person at his last or usual place of abode.

15. The Constable or other Peace Officer who serves the same shall attend at the time and place, and before the Justice or Justices in the Summons mentioned, to depose, if necessary, to the service of the Summons.

16. If the person served does not appear before the Justice or Justices, at the time and place mentioned in the Summons, in obedience to the same, the Justice or Justices may issue his or their Warrant (D) for apprehending the party so summoned, and bringing him before him or them, or before some other Justice or Justices for the same Territorial Division to answer the charge in the information and complaint mentioned, and to be further dealt with according to law.

17. Every Warrant (B) hereafter issued by any Justice or Justices of the Peace to apprehend any person charged with any indictable offence, shall be

under the hand and seal, or hands and seals, of the Justice or Justices issuing the same, and may be directed to all or any of the Constables or other Peace Officers of the Territorial Division within which the same is to be executed, or to any such Constable and all other Constables or Peace Officers in the Territorial Division within which the Justice or Justices issuing the same has jurisdiction, or generally to all the Constables or Peace Officers within such last mentioned Territorial Division; and it shall state shortly the offence on which it is founded, and shall name or otherwise describe the offender, and it shall order the person or persons to whom it is directed to apprehend the offender, and bring him before the Justice or Justices issuing the Warrant, or before some other Justice or Justices of the Peace for the same Territorial Division, to answer to the charge contained in the information, and to be further dealt with according to law.

If the warrant is directed to any person, not a constable, he is not bound to execute it, and is not punishable if he does not execute it, but a constable is bound to execute it if directed to him.

Under this section the warrant may be directed to all or any of the constables or other peace officers of the territorial division within which the same is to be executed. This would meet the case of the offence having been committed within the Justices' jurisdiction and of the offender having fled therefrom, and where the intention is to have the warrant backed under the 23rd section. The warrant may also be directed to any such constable (as above mentioned) and all other constables in the territorial division within which the Justice has jurisdiction. The latter direction of the warrant is recommended. It enables the constable to execute the warrant within the jurisdiction of the Justice granting it, though it is not directed specially to such constable by name, and though the place within which such warrant is executed be not within the place for which he is constable or peace officer. See section 20. It also authorizes the execution of the warrant (in case of its being backed under the 23rd section), in any place in Canada where the offender may be found. The 23rd section authorizes the execution of the warrant by the person bringing it, and all others to whom the same was originally directed, and all constables of the territorial division in which the warrant has been endorsed.

Where a warrant was directed to the Constable of Thorold, in the Niagara District, authorizing him to search the plaintiff's house, at the Township of Louth, in the same district, it not appearing that there was more than one person appointed to the office of Constable of Thorold, it was held that the direction to the Constable of Thorold, not naming him, to execute the warrant in the Township of Louth was good, for although a warrant to a peace officer, by his name of office, gives him no authority out of the precincts of his jurisdiction, yet such authority may be expressly given on the face of the warrant, as in this case. *Jones* v. *Ross*, 3 Q. B. (Ont.), 328.

18. It shall not be necessary to make the Warrant returnable at any particular time, but the same may remain in force until executed.

19. Such Warrant may be executed by apprehending the offender at any place in the Territorial Division within which the Justice or Justices issuing the same have jurisdiction, or in case of fresh pursuit, at any place in the next adjoining Territorial Division, and within seven miles of the border of the first mentioned Territorial Division, without having the Warrant backed, as hereinafter mentioned.

The seven miles are measured, not by the nearest practicable road but, by a straight line from point to point on the horizontal plane, "as the crow flies." *Lake* v. *Butler*, 24 L. J., N.S., Q.B., 273; *R.* v. *Walden*, 9 Q. B., 76.

20. In case any Warrant be directed to all Constables or other Peace Officers in the Territorial Division within which the Justice or Justices have jurisdiction, any Constable or other Peace Officer for any place within such Territorial Division may execute the warrant at any place within the jurisdiction for which the Justice or Justices acted when he or they granted such Warrant, in like manner as if the Warrant had been directed specially to such Constable by name, and notwithstanding the place within which such Warrant is executed be not within the place for which he is Constable or Peace Officer.

Where an offence was committed in the county of G., and warrants were issued for the arrest of the guilty parties, persons from another county who came to assist the Constables of the county of G. in making arrests, were held entitled to the same protection as the constables. *R.* v. *Chasson*, 3 Pugsley, 546.

21. No objection shall be taken or allowed to any Summons or Warrant for any defect therein, in substance or in form, or for any variance between it and the evidence adduced on the part of the prosecution, before the Justice or Justices who takes the examinations of the Witnesses in that behalf as hereinafter mentioned.

22. But if it appears to the Justice or Justices that the party charged has been deceived or misled by any such variance, such Justice or Justices, at the request of the party charged, may adjourn the hearing of the case to some future day, and in the meantime may remand the party, or admit him to bail as hereinafter mentioned.

23. If the person against whom any Warrant has been issued, cannot be found within the jurisdiction of the Justice or Justices by whom the same was issued, or if he escapes into, or is supposed or suspected to be in, any place within Canada, out of the jurisdiction of the Justice or Justices issuing the Warrant, any Justice of the Peace within the jurisdiction of whom the person so escapes, or in which he is or is suspected to be, upon proof alone being made on oath or affirmation of the handwriting of the Justice who issued the same, without any security being given, shall make an endorsement (K) on the Warrant, signed with his name, authorizing the execution of the Warrant within the jurisdiction of the Justice making the endorsement, and such endorsement shall be sufficient authority to the person bringing such Warrant, and to all other persons to whom the same was originally directed, and also to all Constables and other Peace Officers of the Territorial Division where the Warrant has been so endorsed, to execute the same in such other Territorial Division and to carry the person against whom the Warrant issued, when apprehended, before the Justice or Justices of the Peace who first issued the Warrant, or before some other Justice or Justices of the Peace for the same Territorial Division, or before some Justice or Justices of the Territorial Division in which the offence mentioned in the Warrant appears therein to have been committed.

If the person against whom the warrant is issued cannot be found in the county in which it has been backed, it may be again backed in the same manner in any other county, and so from county to county until the offender is apprehended, and notwithstanding such backings of the warrant, the offender may be afterwards apprehended thereon in the county in which it originally issued.

24. If the Prosecutor or any of the witnesses for the prosecution be then in the Territorial Division where such person has been apprehended, the Constable, or other person or persons who have apprehended him may, if so

directed by the Justice backing the Warrant, take him before the Justice who backed the Warrant, or before some other Justice or Justices for the same Territorial Division or place ; and the said Justice or Justices may thereupon take the examination of such prosecutor or witnesses, and proceed in every respect in manner hereinafter directed with respect to persons charged before a Justice or Justices of the Peace, with an offence alleged to have been committed in another Territorial Division than that in which such persons have been apprehended.

25. If it be made to appear to any Justice of the Peace, by the oath or affirmation of any creditable person, that any person within the Dominion is likely to give material evidence for the prosecution and will not voluntarily appear for the purpose of being examined as a witness at the time and place appointed for the examination of the witnesses against the accused, such Justice shall issue his Summons (L 1) to such person, requiring him to be and appear at a time and place therein mentioned, before the said Justice, or before such other Justice or Justices of the Peace for the same Territorial Division as may then be there, to testify what he knows concerning the charge made against the accused party.

It will be observed that under this section only the witnesses for the prosecution can be subpœnaed. The witness must be within the Dominion ; it must appear that he is likely to give material evidence for the prosecution, and will not voluntarily appear to do so.

The provisions of the section cannot be invoked until an information is laid against the accused, and a summons or warrant is issued against him.

The Act 39 Vic., chap. 36, makes provision for the attendance of witnesses at criminal trials. The subpœna or summons to a witness should be addressed to him by his name and description. The day on which he is thereby ordered to appear should be stated as well as the place, giving such a designation or description thereof as that he can easily find it, if in a city, town, village or parish. It should also be dated, signed, and sealed by the Justice. In the event of the person served with a subpœna neglecting or refusing to appear, the Justice can issue a warrant for his apprehension. The formalities to be observed before such warrant can be issued are the same as prescribed by section 2, to precede the issue of the warrant where the person has failed after service to appear on an ordinary summons, and such warrant can be backed as provided by section 23. See s. 26, Kerr's Acts, 74-5.

A witness cannot refuse to attend on being served with a summons or subpœna, until his expenses are paid. *R.* v. *James*, 1 C. & P., 322.

26. If any person so summoned neglects or refuses to appear at the time and place appointed by the Summons, and no just excuse be offered for such neglect or refusal (after proof upon oath or affirmation of the Summons having been served upon such person, either personally or left with some person for him at his last or usual place of abode), the Justice or Justices before whom such person should have appeared may issue a Warrant (L. 2) to bring such person, at a time and place to be therein mentioned before the Justice who issued the Summons, or before such other Justice or Justices of the Peace for the same Territorial Division as may then be there, to testify as aforesaid, and the said Warrant may, if necessary, be backed as hereinbefore mentioned, in order to its being executed out of the jurisdiction of the Justice who issued the same.

27. If the Justice be satisfied by evidence upon oath or affirmation that it is probable the person will not attend to give evidence unless compelled so to do, then, instead of issuing such Summons, the Justice may issue his Warrant (L 3) in the first instance, and the Warrant, if necessary, may be backed as aforesaid.

28. If on the appearance of the person so summoned, either in obedience to the Summons or by virtue of the Warrant, he refuses to be examined upon oath or affirmation concerning the premises, or refuses to take such oath or affirmation, or having taken such oath or affirmation, refuses to answer the questions concerning the premises then put to him without giving any just excuse for such refusal, any Justice of the Peace then present and there having jurisdiction, may, by Warrant (L 4), commit the person so refusing to the common gaol or other place of confinement, for the Territorial Division where the person so refusing then is, there to remain and be imprisoned for any time not exceeding ten days, unless he in the meantime consents to be examined and to answer concerning the premises.

29. In all cases where any person appears or is brought before any Justice or Justices of the Peace charged with any indictable offence, whether committed in Canada or upon the high seas, or on land beyond the sea, and whether such person appears voluntarily upon Summons or has been apprehended, with or without Warrant, or is in custody for the same or any other offence, such Justice or Justices before he or they commit such accused person to prison for trial, or before he or they admit him to bail, shall, in the

presence of the accused person (who shall be at liberty to put questions to any witness produced against him), take the statement (M) on oath or affirmation of those who know the facts and circumstances of the case, and shall put the same in writing, and such depositions shall be read over to and signed respectively by the witnesses so examined, and shall be signed also by the Justice or Justices taking the same.

It will be observed that the depositions under this section must be taken in the presence of the accused person, and there is therefore no power to proceed *ex parte* in indictable cases.

In England, the manner of taking depositions varies; in some places it is usual, in all indictable cases, to take down the evidence in the form of a deposition at once; in others, abbreviated notes are taken of the examination before the magistrate, copied verbatim, and afterwards read over to the witnesses in the presence of the magistrate and the accused; the accused having every opportunity of cross-examining the witnesses, and of objecting as well as the witnesses if the evidence is taken down incorrectly. The former mode is the more correct, but the latter has been approved, and depositions so taken have been held admissible. *R.* v. *Bates*, 2 F. & F., 317. If the latter plan is adopted, the deposition should be merely a plain copy of the notes, and the clerk should not in the absence of the magistrate ask the witnesses any questions to complete the depositions (*R.* v. *Christopher*, 1 Den. C.C., 536), though the accused be present at the time (*R.* v. *Watts*, 9 L.T., N.S., 453); for that will make the depositions inadmissible, even if they are subsequently read over to the witnesses in the presence both of the magistrate and the accused.

The evidence should be taken down as nearly as possible in the witness's own words, and the depositions should contain the full evidence, cross-examination as well as examination-in chief. Any interruption by the accused should be taken down, and may be evidence against him. *R.* v. *Stripp*, Dears., 648.

At the close of the witness's examination, it would be well for the Justice to put any questions—answers to which would in his opinion tend to throw light on the facts and circumstances of the case. The accused person should then be asked by the Justice if he has any questions in cross-examination to put to the witness; if he declares that he does not wish to cross-examine, that fact should be noted in the deposition, but if he declares that he desires to cross-examine, his questions, when pertinent to the matter in issue, must be answered by the witness, and must be reduced to writing by the Justice together with the answers of the witness thereto. Care must be taken to distinguish between the examination and cross-examination of the witness; if necessary, the witness can be re-examined, the deposition must then be read over to and signed by the witness and by the Justice taking the same, all in the presence of the accused. *R.* v. *Watts*, 9 L.T., N.S., 453; Kerr's Acts, 78–9.

The Justice is bound to examine all the parties who know the facts and circumstances of the case. The depositions of the witness should be taken carefully; as far as possible, the very words made use of should be preserved. It is not, however, necessary to take down all that a witness may state, since that which is clearly irrelevant or not admissible as evidence, ought not to be admitted. If, however, any doubt should arise as to admissibility, the better plan is to take it and leave it to another tribunal to decide whether it shall be used or not (*ib.*).

Under this section, it is not necessary that *each* deposition should be signed by the Justice taking it. Therefore, where a number of depositions taken at the same hearing on several sheets of paper, were fastened together, and signed by the Justices taking them, once only, at the end of all the depositions, in the form given in the Schedule M, it was held that one of these depositions was admissible in evidence under section 30 of the Act, after the death of the witness making it, although no part of it was on the sheet signed by the Justice. *R.* v. *Parker*, L.R., 1 C. C. R., 225; *R.* v. *Richards*, 4 F. & F., 860, overruled.

Although the prisoner be cautioned, as provided by the 31st section, before he makes his statement, yet if his statement amount to a confession, and he was induced to make it by any previous promise of favour or threat, it cannot be read in evidence against him; unless, indeed, before he made the statement he had been undeceived as to the threat or promise, and told that he has nothing to fear from the one or hope from the other. The 32nd section of the statute was intended to remove this difficulty, and compliance with its provisions is only necessary in cases where such a threat or promise has been holden out; and in order to undeceive the prisoner in respect to it, and make his confession evidence against him notwithstanding. In all other cases it is sufficient to give the caution required by the 31st section, after which any confession not induced by threat or promise may be given in evidence against the prisoner. *R.* v. *Sansome*, 1 Den C. C., 545; *R.* v. *Bond*, *ib.* 517.

Under the 30th section the deposition of a witness who is dead may be read before the Grand Jury for the purpose of finding a bill, as well as before the Petty Jury at the trial. *R.* v. *Clements*, 20 L.J., M.C., 193. The presence of the accused and the Justice is indispensable. *R.* v. *Watts*, 33 L.J., M.C., 63. Although the cases of death, illness, and absence from Canada are alone expressly stated in this section as those in which the deposition of a witness may be read against a prisoner on his trial, it is probable that such deposition may also be read in evidence if the witness be bed-ridden, though otherwise not in ill-health (*R.* v. *Stephenson*, 31 L.J., M.C., 147), or if he have become insane, or if he be kept out of the way by the prisoner (*R.* v. *Scaife*, 20 L. J., M.C., 229; 17 Q. B., 238), or by some person on his behalf at the time of the trial; and it is admissible where the witness, having been struck by paralysis, is unable to speak though still able to travel (*R.* v. *Cockburn*, Dears. & B. 203); but it must relate to the charge on which the prisoner is being tried. *R.* v. *Langbridge*, 1 Den. C.C., 448.

It was proposed to read the deposition of a witness, on the ground that the witness was so ill as not to be able to travel. The evidence upon that point was as follows:—The medical attendant of the witness was called and said, "I know M. L., she is very nervous and seventy-four years of age. I think she would faint at the idea of coming into Court, but I think that she could go to London to see a doctor without difficulty or danger. I think the idea of seeing so many faces would be dangerous to her, and that she is so nervous that it might be dangerous to her to be examined at all. I think she could distinguish between the Court going to her house, and she herself coming to the Court." The witness, whose deposition it was proposed to read, lived not far from the Court. The deposition was held inadmissible. *R.* v. *Farrell*, L. R., 2 C. C. R., 116.

Upon the trial of the prisoner for obtaining money by false pretences, it was proved by a female servant and the brother of the prosecutrix, that she was daily expecting her confinement, and the latter stated that she was "poorly otherwise," and was therefore too ill to travel, it was held upon this evidence, the Statute 32 & 33 Vic. chap. 30, s. 30, authorized the presiding Judge to receive the depositions of the prosecutrix taken before the committing magistrate; that there may be incidents in regard to parturition, to bring the case within the statute; that it is in the discretion of the presiding Judge to determine, whether the evidence of illness is sufficient that it is not necessary in such case to produce medical evidence. *R.* v. *Stevenson*, L. & C., 165.

Formerly depositions were receivable only when the indictment was substantially for the same offence, as that which the defendant was charged with before the Justice. Now by the 32 & 33 Vic., chap. 29, s. 58, depositions taken in the preliminary or other investigation, of any charge against any person may be read as evidence in the prosecution of such person for any other offence whatsoever.

The statement of a deceased witness taken on oath by a magistrate, detailing the circumstances under which a felony was committed, is admissible in evidence on the trial under the (N. B.) 1 Rev. Stat. chap. 156, s. 7, though it is headed "the complaint of" &c., instead of "the examination" of the deceased, and does not state on its face to have been taken in the presence of the accused, it being proved that it was taken in his presence. *R.* v. *Miller*, 5 Allen, 87.

Justices of the Peace are liable in damages for illegal and malicious commitment, made without previous examination of witnesses before them, in the presence of the accused, as required by this (29th) section. *Lacombe* v. *Ste. Marie*, 15 L. C. J., 276.

30. The Justice or Justices shall, before any witness is examined, administer to such witness the usual oath or affirmation, which such Justice or Justices are hereby empowered to do; and if upon the trial of the person accused, it be proven upon the oath or affirmation of any credible witness, that any person whose deposition has been taken as aforesaid is dead, or is so ill as not to be able to travel, or is absent from Canada, and if it be also proved that such deposition was taken in presence of the person accused, and that he, his Counsel or Attorney, had a full opportunity of cross-examining the witness, then if the deposition purports to be signed by the Justice by or before whom the same purports to have been taken, it shall be read as evidence in the prosecution without further proof thereof, unless it be proved that such deposition was not in fact signed by the Justice purporting to have signed the same.

The deposition is not admissible on the ground merely that the prosecutor, after using every possible endeavour, cannot find the witness.

The Justice must proceed in the manner pointed out by this section. A defendant, arrested on a warrant, was brought before a Justice who examined him, but took no evidence either of the prosecutor or witnesses, and committed defendant to gaol, saying he could not bail. The defendant did not ask to have any hearing or investigation, or produce or offer to produce any evidence, or to give bail. It was held that the commitment, without the appearance of the prosecutor, or examination of any witnesses, or of the defendant, according to this section, or any legal confession, was an act wholly in excess of the jurisdiction of the magistrate and illegal. *Connors* v. *Darling*, 23 Q. B. (Ont.), 541.

31. After the examinations of all the witnesses for the prosecution have been completed, the Justice, or one of the Justices by or before whom the examinations have been completed, shall, without requiring the attendance of the witnesses, read or cause to be read to the accused, the depositions taken against him, and shall say to him these words, or words to the like effect: "Having heard the evidence, do you wish to say anything in answer "to the charge? You are not obliged to say anything unless you desire to do so, "but whatever you say will be taken down in writing, and may be given in "evidence against you upon your trial;" and whatever the prisoner then says in answer thereto shall be taken down in writing (N) and read over to him, and shall be signed by the Justice or Justices, and kept with the depositions of the witnesses, and shall be transmitted with them as hereinafter mentioned.

When a prisoner is willing to make a statement, it is the magistrate's duty to receive it, but he ought, before doing so, entirely to get rid of any impression that may have been on the prisoner's mind that the statement may be used for his own benefit, and he ought also to be told that what he thinks fit to say will be taken down, and may be used against him on the trial. The mode of doing this is now prescribed in terms by the 32 & 33 Vic., chap. 30, ss. 31 & 32. The caution contained in s. 32 is not necessary, unless it appears that some inducement or threat had previously been held out to the accused. *R.* v. *Sansome*, 1 Den., 545.

The 66th section of the statute declares that the several forms given in the schedule, or forms to the like effect shall be good, valid, and sufficient in law. The form (N) of the statement of the accused before the magistrate contains the cautions specified in s. 31, and not that in s. 32. Therefore a statement returned, purporting to be signed by the magistrate, and bearing on the face of it the caution provided for by s. 31, is admissable by s. 34, without further proof. *R.* v. *Bond*, 1 Den., 517.

The object of taking depositions under the 32 & 33 Vic., chap. 30, is not to afford information to the prisoner, but to preserve the evidence, if any of the witnesses is unable to attend the trial, or dies. This being the ground on which they are taken, until recently the prisoner had no right to see them. *R.* v. *Hamilton*, 16 C. P. (Ont.), 364.

Now he is entitled to inspect the depositions, that he may know why he is committed. See 32 & 33 Vic., chap. 29, s. 46.

The caution required to be given by this section is, by its terms, applicable to accused persons only, and has no application whatever to witnesses. Therefore, the depositions of a witness, regularly taken, but without any caution, may be used against him if he afterwards becomes the accused. *R.* v. *Coote*, 18 L. C. J., 103. L.R., 4 P. C. App., 599.

The caution does not apply to questions which criminate *(ib)*.

32. The Justice or Justices shall, before the accused person makes any statement, state to him and give him clearly to understand that he has nothing to hope from any promise of favour, and nothing to fear from any threat which may have been held out to him to induce him to make any admission or confession of his guilt, but that whatever he then says may be

given in evidence against him upon his trial, notwithstanding such promise or threat.

The only effect of this, however, is to enable the prosecutor to give in evidence upon the trial any confession of the prisoner made after it, notwithstanding any promise or threat previously made, the omission of it does not in the slightest degree prevent the prosecutor from giving in evidence a confession made before the Justice in the prisoner's statement above mentioned, after the usual cautions (*R.* v. *Sansome*, 19 L. J., M. C., 143), or a confession made at any other time which was not induced by any promise or threat.

If the form prescribed by the statute has not been followed, then the caution, the prisoner's statement, and the magistrate's signature must be proved as at common law (*R.* v. *Boyd*, 19 L. J., 141), namely, by the magistrate or his clerk, or by some person who was present at the examination. *R.* v. *Hearn*, C. & M., 109.

33. Nothing herein contained shall prevent any prosecutor from giving in evidence any admission or confession, or other statement made at any time by the person accused or charged, which by law would be admissible as evidence against him.

34. Upon the trial of the accused person, the examinations may, if necessary, be given in evidence against him without further proof thereof, unless it be proved that the Justice or Justices purporting to have signed the same, did not in fact sign the same.

35. The room or building in which the Justice or Justices take the examination and statement shall not be deemed an open Court for that purpose; and the Justice or Justices, in his or their discretion, may order that no person shall have access to or be or remain in such room or building without the consent or permission of such Justice or Justices, if it appear to him or them that the ends of justice will be best answered by so doing.

Under this section, the Justice may, in his discretion, order that no person shall have access to the room or building in which the examination is being taken, or shall be or remain in it without his consent or permission, if it appear to him that the ends of justice will be best answered by doing so. The Justices may exclude an attorney or counsel if they please (*R.* v. *Coleridge*, 1 B. & C., 37; *Collier* v. *Hicks*, 2 B. & Ad., 663; see also *Re Judge*, C.

C. York, 31 Q.B. (Ont.),267); but in no circumstances the accused. *R.* v. *Commins*, 4 D & R., 94.

The law is different in the case of summary convictions. See 32 & 33 Vic., chap. 31, s. 29.

36. Any Justice or Justices, before whom any witness is examined, may bind by Recognizance (O 1) the prosecutor, and every such witness, (except married women and infants) who shall find security for their appearance, if the Justice or Justices see fit, to appear at the next Court of competent Criminal Jurisdiction at which the accused is to be tried, then and there to prosecute, or prosecute and give evidence, or to give evidence, as the case may be, against the party accused, which Recognizance shall particularly specify the place of residence and the addition or occupation of each person entering into the same.

In reference to the provisions of the 32 & 33 Vic., chap. 29, s. 28, and 40 Vic., chap. 26, ss. 1 & 2, it is important that the prosecutor be bound by recognizance, as in this section provided, to prosecute and give evidence against the accused. In the cases of perjury, subornation of perjury, conspiracy, obtaining money or other property by false pretences, keeping a gambling house, keeping a disorderly house, or any indecent assault, or the offences of nuisance and of forcible entry or detainer, no bill of indictment shall be presented to or found by any grand jury, unless the prosecutor has been bound to give evidence, &c., or unless the person accused has been committed to or detained in custody, or has been bound by recognizance to appear to answer to an indictment to be preferred against him for such offence, or unless the indictment is preferred by direction of the Attorney or Solicitor-General, or a Judge of the Court, or with the consent of the Court. (*Ib.*)

37. The Recognizance, being duly acknowledged by the person entering into the same, shall be subscribed by the Justice or Justices before whom the same is acknowledged, and a notice (O 2) thereof, signed by the said Justice or Justices, shall at the same time be given to the person bound thereby.

A recognizance is an obligation of record, whereby a man acknowledges that he is indebted to our Lady the Queen in a certain sum of money, which obligation is to be at an end upon the party performing whatever is required of him by a certain condition written either at the foot or on the back of the recognizance.

And in all cases where a Justice of the Peace is authorized or required to bind a person or make him give security to do anything, he may do so by recognizance, and it is the ordinary and proper form of doing it. Thus binding a man over to prosecute, or a witness to give evidence, is by recognizance. Sureties to keep the peace or be of good behaviour, are by recognizance.

A Justice cannot be ordered by *mandamus* to go a distance to take a recognizance of a party committed by him to prison. *Ex parte Hays*, 26 J. P. 309.

The recognizance is taken by stating to the party the substance of it, but in the second person, "You A. B. acknowledge yourself to owe to our Sovereign Lady the Queen," &c. The Justices must then give to each of the parties, sureties, &c., the notice (O. 2) required by this section.

The party need not sign the recognizance, and the verbal acknowledgment is the date of it. *R.* v. *St. Albans*, 8 A & E., 933.

38. The several Recognizances so taken, together with the written information, if any, the depositions, the statement of the accused, and the Recognizance of Bail, if any, shall be delivered by the said Justice or Justices, or he or they shall cause the same to be delivered to the proper officer of the Court in which the trial is to be had, before or at the opening of the Court on the first day of the sitting thereof, or at such other time as the Judge, Justice, or person who is to preside at such court, or at the trial, orders and appoints.

The recognizances intended are the personal recognizances of the persons so bound over. The practical mode of taking the recognizance is as follows: The Justice, or his clerk in the Justice's presence, states to the party bound (and to his sureties if there are any), the substance of the recognizance. The parties bound assent to, but do not sign the recognizance, the Justice alone appending his signature thereto, and the notice is then given in the form (O. 2), to the prosecutor or witnesses. Care must be taken to suit the recognizance to the situation of the party bound, according to the variations of the form (O. 1), Kerr's Acts, 87. See as to returning depositions, *Burgoyne* v. *Moffatt*, 5 Allen, 13. A coroner is required to comply with this section in cases of examinations before him. See sec. 60.

Where a charge of an offence committed in another jurisdiction is heard by a Justice within whose jurisdiction an offender has been apprehended under a warrant backed under the 23rd section of the Act, the recognizances, depositions, &c., when returned to the Justice having jurisdiction where the offence was committed, must be transmitted to the proper officer of the court where the case is to be tried, pursuant to the provisions of the above section. See sec. 47.

39. If any witness refuses to enter into Recognizance, the Justice or Justices of the Peace by his or their warrant (P 1), may commit him to the Common Gaol for the Territorial Division in which the accused party is to be tried, there to be imprisoned and safely kept until after the trial of such accused party, unless in the meantime such witness duly enters into a Recognizance before some one Justice of the Peace for the Territorial Division in which such gaol is situate.

40. If afterwards, for want of sufficient evidence in that behalf or other cause, the Justice or Justices before whom the accused party has been brought, do not commit him or hold him to bail for the offence charged, such Justice or Justices or any other Justice or Justices for the same Territorial Division, by his or their order (P 2) in that behalf, may order and direct the Keeper of the Gaol where the witness is in custody, to discharge him from the same, and such Keeper shall thereupon forthwith discharge him accordingly.

After all the evidence is taken and there appears to be no case against the prisoner, the discharge is verbally made, no document or writing of any kind being required.

41. If from the absence of witnesses, or from any other reasonable cause, it becomes necessary or advisable to defer the examination or further examination of the witnesses for any time, the Justice or Justices before whom the accused appears or has been brought, may, by his or their warrant (Q 1) from time to time, remand the party accused for such time as by such Justice or Justices in his or their discretion may be deemed reasonable, not exceeding eight clear days at any one time, to the common gaol in the Territorial Division for which such Justice or Justices are then acting.

There is no power at one time to remand for a period exceeding eight clear days, but at the expiration of such time there may be a further remand for eight days, and so on. A remand for an unreasonable time would be void. *Connors* v. *Darling*, 23 Q. B. (Ont.), 547-51.

Committing Magistrates are not responsible for the condition of the lock-ups, and a Justice who remands a prisoner under this section, without any express direction to take him to the lock-up, is not responsible for the prisoner's sufferings in the lock-up, if the constable takes him there instead of to the common gaol of the county. *Crawford* v. *Beattie*, 39 Q. B. (Ont.), 13.

42. If the remand be for a time not exceeding three clear days, the Justice or Justices may verbally order the Constable or other person in whose custody the accused party may then be, or any other Constable or person to be named by the Justice or Justices in that behalf, to keep the accused party in his custody, and to bring him before the same or such other Justice or Justices as may be there acting, at the time appointed for continuing the examination.

43. Any such Justice or Justices may order the accused party to be brought before him or them, or before any other Justice or Justices of the Peace for the same Territorial Division, at any time before the expiration of the time for which such party has been remanded, and the Gaoler or Officer in whose custody he then is, shall duly obey such order.

44. Instead of detaining the accused party in custody during the period for which he has been so remanded, any one Justice of the Peace before whom such party has appeared or been brought, may discharge him, upon his entering into a Recognizance (Q 2, 3) with or without a surety or sureties, at the discretion of the Justice, conditioned for his appearance at the time and place appointed for the continuance of the examination.

A recognizance of bail only obliges the prisoner to appear to plead to such indictment as may be found against him. If, therefore, no indictment is found, his non-appearance will not forfeit the recognizance. *R.* v. *Ritchie*, 1 U. C. L. J., N. S., 272.

After the accused has appeared and pleaded not guilty to the indictment, no default can be recorded against him without notice, unless it be on a day appointed for his appearance. *R.* v. *Croteau*, 9 L. C. R., 67.

By the terms of this section it is entirely in the Justice's discretion, in every case, whether he will allow the accused to go on bail during an adjournment of the hearing. It is otherwise when the Justice has completed the examination and committed for trial, for then (as will be seen by sections 52 and 56), the accused is, in cases of misdemeanor, entitled to bail, but in felonies he is not so entitled. As a general rule it may be said that in practice it is not usual on a remand (especially where the precise nature or extent of the charge is undeveloped), for magistrates to admit to bail in those cases in which an accused is not entitled to be bailed after committal, unless the amount of property involved is very small. Kerr's Acts, 90.

45. If the accused party does not afterwards appear at the time and place mentioned in the Recognizance, the said Justice or any other Justice of the Peace who may then and there be present, having certified (Q 4) upon the back of the Recognizance the non-appearance of such accused party, may transmit the Recognizance to the Clerk of the Court where the accused person is to be tried, or other proper officer appointed by law, to be proceeded upon in like manner as other recognizances, and such certificate shall be deemed sufficient *primâ facie* evidence of the non-appearance of the accused party.

46. Whenever a person appears or is brought before a Justice or Justices of the Peace in the Territorial Division wherein such Justice or Justices have jurisdiction, charged with an offence alleged to have been committed by him within any Territorial Division in Canada wherein such Justice or Justices have not jurisdiction, such Justice or Justices shall examine such witnesses and receive such evidence in proof of the charge as may be produced before him or them within his or their jurisdiction ; and if in his or their opinion, such testimony and evidence be sufficient proof of the charge made against the accused party, the Justice or Justices shall thereupon commit him to the Common Gaol for the Territorial Division where the offence is alleged to have been committed, or shall admit him to bail as hereinafter mentioned, and shall bind over the prosecutor (if he has appeared before him or them) and the witnesses, by recognizance as hereinbefore mentioned.

47. If the testimony and evidence be not, in the opinion of the Justice or Justices, sufficient to put the accused party upon his trial for the offence with which he is charged, then the Justice or Justices shall, by Recognizance, bind over the witness or witnesses whom he has examined to give evidence as hereinbefore mentioned ; and such Justice or Justices shall, by Warrant (R 1), order the accused party to be taken before some Justice or Justices of the Peace in and for the Territorial Division where the offence is alleged to have been committed, and shall at the same time deliver up the information and complaint, and also the depositions and Recognizances so taken by him or them to the Constable who has the execution of the last mentioned Warrant,

to be by him delivered to the Justice or Justices before whom he takes the accused, in obedience to the Warrant, and the depositions and Recognizances shall be deemed to be taken in the case, and shall be treated to all intents and purposes as if they had been taken by or before the last mentioned Justice or Justices and shall together with the depositions and Recognizances taken by the last mentioned Justice or Justices in the matter of the charge against the accused party, be transmitted to the Clerk of the Court or other proper officer where the accused party ought to be tried, in the manner and at the time hereinbefore mentioned, if the accused party should be committed for trial upon the charge, or be admitted to bail.

48. In case such accused party be taken before the Justice or Justices last aforesaid, by virtue of the said last mentioned Warrant, the Constable or other person or persons to whom the said Warrant is directed, and who has conveyed such accused party before such last mentioned Justice or Justices, shall upon producing the said accused party before such Justice or Justices and delivering him into the custody of such person as the said Justice or Justices direct or name in that behalf, be entitled to be paid his costs and expenses of conveying the said accused party before the said Justice or Justices.

49. Upon the Constable delivering to the Justice or Justices the Warrant, information (if any), depositions and Recognizances. and proving on oath or affirmation the hand-writing of the Justice or Justices who has subscribed the same, such Justice or Justices before whom the accused party is produced, shall thereupon furnish such Constable with a receipt or certificate (R 2), of his or their having received from him the body of the accused party, together with the Warrant, information (if any), depositions and Recognizances, and of his having proved to him or them, upon oath or affirmation, the hand-writing of the Justice who issued the Warrant.

50. The said Constable, on producing such receipt or certificate to the proper officer for paying such charges, shall be entitled to be paid all his reasonable charges, costs and expenses of conveying such accused party into such other Territorial Division, and of returning from the same.

51. If such Justice or Justices do not commit the accused party for trial, or hold him to bail, then the Recognizances taken before the first mentioned Justice or Justices shall be void.

52. When any person appears before any Justice of the Peace charged with a felony, or suspicion of felony, other than treason or felony punishable with death, or felony under the Act for the better protection of the Crown and of the Government, and the evidence adduced is in the opinion of such Justice, sufficient to put such accused party on his trial, but does not furnish such a strong presumption of guilt as to warrant his committal for trial, the Justice,

jointly with some other Justice of the Peace, may admit such person to bail upon his procuring and producing such surety or sureties as in the opinion of the two Justices will be sufficient to ensure the appearance of the person charged, at the time and place when and where he ought to be tried for the offence ; and thereupon the two Justices shall take the Recognizances (S 1, 2,) of the accused person and his sureties, conditioned for his appearance at the time and place of trial, and that he will then surrender and take his trial and not depart the Court without leave ; and when the offence committed or suspected to have been committed is a misdemeanor, any one Justice before whom the accused party appears may admit to bail in manner aforesaid ;— And such Justice may, in his discretion, require such bail to justify upon oath as to their sufficiency, which oath the said Justice may administer, and in default of such person procuring sufficient bail, then such Justice may commit him to prison, there to be kept until delivered according to law.

Under this and the 56th section, it is only the Justice who took the evidence that can bail.

Under the 59th section of the Act, certain functionaries, such as any Police Magistrate, District Magistrate, or Stipendiary Magistrate, have the power of two Justices of the Peace, and may admit to bail.

The amount of bail is fixed by the Justice, the character of the charge and evidence, position of the accused being considered. Sureties are usually householders, but it is in the discretion of the Justice to accept whom he will ; he may examine proposed sureties on oath, but the examination should tend to the sufficiency of the surety, and not to character. *R.* v. *Badger*, 4 Q. B. 468.

The qualification of property rather than of character is the main consideration. *R.* v. *Saunders*, 2 Cox, 249. The Justices may if they think fit, require twenty-four or forty-eight hours notice of the bail proposed to be given to the other side.

The number of bail is usually two men of ability, but the Court of Queen's Bench, on a commitment for treason or felony, often requires four. *R.* v. *Shaw*, 6 D. & R., 154.

In determining as to the propriety of taking bail, the nature of the crime and punishment, and the weight of evidence are to be considered. *Re Robinson*, 23 L. J. M. C., 25; *R.* v. *Barronet*, 1 E. & B. 1. In the case of murder, Justices never admit to bail if the evidence be strong against the accused, and the same in the case of stabbing or wounding where death is likely to ensue.

Prisoners charged with murder cannot be admitted to bail, unless it be under very extreme circumstances, as where facts are brought before the Court to show that the bill cannot be sustained. The fact that prisoners indicted for wilful murder cannot be tried until the next term, is no ground for admitting them to bail. *R.* v. *Murphy*, 1 James, 158. But accessories after the fact, who have merely harboured prisoners guilty of murder, may be admitted to bail (*ib.*)

A prisoner charged with murder may in some cases in the exercise of a sound discretion be admitted to bail. On an application for bail, the Court may look into the information, and, if they find good ground for a charge of felony, may remedy a defect in the commitment, by charging a felony in it so that the prisoner would not be entitled to bail on the ground of the defective commitment. *R.* v. *Higgins*, 4 O. S., 83. A person charged with having murdered his wife in Ireland will not be admitted to bail, until a year has elapsed from the time of the first imprisonment, although no proceedings have in the meantime been taken by the Crown, and no answer has been received to a communication from the Provincial to the Home Government on the subject. *R.* v. *Fitzgerald*, 3 O. S., 300.

Where a person charged with murder applies for bail, the Judge will look to the gravity of the offence, the weight of the evidence and the severity of the punishment, and may refuse bail. *Ex parte Corriveau*, 6 L. C. R., 249.

A prisoner charged with felony may be released on bail, if it is satisfactorily established, that, unless liberated, he will in all probability not live until the time fixed for his trial. *Ex parte Blossom*, 10 L. C. J., 71.

A prisoner confined upon a charge of arson, may be admitted to bail after a bill found by a Grand Jury, if the depositions against him are found to create but a very slight suspicion of his guilt. *Ex parte Maguire*, 7 L. C. R., 57.

Bail was granted after commitment on a charge of arson, where it was not proved by the depositions produced that the prisoner was guilty, though the depositions also failed to show that he was innocent. *Ex parte Onasakeurat*, 21 L. C. J., 219.

A prisoner in custody for larceny may be admitted to bail, when the evidence discloses very slight grounds for suspicion. *R.* v. *Jones*, 4 O. S. 18.

The Con. Stats. L. C., chap. 95 excepts persons committed for treason or felony, as well as persons convicted or in execution by legal process, who are not entitled to bail in term or vacation. *Ex parte Blossom*, 10 L. C. J., 43.

The Court may order bail in a case of perjury. *R.* v. *Johnson*, 8 L. C. J. 285. By the words of the Con. Stats. L. C. chap. 95, it is obligatory upon the Judge in a case of misdemeanor to admit to bail. *Ex parte Blossom*, 10 L. C. J., 31.

All misdemeanors whether common or otherwise are bailable. Under this section it is obligatory upon Justices of the Peace to admit to bail in all cases of misdemeanor. The Statute is equally binding upon the Judges of the Superior Courts.

The word "shall," in section 56 of this Statute is imperative. *Ex parte Blossom*, 10 L. C. J. 35, 67-8, 73.

Several persons were accused of a misdemeanor, and in the opinion of the Judge presiding, the evidence adduced was positive against them. Two juries had been discharged because they could not agree upon a verdict. The Court ordered them to be committed to gaol without bail or mainprize, to be tried again at the next term and not to be discharged without further order from the Court. *R.* v. *Blossom*, 10 L. C. J., 29.

A prisoner was charged with conspiracy to kidnap one G. N. S. and steal and carry him away into the United States. The Grand Jury found a true bill against him for misdemeanor. He was twice tried for the offence, on the first occasion the jury after three days' deliberation, being unable to agree, were discharged; and on the second occasion, the jury did not agree after three days' deliberation, and were also discharged. It was held that under these circumstances the prisoner was entitled to bail by virtue of the Con. Stats. L. C., chap. 95. The circumstances raising a presumption of his innocence. *Ex parte Blossom*, 10 L. C. J., 30.

The word "may" in this (52nd) section must be considered as conferring a power, and not as giving a discretion. The object of the Act is to declare that one Justice cannot bail in felony, but may in misdemeanor. *Ex parte Blossom*, 10 L. C. J., 67.

If an offence is bailable, and the party, at the time of his apprehension, is unable to obtain immediate sureties, he may at any time on producing proper persons as sureties be liberated from confinement. *Ib.*, 68.

The reason why parties are committed to prison by Justices before trial, is for the purpose of ensuring or making certain their appearance to take their trial, and the same principle is to be adopted on an application for bail. It is not a question as to the guilt or innocence of the prisoner. On this account it is necessary to see whether the offence is serious and severely punishable, and whether the evidence is clear and conclusive. *R.* v. *Brynes*, 8 U. C. L.J., 76; *R.* v. *Scaife*, 9 Dowl. P.C., 553.

When the charge against a prisoner is that he procured a person to set fire to his house, with intent to defraud an insurance company, and it is shown that the prisoner attempted to bribe the constable to allow him to escape, the probability of his appearing to stand his trial is too slight for the Judge to order bail. *R* v. *Brynes*, *supra*. The principle upon which a party committed to take his trial for an offence may be bailed, is founded chiefly upon the legal probability of his appearing to take his trial. Such probability does not exist in contemplation of law when a crime is of the highest magnitude, the evidence in support of the charge strong, and the punishment the severest known to the law. *Ex parte Maguire*, 7 L. C. R., 59.

On an application by prisoners in custody on a charge of murder under a coroner's warrant, it is proper to consider the probability of their forfeiting their bail if they know themselves to be guilty; and where in such a case there is such a presumption of the guilt of the prisoner as would warrant a Grand Jury in finding a true bill, they should not be admitted to bail. *R.* v. *Mullady*, 4 P.R. (Ont.), 314.

It has been held that although a statute may require the presence of three Justices to convict of an offence, yet one has power to bail the offender; and a second arrest for the same charge by the same complainant before the time appointed for the hearing is illegal. *King* v. *Orr*, 5 O.S. 724. But under the above section one Justice cannot bail except in the case of a misdemeanor.

It is a misdemeanor for Justices or Judges to exact excessive bail; and the party may also bring an action or apply for a criminal information.

It was held before the passing of the 16 Vic., chap. 179, that Magistrates were not liable for refusing to admit to bail on a charge of misdemeanor, in the absence of any proof of malice. *Conroy* v. *McKenney*, 11 Q.B. (Ont.), 439; see *McKinley* v. *Munsie*, 15 C. P. (Ont.), 230; see *R.* v. *Mosier*, 4 P. R. (Ont.), 64, as to bail.

A Justice of the Peace might perhaps in a matter in which he could properly act, and in which he was bound to admit a person charged with an offence to bail, be prosecuted for maliciously refusing to take bail. *McKinley* v. *Munsie*, 15 C. P. (Ont.) 236.

Where plaintiff was arrested and imprisoned by a Magistrate on an information laid by defendant himself, a Magistrate, who was present when the Magistrate refused to grant bail, it was held in the absence of any evidence, that the defendant had directed the officer to take the plaintiff to prison, or had influenced the other Magistrate in sending him there, or that the officer was present when the defendant and the other Magistrate declined to take bail, and said they would send the plaintiff to prison, or that he even knew that defendant had said anything about it, that the mere refusal of the defendant to admit the plaintiff to bail was not evidence to go to the jury, that the defendant authorized the illegal arrest and imprisonment of the plaintiff. *Ib.* 230.

53. In all cases of felony, or suspicion of felony, other than treason or felony, punishable with death, or felony under the Act for the better protection of the Crown and of the Government, and in all cases of misdemeanor, where the party accused has been finally committed as hereinafter provided, any Judge of any Superior or County Court, having jurisdiction in the District or County, within the limits of which such accused party is confined, may, in his discretion, on application made to him for that purpose, order such accused party or person to be admitted to bail on entering into Recognizance with sufficient sureties before two Justices of the Peace, in such amount as the Judge directs, and thereupon the Justices shall issue a Warrant of Deliverance (S 3), as hereinafter provided, and shall attach thereto the order of the Judge directing the admitting of such party to bail.

In Prince Edward Island, by the 40 Vic. chap. 4, s. 4, any Judge of the Supreme Court, or County Court, shall have power to order the admission of an accused party to bail under sections fifty-three and sixty-one of the Act 32 & 33 Vic. chap. 30. And generally any power vested by any of the Acts thereby extended in any Court, Magistrate or Tribunal, may be exercised respectively by any Court, Magistrate or Tribunal of like name or kind in the said Province.

54. No Justices of the Peace, or County Judge shall admit any person to bail accused of treason or felony punishable with death, or felony under the Act for the better protection of the Crown and of the Government, nor shall any such person be admitted to bail, except by order of a Superior Court of Criminal Jurisdiction for the Province in which the accused person stands committed, or of one of the Judges thereof, or in the Province of Quebec, by order of a Judge of the Court of Queen's Bench or Superior Court; and nothing herein contained, shall prevent such Courts or Judges admitting any person accused of misdemeanor or felony to bail when they may think it right so to do.

55. In all cases where a Justice or Justices of the Peace admit to bail any person who is then in any prison charged with the offence for which he is so admitted to bail, the Justice or Justices shall send to or cause to be lodged with the Keeper of such prison, a Warrant of Deliverance (S 3), under his or their hand and seal or hands and seals, requiring the said Keeper to discharge the person so admitted to bail if he be detained for no other offence, and upon such Warrant of Deliverance being delivered to or lodged with such Keeper he shall forthwith obey the same.

56. When all the evidence offered upon the part of the prosecution against the accused party has been heard, if the Justice or Justices of the Peace then present are of opinion that it is not sufficient to put the accused party upon his trial for any indictable offence, such Justice or Justices shall forthwith order the accused party, if in custody, to be discharged as to the Information then under inquiry; but if in the opinion of such Justice or Justices the evidence is sufficient to put the accused party upon his trial for an indictable offence, although it may not raise such a strong presumption of guilt as would induce them to commit the accused for trial without bail, or if the offence with which the party is accused is a misdemeanor, then the Justices shall admit the party to bail as hereinbefore provided, but if the offence be a felony, and the evidence given is such as to raise a strong presumption of guilt, then the Justice or Justices shall by his or their Warrant (T 1), commit him to the Common Gaol for the Territorial Division to which he may by law be com-

mitted, or in the case of an indictable offence committed on the high seas or on land beyond the sea, to the Common Gaol of the Territorial Division within which such Justice or Justices have jurisdiction, to be there safely kept until delivered by due course of law: Provided that in cases of misdemeanor the Justice or Justices who have committed the offender for trial, may, at any time before the first day of the sitting of the Court at which he is to be tried, bail such offender in manner aforesaid, or may certify on the back of the Warrant of committal the amount of bail to be required, in which case any other Justice of the Peace for the same Territorial Division may admit such person to bail in such amount, at any time before such first day of the sitting of the Court aforesaid.

It would seem that a discharge under this section does not operate as a bar to the same person being again brought up before another Justice and committed upon the same charge upon the same or different evidence. *R.* v. *Morton*, 19 C. P. (Ont.) 26.

Justices ought not to balance the evidence and decide according as it preponderates, for this would, in fact, be taking upon themselves the functions of the Petty Jury and be trying the case. They should consider whether or not the evidence makes out a strong, or probable, or conflicting case of guilt. In the first case they should commit, in the second and third they should admit to bail. If, however, from the slender nature of the evidence, the unworthiness of the witnesses, or the conclusive proof of innocence produced on the part of the accused, by way of confession and avoidance, they feel that the case is not sustained, and that if they send it for trial he must be acquitted, they should discharge the accused. Kerr's Acts, 100, 1.

If the evidence goes to prove an offence which the Justices cannot decide summarily, they ought to dismiss the complaint or commit the person charged for trial. *Re Thompson*, 30 L. J., M.C., 19. If the warrant be defective or bad a new warrant may be made out and lodged with the gaoler to cure the defect, and this even in a case where the warrant is in the nature of a conviction as well as commitment as under the Vagrant Act. *Ex parte Cross*, 26 L. J., M.C., 201.

57. The Constable or any of the Constables or other persons to whom any Warrant of Commitment authorized by this or any other Act or law is directed, shall convey the accused person therein named or described to the gaol

or other prison mentioned in such Warrant, and there deliver him, together with the Warrant to the Keeper of such gaol or prison, who shall thereupon give the Constable or other person delivering the prisoner into his custody a receipt (T 2) for the prisoner setting forth the state and condition of the prisoner when delivered into his custody.

58. At any time after all the examinations have been completed, and before the first sitting of the Court at which any person so committed to prison or admitted to bail is to be tried, such person may require and shall be entitled to have from the Officer or person having the custody of the same, copies of the depositions on which he has been committed or bailed, on payment of a reasonable sum for the same, not exceeding the rate of five cents for each folio of one hundred words.

See *ante*, p. 14.

59. Any Judge of the Sessions of the Peace for the City of Quebec or for the City of Montreal, or any Police Magistrate, District Magistrate or Stipendiary Magistrate, appointed for any Territorial Division, or any Magistrate authorized by the law of the Province in which he acts, to perform acts usually required to be done by two or more Justices of the Peace, may do alone whatever is authorized by this Act to be done by any two or more Justices of the Peace, and the several forms in this Act contained may be varied so far as necessary to render them applicable to such case.

See also 32 & 33 Vic., chap. 36, s. 8.

60. Every Coroner, upon any inquisition taken before him, whereby any person is indicted for manslaughter or murder, or as an accessory to murder before the fact, shall, in presence of the party accused, if he can be apprehended, put in writing the evidence given to the Jury before him, or as much thereof as may be material, giving the party accused full opportunity of cross-examination; and the Coroner shall have authority to bind by recognizance all such persons as know or declare anything material touching manslaughter or murder, or the offence of being accessory to murder, to appear at the next Court of Oyer and Terminer, or Gaol Delivery, or other Court or term or sitting of a Court at which the trial is to be, then and there to prosecute or give evidence against the party charged; and every such Coroner shall certify and subscribe the evidence, and all the recognizances, and also the inquisition before him taken, and shall deliver the same to the proper Officer of the Court at the time and in the manner specified in the thirty-eighth section of this Act.

61. When any person has been committed for trial by any Justice or Justices, or Coroner, the Prisoner, his Counsel, Attorney or Agent, may notify the committing Justice or Justices, or Coroner, that he will so soon as coun-

sel can be heard, move one of Her Majesty's Courts of Superior Criminal Jurisdiction for the Province in which such person stands committed, or one of the Judges thereof, or in the Province of Quebec, a Judge of the Court of Queen's Bench, or of the Superior Court, or in the Provinces of Ontario or New Brunswick, the Judge of the County Court if it is intended to apply to such Judge under the fifty-third section of this Act, for an order to the Justices of the Peace, or Coroner for the Territorial Division where such Prisoner is confined, to admit such Prisoner to bail, whereupon such committing Justice or Justices, or Coroner, shall, with all convenient expedition, transmit to the office of the Clerk of the Crown, or the Chief Clerk of the Court, or the Clerk of the County Court or other proper officer (as the case may be), close under the hand and seal of one of them, a certified copy of all informations, examinations, and other evidences, touching the offence wherewith the Prisoner has been charged, together with a copy of the Warrant of commitment and inquest, if any such there be, and the packet containing the same shall be handed to the person applying therefor, in order to its transmission, and it shall be certified on the outside thereof to contain the information touching the case in question.

As to Prince Edward Island, the 40 Vic. chap 4, s. 4, provides that any Judge of the Supreme Court or County Court shall have power to order the admission of an accused party to bail, under sections 53 and 61 of this Act.

62. Upon such application to any such Court or Judge as in the last preceding section mentioned, the same order touching the prisoner being bailed or continued in custody shall be made as if the party were brought up upon a *Habeas Corpus*.

63. If any Justice or Coroner neglects or offends in any thing contrary to the true intent and meaning of any of the provisions of the sixtieth and following sections of this Act, the Court to whose Officer any such examination, information, evidence, bailment, recognizance, or inquisition ought to have been delivered, shall, upon examination and proof of the offence, in a summary manner, set such fine upon every such Justice or Coroner as the Court thinks meet.

64. The provisions of this Act relating to Justices and Coroners shall apply to the Justices and Coroners not only of Districts and Counties at large, but also of all other Territorial Divisions and Jurisdictions.

65. The words "Territorial Division," whenever used in this Act shall mean County, Union of Counties, Township, City, Town, Parish or other Juridical Division or place to which the context may apply.

66. The several forms in the Schedule to this Act contained, or forms to the like effect, shall be good, valid and sufficient in law.

The Interpretation Act, 31 Vic. chap. 1, s. 7, thirty-firstly, provides where forms are prescribed slight deviations therefrom, not affecting the substance or calculated to mislead, shall not vitiate them.

67. This Act shall commence and take effect on the first day of January, in the year of our Lord, one thousand eight hundred and seventy.

SCHEDULES.

(A) *Vide* ss. 1 *and* 9.

INFORMATION AND COMPLAINT FOR AN INDICTABLE OFFENCE.

Canada,
Province of
District (*or* County,
United Counties, *or*
as the case may be,)
of

The information and complaint of C. D. of (*yeoman*), taken day of , in the year of our Lord , before the undersigned, (*one*) of Her Majesty's Justices of the Peace, in and for the said District (*or* County, *or as the case may be*,) of who saith that (*&c.*, *stating the offence.*)

Sworn (*or* affirmed) before (*me*) the day and year first above mentioned, at

J. S.

STATEMENT OF OFFENCES IN INFORMATIONS.

In the following forms, the place of the commission of the offence is stated in the body of the information. This is not absolutely required—when the District, County or place is named in the margin of the information as in the form A. it is the venue for all the facts stated in the body of the information. 32 & 33 Vic. chap. 29, s. 15. *See R.* v. *Cavanagh*, 27 C. P. (Ont.) 537.

Murder.

A. B., on the day of , in the year of our Lord, one thousand eight hundred and , at , in the County (*or* District) of , did feloniously, wilfully, and of his malice aforethought, kill and murder one C. D.

Manslaughter.

Same as last form, omitting " wilfully, and of malice aforethought," *and substituting the word* " slay " *for the word* " murder."

Bodily Harm.

J. B., on the day of , at did feloniously administer to (*or* cause to be taken by) one A. B., poison (or other destructive thing), and did thereby cause grievous bodily harm to the said A. B., with intent feloniously, wilfully, and of his malice aforethought, to kill and murder the said A. B. (*or* C. D.)

Rape.

A. B., on the day of , at , by force and against her will, feloniously ravished and carnally knew C. D., a woman above the age of *twelve* years.

Simple Larceny.

A. B., on the day of , at , did feloniously steal, take and carry away a *gold watch*, the property of C. D.

Robbery.

A. B., on the day of , at , in and upon one C. D., feloniously did make an assault and him the said C. D., in bodily fear, and danger of his life, then feloniously did put, and the money of the said C. D., to the amount of ten dollars from the person, and against the will of the said C. D., then feloniously and violently, did steal, take, and carry away against the form, &c., and that the said A. B., at the time of, or immediately before or after such robbery (*if the case be so*), the said C. D., feloniously did wound against the form of the statute in such case made and provided.

Burglary.

A. B., on the day of , at , did feloniously and burglariously break into and enter the dwelling house of C. D., in the night time, with intent, the goods and chattels of the said C. D., in the said dwelling house, then and there being found, then and there feloniously and burglariously to steal, take and carry away (*or as the case may be*).

Stealing money.

A. B., on the day of , at , did feloniously steal a certain sum of money, to wit, to the amount of dollars, the property of one C. D. (*or as the case may be*).

Embezzlement.

A. B., on the day of , at , being a servant (*or* clerk) then employed in that capacity by one C. D., did then and there in virtue thereof, receive a certain sum of money to wit, to the amount of for and on account of the said C. D., and the said money did fraudulently and feloniously embezzle.

False Pretences.

A. B., on the day of , at , unlawfully, fraudulently and knowingly by false pretences, did obtain from one C. D., *six yards of muslin*, of the goods and chattels of the said C. D., with intent to defraud.

Offences against the Habitation.

A. B., on the day of , at , did unlawfully, feloniously and maliciously set fire to the dwelling house of C. D., and the said C. D., (*or some other person by name, or if the name be unknown,* some person) being therein.

Malicious Injuries to Property.

A. B., on the day of , at , did unlawfully, feloniously, and maliciously set fire, or attempt to set fire to a certain building or erection, that is to say (a house *or* barn *or* bridge, *or as the case may be*), the property of one C. D. (*or as the case may be*).

Forgery.

A. B. on the day of , at , did feloniously forge (*or* utter, knowing the same to be forged), a certain *promissory note, etc.* (*or* feloniously, wilfully, and without the consent of the owner, did make an *alteration* in a certain written instrument with intent to defraud, which said alteration is as follows, that is to say, *or as the case may be*).

Coining.

A. B., on the day of , at , did feloniously counterfeit a gold coin of the United Kingdom, called a *sovereign*, current by law in Canada, with intent to defraud,

had in his possession rfe of a gold coin of the United Kingdom, called a *sovereign*, current by law in Canada, knowing the same to be counterfeit, and with intent to defraud by uttering the same

Perjury.

Heretofore to wit, at the (*Assizes*) holden for the County (*or* District) of , on the day of , in the year of Our Lord one thousand eight hundred and , before , (*one of the Judges of Our Lady the Queen*), a certain issue between one E. F. and one J. H. in a certain action of *covenant*, was tried, upon which trial A. B. appeared as a witness for and on behalf of the said E. F., and was then and there duly *sworn* before the said , and did then and there, upon his *oath* aforesaid, falsely, wilfully, and corruptly depose and *swear* in substance and to the effect following, "*that he saw the said G. H. duly execute the deed on which the said action was brought*," whereas, in truth, the said A. B. did not see the said G. H. execute the said deed, and the said deed was not executed by the said G. H., and the said A. B. did thereby commit wilful and corrupt perjury.

Subornation of Perjury.

Same as last form to the end and then proceed;—That before the committing of the said offence by the said A. B., to wit, on the day of , at , C. D., unlawfully, wilfully, and corruptly did cause and procure the said A. B. to do and commit the said offence in manner and form aforesaid.

Offences against the Public Peace.

A. B., on the day of , at , with *two* or more persons, did riotously and tumultuously assemble together to the disturbance of the public peace, and unlawfully, feloniously, and with force did demolish, pull down, or destroy (*or* attempt or begin to demolish, etc.), a certain building or erection of C. D.

Offences against the Administration of Justice.

A. B., on the day of , at , did feloniously, unlawfully, and corruptly take or receive money under pretence of helping C. D. to a chattel (*or* money, etc.) that is to say a horse (*or* five dollars, *or* a note, *or* a carriage), which had been stolen (*or as the case may be*), the said A. B. not having used all due diligence to cause the person by whom the said goods were so stolen to be brought to trial for the same.

Bigamy or Offences against the Law for the Celebration of Marriage.

A. B., on the day of , at , being then married, did feloniously marry C. D. during the lifetime of the wife of the said A. B.—(*or* not being duly authorized did celebrate (*or* assist in the celebration of), a marriage between C.D. and E.F.,—*or* being duly authorized to marry did celebrate marriage between C. D. and E. F. before proclamation of banns according to law, *or* without a license for such marriage under the hand and seal of the Governor.

Offences relating to the Army.

A. B., not being an enlisted soldier, on the day of , at did persuade (*or* procure) C. D., a soldier, to desert the Queen's service (*or as the case may be*).

Offences against Public Morals and Decency.

A. B., on the day of , at , did keep a common gaming, bawdy, *or* disorderly house (*or* rooms).

INFORMATION AGAINST AN ACCESSORY AFTER THE FACT TO A FELONY WITH THE PRINCIPAL (not in Statute, Oke's Form, p. 487, No. 2).

Proceed as in No. 1, supra, and after describing the offence of the principal, state thus:—And that C. S., of, etc., well knowing the said A. B. to have committed the felony aforesaid, afterwards, to wit, on the day of instant, at the of aforesaid, feloniously did receive, harbour, and maintain the said A. B.

THE LIKE WITHOUT THE PRINCIPAL OR WHERE THE PRINCIPAL UNKNOWN (not in Statute, Oke's Forms, p. 487, No. 3).

Proceed as in No. 1, supra, to the statement of the offence, then thus:—That one A. B., of, etc., (or some person or persons whose name or names is or are unknown), on the day of at the of etc., feloniously did (*describe the offence of the principal*), and that E. S., of well knowing the said A. B. (or person unknown) to have committed the felony aforesaid, afterwards, to wit, on the day of at the of aforesaid, feloniously did receive, harbour, and maintain the said A. B. (or person unknown).

General Form.

Describe the offence in the terms in which it is described in the law, or state such facts as constitute the offence intended to be charged, and if the offence be felony, state the act to have been done feloniously.

(B) *See* ss. 1, 17.

WARRANT TO APPREHEND A PERSON CHARGED WITH AN INDICTABLE OFFENCE.

Canada,
Province of
District (*or* County,
United Counties, *or*
as the case may be,)
of

To all or any of the Constables or other Peace Officers in the District (*or* County, United Counties, *or as the case may be*,) of :

Whereas A. B., of (*labourer*), hath this day , been charged upon oath before the undersigned, (*one*) of Her Majesty's Justices of the Peace in and for the said District (*or* County, United Counties, *or as the case may be*) of , for that he, on , at , did (*&c., stating shortly the offence*); These are therefore to command you, in Her Majesty's name, forthwith to apprehend the said A. B., and to bring him before (*me*) or some other of Her Majesty's Justices of the Peace in and for the said District *or* County, United Counties, *or as the case may be*,) of , to answer unto the said charge, and to be further dealt with according to law.

Given under (*my*) Hand and Seal, this day of , at , in the District (*County, &c.*,) aforesaid.

J. S. [L. S.]

(C) *See* ss. 2, 13.

SUMMONS TO A PERSON CHARGED WITH AN INDICTABLE OFFENCE.

Canada,
District (*or* County,
United Counties, *or*
as the case may be,)
of

To A. B. of , (*labourer*):

Whereas you have this day been charged before the undersigned (*one*) of Her Majesty's Justices of the Peace in and for the said District (*or* County, United Counties, *or as the case may be*,) of for that you on , at , (*&c., stating shortly the offence*); These are therefore to command you, in Her Majesty's name, to be and appear before (*me*) on , at o'clock in the (*fore*) noon, at , or before such other Justice or Justices of the Peace of the same District (*or* County, United

Counties, *as the case may be,*) of , as may then be there to answer to the said charge, and to be further dealt with according to law. Herein fail not.

Given under (*my*) Hand and Seal, this day of , in the year of Our Lord , at , in the District (*or* County, *&c.*,) aforesaid.

J. S. [L. S.]

---

(1) DEPOSITION OF THE CONSTABLE OF THE SERVICE OF THE SUMMONS (not in Statute, Oke's For. No. 9. p. 11).

Canada,
Province of ,
District (*or* County,
United Counties, *or*
as the case may be,)
of

The deposition of J. N. Constable of the of C., in the said (*county,*) taken upon oath before me the undersigned, one of Her Majesty's Justices of the Peace for the said (*county*) of C., at N., in the same (*county*), this day of 18 , who saith that he served A. B., mentioned in the annexed (*or* within) summons, with a duplicate thereof, on the day of last personally (*or* " by leaving the same with N. O., a grown person, at the said A. B's usual *or* last place of abode at N., in the county S.").

Before me J. S.

J. N.

(D 1) *See* ss. 2, 16.

WARRANT WHEN THE SUMMONS IS DISOBEYED.

Canada,
Province of ,
District (*or* County,
United Counties, *or*
as the case may be,)
of

To all or any of the Constables, or other Peace Officers in the said District (*or* County, United Counties, *or as the case may be,*) of :

Whereas on the day of (instant *or* last past) A. B. of the , was charged before (*me* or *us,*) the undersigned, (*or name the Magistrate or Magistrates, or as the case may be*) (*one*) of Her Majesty's Justices of the Peace in and for the said District) *or* County, United Counties, *as the case may be*) of for that (*&c., as in the Summons*); And whereas (I, *or* he, *the said Justice of the Peace, or* we *or* they, *the said Justices of the Peace*) did then issue (*my, our, his* or *their*) Summons to the said A. B., commanding him, in Her Majesty's name, to be and appear before (*me*) on at , o'clock in the (*fore*) noon. at , or before such other Justice or Justices of the Peace as should then be there, to answer to the said charge, and to be further dealt with according to law ; And whereas the said A. B. hath neglected to be or appear at the time and place appointed in and by the said Summons, although t hath now been proved to (*me*) upon oath, that the said Summons was duly served upon the said A. B. ; These are therefore to command you in Her Majesty's name forthwith to apprehend the said A. B., and to bring him before (*me*) or some other of Her Majesty's Justices of the Peace in and for the said District (*or* County, United Counties, *or as the case may be*,) of , to answer the said charge, and to be further dealt with according to law.

Given under (*my*) Hand and Seal, this day of , in the year of Our Lord , at , in the District (*or* County, &c.,) of aforesaid.

J. S. [L. S.]

(D 2) *See* s. 3.

WARRANT TO APPREHEND A PERSON CHARGED WITH AN INDICTABLE OFFENCE COMMITTED ON THE HIGH SEAS OR ABROAD.

For offences committed on the high seas the warrant may be the same as in ordinary cases, but describing the offence to have been committed "on the high seas, out of the body of any District or County of Canada and within the jurisdiction of the Admiralty of England."

For offences committed abroad, for which parties may be indicted in Canada, the Warrant also may be the same as in ordinary cases, but describing the offence to have been committed "on land out of Canada, to wit : at , in the Kingdom of , *or* at , in the Island of , in the West Indies, *or* at , in the East Indies," *or as the case may be.*

(E 1) *See* s. 12.

INFORMATION TO OBTAIN A SEARCH WARRANT.

Canada,
Province of ,
District (*or* County,
United Counties, *or*
as the case may be,)
of

The information of A. B., of the , of , in the said District (*or* County, *&c.*,) (*yeoman*), taken this day of , in the year of our Lord , before me, W. S., Esquire, one of Her Majesty's Justices of the Peace, in and for the District (*or* County, United Counties, *or as the case may be,*) of , who saith that on the day of *insert the description of articles stolen*) of the goods and chattels of Deponent, were feloniously stolen, taken and carried away, from and out of the (*Dwelling House, &c.,*) of this Deponent, at the (*Township, &c.,* aforesaid, by (some person or persons unknown, *or name the person,*) and that he hath just and reasonable cause to suspect, and doth suspect that the said goods and chattels, or some part of them, are concealed in the (*Dwelling House, &c., of C. D.*) of , in the said District (*or* County) (*here add the causes of suspicion, whatever they may be*;) Wherefore, (*he*) prays that a Search Warrant may be granted to him to search (*the Dwelling House, &c.,*) of the said C. D. as aforesaid, for the said goods and chattels so feloniously stolen, taken and carried away as aforesaid.

Sworn (*or* affirmed) before me the day and year first above mentioned, at in the said District, (*or* County) of

W. S.,
J. P.

(E 2) *See* s. 12.

SEARCH WARRANT.

Canada,
Province of ,
District (*or* County,
United Counties
or as the case may be,)
of

To all or any of the Constables, or other Peace Officers, in the District (*or* County, United Counties, *or as the case may be*), of :

Whereas A. B. of the , of , in the said District (*or* County, *&c.,*) hath this day made oath before me, the undersigned, one of Her Majesty's Justices of the Peace, in and for the said District (*or* County, United Counties, *or as the case may be*,) of , that on the day of , (*copy information as far as place of supposed concealment*); These are therefore in the name of our Sovereign Lady the Queen, to authorize and require you, and each and every of you, with necessary and proper assistance, to enter in the day time into the said (*Dwelling House, &c.*,) of the said, *&c.*, and there diligently search for the said goods and chattels, and if the same, or any part thereof, shall be found upon such search, that you bring the goods so found, and also the body of the said C. D. before me, or some other Justice of the Peace, in and for the said District (*or* County, United Counties, *or as the case may be*) of , to be disposed of and dealt with according to law.

Given under my Hand and Seal, at , in the said District (*or* County, *&c.*,) this day of , in the year of our Lord, one thousand eight hundred and

W. S.,
J. P.
(*Seal.*)

(F) *See* s. 4.

CERTIFICATE OF INDICTMENT BEING FOUND.

I hereby certify that a Court of (Oyer and Terminer, *or* General Gaol Delivery, *or* General Sessions of the Peace) holden in and for the District (*or* County, United Counties, *or as the case may be*,) of , at , in the said District, (County, *&c.*,) on , a Bill of Indictment was found by the Grand Jury against A. B., therein described as A. B., late of (*labourer*) for that he (*&c., stating shortly the offence*,) and that the said A. B. hath not appeared or pleaded to the said indictment.

Dated this , day of , one thousand eight hundred and .

Z. X.,

Clerk of the Crown, *or* Deputy Clerk of the Crown for the District (*or* County, United Counties, *or as the case may be*),

or

Clerk of the Peace of and for the said District (*or* County, United Counties *or as the case may be*).

(G) *See* s. 4.

WARRANT TO APPREHEND A PERSON INDICTED.

Canada,
Province of
District (*or* County,
United Counties, *or*
as the case may be)
of

To all or any of the Constables, or other Peace Officers, in the said District (*or* County, United Counties, *as the case may be*) of :

Whereas it hath been duly certified by J. D., Clerk of the Crown of (*name the Court*) (*or* E. G. Deputy Clerk of the Crown, *or* Clerk of the Peace, *as the case may be*) in and for the District (*or* County, United Counties, *or as the case may be*) of that (*&c., stating the certificate*) ; These are therefore to command you in Her Majesty's name forthwith to apprehend the said A. B., and to bring him before (*me*), or some other Justice or Justices of the Peace in and for the said District (*or* County, United Counties, *or as the case may be*), to be dealt with according to law.

Given under my Hand and Seal, this day of , in the year of our Lord , at , in the District (*or* County, *&c.*, aforesaid.

J. S. [L. S.]

---

(2) DEPOSITION THAT THE PERSON APPREHENDED IS THE SAME WHO IS INDICTED (not in Statute, Okes For. p. 491).

Canada,
Province of
District (*or* County,
United Counties, *or*
as the case may be),
of

The deposition of J. N., of the of , in (*County*) of , constable, taken upon oath before me, the undersigned, one of Her Majesty's Justices of the Peace for the said (*County*) of , in the same (*County*), this day of , A. D. 18 :

Who saith, I well know A. B., of &c., described in the certificate of J. D., Clerk of the Crown of (*or* Clerk of the Peace of, *as the case may be*), now produced by me ; that I never heard mention of any other person of the same name as the said A. B., living at or near the of * (*or as* *the case may be*); that A. B., apprehended (by me) and now here present, is the same person who is charged in the indictment referred to in the said certificate.

Taken and sworn before me, the day and year and at the place above mentioned. } J. N.

J. S.

(H) *See* s. 5.

WARRANT OF COMMITMENT OF A PERSON INDICTED.

Canada,
Province of
District (*or* County,
United Counties, *or*
as the case may be)
of

To all or any of the Constables, or other Peace Officers in the said District (*or* County, *&c.*,) of , and the Keeper of the Common Gaol, at , in the said District (*or* County, United Counties, *or as the case may be*) of :

Whereas by a Warrant under the Hand and Seal of (*one*) of Her Majesty's Justices of the Peace in and for the said District (*or* County, United Counties, *or as the case may be*) of under Hand and Seal , dated , after reciting that it had been certified by J. D. (*&c., as in the certificate*), ( ) the said Justice of the Peace commanded all or any of the Constables, in Her Majesty's name, forthwith to apprehend the said A. B. and to bring him before (*him*) the said Justice of the Peace in and for the said District (*or* County, United Counties *or as the case may be*), of or before some other Justice or Justices in and for the said District (*or* County, United County (*or as the case may be*), to be dealt with according to law ; And whereas the said A. B., hath been apprehended under and by virtue of the said Warrant, and being now brought before (*me*) it is hereupon duly proved to (*me*) upon oath that the said A. B., is the same person who is named and charged by , in the said indictment ; These are therefore to command you the said Constables and Peace Officers, or any of you, in Her Majesty's name, forthwith to take and convey the said A. B., to the said Common Gaol at , in the said District (*or* County, United Counties, *or as the case may be*), of , and there to deliver him to the Keeper thereof, together with this Precept ; and (*I*) hereby command you the said Keeper to receive the said A. B., into your custody in the said Gaol, and him there safely to keep until he shall thence be delivered by due course of law.

Given under *(my)* Hand and Seal, this day of , in the year of Our Lord , at , in the District *(or* County, *&c.,)* aforesaid.

J. S. [L. S.]

---

(3) DEPOSITION THAT THE PERSON INDICTED IS THE SAME WHO IS IN CUSTODY FOR SOME OTHER OFFENCE. (Not in Statute, Oke's For. p. 492.)

Proceed as in the form No. 2 to the asterisk,* then thus :—that A. B., now confined in the *(common gaol)* at , in the *(county)* of , is the same person who is indicted and referred to in the said certificate.

---

(1) *See* s. 6.

WARRANT TO DETAIN A PERSON INDICTED WHO IS ALREADY IN CUSTODY FOR ANOTHER OFFENCE.

Canada,
Province of
District *(or* County, United Counties, *or as the case may be)* of

To the Keeper of the Common Gaol at , in the said District *(or* County, United Counties, *or as the case may be)*, of :

Whereas it hath been duly certified by J. D., Clerk of the Crown of *(name the Court) or* Deputy Clerk of the Crown, *or* Clerk of the Peace of and for the District *(or* County, United Counties, *or as the case may be)*, of that *&c., stating the Certificate)*; And whereas *(I am)* informed that the said A. B., is in your custody in the said Common Gaol at aforesaid, charged with some offence, or other matter ; and it being now duly proved upon oath before *(me)* that the said A. B., so indicted as aforesaid, and the said A. B., in your custody as aforesaid, are one and the same person; These are therefore to command you, in Her Majesty's name, to detain the said A. B., in your custody in the Common Gaol aforesaid, until by Her Majesty's Writ of *Habeas Corpus*, he shall be removed therefrom for the purpose of being tried upon the said indictment, or until he shall otherwise be removed or discharged out of your custody by due course of law.

Given under *(my)* Hand and Seal, this day of , in the year of Our Lord , at , in the District *(or* County, etc.) aforesaid.

J. S. [L.S.]

(K) *See* s. 23.

ENDORSEMENT IN BACKING A WARRANT.

Canada,
Province of ,
District (*or* County,
United Counties *or*
as the case may be)
of

Whereas good proof upon oath hath this day been made before me, one of Her Majesty's Justices of the Peace in and for the said District (*or* County, United Counties, *or as the case may be*) of that the name of J. S., to the within Warrant subscribed, is of the handwriting of the Justice of the Peace within mentioned; I do therefore hereby authorize W. T. who bringeth to me this Warrant and all other persons to whom this Warrant was originally directed, or by whom it may be lawfully executed, and also all Constables and other Peace Officers of the said District (*or* County, United Counties, *or as the case may be*) of , to execute the same within the said last-mentioned District (*or* County, United Counties, *or as the case may be*).

Given under my Hand, this day of , in the year of Our Lord , at , in the District (*or County, etc.*) aforesaid.

J. L.

---

(4) DEPOSITION THAT A PERSON IS A MATERIAL WITNESS.

(Not in Statute. Oke's For. p. 14.)

Canada,
Province of ,
District (*or* County,
United Counties, *or*
as the case may be),
of

The deposition of J. N., of the of C., in the said County (*farmer*), taken on oath before me the undersigned, one of Her Majesty's Justices of the Peace in and for the said County of C., at N., in the said County, this day of , 18 , who saith that E. F., of the of C. aforesaid (*grocer*), is likely to give material evidence on behalf of the prosecution, in this behalf, touching the matter of the annexed (*or* "within") information (*or* "complaint"); And that this deponent verily believes that the said E. F.

will not appear voluntarily for the purpose of being examined as a witness (*or if a warrant be granted in the first instance,* "without being compelled so to do)."

Before me, J. S. J. N.

(L 1) *See* s. 25.

SUMMONS TO A WITNESS.

Canada,
Province of ,
District (*or* County,
United Counties (*or as the case may be*
of

To E. F., of , (*labourer*):

Whereas information hath been laid before the undersigned, one of Her Majesty's Justices of the Peace in and for the said District (*or* County, United Counties, *or as the case may be*], of , that A.B. (*&c., as in the Summons or Warrant against the accused*), and it hath been made to appear to me upon *oath*, that you are likely to give material evidence for (*prosecution*); These are therefore to require you to be and to appear before me on next, at o'clock in the (*fore*) noon, at , or before such other Justice or Justices of the Peace of the same District (*or* County, United Conntics, *or as the case may be*), of , as may then be there, to testify what you shall know concerning the said charge so made against the said A. B. as aforesaid. Herein fail not.

Given under my Hand and Seal, this day of , in the year of Our Lord , at , in the District (*or* County, *&c.*) aforesaid.

J. S. [L.S.]

(L 2) *See* s. 26.

WARRANT WHEN A WITNESS HAS NOT OBEYED THE SUMMONS.

Canada,
Province of ,
District (*or* County,
United Counties, *or as the case may be*),
of

To all or any of the Constables or other Peace Officers, in the said District (*or* County, United Counties, *or as the case may be*) of

Whereas information having been laid before , (*one*) of Her Majesty's

Justices of the Peace in and for the said District (*or* County, &c.) of , that A.B. (*&c., as in the Summons*) ; And it having been made to appear to (*me*) upon oath that E. F., of , (*labourer*), was likely to give material evidence for the prosecution, (*I*) did duly issue (*my*) summons to the said E. F., requiring him to be and to appear before (*me*) on , at , or before such other Justice or Justices of the Peace for the same District (*or* County, United Counties, *or as the case may be*), as might then be there, to testify what he should know respecting the said charge so made against the said A. B. as aforesaid ; And whereas proof has this day been made upon oath before (*me*) of such summons having been duly served upon the said E. F. ; and whereas the said E. F. hath neglected to appear at the time and place appointed by the said Summons, and no just excuse has been offered for such neglect ; these are therefore to command you to bring and have the said E. F. before (*me*) on , at o'clock in the (*fore*) noon, at , or before such other Justice or Justices for the same District (*or* County, United Counties, *or as the case may be*), as may then be there, to testify what he shall know concerning the said charge so made against the said A. B. as aforesaid.

Given under (*my*) Hand and Seal, this day of , in the year of Our Lord , at , in the District (*or* County, *&c.*), aforesaid.

J. S. [L.S.]

(L 3) *See* s. 27.

WARRANT FOR A WITNESS IN THE FIRST INSTANCE.

Canada,
Province of ,
District (*or* County,
United Counties, *or*
as the case may be,)
of

To all or any of the Constables, or other Peace Officers in the said District (*or* County, United Counties, *or as the case may be*,) of

Whereas information has been laid before the undersigned, (*one*) of Her Majesty's Justices of the Peace, in and for the said District (*or* County. United Counties, *or as the case may be*,) of that (*&c., as in the summons*) ; and it having been made to appear to (*me*) upon oath, that E. F. of , (*labourer*), is likely to give material evidence for the prosecution, and that it is probable that the said E. F. will not attend to give evidence unless compelled to do so : These are therefore to command you to to bring and have the said E. F. before (*me*) on at o'clock in the (*fore*) noon, at , or before such other Justice or Justices of the Peace for the same District (*or* County, United Counties, *or as the case may be*,) as may then be there, to testify what he shall know concerning the said charge so made against the said A. B. as aforesaid.

Given under my Hand and Seal, this day of in the year of Our Lord , at in the District (*or* County, *&c.*,) aforesaid.

J. S. [L. S.]

(L 4) *See* s. 28.

WARRANT OF COMMITMENT OF A WITNESS FOR REFUSING TO BE SWORN, OR TO GIVE EVIDENCE.

Canada,
Province of .
District (*or* County, United Counties, *or as the case may be*) of

To all or any of the Constables, or other Peace Officers, in the District (*or* County, United Counties, *or as the case may be*) of , and to the Keeper of the Common Gaol at , in the said District (*or* County, United Counties, *or as the case may be*] of :

Whereas A. B. was lately charged before [*one*] of Her Majesty's Justices of the Peace in and for the said District [*or* County, United Counties, *or as the case may be*] of for that [*&c., as in the Summons*]; And it having been made to appear to [*me*] upon oath that E. F. of was likely to give material evidence for the prosecution, [*I*] duly issued [*my*] Summons to the said E. F. requiring him to be and appear before me on , at , or before such other Justice or Justices of the Peace for the same District [*or* County, United Counties, *or as the case may be*] as should then be there, to testify what he should know concerning the said charge so made against the said A. B. as aforesaid; and the said E. F. now appearing before [*me*] [*or* being brought before [*me*] by virtue of a Warrant in that behalf to testify as aforesaid,] and being required to make oath or affirmation as a witness in that behalf, hath now refused so to do, [*or* being duly sworn as a witness doth now refuse to answer certain questions concerning the premises which are now here put to him, and more particularly the following] without offering any just excuse for such refusal; These are therefore to command you, the said Constables, Peace Officers, or any one of you, to take the said E. F. and him safely convey to the Common Gaol at , in the District *(or County, &c.,)* aforesaid, and there to deliver him to the Keeper thereof, together with this Precept; And [*I*] do hereby command you, the said Keeper of the said Common Gaol to receive the said E. F. into your custody in the said Common Gaol, and him there safely keep for the space of days, for his said contempt, unless he shall in the meantime consent to be examined, and to answer concerning the premises; and for your so doing, this shall be your sufficient Warrant.

Given under [*my*] Hand and Seal, this day of in the year of Our Lord , at in the District [County, *&c.*,] aforesaid.

J. S. [L.S.]

---

(5) WARRANT OF COMMITMENT OF A WITNESS FOR REFUSING TO BE SWORN OR TO GIVE EVIDENCE WHO ATTENDS WITHOUT A SUMMONS. (Not in Statute, Oke's For. p. 400.)

Canada,
Province of ,
District (*or* County,
United Counties, *or*
as the case may be,)
of

To all or any of the Constables, or other Peace Officers, in the District (*or* County, United Counties, *or as the case may be*,) of and to the Keeper of the Common Gaol at , in the said District (*or* County, United Counties, *or as the case may be*) of

Whereas A. B. was this day brought before me, the undersigned, (*one*) of Her Majesty's Justices of the Peace in and for the said (*County*) of , for that he the said A.B. on &c., at &c., (*here state the charge as in the Summons, Warrant or caption of the depositions*); And whereas one E. F. of &c., here in the presence of the said A.B. now under examination before me the said Justice on the charge aforesaid, now voluntarily appears as a witness for the prosecution in that behalf, and the said E.F. appearing to me, upon oath, likely to give material evidence for the prosecution, but being required to make oath or affirmation as a witness in that behalf, hath now refused so to do, (*or* being duly sworn as a witness, doth now refuse to answer certain questions concerning the premises, which are here put to him,) without offering any just cause for such his refusal: These are therefore to command you the said Constable to take the said E. F., and him safely convey to the (*Com-*

mon Gaol) at , in the (*County*) aforesaid, and there deliver him to the said Keeper thereof with this precept, and I do hereby command you the said Keeper of the said (*Common Gaol*) to receive the said E. F. into your custody in the said (*Common Gaol*), and him there safely keep for the space of days for his said contempt, unless he shall in the meantime consent to be examined and to answer concerning the premises; and for your so doing this shall be your sufficient Warrant.

Given under my Hand and Seal, this day of , in the year of our Lord , at in the (*County*) aforesaid.

J. S. [L. S.]

(M) See s. 29.

DEPOSITIONS OF WITNESSES.

Canada,
Province of
District [*or* County,
United Counties, *or*
as the case may be,]
of

The examination of C. W. of , [*farmer*], and E. F. of , [*labourer*], taken on [*oath*] this day of , in the year of Our Lord , at , in the District [*or* County, *&c.*, *or as the case may be*) aforesaid, before the undersigned, [*one*] of Her Majesty's Justices of the Peace for the said District [*or* County, United Counties, *or as the case may be,*] in the presence and hearing of A. B. who is charged this day before [*me*] for that he the said A. B. at * [*&c., describe the offence as in a Warrant of Commitment.*]

This Deponent, C. D., upon his [*oath*] saith as follows: [*&c., stating the deposition of the witness as nearly as possible in the words he uses. When his deposition is completed, let him sign it.*]

And this Deponent, E. F. upon his [*oath*] saith as follows: [*&c.*]

The above depositions of C. D. and E. F. were taken and [*sworn*] before me, at , on the day and year first above mentioned.

J. S.

---

(6) DEPOSITIONS OF THE WITNESSES ON THE REMAND DAY. (Not in Statute.)

This will be on the like caption as the preceding, but instead of repeating the offence say from the asterisk : with the felony (*or* misdemeanor) before mentioned.

The jurat will be as follows:—The above depositions of F.G., &c., were taken and sworn before me at , on the day of 18 , the depositions of C.D., and E.F., taken on the day of 18 , (and the depositions of C.H. and L.M. taken on the day of 18 ,) being at the same time severally read over and resworn in the presence and hearing of the before-named prisoner.

J. S.

Where the same justice hears the further evidence on the remand day, there would be no necessity for the former depositions to be re-sworn, and consequently no allusion to it in the jurat.

If on the remand day there is a committal for trial by another justice without any additional evidence, place the following jurat: "The foregoing depositions of C.D. and E.F. taken on &c. (and the depositions of F.G., &c., taken on &c.,) were severally read over and re-sworn before me at , on the day of 18 , in the presence and hearing of the before-named prisoner.

J. L.

(N) *See* s. 31.

STATEMENT OF THE ACCUSED.

Canada,
Province of ,
District (*or* County,
United Counties, *or*
as the case may be,)
of

A. B. stands charged before the undersigned, (*one*) of Her Majesty's Justices of the Peace, in and for the District (*or* County, United Counties, *or as the case may be*) aforesaid, this day of , in the year of our Lord , for that the said A. B., on , at , *&c.*, (*as in the captions of the depositions;*) And the said charge being read to the said A. B., and the witnesses for the prosecution, C. D. and E F., being severally examined in his presence, the said A. B. is now addressed by me as follows: "Having heard the evidence, do you wish "to say anything in answer to the charge? You are not obliged to say any- "thing, unless you desire to do so; but whatever you say will be taken down "in writing, and may be given in evidence against you at your trial." Whereupon the said A. B. saith as follows: (*Here state whatever the prisoner may say, and in his very words as nearly as possible. Get him to sign it if he will.*)

A. B.

Taken before me, at , the day and year first above mentioned.

J. S.

(7) MEMORANDUM TO BE WRITTEN ON DOCUMENTS PRODUCED IN EVIDENCE.
(Not in Statute. Oke's For. p. 502. No. 44.)

This is the plan (*or as the case may be*) produced to me, the undersigned, (*one*) of Her Majesty's Justices of the Peace for the (*County*) of , on the examination of A. B., charged with arson, (forgery, &c.,) and referred to in the examination of C. D. touching the said charge, taken before me this day of 18

J. S.

(O 1) *See* s. 36.

RECOGNIZANCE TO PROSECUTE OR GIVE EVIDENCE.

Canada,
Province of ,
District (*or* County,
United Counties, *or*
as the case may be,)
of

Be it remembered, That on the day of , in the year of our Lord , C. D. of , in the of , in the (*Township*) of , in the said District (*or* County, *&c.*,) of , (*farmer*), personally came before me, one of Her Majesty's Justices of the Peace in and for the said District (*or* County, United Counties, *or as the case may be*), of , and acknowledge himself to owe to Our Sovereign Lady the Queen, Her Heirs and Successors, the sum of of good and lawful current money of Canada, to be made and levied of his goods and chattels, lands and tenements, to the use of our said Sovereign Lady the Queen, Her Heirs and Successors, if the said C. D. shall fail in the condition endorsed.

Taken and acknowledged the day and year first above mentioned, at, before me.

J. S.

CONDITION TO PROSECUTE.

The condition of the within (*or* above) written recognizance is such that whereas one A. B. was this day charged before me, J. S., Justice of the Peace within mentioned, for that (*&c., as in the caption of the depositions*); if therefore, he the said C. D. shall appear at the next Court of Oyer and Terminer *or* General Gaol Delivery, (*or* at the next Court of General *or* Quarter Sessions of the Peace), to be holden in and for the District (*or* County, United Counties, *or as the case may be*) of * , and there prefer or cause to be preferred a Bill of Indictment for the offence aforesaid, against the said A. B. and there also duly prosecute such indictment, then the said Recognizance to be void or else to stand in full force and virtue.

CONDITION TO PROSECUTE AND GIVE EVIDENCE.

(*Same as the last form, to the asterisk,* and then thus :*)—" And there prefer " or cause to be preferred a Bill of Indictment against the said A. B. for the " offence aforesaid, and duly prosecute such Indictment, and give evidence " thereon, as well to the Jurors who shall then enquire into the said offence, " as also to them who shall pass upon the trial of the said A. B., then the " said Recognizance to be void, or else to stand in full force and virtue."

CONDITION TO GIVE EVIDENCE.

(*Same as the last form but one, to the asterisk,* and then thus :*)—" And there " give such evidence as he knoweth upon a Bill of Indictment to be then and " there preferred against the said A. B. for the offence aforesaid, as well to " the Jurors who shall there enquire of the said offence, as also to the Jurors " who shall pass upon the trial of the said A. B. if the said Bill shall be found " a True Bill, then the said Recognizance to be void, otherwise to remain in " full force and virtue."

(O 2) *See* s. 37.

NOTICE OF THE SAID RECOGNIZANCE TO BE GIVEN TO THE PROSECUTOR AND HIS WITNESSES.

Canada,
Province of ,
District (*or* County, United Counties, *or as the case may be,*) of }

Take notice that you C. D. of , are bound in the sum of to appear at the next Court of Oyer and Terminer and General Gaol Delivery, (*or* at the next Court of General Quarter Sessions of the Peace, in and for the District *or* County, United Counties, *or as the case may be*) of to be holden at , in the said District (County, *&c.*,) and then and there (*prosecute and*) give evidence against A. B., and unless you then appear there, (*prosecute and*) give evidence accordingly, the Recognizance entered into by you will be forthwith levied on you.

Dated this day of one thousand eight hundred and

J. S.

THE LIKE WITH VARIATION WHEN THERE IS A SURETY FOR A WITNESS. (Not in Statute. Oke's For. p. 501.)

Take notice, that you C. D. of &c., are bound in the sum of pounds to appear (*or* for the appearance of L. M., of &c., a minor *or* the wife of J. M. of &c., *as the case may be*) at the next Court of General Quarter Sessions of the Peace (*or* Oyer and Terminer and General Gaol Delivery) in and for the said (*County*) of , and then and there to (prosecute and) give evidence against A. B. for (felony), and unless you (he) then appear (appears and prosecutes) and gives evidence accordingly, the Recognizance entered into by you will be forthwith levied on you.

Dated this day of , 18 .

J. S. the Justice of the Peace for the said (*County*) of , before whom the Recognizance was entered into.

(P 1) *See* s. 39.

COMMITMENT OF A WITNESS FOR REFUSING TO ENTER INTO THE RECOGNIZANCE.

Canada,
Province of .
District (*or* County,
United Counties, *or*
as the case may be,)
of

To all or any of the Constables or other Peace Officers in the said District (*or* County, &c.) of , and to the Keeper of the Common Gaol of the said District, (*or* County, *&c.*, *or as the case may be*,) at , in the said District (*or* County, *&c.*, *or as the case may be*,) of

Whereas A. B. was lately charged before the undersigned, (*or name of Jus-*

tice of the Peace) (*one*) of Her Majesty's Justices of the Peace in and for the said District (*or* County, &c.,) of , for that (*&c.; as in the Summons to the witness,*) and it having been made to appear to (*me*) upon oath that E. F., of , was likely to give material evidence for the prosecution, (*I*) duly issued (*my*) Summons to the said E. F., requiring him to be and appear before (*me*) on , at or before such other Justice or Justices of the Peace as should then be there, to testify what he should know concerning the said charge so made against the said A. B. as aforesaid; and the said E. F. now appearing before [*me*] (or being brought before [*me*] by virtue of a Warrant in that behalf to testify as aforesaid,) hath been now examined before (me) touching the premises, but being by (*me*) required to enter into a Recognizance conditioned to give evidence against the said A. B., hath now refused so to do: These are therefore to command you the said Constables or Peace Officers, or any one of you, to take the said E. F. and him safely convey to the Common Gaol at in the District (*or* County, *&c.*,) aforesaid, and there deliver him to the said Keeper thereof, together with this Precept; and I do hereby command you, the said Keeper of the said Common Gaol, to receive the said E. F. into your custody in the said Common Gaol, there to imprison and safely keep him until after the trial of the said A. B. for the offence aforesaid, unless in the meantime the said E. F. shall duly enter into such Recognizance as aforesaid, in the sum of , before some one Justice of the Peace for the said District (*or* County, United Counties, *or as the case may be,*) conditioned in the usual form to appear at the next Court of (Oyer and Terminer or General Gaol Delivery, *or* General *or* Quarter Sessions of the Peace,) to be holden in and for the said District (*or* County, United Counties, *or as the case may be,*) of , and there to give evidence before the Grand Jury upon any Bill of Indictment which may then and there be preferred against the said A. B. for the offence aforesaid, and also to give evidence upon the trial of the said A. B. for the said offence, if a True Bill should be found against him for the same.

Given under my Hand and Seal, this day of , in the year of our Lord , at in the District (*or* County, *&c.*,) aforesaid.

J. S. [L. S.]

(P 2) *See* s. 40.

SUBSEQUENT ORDER TO DISCHARGE THE WITNESS.

Canada,
Province of ,
District *(or* County,
United Counties, *or*
as the case may be,
of

To the Keeper of the Common Gaol at , in the District *(or* County, &c.*)*, of aforesaid :

Whereas by *(my)* order dated the day of *(instant)*, reciting that A. B. was lately before then charged before *(me)* for a certain offence therein mentioned, and that E. F. having appeared before *(me)*, and being examined as a witness for the prosecution on that behalf, refused to enter into Recognizance to give evidence against the said A. B., and I therefore thereby committed the said E. F. to your custody, and required you safely to keep him until after the trial of the said A.B. for the offence aforesaid, unless in the meantime he should enter into such Recognizance as aforesaid ; and whereas for want of sufficient evidence against the said A.B. the said A.B. has not been committed or holden to bail for the said offence, but on the contrary thereof has been since discharged, and it is therefore not necessary that the said E. F should be detained longer in your custody : These are therefore to order and direct you the said Keeper to discharge the said E.F. out of your custody, as to the said commitment, and suffer him to go at large.

Given under my Hand and Seal, this day of , in the year of Our Lord , at , in the District *(or* County, *&c.)*, aforesaid.

J. S. [L.S.]

(Q 1) *See* s. 41.

WARRANT REMANDING A PRISONER.

Canada,
Province of ,
District *(or* County,
United Counties, *or*
as the case may be,
of

To all or any of the Constables and other Peace Officers in the said District *(or* County, United Counties, *or as the case may be)*, of , and to the Keeper of the *(Common Gaol* or *Lock-up House)* , in the said District *or* County, *&c.)* of

Whereas A. B. was this day charged before the undersigned *(one)* of Her

Majesty's Justices of the Peace in and for the said District *(or* County, United Counties, *or as the case may be)*, of , for that *(&c., as in the Warrant to apprehend)*, and it appears to *(me)* to be necessary to remand the said A. B.: These are therefore to command you, in Her Majesty's name, forthwith to convey the said A. B. to the *(Common Gaol* or *Lock-up House)* at , in the said District *(or* County, *&c.)*, and there to deliver him to the Keeper thereof, together with this Precept; and I hereby command you the said Keeper to receive the said A. B. into your custody in the said *(Common Gaol* or *Lock-up House)*, and there safely keep him until the day of *(instant)*, when I hereby command you to have him at , at * o'clock in the *(fore)* noon of the same day before *(me)* or before some other Justice or Justices of the Peace for the said District *(or* County, United Counties, *or as the case may be)*, as may then be there, to answer further to the said charge, and to be further dealt with according to law, unless you shall be otherwise ordered in the meantime.

Given under my Hand and Seal, this day of , in the year of Our Lord , at , in the District *(or* County, *&c.)* of aforesaid.

J. S. [L. S.]

---

(9) ORDER TO BRING UP ACCUSED BEFORE EXPIRATION OF REMAND.

(Not in Statute. Oke's For. p. 496, No. 31).

To the Keeper of the (*Common Gaol*) at , in the said (*County* of

to wit: } Whereas A. B. (hereinafter called the "accused" was on the day of , committed (by me) to your custody in the said (*Common Gaol*) charged for that (*&c., as in the warrant remanding the prisoner*), and by the warrant in that behalf* you were commanded to have him at , on the day of , now next, at o'clock in the forenoon, before such Justice or Justices of the Peace for the said (*County*), as might then be there, to answer further to the said charge, and to be further dealt with according to law.

(*or shortly, from the asterisk,** "he was remanded to the day of next") unless you should be otherwise ordered in the meantime: and whereas it appears to me, the undersigned, one of Her Majesty's Justices of the Peace in and for the said (*County*) of , (*or* me the said Justice), to be expedient the said accused should be further examined before the expiration of the said remand: These are therefore to order you in Her Majesty's name to bring and have the said accused at (*&c., follow from the asterisk in the preceding form, supra, to the end*).

(Q 2) *See* s. 44.

RECOGNIZANCE OF BAIL INSTEAD OF REMAND ON AN ADJOURNMENT OF EXAMINATION.

Canada,
Province of ,
District (*or* County,
United Counties, *or*
as the case may be),
of

Be it remembered, That on the day of , in the year of Our Lord , A. B., of (*labourer*), L. M. of (*grocer*), and N. O. of (*butcher*), personally came before me (*one*) of Her Majesty's Justices of the Peace for the said District (*or* County, United Counties, *or as the case may be*), and severally acknowledged themselves to owe to our Sovereign Lady the Queen, Her Heirs and Successors, the several sums following, that is to say : the said A. B. the sum of , and the said L. M. and N. O. the sum of each, of good and lawful current money of Canada, to be made and levied of their several goods and chattels, lands and tenements respectively, to the use of our said Lady the Queen, Her Heirs and Successors, if he, the said A. B. fail in the condition endorsed.

Taken and acknowledged the day and year first above-mentioned, at before me,

J. S.

CONDITION.

The condition of the within written recognizance is such, that whereas the within bounden A. B. was this day (*or* on last past) charged before me for that (*&c., as in the Warrant*) : And whereas the examination of the Witnesses for the prosecution in this behalf is adjourned until the day of (*instant*) ; If therefore the said A. B. shall appear before me on the said day of (*instant*), at o'clock in the (*fore*) noon, or before such other Justice or Justices of the Peace for the said District (*or* County *or* United Counties, of *or as the case may be*), as may then be there, to answer (*further*) to the said charge, and to be further dealt with according to law, the said recognizance to be void, or else to stand in full force and virtue.

(Q 3) *See* s. 44.

NOTICE OF RECOGNIZANCE TO BE GIVEN TO THE ACCUSED AND HIS SURETIES.

Canada,
Province of ,
District (*or* County,
United Counties, *or*
as the case may be)
of

Take notice that you A B., of , are bound in the sum of , and your Sureties L. M. and N. O. in the sum of , each, that you A. B. appear before me J. S. one of Her Majesty's Justices of the Peace for the District (*or* County, United Counties, *or as the case may be*), of , on , the day of (*instant*,) at o'clock in the (*fore*) noon, at , or before such other Justice or Justices of the same District, (*or* County, United Counties, *or as the case may be*) as may then be there, to answer (*further*) to the charge made against you by C. D. and to be further dealt with according to law ; and unless you A. B. personally appear accordingly, the Recognizance entered into by yourself and Sureties will be forthwith levied on you and them

Dated this day of , one thousand eight hundred and

J. S.

(Q 4) *See* s. 45.

CERTIFICATE OF NON-APPEARANCE TO BE ENDORSED ON THE RECOGNIZANCE.

I hereby certify that the said A. B. hath not appeared at the time and place, in the above condition mentioned, but therein hath made default, by reason whereof the within written Recognizance is forfeited.

J. S.

(R 1) *See* s. 47.

WARRANT TO CONVEY THE ACCUSED BEFORE A JUSTICE OF THE COUNTY IN WHICH THE OFFENCE WAS COMMITTED.

Canada,
Province of ,
District (*or* County,
United Counties, *or*
as the case may be,)
of

To all or any of the Constables, or other Peace Officers in the said District (*or* County, United Counties, *or as the case may be*) of

Whereas A. B. of (*labourer*), hath this day been charged before the undersigned (*one*) of Her Majesty's Justices of the Peace in and for the said District (*or* County, United Counties, *or as the case may be*) of , for that (*&c., as in the Warrant to apprehend*); And whereas (*I*) have taken the deposition of C. D. a witness examined by (*me*) in this behalf, but inasmuch as (*I*) am informed that the principal witnesses to prove the said offence against the said A. B. reside in the District (*or* County, United Counties, *or as the case may be,*) of where the said offence is alleged to have been committed: These are therefore to command you, in Her Majesty's name, forthwith to take and convey the said A. B. to the said District (*or* County, United Counties, *or as the case may be,*) of and there carry him before some Justice or Justices of the Peace in and for that District (*or* County, United Counties, *or as the case may be,*) and near unto the (*Township of*) where the offence is alleged to have been committed, to answer further to the said charge before him or them, and to be further dealt with according to law; and (*I*) hereby further command you to deliver to the said Justice or Justices the information in this behalf, and also the said deposition of C. D. now given into your possession for that purpose, together with this Precept.

Given under my hand and seal, this day of , in the year of our Lord , at , in the District (*or* County, *&c.,*) of aforesaid.

J. S. [L. S.]

(R 2) *See* s. 49.

RECEIPT TO BE GIVEN TO THE CONSTABLE BY THE JUSTICE FOR THE COUNTY IN WHICH THE OFFENCE WAS COMMITTED.

Canada,
Province of ,
District (*or* County,
United Counties, *or*
as the case may be)
of

I, J. P., one of Her Majesty's Justices of the Peace, in and for the District (*or* County, &c.) of , hereby certify that W. T., Constable, *or* Peace Officer, of the District (*or* County, United Counties, *or as the case may be*) of , has on this day of , one thousand eight hundred and , by virtue of and in obedience to a Warrant of J. S., Esquire, one of Her Majesty's Justices of the Peace in and for the District (*or* County, United Counties, *or as the case may be*) of produced before me, one A. B. charged before the said J. S.

with having (*&c., stating shortly the offence,*) and delivered him into the custody of by my direction, to answer to the said charge, and further to be dealt with according to law, and has also delivered unto me the said Warrant, together with the information (*if any*) in that behalf, and the deposition (*s*) of C. D. (*and of*) in the said Warrant mentioned, and that he has also proved to me upon oath, the hand-writing of the said J. S. subscribed to the same.

Dated the day and year first above mentioned, at , in the said District (*or* County, *&c.*) of .

J. P.

(S 1) *See* s. 52.

RECOGNIZANCE OF BAIL.

Canada,
Province of
District (*or* County,
United Counties, *or*
as the case may be)
of

Be it remembered, that on the day of in the year of Our Lord , A. B. of , (*labourer,*) L. M. of (*grocer,*) and N. O. of , (*butcher,*) personally came before (*us*) the undersigned, (*two*) of Her Majesty's Justices of the Peace for the District (*or* County, United Counties, *or as the case may be,*) of and severally acknowledged themselves to owe to our Sovereign Lady the Queen, Her Heirs and Successors, the several sums following, that is to say : the said A. B. the sum of and

The said L. M. and N. O. the sum of each of good and lawful current money of Canada to be made and levied of their several goods and chattels, lands and tenements respectively, to the use of our said Sovereign Lady the Queen, Her Heirs and Successors, if he, the said A. B. fail in the condition endorsed.

Taken and acknowledged the day and year first above mentioned, at before us.

J. S.

CONDITION.

The condition of the within written Recognizance is such, that whereas the said A. B. was this day charged before (*us,*) the Justices within mentioned for that (*&c., as in the Warrant*); if therefore the said A. B. will appear at the next Court of Oyer and Terminer (*or* General Gaol Delivery (*or* Court of General or Quarter Sessions of the Peace) to be holden in and and for the District (*or* County, United Counties, *or as the case may be*) of , and there surrender himself into the custody of the Keeper of the *Common Gaol or Lock-up House*) there, and plead to such indictment as may be found against him by the Grand Jury, for and in respect to the charge aforesaid, and take his trial upon the same, and not depart the said Court without leave, then the said Recognizance to be void, or else to stand in full force and virtue.

(S 2) *See* s. 52.

NOTICE OF THE SAID RECOGNIZANCE TO BE GIVEN TO THE ACCUSED AND HIS BAIL.

Take notice that you A. B., of , are bound in the sum of , and your Sureties (L. M. and N. O.) in the sum of , each, that you A. B. appear (*&c., as in the condition of the Recognizance,*) and not depart the said Court without leave; and unless you, the said A. B., personally appear and plead, and take your trial accordingly, the Recognizance entered into by you and your Sureties shall be forthwith levied on you and them.

Dated this day of , one thousand eight hundred and

J. S.

(S 3) *See* ss. 53, 55.

WARRANT OF DELIVERANCE ON BAIL BEING GIVEN FOR A PRISONER ALREADY COMMITTED.

Canada,
Province of ,
District (*or* County,
United Counties, *or as the case may be*)
of

To the Keeper of the Common Gaol of the District (*or* County, United Counties, *or as the case may be*) of at , in the said District (*or* County, United Counties, *or as the case may be*).

Whereas A. B. late of , [*labourer.*] hath before [*us*] [*two*] of Her Majesty's Justices of the Peace in and for the said District [*or* County, United Counties, *or as the case may be*] of , entered into his own Recognizance, and found sufficient sureties for his appearance at the next Court of Oyer and Terminer or General Gaol Delivery [*or* Court of General or Quarter Sessions of the Peace] to be holden in and for the District [*or* County, United Counties, *or as the case may be*] of , to answer Our Sovereign Lady the Queen, for that [*&c., as in the commitment*], for which he was taken and committed to your said Common Gaol: These are therefore to command you, in Her said Majesty's name, that if the said A. B. do remain in your custody in the said Common Gaol for the said cause, and for no other, you shall forthwith suffer him to go at large.

Given under our Hands and Seals, this day of , in the year of Our Lord , at in the District [*or* County, &c.,] aforesaid.

J. S. [L. S.]
J. N. [L. S.]

(T 1) *See* s. 56.

WARRANT OF COMMITMENT.

Canada,
Province of ,
District [*or* County, United Counties, *or as the case may be*] of

To all or any of the Constables, or other Peace Officers in the District [*or* County, United Counties, *or as the case may be*] of , and to the Keeper of the Common Gaol of the District [*or* County, United Counties, *or as the case may be*] at , in the said District [*or* County, &c.,] of :

Whereas A. B. was this day charged before [*me*] J. S. [*one*] of Her Majesty's Justices of the Peace, in and for the said District [*or* County, United Counties, *or as the case may be*] of on the oath of C. D., of [*farmer*,] and others, for that, [*&c., stating shortly the offence*]; These are therefore to command you the said Constables or Peace Officers, or any of you, to take the said A. B. and him safely convey to the Common Gaol at aforesaid, and there deliver him to the Keeper thereof, together with this Precept; And I do hereby command you the said Keeper of the said Common Gaol to receive the said A. B. into your custody in the said Common Gaol, and there safely to keep him until he shall be thence delivered by due course of law.

Given under my Hand and Seal, this day of , n the year of Our Lord , at , in the District [*or* County, &c.,] of aforesaid.

J. S. [L. S.]

(T 2) *See* s. 57.

GAOLERS' RECEIPT TO THE CONSTABLE FOR THE PRISONER.

I hereby certify that I have received from W.T., Constable, of the District [*or* County, &c.,] of , the body of A. B., together with a Warrant under the Hand and Seal of J. S., Esquire, one of Her Majesty's Justices of the Peace for the said District [*or* County, United Counties, *or as the case may be*,] of , and that the said A. B. was [sober, *or as the case may be*,] at the time he was delivered into my custody.

P. K.

Keeper of the Common Gaol of the said District [*or* County, &c.]

---

(10) COMPLAINT OF BAIL FOR A PERSON CHARGED WITH AN INDICTABLE OFFENCE IN ORDER THAT HE MIGHT BE COMMITTED IN DISCHARGE OF THEIR RECOGNIZANCES. (Not in Statute. Oke's For. p. 514, No. 70.)

Proceed as in form No. 9, *ante to the asterisk* altering it to two complaints if there be more than one surety, then thus:* that they the said C. D., and E. F., were on the day of now last past, severally and respectively bound by recognizance before J. P., Esquire, one of Her Majesty's Justices of the Peace for the said (county) of , in the sum of each, upon condition that one A. B., of &c., should appear at the next term of the Court of Queen's Bench (Crown Side), for the District of , (or Court of Oyer and Terminer and General Gaol Delivery, *or* Court of General Quarter Sessions of the Peace), to be holden in and for the (*County*) of , and there surrender himself into the custody of the Keeper of the (*Common Gaol*) there, and plead to such indictment as might be found against him by the grand jury for or in respect to the charge of (stating the charge shortly), and take his trial upon the same and not depart the said Court without leave; and that these complainants have reason to suspect and believe and do verily suspect and believe, that the said A. B. is about to depart from this part of the country; and therefore they pray of me the said Justice that I would issue my warrant of apprehension of the said A. B., in order that he may be surrendered to prison in discharge of them his said bail.

Before me, J. P.

C. D.
E. F.

(11) WARRANT TO APPREHEND THE PERSON CHARGED.

(Not in Statute. Oke's For. p. 514, No. 71. Venue should be as in T, 1.)

To all or any of the Constables and other Peace Officers in the said District (*or* County, United Counties, *or as the case may be*) of , and to C. D. and E. F., severally and respectively.

to wit: } Whereas you the said C. D. and E. F., have this day made complaint to me the undersigned, one of Her Majesty's Justices of the Peace in and for the said (*County*) of , that you the said C. D. and E. F., were, &c., (*as in the complaint,* No. (10), *supra to the end*) : These are therefore to authorize you the said C. D. and E. F., and also to command you the said (*Constable or other* Peace Officer), in Her Majesty's name forthwith to apprehend the said A. B., and to bring him before me or some Justice or Justices of the Peace in and for the said (*County*), to the intent that he may be committed to the (*Common Gaol*) in and for the said (*County*), until the next Court of Oyer and Terminer and General Gaol Delivery (*or* Court of General Quarter Sessions of the Peace, to be holden in and for the said (*County*) of *or &c., as the case may be*), unless he find new and sufficient sureties to become bound for him in such recognizance as aforesaid.

Given under my Hand and Seal, this day of , in the year of our Lord , at , in the (*County*) aforesaid.

J. S. [L.S.]

---

(12) COMMITMENT OF THE PERSON CHARGED ON SURRENDER OF HIS BAIL AFTER APPREHENSION UNDER A WARRANT. (Not in Statute. Oke's For. p. 515, No. 72.)

To all or any of the Constables, or other Peace Officers in the District (*or* County, United Counties, *or as the case may be*) of , and to the Keeper of the Common Gaol of the District (*or* County, United Counties, *or as the case may be*) at , in the said District (*or* County, &c.,) of :

to wit: } Whereas on the day of instant, complaint was made to me the undersigned (*or* J. S.) one of Her Majesty's Justices of the Peace, in and for the said (County) of , by C. D. and E. F., of &c., that (*as in the complaint* No. (10), *supra to the end*), I (*or* the said Justice) thereupon issued my warrant authorizing the said C. D. and E. F., and also commanding the said Constables of , and all other Peace Officers in the said (*County*) of , in Her Majesty's name forthwith to apprehend the said A. B., and to bring him (follow *to end of warrant,* preceding form, *supra*) ; and whereas the said A. B., hath been apprehended under and by virtue of the said Warrant, and being now brought before me the said Justice (*or* me the undersigned, one &c.,) and surrendered by the said C. D. and E. F., his said Sureties, in discharge of their said Recognizances, I have required the said A. B., to find new and sufficient sureties to become bound for him in such Recognizance as aforesaid, but the said A. B. hath now refused so to do ; These are therefore to command you the said Constables (*or other Peace Officers*) in Her Majesty's name, forthwith to take and safely to convey the said A. B., to the said (*Common Gaol*) at , in the said (*County*) and there deliver him to the Keeper thereof, together with this precept ; and I hereby command you the said Keeper to receive the said A. B. into your custody in the said (*Common Gaol*), and him there safely to keep until the next Court of Oyer and Terminer and General Gaol Delivery (*or* Court of General Quarter Sessions of the Peace), to be holden in and for the said (*County*) of , unless in the mean time the said A. B. shall find new and sufficient Sureties to become bound for him in such recognizance as aforesaid.

Given, &c., (*as in the preceding form, supra.*)

---

32 & 33 VIC. CHAP. XXXI.

An Act respecting the duties of Justices of the Peace, out of Sessions, in relation to summary convictions and orders.

[*Assented to 22nd June,* 1869.]

WHEREAS it is expedient to assimilate, amend and consolidate the statute law of the several Provinces of Quebec, Ontario, Nova Scotia and New Brunswick, respecting the duties of Justices of the Peace out of Sessions in relation to summary convictions and orders, and to extend the same as so amended to all Canada : Therefore, Her Majesty, by and with the advice and consent of the Senate and House of Commons of Canada, enacts as follows :

1. In all cases where an information is laid before one or more of Her Majesty's Justices of the Peace for any Territorial Division of Canada, that any person, being within the jurisdiction of such Justice or Justices, has committed or is suspected to have committed any offence or act over which the Parliament of Canada has jurisdiction, and for which he is liable by law, upon a Summary Conviction for the same before a Justice or Justices of the Peace, to be imprisoned or fined, or otherwise punished, and also in all cases where a complaint is made to any such Justice or Justices in relation to any matter over which the Parliament of Canada has jurisdiction, and upon which he or they have authority by law to make any order for the payment of money or otherwise, such Justice or Justices of the Peace may issue his or their Summons [A], directed to such person, stating shortly the matter of the information or complaint, and requiring him to appear at a certain time and place, before the same Justice or Justices, or before such other Justice or Justices of the same Territorial Division as may then be there, to answer to the said information or complaint, and to be further dealt with according to law.

This Act did not come into effect in Manitoba until the 1st day of July, 1871. On and after that day it was in force there, subject to the amendments made in the 32 & 33 Vic., chap. 36, and to those of the 33 Vic., chap. 27. See 34 Vic., chap. 13, Sched. A. The Act was extended to Prince Edward Island by the 40 Vic., chap. 4, and to the District of Keewatin, by the 39 Vic. chap. 21, except so much of the Act or of any Act amending it as gives any appeal from any conviction or order adjudged or made under it ;

and to the North-west Territories, by the Act 38 Vic., chap. 49, except so much of the Act or of any Act amending it as gives any appeal from any conviction adjudged or made under it. The Act, was also extended to British Columbia by the 37 Vic., chap. 42.

This section points out the distinction between an *information* and *complaint*. It is called an information where it is for an offence punishable on summary conviction, a complaint where it is sought to obtain an order merely; a similar distinction exists between *convictions* and *orders*, the former following an information and the latter following a complaint. See *Morant* v. *Taylor*, L. R. 1 Ex. D. 188. Under section 20 of the Act, complaints need not be in writing unless required to be so by some particular Act or law upon which such complaint is framed, but the Justice may, if he thinks fit, require them to be in writing. By section 24, all complaints and informations, unless some particular Act or law otherwise requires, and except in cases where it is herein otherwise provided, may respectively be made or laid without any oath or affirmation as to the truth thereof.

It is not necessary that an information should be on oath or even in writing, unless required to be so by some statute. *Basten* v. *Carew*, 3 B. & C. 649; *Friel* v. *Ferguson*, 15 C. P. (Ont.) 594; *Re Conklin*, 31 Q. B. (Ont.) 168; see section 24. By section 25 of this statute, where a warrant is issued in the first instance, the information must be upon oath. By the same section every information or complaint must be for one offence only, or for one matter of complaint only.

By section 25 every complaint or information may be laid or made by the complainant or informant in person, or by his counsel or attorney or other person authorized in that behalf. The person aggrieved or some specified individual must be the informer, if the statute so states. *R.* v. *Daman*, 2 B & A. 378. But if no prosecutor is described, then any person may inform. *Morden* v. *Porter*, 7 C. B. N. S. 641, even though the penalties go to a specified individuals. *Coles* v. *Coulton*, 2 E. & E. 695.

Where no time is specially limited for making the information or complaint, it must, by section 26, be laid within three months from the time when the matter of the complaint or information arose. The word "month" means calendar month, 31 Vic., chap. 1, sec. 7 fourteenthly. The time counts from the matter which gives rise to the real offence or cause of proceeding. *Hill* v. *Thorncroft*, 3 E. & E. 257; and when it is complete *Jacomb* v. *Dodgson* 27 J. P. 68.

It seems that it is not necessary, under this statute, that the Justice who issues the summons should also hear and determine the matter. "Such other Justice or Justices of the same Territorial Division as may then be there," would seem to have the power to adjudicate. At all events, under the Con. Stat. U.C. chap. 75, s. 12, respecting master and servants, the Justice who issues the summons has no exclusive right to deal with the case. Where on the return of a summons issued by one Justice under this statute, two other Justices were present, who, without any objection from the Justice issuing the summons, heard the complaint with him. The conviction of the latter, in opposition to the judgment of the other two, was quashed. *R.* v. *Milne*, 25 C. P. (Ont.), 94. See also section 87.

In regard to the number of Justices required, the provisions of the particular law on which proceedings are instituted must be observed. In the absence of any direction in the Act or law upon which the complaint or information is framed, one Justice is sufficient. See sections 27 and 28. Where two Justices are required, they must be present and acting together during the whole of the hearing and determination of the case. See section 88. See also 31 Vic. chap. 1, s. 7, twenty-fifthly. Under the 91st section of this Act, certain persons, such as the Recorder, Police or Stipendiary Magistrate, have the power of two Justices of the Peace, and may do alone whatever the Act authorizes two Justices to do. See also section 59 of the 32 & 33 Vic. chap. 30.

Justices of the Peace have no jurisdiction to convict summarily at common law in any case, but in all cases a direct legislative authority must be shewn or the conviction will be illegal. *Bross* v. *Huber*, 18 Q. B. (Ont.), 286. See also *Ferguson* v. *Adams*, 5 Q. B. (Ont.), 194.

The jurisdiction of Justices to hear and determine offences summarily is entirely given by the statutes creating the offence—

although owing to some omission in the statute, summary jurisdiction may not be expressly given, the Justices may still proceed when it may reasonably be implied from the rest of the statute, that such jurisdiction was intended to be given to them. *Cullen* v. *Trimble*, L. R., 7 Q. B., 416.

The information should contain the name, address, and occupation of the informer; the date and place of taking, and description of the Justice receiving it; the name of the accused, or a full description if the name is not known—see section 8, which requires the Warrant to name, or otherwise describe, the offender—the date and place of the commission of the offence, shewing the jurisdiction of the Justice; but stating the place in the margin of the information is sufficient, and it need not be set out in the body. 32 & 33 Vic. chap. 29, s. 15; *R.* v. *Cavanagh*, 27 C. P. (Ont.), 537.

The charge must be set out in such distinct terms that the accused may know exactly what he has to answer; for the accused cannot be convicted of a different offence from that contained in the information. *Martin* v. *Pridgeon*, 28 L. J. M. C., 179; *ex parte Hogue*, 3 L. C. R. 94.

There must also be an allegation of any particular matters necessary to bring the accused under the scope of the Act or law on which the proceedings are founded, *i. e.* when any particular description of person is mentioned in the Act, the accused must be described as such person, and when such words as "maliciously," "knowingly," &c., are used, the offence must be described as having been so committed. In stating the offence in the summons, or Warrant, the nearer the exact words of the statute are followed the better. *Ex parte Perham*, 5 H. & N., 30. If the proceeding is on a second offence the previous conviction should be mentioned.

Certainty and precision are required in the statement, and description of an offence under a penal statute, and an information charging several offences in the disjunctive is bad, though the words of the statute are copied in the information, the statute relating to several offences in the disjunctive. *Ex parte Hogue*, 3 L. C. R. 94. The confession of the defendant to an information defective in the above particulars will not aid or cure the defect.

So an information charging an offence in the alternative, is bad. Therefore, where the information charged the defendant with selling beer *or* ale without a license, the Court held that it was bad, both in matter and substance, and could not be made out by evidence nor helped by intendment. *R.* v. *North*, 6 D & R., 143; *R* v. *Jukes*, 8 T. R., 536.

Where a prosecutor is not obliged to negative the exceptions in a statute, and negatives some of them only, that part of the information will be rejected as surplusage. *R.* v. *Hall*, 1 T. R. 320.

But an information founded on a penal statute must negative the exceptions in the enacting clause creating the penalty, and also those contained in a former clause, to which the enacting clause refers in express terms. *R.* v. *Pratten*, 6 T. R. 559; see also *R.* v. *Breen*, 36 Q. B. (Ont.), 84 post convictions, s. 50.

An information against A will not justify the issue of a warrant for the arrest of B. Where an information was laid against A, the keeper of a disorderly house, and the prayer in the information was for the arrest of A. and all others found or concerned in the house, it was held that this information did not authorize a warrant for the arrest of a person found in the house, but against whom the information was not laid otherwise than in the prayer as above. *Cleland* v. *Robinson*, 11 C. P. (Ont.), 416.

If a statute gives summary proceedings for various offences specified in several sections, an information is bad which leaves it uncertain under which section it took place; and where a statute creates several offences, one of which is charged in an information, a conviction of another offence, the subject of the same penalty will be bad. *Thompson* v. *Durnford*, 12 L. C. J., 285–7.

Where two or more persons may commit an offence under an Act, the information may be jointly laid against them. *R.* v. *Littlechild*, L. R. 6 Q. B., 295. But where the penalty is imposed on each person, it is wrong to convict them jointly, even when they are charged in a joint information, and in such case there may be separate convictions (*ib.*). But under the eighty-ninth section of this Act, when each joint offender is adjudged to forfeit a sum equivalent to the value of the property, no further sum shall be paid to the party aggrieved than the amount forfeited by one of such offenders only; and the corresponding sum forfeited by the other offender shall be applied in the same manner as other penalties are directed to be applied.

The laying of the information is the commencement of a prosecution before a magistrate. *R.* v. *Lennox*, 34 Q.B. (Ont.), 28.

If when the information is sworn to, a blank is left for the defendant's christian name, and this blank is afterwards filled up by the Justice, the information will be void, and the Justice will have no right to issue a warrant thereon, and any warrant issued thereon will be void. *Garrison* v. *Harding*, 1 Pugsley, 166.

An information is unnecessary where the Justices have power to convict on view (*R.* v. *Jones*, 12 A. & E., 684), or where the defendant is already present and before the Justices. *Turner* v. *Postmaster-General*, 5 B. & S. 756.

The laying of the information or complaint will give the magistrate jurisdiction to hear the case if the defendant appears; and though no summons is issued or any steps taken to bring the person complained of before the magistrate. Where the information or complaint is laid, the actual presence of the defendant is all that is required, whether he appears voluntarily or on summons or warrant is immaterial, the magistrate having jurisdiction in either case (*R.* v. *Mason*, 29 Q. B. (Ont.), 431); and if a party appears and defends without any summons being issued, he cannot afterwards object that there was no complaint on oath. *Ex parte Wood*, 1 Allen, 422.

But in order to give jurisdiction over the person of the offender, in the case of a summary conviction, it must either appear that an information has been laid, or that the information has been waived. *Stoness* v. *Lake*, 40 Q. B. (Ont.), 326; *R.* v. *Fletcher*, L. R., 1 C. C. R., 320; *Blake* v. *Beech*, L. R., 1 Ex. D., 320.

The plaintiff, on an information against him, under the (Ont.) 37 Vic., chap. 32, for selling liquor without a license, was brought before the defendants magistrates. It was proved that this was his second offence, though the information did not charge it as such. The plaintiff, represented by counsel, disputed the evidence as to the first conviction, but did not object to the information and the magistrates convicted and adjudged him to be imprisoned for ten days, which they had power to do only for a second offence. It was held that the plaintiff had waived the objection to the information, and that defendants were not liable in trespass. *Stoness* v. *Lake*, 40 Q. B. (Ont.), 320; see also *Appleton* v. *Lepper*, 20 C. P. (Ont.), 142; *Powell* v. *Williamson*, 1 Q. B. (Ont.), 154; *Friel* v. *Ferguson*, 15 C. P. (Ont.), 584.

If no information is laid, and the objection is not waived, the conviction will be illegal. The respondent laid an information before a Justice, that a house was "kept or used as a common gaming house," and thereupon the Justice granted a warrant under which the appellant was arrested at the house in question. He was brought before two Justices, and charged under the "Act for the Suppression of Betting Houses," as "the person" who "having the management of a room" in the house used it "for the purpose of betting with persons resorting thereto." No information was laid, nor was any summons issued under the last named statute, and the appellant did not waive this omission. It was held that the appellant could not, under these circumstances, be legally convicted. *Blake* v. *Beech*, L. R., 1 Ex. D., 320.

Where the information is for one offence, and where, if the defendant appear, the charge against him is for another offence, the proceedings are irregular, and a conviction cannot be upheld. *Martin* v. *Pridgeon*, 1 E. & E., 778. But such an irregularity may be waived. *Turner* v. *Postmaster*, G. 5 B. & S., 756.

Every objection to any information, for any defect apparent on the face thereof, should be taken before the magistrate, when the substance of the information is stated to the defendant under section 37. If not then taken the objection will be waived, and if the objection is taken, the magistrate may forthwith cause the information to be amended in such particular. See *R.* v. *Cavanagh*, 27 C. P. (Ont.), 537, in which it was held that the 32 & 33 Vic., chap. 29, s. 32, applied to informations in cases of summary convictions; see section 1 s.-s. 1. Where, therefore, objection was taken to a conviction for selling liquor without license, that the conviction did not name or otherwise describe the person to whom the liquor was sold, it was held that the objection should have been made before the magistrate, and though a fatal objection, if taken at the proper time, it was removed by the delay. The Court also seemed to be of opinion that section 5 of this Act (32 & 33 Vic., chap. 31) would of itself have been a sufficient answer to the objection. *R.* v. *Cavanagh, supra.*

According to the decision in *R.* v. *Cavanagh*, 27 C. P. (Ont.), 537, that the Act respecting procedure in criminal cases 32 & 33 Vic., chap. 29, applies to informations in cases of summary convictions (see section 1 s.-s. 1); all the provisions of that Act already given in relation to indictable cases (see *ante*, 23-4) will apply to informations under this Act. The 14th section of this Act contains express provision in regard to the statement in informations of the property of partners or municipal corporations. See also 32 & 33 Vic., chap. 29, sections 17 to 22 inclusive.

The principle which *R.* v. *Cavanagh, supra*, sustains, namely, requiring objections to be raised before the magistrate on the original hearing, is further enforced by the 67th section of this Act, which provides that no appeal shall be successful on the ground of variance, unless insisted on before the Justice, and unless it appear that the Justice refused to adjourn, though it was shewn to him that the defendant was deceived or misled. See sections 5 and 12, also section 68.

In *R.* v. *Cavanagh*, 27 C. P. (Ont.), 537, it was held that the information might be amended: see 32 & 33 Vic., chap. 29, s. 32; also *Crawford* v. *Beattie*, 39 Q. B. (Ont.), 13, *ante*, p. 30. But if the information is on oath, it must be re-sworn. *Re Conklin*, 31 Q. B. (Ont.), 160. On an information for an assault under the 32 & 33 Vic., chap. 20, s. 43, it was held that the information might be amended, by adding the words "falsely imprison" so as to convey a charge of false imprisonment. (*Ib.*)

The general rule is, that no person can have an order or conviction made against him without first being summoned, and having an opportunity of defence. *Cooper* v. *W. Board*, 14 C. B., N. S., 180; but his appearing will waive the summons. *R.* v. *Smith*, L. R., 1 C. C. R., 110; see *ante*, p. 100.

It seems that the summons under this section should on its face show the authority of the magistrate issuing it to act. In the Province of Quebec a defendant had been convicted of selling liquor without license. In the absence of Mr. Coursol, Mr. Brehaut had presided. The usual form of words in the summons, requiring the defendant to be and appear before "C. J. Coursol, Esq.," and stating under what authority, had been struck out, and the words "M. Brehaut, P.M.," substituted. On the return of the summons, the defendant pleaded to the jurisdiction, and on this being overruled he pleaded to the merits. The Court held that the plea to the jurisdiction was not a waiver of the plea to the merits, and they quashed the conviction. (*Durnford* v. *Faireau*, 3 L C., L. J., 19. But if the defendant had made a motion instead of pleading to the jurisdiction, the subsequent plea to the merits would be a waiver of the objection to the jurisdiction. *Durnford* v. *St. Marie*, 3 L. C., L. J., 19.)

The words in this section, "order for the payment of money or otherwise," include orders of every kind which a Justice of the Peace has authority to make, and orders other than those for the payment of money. *Morant* v. *Taylor*, L. R., 1 Ex. D., 188. The rule as to words *ejusdem generis* does not apply here, or limit the effect of the words "or otherwise." (*Ib.*)

2. Every such summons shall be served by a Constable or other Peace Officer, or other person to whom the same may be delivered, upon the person to whom it is directed, by delivering the same to the party personally, or by leaving it with some person for him at his last or most usual place of abode.

If the summons cannot be personally served it must be left for him at his present place of abode if he have one, or if not, then at his last place of abode. *R.* v. *Evans*, 19 L. J., M. C., 151; *R.* v. *Higham*, 7 E. & B. 557. It should be served a reasonable time before the day appointed in it for his appearance, but it is for the Justice to decide whether the summons has been served a reasonable time before or not. Two days or more would generally be deemed reasonable, (*Re Williams*, 21 L. J., M. C., 46; *ex parte Hopwood*, 15 Q. B. 121); as to reasonable time see section 7 and note thereon. An objection to the service should be taken at the hearing. *R.* v. *Berry*, 23 J. P. 86. A summons under this Act may be served by any person to whom it is delivered, including either the informant or complainant. The summons should be signed in duplicate, and one of them retained by the party serving.

3. The Constable, Peace Officer, or person who serves the same, shall attend at the time and place, and before the Justice or Justices in the summons mentioned, to depose, if necessary, to the service thereof.

It seems that a commissioner for taking affidavits has no power to swear to the affidavit of service of the summons. *R.* v. *Golding*, 2 Pugsley, 385. Under this section it seems the Justice must swear to the affidavit of service himself.

In every case where an oath or affirmation is directed to be made before a Justice, he has full power and authority to administer the same, and to certify to its being made. 31 Vic., chap. 1, s. 7, sixteenthly.

4. But nothing hereinbefore contained shall oblige any Justice or Justices of the Peace to issue any such Summons in any case where the application for any order of Justices is by law to be made *ex parte*.

5. No objection shall be allowed to any information, complaint or summons, for any alleged defect therein, in substance or in form, or for any variance between such information, complaint or summons, and the evidence adduced on the part of the informant or complainant at the hearing of such information or complaint; but if any such variance appears to the Justice or Justices present and acting at such hearing to be such, that the person summoned and appearing has been thereby deceived or misled, such Justice or Justices, may, upon such terms as he or they think fit, adjourn the hearing of the case to a future day.

There is a similar provision in the Act in reference to warrants. See section 12.

An information by a person who has no authority to make it is the same as no information, and this provision in the Act, curing objections for defects in form, must be held to apply only to informations made by persons who have authority to make them, and not to give validity to an information made by a person without any authority. *Ex parte Eagles*, 2 Hannay, 51.

In all cases after judgment given, and in the event of an appeal, the appellant will not be allowed to succeed for any such variance, unless he proves that the objection was made before the

Justice trying the case, and unless he also proves that such Justice refused to adjourn on its being shown to him that the person summoned &c., was deceived or misled by the variance. See section 67. Under the 68th section the appeal is to be disposed of on its merits, notwithstanding any defect of form.

Any objection will be disposed of, if both parties still consent to the Justice proceeding in the case. *R.* v. *Cheltenham*, 1 Q. B., 467.

Objections should be distinctly taken at first, for a person cannot waive the objection, and renew it when the decision is against him. *Wakefield* v. *West Riding*, L. R., 1. Q. B., 84. If a party appears before Justices and allows a charge which they have jurisdiction to hear, to be proceeded with without objection, he waives the want of a summons. *R.* v. *Shaw*, 11 Jur., N. S., 415.

An information, not under oath, was laid for selling liquor without licence. The defendant's counsel appeared, however, on the day of trial, and though he raised this objection he did not ask a delay or adjournment. The Justice then proceeded with the hearing, the defendant's counsel cross-examined the witnesses, and the Justice, upon clear proof of the offence charged, convicted the defendant. It did not appear that the defendant was in any way misled or prejudiced by the alleged defect in the information. Under these circumstances it was held that the statute cured the defect. *R.* v. *McMillan*, 2 Pugsley, 110. See also *Stoness* v. *Lake*, 40 Q. B. (Ont.), 320; *Crawford* v. *Beattie*, 39 Q. B. (Ont.), 13; *R.* v. *Cavanagh*, 27 C. P. (Ont.), 537. See also *ex parte Dunlap*, 3 Allen, 281. See also sections 21 and 22, which contain further provisions as to adjournment when the defendant appears to have been misled.

6. If the person served with a Summons does not appear before the Justice or Justices at the time and place mentioned in the Summons, and it be made to appear to the Justice or Justices, by oath or affirmation, that the Summons was duly served what the Justice or Justices deem a reasonable time before the time therein appointed for appearing to the same, then the Justice or Justices, upon oath or affirmation being made before him or them, substantiating the matter of the information or complaint to his or their satisfaction, may, if he or they think fit, issue his or their Warrant (B) to apprehend the party so summoned, and to bring him before the same Justice or

Justices or before some other Justice or Justices of the Peace in and for the same Territorial Division, to answer to the said information or complaint, and to be further dealt with according to law; or the Justice or Justices before whom any such information is laid, for any such offence as aforesaid, punishable on conviction, upon oath or affirmation being made before him or them substantiating the matter of the information to his or their satisfaction, may, if he or they think fit, instead of issuing a Summons, issue in the first instance his or their Warrant (C) for apprehending the person against whom the information has been laid, and bringing him before the same Justice or Justices, or before some other Justice or Justices of the Peace in and for the same Territorial Division, to answer to the information and to be further dealt with according to law; Provided that where a Warrant is issued in the first instance, the Justice issuing it shall furnish a copy or copies thereof, and cause a copy to be served on each party arrested at the time of such arrest.

The latter part of this section, which authorizes the issue of a warrant in the first instance, is confined to informations and does not extend to complaints or orders.

Under the 1 Vic., chap. 21, s. 27 a magistrate could not cause the arrest of a party in the first instance on a charge of neglect to perform statute labour. That Act required the prior issue of a summons. *Cronkhite* v. *Somerville*, 3 Q. B (Ont.), 129.

Where an Act of Parliament gives a Magistrate jurisdiction over an offence, it impliedly gives him power to make out a Warrant, and bring before him any person charged with such offence. *Bane* v. *Methuen*, 2 Bing. 63.

Complaint under oath of an assault was made before a Justice on which he issued a summons, the defendant not appearing, the Justice on proof of service of the summons issued the warrant B, under this section, upon which the defendant was arrested, brought before the Justice and convicted—he protesting against the proceedings. It was held that as there was a complaint under oath, the Justice had authority to issue a warrant in the first instance, and that his having used the form (B) instead of (C), did not make the arrest illegal, and that he had power to convict, though the summons served was defective in not stating the day the defendant was to appear. *R.* v. *Perkins*, Stephens Dig. N. B., 256.

7. If where a Summons has been issued, and upon the day and at the place

therein appointed for the appearance of the party summoned, the party fails to appear in obedience to the Summons, then, if it be proved upon oath or affirmation to the Justice or Justices present, that a Summons was duly served upon the party a reasonable time before the time appointed for his appearance, the Justice or Justices of the Peace may proceed *ex parte* to the hearing of the information or complaint, and adjudicate thereon, as fully and effectually to all intents and purposes as if the party had personally appeared before him or them in obedience to the Summons.

Justices ought to be very cautious how they proceed in the absence of a defendant who has been summoned only, unless they have strong ground for believing that the summons has reached him, and that he is wilfully disobeying it; and this rule applies, though under the second section of the statute, the summons may be legally served by leaving the same at the last or most usual place of abode of the defendant. The defendant was a fisherman, and went to sea in pursuit of his calling on the 9th of March. On the same day a summons for an assault was taken out against him requiring him, to appear to answer the charge upon the 12th. On that day it having been proved that a summons was served on the defendant on the 10th by leaving it with his mother at his usual place of abode, the Justice convicted him in his absence, though it did not appear that the defendant's mother knew the nature of the summons. The defendant returned on the 9th of April, and was arrested under the conviction, but the Court held that there was no evidence that a reasonable time had elapsed between the time of the service of the summons and the day for hearing, and that the Justices had therefore no jurisdiction to convict. *R.* v. *Smith*, L. R. 10 Q. B., 604. It will be observed that the sixth section of the Act gives the Justice tice power to issue a warrant on the non-appearance of the party in obedience to the summons. It is recommended that this course be pursued by the Justices in every case before conviction. It is sanctioned also by the 32nd section of this Act.

Where a statute fixed no period for delay between the service and the return of the summons, it was held that a service on the defendant at his domicile, twenty miles from the place where he was by the writ summoned to appear on the following day, at ten o'clock in the forenoon, the service being effected about three o'clock in the afternoon of the day preceding, was not reasonable, and the plaintiff could not legally proceed *ex parte*. *Ex parte Church*, 14 L. C. R., 318.

8. Every Warrant to apprehend a Defendant that he may answer to an information or complaint shall be under the hand and seal or hands and seals of the Justice or Justices issuing the same, and may be directed to any one or more, or to all of the Constables (or other Peace Officers, of the Territorial Division within which it is to be executed, or to such Constable and all other Constables in the Territorial Division within which the Justice or Justices who issued the Warrant hath or have jurisdiction, or generally to all the Constables (or Peace Officers) within such Territorial Division, and it shall state shortly the matter of the information or complaint on which it is founded, and shall name or otherwise describe the person against whom it has been issued, and it shall order the Constables (or other Peace Officers) to whom it is directed to apprehend the Defendant, and to bring him before one or more Justice or Justices of the Peace, of the same Territorial Division, as the case may require, to answer to the information or complaint and to be further dealt with according to law.

See observations under section 17 of the 32 & 33 Vic., chap. 30, *ante*, p. 33-4.

9. It shall not be necessary to make the Warrant returnable at any particular time, but the same may remain in full force until executed; and the Warrant may be executed by apprehending the Defendant at any place in the Territorial Division within which the Justices who issued the same have jurisdiction, or, in case of fresh pursuit, at any place in the next adjoining Territorial Division within seven miles of the border of the first mentioned Territorial Division, without having the Warrant backed as hereinafter mentioned.

10. In all cases where the Warrant is directed to all Constables or Peace Officers in the Territorial Division within which the Justice or Justices who issued the same have jurisdiction, any Constable or Peace Officer for any place within the limits of the jurisdiction may execute the Warrant in like manner as if the Warrant was directed specially to him by name, and notwithstanding that the place in which the Warrant is executed be not within the place for which he is a Constable or Peace Officer.

11. If any person against whom any Warrant has been issued be not found within the jurisdiction of the Justice or Justices by whom it was issued, or, if he escapes into, or is, or is suspected to be in any place within Canada, out of the jurisdiction of the Justice or Justices who issued the Warrant, any Justice of the Peace, within whose jurisdiction such person may be or be sus-

pected to be, upon proof upon oath or affirmation of the handwriting of the Justice or Justices issuing the Warrant, may make an endorsement upon it, signed with his name, authorizing the execution of the Warrant within his jurisdiction ; and such endorsement shall be a sufficient authority to the person bringing the Warrant, and to all other persons to whom it was originally directed, and to all Constables or other Peace Officers of the Territorial Division wherein the endorsement has been made, to execute the same in any place within the jurisdiction of the Justice of the Peace endorsing the same, and to carry the offender, when apprehended, before the Justice or Justices who first issued the Warrant or some other Justice having the same jurisdiction.

12. No objection shall be taken or allowed to any Warrant issued as aforesaid, for any alleged defect therein in substance or in form, or for any variance between it and the evidence adduced on the part of the Informant or Complainant, but if it appears to the Justice or Justices present and acting at the hearing, that the party apprehended under the Warrant has been deceived or misled by any such variance, such Justice or Justices may, upon such terms as he or they think fit, adjourn the hearing of the case to some future day, and in the meantime commit (D) the Defendant to the Common Gaol, or other prison, or place of security within the Territorial Division or place wherein the Justice or Justices may be acting, or to such other custody as the Justice or Justices think fit, or may discharge him upon his entering into a Recognizance (E), with or without surety or sureties, at the discretion of the Justice or Justices, conditioned for his appearance at the time and place to which the hearing is so adjourned.

13. In all cases where a Defendant is discharged upon Recognizance and does not afterwards appear at the time and place in the Recognizance mentioned, the Justice who took the Recognizance, or any Justice or Justices who may then be present, having certified (F) upon the back of the Recognizance the non-appearance of the Defendant, may transmit such Recognizance to the proper Officer in the Province appointed by law to receive the same, to be proceeded upon in like manner as other Recognizances, and such Certificate shall be deemed sufficient *prima facie* evidence of the non-appearance of the said Defendant, and the Justice or Justices may issue his or their Warrant for the apprehension of the Defendant on the information or complaint.

14. In any information or complaint or proceedings thereon, in which it is necessary to state the ownership of any property belonging to or in possession of partners, joint tenants, parceners or tenants in common, or *par indivis*, it shall be sufficient to name one of such persons, and to state the property to belong to the person so named and another, or others, as the case may be ; and whenever in any information or complaint or the proceedings thereon, it

is nececssary to mention, for any purpose whatsoever, any partners, joint tenants, parceners or tenants in common, or *par indivis*, it shall be sufficient to describe them in the manner aforesaid ; and whenever in any information or complaint, or the proceedings thereon, it is necessary to describe the ownership of any work or building made, maintained or repaired at the expense of the Corporation or inhabitants of any Territorial Division or place, or of any materials for the making, altering or repairing the same, they may be therein described as the property of the inhabitants of such Territorial Division or place.

15. Every person who aids, abets, counsels or procures the commission of any offence which is punishable on summary conviction, shall be liable to be proceeded against and convicted for the same, either together with the principal offender, or before or after his conviction, and shall be liable, on conviction, to the same forfeiture and punishment as the principal offender, and may be proceeded against and convicted either in the Territorial Division or place where the principal offender may be convicted, or in that in which the offence of aiding, abetting, counselling or procuring was committed.

Where a master intends a servant to commit some offence, he should be summoned as principal, and the servant as aiding and abetting, (*Wilson* v. *Stewart*, 3 B. & S.,913); or the master may be charged with aiding the servant. *Howells* v. *Wynne*, 15 C.B.N.S. 3. In some cases the master may be responsible for the criminal act of his servant, though done without his knowledge,—as, for example, under the Licensing Act. *Mullins* v. *Collins*, 38 J. P., 34.

A conviction cannot be procured under this section, unless the principal offence has been committed. Though there may be accessories after the fact in regard to felonies, there can be none such in the case of an offence punishable on summary conviction, as the above section only applies to aiding, &c., the commission of any offence. Kerr's Acts, 165.

16. If it be made to appear to any Justice of the Peace, by the oath or affirmation of any credible person, that any person within the jurisdiction of such Justice is likely to give material evidence on behalf of the prosecutor or complainant or defendant, and will not voluntarily appear as a witness at the time and place appointed for the hearing of the information or complaint, the Justice shall issue his Summons (G 1) to such person, requiring him to be and appear at a time and place mentioned in the Summons, before the said Justice, or any other Justice or Justices of the Peace for the Territorial Division who may then be there, to testify what he knows concerning the information or complaint.

Under this section the witness must be within the jurisdiction of the Justice, but either party, either prosecutor or defendant, may invoke the provisions of the section.

The plain rule is that witnesses for the defence, in the absence of any provision expressly taking away the right to examine them, are admissible as a matter of unquestionable right. Where, therefore, a party was convicted under the Public Health Act (Ont.), 36 Vic., chap. 43, the magistrates refusing to hear witnesses for the defence, on the ground that the statute made no provision for such witnesses being called, the complaint was re-opened by the Court. *Re Holland*, 37 Q. B. (Ont.), 214.

A Justice cannot be ordered to attend at the house of an infirm witness to take his deposition. *Ex parte Kimbolton*, 25 J.P., 759.

Every prosecutor of any information who has not a pecuniary interest in the result, and every complainant, whatever his interest may be, is a competent witness, and a liability for costs will not exclude a prosecutor, see sec. 45. The 32 & 33 Vic., chap. 29, s. 58, and following sections, contain the law as to witnesses and evidence in criminal cases. As a general rule crime or interest does not exclude a witness, see sec. 62. The sixty-fourth section of this Act was amended by the 40 Vic., chap. 26.

The Justice under this section can, as we have already seen, issue his summons to witnesses for the informant, complainant, or defendant, whilst under the 32 & 33 Vic., chap. 30, he can only summon witnesses for the prosecution, but the person so to be summoned must by the oath or affirmation of the person whose deposition supports the application, be shewn to be within the jurisdiction, *i.e.*, the territorial division, of the Justice to whom it is made; whilst under the 32 & 33 Vic., chap. 30, he can summon any one within the limits of Canada.

The power of the Justice under this section to issue summons and warrant is conditional upon its being made to appear by the *oath* or *affirmation* of any credible person, that any person within the jurisdiction of such Justice is likely to give material evidence on behalf of the prosecutor, and will not voluntarily appear; without such oath the summons or warrant is unauthorized. *Cross v. Wilcox*, 39 Q. B. (Ont.), 193.

These sections in no manner apply to the case of a prosecutor unwilling to proceed, and entitled so to refuse (as for instance where the charge is of assault only), but only to the case of a material witness other than the prosecutor refusing to attend, where the prosecutor is desirous of proceeding. *Cross* v. *Wilcox*, 39 Q. B. (Ont.), 187. A magistrate who by warrant causes the arrest of the prosecutor to *answer the charge contained in the information*, and to be further dealt with according to law, exceeds his jurisdiction and is liable in trespass.

17. If any person so summoned neglects or refuses to appear at the time and place appointed by the Summons, and no just excuse be offered for such neglect or refusal, then (after proof upon oath or affirmation of the Summons having been served upon him, either personally or by leaving the same for him with some person at his last or most usual place of abode) the Justice or Justices before whom such person should have appeared may issue a Warrant (G 2) to bring and have such person, at a time and place to be therein mentioned, before the Justice who issued the Summons, or before any other Justice or Justices of the Peace for the same Territorial Division who may be then there, to testify as aforesaid, and the said Warrant may, if necessary, be backed as hereinbefore mentioned, in order to its being executed out of the jurisdiction of the Justice who issued the same.

18. If the Justice is satisfied, by evidence upon oath or affirmation, that it is probable that the person will not attend to give evidence without being compelled so to do, then instead of issuing a Summons he may issue his Warrant (G 3) in the first instance, and the Warrant may, if necessary, be backed as aforesaid.

19. If on the appearance of the person so summoned before the last mentioned Justice or Justices, either in obedience to the Summoms, or upon being brought before him or them, by virtue of the Warrant, such person refuses to be examined upon oath or affirmation concerning the premises, or refuses to take an oath or affirmation, or having taken the oath or affirmation refuses to answer such questions concerning the premises as are then put to him, without offering any just excuse for his refusal, any Justice of the Peace then present, and having jurisdiction, may, by Warrant (G 4), commit the person so refusing to the Common Gaol or other prison for the Territorial Division where the person then is, there to remain and be imprisoned for any time not exceeding ten days, unless in the meantime, he consents to be examined and to answer concerning the premises.

A Justice of the Peace may commit a *feme covert* who is a

material witness on a charge of felony brought before him, and who refuses to appear at the Sessions to give evidence, or to find sureties for her appearance. *Bennet* v. *Watson*, 3 M. & S. 1.

A magistrate has no right to issue a warrant for the apprehension of a person to attend to find bail for his appearance as a witness at the Assizes, although it is sworn that the witness is material and has refused to obey a summons which had previously been issued to give evidence before the magistrate. *Evans* v. *Rees*, 12 A. & E., 55.

20. In all cases of complaint upon which a Justice or Justices of the Peace may make an order for the payment of money or otherwise, it shall not be necessary that such complaint be in writing unless it be required to be so by some particular Act or Law upon which such complaint is framed.

21. In all cases of informations for offences or acts punishable upon summary conviction, any variance between the information and the evidence adduced in support thereof as to the time at which such offence or act is alleged to have been committed, shall not be deemed material, if it be proved that such information was in fact laid within the time limited by law for laying the same; and any variance between the information and the evidence adduced in support thereof, as to the place in which the offence or act is alleged to have been committed, shall not be deemed material, if the offence or act be proved to have been committed within the jurisdiction of the Justice or Justices by whom the information is heard and determined.

As to these allegations of time and place and variances between the information and evidence, in relation to the same respectively, see *R.* v. *Cavanagh*, 27 C. P. (Ont.), 537; see also the 32 & 33 Vic., chap. 29, s. 23, and the observations already made as to informations under section 1 of this Act, *ante*, p. 101-2.

22. If any such variance, or any other variance between the information and the evidence adduced in support thereof, appears to the Justice or Justices present, and acting at the hearing, to be such that the party charged by the information has been thereby deceived or misled, the Justice or Justices, upon such terms as he or they think fit, may adjourn the hearing of the case to some future day, and in the meantime commit (D) the Defendant to the Common Gaol, or other prison, or to such other custody as the Justice or Justices think fit, or may discharge him upon his entering into a Recognizance (E), with or without Surety or Sureties, at the discretion of the Justice or Justices, conditioned for his appearance at the time and place to which the hearing is adjourned.

If Justices of the Peace adjourn their proceedings to a day subsequently to the repeal of an Act of Parliament under which they act their jurisdiction will cease. *R.* v. *Loudon*, 3 Burr. 1456.

23. In all cases where a Defendant has been discharged upon Recognizance as aforesaid, and does not afterwards appear at the time and place in the Recognizance mentioned, the Justice who took the Recognizance, or any other Justice or Justices who may then be there present, having certified (F) upon the back of the Recognizance the non-appearance of the Defendant, may transmit the Recognizance to the proper Officer in the Province appointed by law to receive the same, to be proceeded upon in like manner as other Recognizances, and the Certificate shall be deemed sufficient *prima facie* evidence of the non-appearance of the Defendant.

24. All complaints upon which a Justice or Justices of the Peace are authorized by law to make an order, and all informations for any offence or act punishable upon summary conviction, unless some particular Act or Law otherwise requires, and except in cases where it is herein otherwise provided, may respectively be made or laid without any oath or affirmation as to the truth thereof.

See *Ex parte Cousine*, 7 L. C. J., 112; *R.* v. *McConnell*, 6 O.S., 629. The word "herein" used in any section of an Act, is to be understood to relate to the whole Act, and not to that section only. 31 Vic., chap. 1, sec. 6, s.-s. 4.

25. But in all cases of informations, where the Justice or Justices, receiving the same, thereupon issue his or their Warrant in the first instance, to apprehend the Defendant, and in every case where the Justice or the Justices issue his or their Warrant in the first instance, the matter of the information shall be substantiated by the oath or affirmation of the informant, or by some witness or witnesses on his behalf, before the Warrant shall be issued; and every complaint shall be for one matter of complaint only and not for two or more matters of complaint, and every information shall be for one offence only, and not for two or more offences, and every complaint or information may be laid or made by the complainant or informant in person, or by his Counsel or Attorney, or other person authorized in that behalf.

This section does not prevent a principal and an aider or abettor from being charged in the same information.

The provision in this section, that every information shall be for one offence only does not refer to the number of offenders, and it seems to be quite legal to include several persons in one information or complaint (and conviction or order) when they are all charged with the same offence or matter, committed at the same time and place. *R.* v. *Bacon*, 21 J. P., 404; *R.* v. *Cridland*, 7 E. & B., 853.

According to the decision in *ex parte Cariguan*, 5 L. C. R., 479, the provision in this section, that every information or complaint must be for one offence, only applies when a warrant is issued in the first instance, and a complaint or information may be made or laid for two offences, provided the object be not to arrest the defendant in the first instance.

A complaint can only have reference to one matter, and not to two or more, and an information to but one offence; not to two or more unless the law under which the one or the other is made permit it. *Pacaud* v. *Roy*, 15 L. C. R., 205.

26. In all cases where no time is specially limited for making any complaint or laying any information in the Act or Law relating to the particular case, the complaint shall be made and the information shall be laid within three months from the time when the matter of the complaint or information arose, except in that part of the County of Saguenay which extends from Portneuf in the said county, to the eastward as far as the limits of Canada, including all the Islands adjoining thereto, where the time within which such complaint shall be made, or such information shall be laid, shall be extended to twelve months from the time when the matter of the complaint or information arose.

The corresponding section of the English Act was held not to apply to warrants of distress for rates. *Sweetman* v. *Guest*, L. R., 3 Q. B., 262. See also on this section, *Pacaud* v. *Roy*, 15 L. C. R., 205.

27. Every complaint and information shall be heard, tried, determined and adjudged by one Justice or two or more Justices of the Peace, as may be directed by the Act or Law upon which the complaint or information is framed, or by any other Act or Law in that behalf.

28. If there be no such direction in any Act or Law, then the complaint or information may be heard, tried, determined and adjudged by any one Justice for the Territorial Division where the matter of the complaint or information arose.

29. The room or place in which the Justice or Justices sit to hear and try

any complaint or information, shall be deemed an open and public Court to which the public generally may have access, so far as the same can conveniently contain them.

30. The party against whom the complaint is made, or information laid, shall be admitted to make his full answer and defence thereto, and to have the witnesses examined and cross-examined by Counsel or Attorney on his behalf.

This section does not give a defendant the right to have a case adjourned in order to procure the assistance of attorney or counsel, although he has had no opportunity of procuring it. *R.* v. *Biggins*, 5 L.T., N.S., 605.

31. Every Complainant or Informant in any such case shall be at liberty to conduct the complaint or information, and to have the witnesses examined and cross-examined by Counsel or Attorney on his behalf.

32. If on the day and at the place appointed by the Summons for hearing and determining the complaint or information, the Defendant against whom the same has been made or laid does not appear when called, the Constable, or other person who served him with the summons, shall declare upon oath in what manner he served the Summons; and if it appear to the satisfaction of the Justice or Justices that he duly served the Summons, then the Justice or Justices may proceed to hear and determine the case in the absence of the Defendant, or the Justice or Justices, upon the non-appearance of the Defendant, may, if he or they think fit, issue his or their Warrant in manner hereinbefore directed, and shall adjourn the hearing of the complaint or information until the Defendant is apprehended.

33. When the Defendant has been apprehended under the Warrant, he shall be brought before the same Justice or Justices, or some other Justice or Justices of the Peace for the same Territorial Division, who shall thereupon, either by his or their Warrant (H) commit the Defendant to the Common Gaol, or other prison, or if he or they think fit, verbally to the custody of the Constable or other person who apprehended him, or to such other safe custody as he or they deem fit, and may order the Defendant to be brought up at a certain time and place before him or them, of which order the Complainant or Informant shall have due notice, but no committal under this section shall be for more than one week.

Information having been laid on oath before the defendant, a Justice of the Peace, against the plaintiff, he issued a summons and copy, but the copy was defective in not containing the return day. The constable made oath before the Justice that he had served a true copy of the summons, whereupon the plaintiff not appearing at the return, the defendant issued the warrant in form B in the statute (32 & 33 Vic., chap. 31), for the plaintiff's arrest. On being brought before the defendant the plaintiff refused to enter into a recognizance, though the Justice offered to take his own recognizance. The Justice thereupon by warrant, form H, under this section of the statute, remanded the plaintiff to the "Common Gaol at Kingston," King's County, for five days, from which he was discharged by a Judge's order. An Act had just been passed, not known to the defendant, removing the shire town from Kingston, and making the Common Gaol of St. John or Westmoreland the Common Gaol of Kings. The Court held that the Justice was not liable in the absence of malice or want of reasonable and probable cause, and that the plaintiff's imprisonment was legal as a remand for safe custody under this section of the statute. *Birch* v. *Perkins*, 2 Pugsley, 327.

The commitment, therefore, under this section, need not necessarily be to the Common Gaol of the county for which the Justice acts. It may be to another prison or verbally to the custody of the constable, "or to such other safe custody" as the Justice may think fit (*ib.*).

A warrant of commitment for an indefinite time, or which directs the prisoner to be kept in custody until the costs are paid, without stating the amount, is bad. *Dawson* v. *Fraser*, 7 Q. B. (Ont.), 391; see also *Dickson* v. *Crabb*, 24 Q. B. (Ont.), 494; followed in *Moffatt* v. *Barnard*, 24 Q.B. (Ont.), 498.

A warrant reciting a coroner's inquisition, and stating the offence as follows:—that C "stands charged with having inflicted blows on the body of the said F," and not showing the place where the blows, if any, were inflicted, or the offence, if any, was committed, is bad. *Re Carmichael*, 10 U.C.L.J., 325. The warrant should show the place. *Re Beebe*, 3 P. R. (Ont.), 270.

Omitting to state the conviction of a defendant in his warrant of commitment, will not subject a Justice to an action for false imprisonment, provided the actual conviction is proved upon his defence. *Whelan* v. *Stevens*, Taylor, 245.

A warrant, for non-performance of statute labour, to imprison for the remainder of the penalty, for twelve days absolutely, and not unless the fine and costs should be sooner paid ; and after alleging summons, appearance, conviction, and warrant of distress, averred that part of the sum directed to be levied had been made, and that the plaintiff had no more goods, it was held that the warrant was clearly bad, because it was after part of the fine had been paid, and was for an absolute time, and not unless fine and costs should be sooner paid. *Trigerson* v. *Board*, P.C., 6 O.S. 405.

Under the Summary Punishment Act, magistrates could not issue their warrant to imprison absolutely for so many days, but only to imprison for so many days, unless the fine and costs be sooner paid. *Ferguson* v. *Adams*, 5 Q.B. (Ont.), 194.

34. If upon the day and at the place so appointed, the Defendant appears voluntarily in obedience to the Summons in that behalf served upon him, or is brought before the Justice or Justices by virtue of a Warrant, then, if the Complainant or Informant, having had due notice, does not appear by himself, his Counsel or Attorney, the Justice or Justices shall dismiss the complaint or information, unless for some reason he or they think proper to adjourn the hearing of the same to some other day, upon such terms as he or they think fit, in which case the Justice or Justices may commit (D) the Defendant in the meantime to the Common Gaol, or other prison, or to such other custody as he or they think fit, or may discharge him upon his entering into a Recognizance (E) with or without surety or sureties, at the discretion of the Justice or Justices, conditioned for his appearance at the time and place to which such hearing may be adjourned.

35. If the Defendant does not afterwards appear at the time and place mentioned in his Recognizance, then the Justice who took the Recognizance, or any Justice or Justices then and there present, having certified (F) on the back of the Recognizance the non-appearance of the Defendant, may transmit the Recognizance to the proper officer appointed to receive the same, to be proceeded upon in like manner as other recognizances, and such certificate shall be deemed sufficient *prima facie* evidence of the non-appearance of the Defendant.

36. If both parties appear, either personally or by their respective Counsel or Attorneys, before the Justice or Justices who are to hear and determine the complaint or information, then the said Justice or Justices shall proceed to hear and determine the same.

37. In case the Defendant be present at the hearing, the substance of the

information or complaint shall be stated to him, and he shall be asked if he has any cause to show why he should not be convicted, or why an order should not be made against him, as the case may be.

38. If he thereupon admits the truth of the information or complaint, and shews no sufficient cause why he should not be convicted, or why an order should not be made against him, as the case may be, the Justice or Justices present at the hearing, shall convict him or make an order against him accordingly.

39. If he does not admit the truth of the information or complaint, the Justice or Justices shall proceed to hear the Prosecutor or Complainant and such witnesses as he may examine, and such other evidence as he may adduce in support of his information or complaint, and shall also hear the defendant and such witnesses as he may examine, and such other evidence as he may adduce in his defence, and also hear such witnesses as the Prosecutor or Complainant may examine in reply, if such Defendant has examined any witnesses or given any evidence other than as to his (the Defendant's) general character.

Although this section does not say how the examination shall be taken, yet it seems to be the duty of the magistrate to take the examination and evidence in writing. *R.* v. *Flannigan*, 32 Q. B. (Ont.), 593-599.

Under this section the prosecutor or complainant has no right to go into evidence in reply, unless the defendant has examined witnesses other than as to his general character.

40. The Prosecutor or Complainant shall not be entitled to make any observations in reply, upon the evidence given by the Defendant, nor shall the Defendant be entitled to make any observations in reply upon the evidence given by the Prosecutor or Complainant in reply.

41. The Justice or Justices, having heard what each party has to say, and the witnesses and evidence adduced, shall consider the whole matter, and, unless otherwise provided, determine the same, and convict or make an Order upon the Defendant, or dismiss the information or complaint as the case may be.

42. If he or they convict or make an order against the Defendant, a minute or memorandum thereof shall then be made, for which no fee shall be paid, and the conviction (I 1, 2, 3) or order (K 1, 2, 3) shall afterwards be drawn up by the Justice or Justices in proper form, under his or their hand and seal or hands and seals.

It would seem that a conviction by a Justice may be quashed, unless it is sealed. *Haacke* v. *Adamson*, 14 C. P. (Ont.), 201; *McDonald* v. *Stuckey*, 31 Q. B. (Ont.), 577.

Justices out of sessions are in many cases required to make orders in matters not criminal, but this jurisdiction must be given either by the express words of some statute, or by necessary implication from them. An order of Justices consists of three parts: the first recites the facts which, according to the statute on which the order is framed, give the Justice jurisdiction to make it; the second states the appearance, hearing and finding; and the last, the adjudication and order. Great care must be taken with the part of the order reciting the facts which give the jurisdiction, for it is essential that the order show upon the face of it that the Justices had jurisdiction to make it, otherwise it will be bad (*R.* v. *Spackman*, 2 Q. B., 301); or if in fact the Justices had not jurisdiction, although it be represented on the face of the order that they had—the order may be impugned upon affidavit and quashed, although it appear good on the face of it. *R.* v. *Bolton*, 1 Q. B., 66. An order may be good in part and bad in the rest. *R.* v. *Over*, 14 Q. B., 425. It must appear also that the person upon whom the order was made, either was present at the hearing or was summoned in order to show that he had an opportunity of resisting the order if he objected to it, unless indeed the order be intended by the statute to be *ex parte*, and be made upon the application of the party to whom it is to be directed.

In the last part the only care requisite is, that the matter of complaint be adjudged to be true (*R.* v. *Williams*, 21 L. J., M. C., 150; and that the order be strictly such as is warranted by the statute. The 32 & 33 Vic. chap. 31, s. 51, provides in case an order be made, and no particular form of order is given by the Act or law, giving authority to make such order, and in all cases of orders made under the authority of any Act or law hitherto passed, whether any particular form of order is therein given or not, the Justice by whom the order is made, may draw up the same in such one of the forms of orders (K 1, 2, 3), as may be applicable to the case or to the like effect. Where an order of a Justice or Justices legally made, requires a person to do any certain act, and, upon being personally served with the order and required to do the act he refuse or neglect to do it, this is a misdemeanor at common law, punishable upon indictment by fine or imprisonment or both. *R.* v. *Bidwell*, 17 L. J., M. C., 99; *R.* v. *Ferrall*, 20 L. J., M. C., 39; *R.* v. *Walker*, L. R., 10 Q. B., 355.

A defendant who has been convicted is not entitled of right to a copy of the conviction, to enable him to appeal against it. *R.* v. *Huntingdon*, 5 D. & R., 588. He is, however, under this section, entitled to a minute, or memorandum of the conviction, without any fee, and if he wants the copy of conviction for purposes of defence in any action, a Justice who refuses it may have to pay the costs of a *certiorari* to obtain it. *R.* v. *Huntingdon*, *supra*. A copy given to the defendant will not be binding, since the Justices may draw it up in an amended form any time before a return to a *certiorari*, though after a commitment or distress, and after return to the sessions. *R.* v. *Richards*, 5 Q. B., 926; *R.* v. *Johnson*, 3 B. & S., 947.

A Justice is liable to an action if he prevent, by undue delay and after notice, the defendant from prosecuting his appeal. *Prosser* v. *Hyde*, 1 T. R., 414.

The blanks in the conviction should be filled up before signature. *Bott* v. *Ackroyd*, 28 L. J., M. C., 207.

The magistrate need not fix the amount of penalty at the moment of conviction. It is enough that it be fixed in the conviction when drawn up. *R.* v. *Liston*, 5 T. R., 338.

The Justices can mitigate a penalty where no minimum is fixed by the statute.

43. If the Justice or Justices dismiss the information or complaint, he or they may, when required so to do, make an order of dismissal of the same (L), and shall give the Defendant a Certificate thereof (M), which Certificate upon being afterwards produced, shall, without further proof, be a bar to any subsequent information or complaint for the same matter, against the same party.

The certificate of dismissal in this section refers to a dismissal on the merits. *Foster* v. *Hull*, 33 J. P., 629.

44. If the information or complaint in any case negatives any exemption, exception, proviso, or condition in the Statute on which the same is framed,

it shall not be necessary for the Prosecutor or Complainant to prove such negative, but the Defendant may prove the affirmative thereof in his defence, if he would have advantage of the same.

45. Every Prosecutor of any information not having any pecuniary interest in the result, and every Complainant in any complaint, whatever his interest may be in the result of the same, shall be a competent witness to support such information or complaint; and every witness at any hearing shall be examined upon oath or affirmation, and the Justice or Justices before whom any witness appears for the purpose of being examined, shall have full power and authority to administer to every witness the usual oath or affirmation; provided that no Prosecutor shall be deemed incompetent as a witness on the ground only that he may be liable to costs.

A difference is here created between summary convictions and orders. In seeking to obtain a conviction the informant, if he has no pecuniary interest, can be a witness, but if he seeks thereby compensation for a wrong he cannot testify, and the same rule applies to the informant's wife. On the other hand a complainant seeking an order, whatever his interest may be, is a competent witness, and his wife is also competent. Kerr's Acts, 202.

This section requires that the witnesses shall be examined on oath. Where magistrates first took the examination of witnesses not on oath, in support of a conviction, and afterwards swore them to the truth of their evidence, the Court expressed its disapprobation of the practice. *R.* v. *Kiddy*, 4 D. & R., 734.

It is to be observed that, under the 90th section of this Act, the evidence of the party aggrieved, and also the evidence of any inhabitant of the district, county or place in which any offence was committed, shall be admitted in proof of the offence, notwithstanding that any forfeiture or penalty, incurred by the offence, may be payable to any public fund of such district, county or place.

46. Before or during the hearing of any information or complaint, any one Justice or the Justices present may, in his or their discretion, adjourn the hearing of the same to a certain time and place to be then appointed and stated in the presence and hearing of the party or parties, or of their respective Attorneys or Agents then present, and in the meantime the Justice or Justices may suffer the Defendant to go at large or may commit (D) him to the Common Gaol or other prison, within the Territorial Division for

which the Justice or Justices are then acting, or to such other safe custody as the Justice or Justices think fit, or may discharge the Defendant upon his recognizance (E), with or without sureties, at the discretion of the Justice or Justices, conditioned for his appearance at the time and place to which such hearing or further hearing is adjourned, but no such adjournment shall be for more than one week.

A prosecution for selling liquor without license was instituted before A, a Justice of the Peace, who, on the return of the summons, adjourned the trial. The defendant then went before another Justice, and admitted the sale, whereupon such Justice imposed a fine upon him. At the adjourned hearing before A, the defendant pleaded this conviction in bar, but A notwithstanding proceeded with the case, and convicted the defendant, and this conviction was held good. *R.* v. *Roberts*, Stephens' Dig. N. B., 258.

One Justice of the Peace has power at the return day of the summons to adjourn the proceedings to a future day under the Summary Conviction Act in New Brunswick (1 Rev. Stat., chap. 138, s. 21), though jurisdiction to hear the case is given to two Justices. *Ex parte Holder*, Stephens' Dig. N. B., 256.

The same rule would seem to apply to this section of the statute.

Where a person was brought before a magistrate on a charge of threatened assault, and was ordered by the magistrate to find sureties to keep the peace, which, not being immediately able to do, he remained in the custody of a police constable for three hours, during which time the magistrate frequently visited him to ascertain if he had found bail, and at night not having found bail, he was taken to gaol, where he remained until the following morning, when he was discharged on bail being procured. It was held that the warrant for commitment was good without being in writing, and that the magistrate was therefore not liable in trespass. *Lynden* v. *King*, 6 O. S., 566. But when a magistrate allows a prisoner to depart without examining into the charge against him with a direction to appear next morning at the police office, and in the meantime on the ground that he was assaulted by the prisoner when in custody before him, gives a verbal order to a constable to apprehend him and take him to the station-house or gaol; such imprisonment is illegal, and the magistrate cannot justify the arrest. *Powell* v. *Williamson*, 1 Q. B. (Ont.), 154.

47. If, at the time and place to which the hearing or further hearing has been adjourned, either or both of the parties do not appear, personally or by his or their Counsel or Attorneys respectively, before the Justice or Justices or such other Justice or Justices as may then be there, the Justice or Justices then there present may proceed to the hearing or further hearing as if the party or parties were present.

48. If the Prosecutor or Complainant do not appear, the Justice or Justices may dismiss the information with or without costs, as to him or them seems fit.

49. In all cases when a defendant is discharged upon his recognizance, and does not afterwards appear at the time and place mentioned in the recognizance, the Justice or Justices who took the recognizance, or any other Justice or Justices who may then be there present, having certified (F) on the back of the recognizance the non-appearance of the accused party, may transmit such recognizance to the proper officer appointed to receive the same by the laws of the Province in which the recognizance was taken, to be proceeded upon in like manner as other recognizances, and such certificate shall be deemed sufficient *prima facie* evidence of the non-appearance of the Defendant.

50. In all cases of conviction where no particular form of conviction is given by the Act or Law creating the offence or regulating the prosecution for the same, and in all cases of conviction upon Acts or Laws hitherto passed, whether any particular form of conviction has been therein given or not, the Justice or Justices who convict, may draw up his or their conviction, on parchment or on paper, in such one of the forms of conviction (I 1, 2, 3,) as may be applicable to the case, or to the like effect.

Where an Act of Parliament gives the form of conviction for any offence prohibited by the Act, that form must be followed, and a warrant granted on a conviction drawn up in any other form is illegal, and the Justice and those acting under it, are trespassers. *Danson* v. *Gill*, 1 East, 64; *Goss* v. *Jackson*, 3 Esp., 198.

In the use of the forms of conviction given by this Act, it must be remembered that they are applicable to all previous penal statutes, whether they contain particular forms of convictions or orders or not; and to all subsequent statutes not containing particular forms of convictions or orders. *Ex parte Allison*, 10 Ex., 551. If by any subsequent statute a particular form be prescribed as indispensably necessary, such provision must be strictly complied with. *R.* v. *Jefferies*, 4 T. R, 169.

The blanks in the form of a conviction for a penalty and costs to be levied by distress, and in default of sufficient distress by imprisonment, are to be filled up as follows :—

1. The name of the Province and Territorial Division within which the conviction was rendered.

2. The date of the conviction, giving the day, month, and year in full, without using figures.

3. The place where the conviction was so rendered, showing also the territorial division within which the said place is situate.

4. The name, residence and occupation of each of the defendants.

5. The number of the Justices convicting.

6. The statement of the offence.

This is the most difficult portion of the conviction to draw, and great attention must be paid to the following points, Kerr's Acts, 186, 187: The day on which the act was committed should be stated; but a conviction for selling liquor without license "on a certain day between the 31st July and 1st September in same year, to wit, on the first day of August," is sufficient, and it is not necessary to prove the exact day of sale. *R.* v. *Justices*, 2 Pugsley, 485.

The place for which the Justice acts must be shown, and it must be alleged that the offence was committed within the limits of his jurisdiction, or facts must be stated which give jurisdiction beyond those limits.

But alleging the act to be done at a certain place in the Township of A is sufficient, if a public statute shows that that township is within the county for which the Justice is appointed. *R.* v. *Shaw*, 23 Q.B. (Ont.), 616; see also *R.* v. *Edwards*, 1 East, 278; *R.* v. *Hazell*, 13 East, 139.

When by special statute jurisdiction is given to Justices of the territorial division within which an offender is found, the offence having been by him committed in another territorial division, in addition to setting out the place where the offence is committed, it is necessary to set out the fact of his having been found at some place within the territorial division of the convicting Justice. *Re Peerless*, 1 Q.B., 143.

The description of the offence must include in express terms every ingredient required by the statute to constitute the offence, nothing being left to intendment, inference, or argument. *R.* v. *Turner*, 4 B. & Ald., 510; *Charles* v. *Greene*, 13 Q. B., 216.

Where knowledge is made a material component in the offence, it must be distinctly alleged. *R.* v. *Jukes*, 8 T.R., 536; *Chaney* v. *Payne*, 2 Q. B., 712.

When the statute under which the information is laid in describing the offence contains the words "maliciously," "wilfully," "knowingly," or words of similar import, the defendant should be stated in the description of the offence, to have committed it maliciously, &c., as the case may be. Paley, 143.

Where written instruments form the gist of the offence, the conviction must set them out that it may clearly appear that the instrument is one of the description contemplated by the statute. It does not appear that the 32 & 33 Vic., chap. 29, s. 24, would apply to convictions.

Immediately after the statement of the offence in Form I 1, comes the adjudication of punishment, being the penalty and compensation, if any, adjudged and ordered by the Justice to be forfeited and paid by the defendant.

In the adjudication the Justice must measure the penalty he inflicts by his authority under the statute, inflicting the penalty for the offence of which he convicts the defendant. If the penalty is a sum certain, the defendant should be adjudged to forfeit and pay that sum certain; if, on the other hand, the statute in such cases gives the Justice the power of inflicting a penalty of not more, for instance, than ten dollars, and not less than one dollar, the Justice, if he convicts, must impose a penalty of either of these sums or of any sum between them. But if he imposes a penalty either greater than the higher or less than the lower limit, the conviction is bad. *R.* v. *Patchett*, 5 East, 341. In all cases the clause of the statute fixing the penalty should be carefully and strictly pursued. Oke's Syn., 146; Kerr's Acts, 192, 193.

The 25th section of the statute, in limiting the information or complaint, to one offence or matter of complaint, also limits the conviction to one offence, save where the contrary is provided by a subsequent statute. In all cases then the wording of the statute creating the offence is to be carefully considered in order to determine whether distinct penalties are incurred for each of the several acts charged, or whether they form but one aggregate offence, and require but one penalty. See *Collins* v. *Hopwood*, 15 M. & W., 459; Paley 218, 221. But of late years the distinction formerly recognised as existing between joint and several offences has been done away with, and the Courts treat all persons committing an offence together as liable each to the full penalty imposed by the statute on the person committing such offence, so that in all such cases it is the better plan to have an information and summary case for each person charged. *Mayhew* v. *Wordley*, 14 C. B., N. S., 550; Kerr's Acts, 197.

It is sufficient, if a conviction follows the forms set out in the statutes, for the forms are intended as guides to Justices, and otherwise they would prove only snares to entrap persons. *R.* v. *Shaw*, 23 Q. B. (Ont.), 618; *Reid* v. *McWhinnie*, 27 Q. B. (Ont.), 289; *R.* v. *Hyde*, 16 Jur., 337; *ex parte Eagles*, 2 Hannay, 53; *R.* v. *Johnson*, 8 Q. B., 102; *Moore* v. *Jarron*, 9 Q. B. (Ont.). 233; *R.* v. *Strachan*, 20 C. P. (Ont.), 182; *Moffat* v. *Barnard*, 24 Q. B. (Ont.), 498; *Egginton* v. *Lichfield*, 5 E. & B., 103.

The name of the informant or complainant must in some form or other appear on the face of the conviction. *Re Hennesy*, 8 U. C. L. J., 299.

The offence of which the defendant is convicted must be stated with certainty, otherwise the conviction will be quashed. *Eastman* v. *Reid*, 6 Q. B. (Ont.), 611.

A conviction must not be in the alternative. *R.* v. *Craig*, 21 Q. B. (Ont.), 552. A conviction adjudging the defendant to be imprisoned for twenty-five days, *or* payment of £5, and costs, in the alternative is bad. *R.* v. *Sadler*, 2 Chit., 519; *R.* v. *Wortman*, 4 Allen, 73; *R.* v. *Pain*, 7 D. & R., 678.

All exceptions contained in the *enacting* clause of a statute, must be negatived in the conviction. For instance, if a statute imposes a penalty for selling liquor without license, except upon a requisition for medicinal purposes, the absence of such requisition must be shewn in the conviction. *R.* v. *White,* 21 C. P. (Ont.), 354.

This rule, however, applies only where the exception is contained in the same section of the statute as that constituting the offence, and where the exception is in a different subsequent section, it need not be negatived in the conviction. *R.* v. *Breen*, 36 Q. B. (Ont.), 84. Even where the exception in such subsequent section is incorporated by reference with the enacting clause, for the reference must be *in* the enacting clause itself, and not *to* it. See also *R.* v. *Strachan*, 20 C. P. (Ont.), 182.

A conviction under a by-law must shew the by-law, that the Court may judge of its sufficiency. *R.* v. *Ross*, R. & J. Dig., 1979. And it must also shew by what municipality the by-law was passed. *R.* v. *Osler*, 32 Q. B. (Ont.), 324.

Where a form of conviction is not sanctioned by any statute, it must be legal according to the principles of the common law, and a conviction which did not express that the party had been summoned, nor that he appeared, nor that the evidence was given in his presence, cannot be supported. *Moore* v. *Jarron*, 9 Q. B. (Ont.), 233. But where the general form of conviction prescribed by this section is used, it is clearly not necessary to shew that the defendant was summoned or heard or any evidence given. *R.* v. *Caister* 30 Q. B. (Ont.), 247.

The charge in a conviction must be certain, and so stated, as to be pleadable in the event of a second prosecution for the same offence. *R.* v. *Hoggard*, 30 Q. B. (Ont.), 152.

A magistrate, in order to have a good justification under a conviction and warrant, must give in evidence a conviction not illegal on the face of it, and a warrant of distress supported by that conviction, and not on the face of it, an illegal warrant. *Eastman* v. *Reid*, 6 Q. B. (Ont.), 611.

In describing the offence in convictions it is not sufficient to state as the offence that which is only the legal result of certain facts, but the facts themselves must be specified, for instance, a conviction that the defendant used blasphemous language is not good, the exact words used should be set out in the conviction. *Re Donelly*, 20 C. P. (Ont.), 165.

In framing a conviction where it is immaterial by what means the act prohibited has been effected, it is in general sufficient to follow the words of the statute where it gives a particular description of the offence. But there are exceptions to this rule. Thus under the Act respecting Vagrants 32 & 33 Vic., chap. 28, a conviction of a common prostitute in the very words of the statute was holden insufficient, and that it should also shew a request made on the woman to give a satisfactory account of herself. *R.* v. *Leveeque*, 30 Q. B. (Ont.) 509. And where an Act describing the offence makes use of general terms which embrace a variety of circumstances, it is not enough to follow the words of the statute, but it is necessary to state what particular fact prohibited has been committed or the circumstances under which the act is an offence. *Re Donelly*, 20 C P. (Ont.), 167; *R.* v. *Scott* 4 B. & S. 368; *R.* v. *Nott*, 4 Q. B., 768. When circumstances explanatory of the words of the statute are necessary tobe shewn in order to bring the case within the statute such circumstances must be plainly and distinctly averred. *R.* v. *Wield*, 6 East, 417; *Fletcher* v. *Calthrop*, 6 Q. B. 880.

One of several persons in partnership may be convicted of an offence committed by the firm for all wrongs are several as well as joint. *Mullins* v. *Bellamere*, 7 L. C. J., 228. For a statutory illustration of this principle, see 32 & 33 Vic. chap. 21, s. 91, as to frauds by millers, factors, warehousemen, &c.

A conviction cannot at common law be amended. *R* v. *Jukes* 8 T. R., 625. The magistrate, however, before he returns it to the sessions or upon a *certiorari* may draw it up in a more formal manner than he had at first drawn it. *Chaney* v. *Payne*, 1 Q. B., 712; *Charter* v. *Greame*, 13 Q. B., 216.

If the commitment be bad upon the face of it, the party may apply for a *habeas corpus*, and thereupon be discharged. But a good commitment may be substituted for a bad one, on the return to the writ. *R.* v. *Smith* 3 H. & N. 227. But if instead of convicting the defendant the Justice refuse to convict him and dismiss the case there is no mode of reviewing his decision ; the court will neither grant a *mandamus* requiring the magistrate to rehear the case nor award a *certiorari* to bring up the proceedings. *Ex parte B. & F. P. I. Co.*, 7 Dowl., 614.

It may be observed that although a conviction may be drawn up in a regular form, at any time before it is returned to sessions, an order or warrant of commitment cannot. *R.* v. *Barker*, 1 East, 186 ; *R.* v. *Cheshire*, 5 B. & Ad., 439 ; *Hutchinson* v. *Lowndes*, 4 B. & Ad., 118. Although a magistrate may draw up a conviction in a more formal manner than was done in the first instance, and may return the amended form as his conviction to the sessions or the Court of Queen's Bench upon a *certiorari*, or probably he may return an amended conviction to the sessions even after having returned an erroneous one. *Selwood* v. *Mount*, 9 C. & P., 75. Yet he cannot do this after the first conviction has been quashed, either upon appeal or by the Court of Queen's Bench, or after the defendant has been discharged by the Court of Queen's Bench by reason of a bad conviction being recited in the warrant of commitment. *Chaney* v. *Payne*, 10 L. J., M., C. 114.

After a first conviction has been returned to the sessions and filed, the Justices may if they think it defective make out and file a second. *Wilson* v. *Graybiel*, 5 Q. B. (Ont.), 227.

A conviction will be quashed if the summons states no place where the offence was committed, although the place appear on the face of the conviction. *Ex parte Leonard*, 6 L. C. R. 480.

51. In case an order be made, and no particular form of order is given by the Act or Law giving authority to make such order, and in all cases of orders made under the authority of any Acts or Laws hitherto passed, whether any particular form of order is therein given or not, the Justice or Justices by whom the order is made, may draw up the same in such one of the forms of orders (K 1, 2, 3) as may be applicable to the case, or to the like effect.

This section of the Act relates to orders generally and is not confined to orders for the payment of money and those of a like kind. See *Morant* v. *Taylor*, 1 Ex. D., 188.

It is not necessary that an order of Justices should be sealed with wax; an impression made in ink with a wooden block in the usual place of a seal is sufficient when the document purports to be given under the hands and seals of the Justices, and is in fact signed and delivered by them. *R.* v. *St. Paul*, 7 Q. B., 232.

The Court will make every reasonable intendment in favour of an order of Justices. *R.* v. *Aire*, 2 T. R., 666. But an order is void if it does not appear in the order itself that the Justice had jurisdiction to make it. *R.* v. *Hulcott*, 6 T. R., 587.

Justices may supersede their own order when improvidently made. *R.* v. *Norfolk*, 1 D. & R., 69. If two orders are made by mistake at the sitting of magistrates, it is competent to them to declare at the time which is the right one. *Wilkins* v. *Hemsworth*, 7 A. & E., 807.

No order can be made in the absence of the party whose interests are affected by it. *R.* v. *Totness*, 14 L. J., M. C., 148.

An order may be good in part and void for the residue. *R.* v. *Fox*, 6 T.R., 148. An order of Justices bad in part may be enforced as to the good part, provided that on the face of the order the two parts are clearly separable, and it is not necessary in such case to quash the bad part of the order before enforcing the residue. *R.* v. *Green*, 20 L. J., M. C., 168.

The signature is an essential part of the order, and the order cannot be considered as made until it is reduced into writing and signed by the Justice. *R.* v. *Flintshire*, 10 Jur., 475.

52. In all cases when by any Act or Law authority is given to commit a person to prison, or to levy any sum upon his goods or chattels by distress, for not obeying an order of a Justice or Justices, the Defendant shall be served with a copy of the Minute of the Order before any warrant of commitment or of distress is issued in that behalf, and the Order or Minute shall not form any part of the warrant of commitment or of distress.

This section of the statute applies to *orders* and not *convictions*, and on conviction of the defendant of an unlawful assault under the 32 & 33 Vic., chap. 20, s. 43, it is not necessary that he should be served with a copy of the minutes of the conviction before he is imprisoned, this section not applying to convictions. *R.* v. *O'Leary*, 3 Pugsley, 264.

53. In all cases of summary conviction, or of Orders made by a Justice or Justices of the Peace, the Justice or Justices making the same, may in his or their discretion, award and order in and by the conviction or order, that the defendant shall pay to the prosecutor or complainant such costs as to the said Justice or Justices seem reasonable in that behalf, and not inconsistent with the fees established by law to be taken on proceedings had by and before Justices of the Peace.

A conviction adjudging the defendant to pay a sum for costs, without saying to whom the costs are to be paid, is void under this section. The conviction should order the costs to be paid to the complainant. *R.* v. *Mabey,* 37 Q.B. (Ont.), 248.

54. In cases where the Justice or Justices instead of convicting or making an order, dismiss the information or complaint, he or they, in his or their discretion, may, in and by his or their order of dismissal, award and order that the prosecutor or complainant shall pay to the defendant such costs as to the said Justice or Justices seem reasonable and consistent with law.

Before this enactment the party could not be punished for non-payment of costs in the same way as for non-payment of penalty. *R.* v. *Burton,* 13 Q.B., 389.

A warrant of commitment for non-payment of penalty and costs, where the conviction did not mention costs, would be illegal. *Leary* v. *Patrick,* 15 Q.B., 266.

A warrant of commitment for non-payment of a penalty cannot be executed on a Sunday. *Egginton* v. *Lichfield,* 2 E. & B., 717.

55. The sums so allowed for costs shall in all cases be specified in the conviction or order, or order of dismissal, and the same shall be recoverable in the same manner and under the same warrants as any penalty adjudged to be paid by the conviction or order is to be recovered.

A warrant to commit for non-payment of the costs of an appeal to the sessions, unless such sum and all the costs of distress and commitment and conveying the party to gaol be sooner paid, should show the *amount* of the costs of distress, commitment, and conveyance to gaol. *Dickson* v. *Crabb,* 24 Q. B. (Ont.), 494; see also *Dawson* v. *Fraser,* 7 Q.B. (Ont.), 391; see also sections 62, 64, and 65; *Re Bright,* 1 U.C.,L.J.,N.S., 240; *Re Smith, ib.* 241; *R* v. *Ferguson,* 3 O. S., 220.

In a conviction for a penalty to be levied by distress, and in default of sufficient distress, imprisonment, it is no objection that the conviction specifies the amount of costs of conveying the party to gaol in default of sufficient distress; specifying the amount is only a notification to the defendant what he shall have to pay in the event of no distress and he is arrested. *Reid* v. *McWhinnie*, 27 Q.B. (Ont.), 289.

56. In cases where there is no such penalty to be recovered, such costs shall be recoverable by distress and sale of the goods and chattels of the party, and in default of distress, by imprisonment, with or without hard labour, for any time not exceeding one month, unless the costs be sooner paid.

57. Where a conviction adjudges a pecuniary penalty or compensation to be paid, or where an order requires the payment of a sum of money, and by the Act or Law authorizing such conviction or order, the penalty, compensation, or sum of money is to be levied upon the goods and chattels of the Defendant, by distress and sale thereof; and also in cases where, by the Act or Law in that behalf, no mode of raising or levying the penalty, compensation or sum of money, or of enforcing the payment of the same, is stated or provided, the Justice or any one of the Justices making such conviction or order, or any Justice of the Peace for the same Territorial Division, may issue his Warrant of Distress (N 1, 2) for the purpose of levying the same, which Warrant of Distress shall be in writing, under the hand and seal of the Justice making the same.

This section applies to a conviction under the 32 & 33 Vic., chap. 20, s. 37, for making a disturbance in a place of worship, and where the Justice is satisfied that the party has no goods, he has authority to commit to gaol, without first issuing a warrant to levy fine and costs. *Moffatt* v. *Barnard*, 24 Q. B. (Ont.), 498. See also s. 59.

Where a statute requires the issue of a warrant of distress before a warrant of commitment, the issue of the latter, without first issuing the former, will be invalid, and the prisoner committed will be discharged. *R.* v. *Blakely*, 6 P. R. (Ont.), 244.

58. If, after delivery of the warrant of distress to the Constable or Constables to whom the same has been directed to be executed, sufficient distress cannot be found within the limits of the jurisdiction of the Justice granting the warrant, then upon proof being made upon oath or affirmation of the handwriting of the Justice granting the warrant, before any Justice of any other Territorial Division, such Justice shall thereupon make an endorsement (N 3) on the warrant, signed with his hand, authorizing the execution of the warrant within the limits of his jurisdiction, by virtue of which warrant and endorsement the penalty or sum, and costs, or so much thereof as may not have been before levied or paid, shall be levied by the person bringing the warrant, or by the person or persons to whom the warrant was originally directed, or by any Constable or other Peace Officer of the last mentioned Territorial Division, by distress and sale of the goods and chattels of the Defendant therein.

59. Whenever it appears to any Justice of the Peace to whom application is made for any warrant of distress, that the issuing thereof would be ruinous to the Defendant and his family, or whenever it appears to the Justice, by the confession of the Defendant or otherwise, that he hath no goods and chattels whereon to levy such distress, then the Justice, if he deems it fit, instead of issuing a warrant of distress, may (O 1, 2) commit the Defendant to the Common Gaol, or other prison in the Territorial Division, there to be imprisoned with or without hard labour, for the time and in the manner the Defendant could by law be committed in case such warrant of distress had issued, and no goods or chattels had been found whereon to levy the penalty or sum and costs.

Under the Fishery Act of the Dominion, 31 Vic., chap. 60, a warrant of commitment may issue in the first instance, without previous issue of a warrant of distress—the statute not requiring that a distress warrant should first issue. *Arnott* v. *Bradly*, 23 C. P. (Ont.), 1.

So a conviction for an unlawful assault under the 32 & 33 Vic., chap. 20, s. 43, may adjudge the defendant to be imprisoned in the first instance. *R.* v. *O'Leary*, 3 Pugsley, 264.

Where by an Act power is conferred upon Justices to issue a distress warrant "if they shall think fit," they must not refuse to issue it, merely because they think the Act of Parliament does an injustice in giving such power in the particular case. *R.* v. *Boteler*, 4 B. & S., 959.

If the warrant is specially directed to the person who is to execute it, or generally to all other constables or peace officers of the division, any person coming within this description may lawfully execute it, but where it is directed to the Constable of A that is the Constable of such Division, it cannot lawfully be executed by any other person. *R.* v. *Sanders*, L. R., 1 C. C. R., 75.

60. In all cases where a Justice of the Peace issues any warrant of distress, he may suffer the Defendant to go at large, or verbally, or by a written warrant in that behalf, may order the Defendant to be kept and detained in safe custody, until return has been made to the warrant of distress, unless the Defendant gives sufficient security, by recognizance or otherwise, to the satisfaction of the Justice, for his appearance before him at the time and place appointed for the return of the warrant of distress, or before such other Justice or Justices for the same Territorial Division, as may then be there.

61. In all such cases where a Defendant gives security by recognizance, and does not afterwards appear at the time and place in the said recognizance mentioned, the Justice who hath the same, or any Justice or Justices who may then be there present, upon certifying (F) on the back of the recognizance, the non-appearance of the Defendant, may transmit the recognizance to the proper officer appointed by law to receive the same, to be proceeded upon in like manner as other recognizances, and such certificate shall be deemed sufficient *prima facie* evidence of the non-appearance of the Defendant.

62. If at the time and place appointed for the return of any warrant of distress, the Constable who has had execution of the same returns (N 4) that he could find no goods or chattels whereon he could levy the sum or sums therein mentioned, together with the costs of, or occasioned by, the levy of the same, the Justice of the Peace before whom the same is returned may issue his warrant of commitment (N 5) directed to the same or any other Constable, reciting the conviction or order shortly, the issuing of the warrant of distress, and the return thereto, and requiring the Constable to convey the Defendant to the Common Gaol, or other prison of the Territorial Division for which the Justice is then acting, and there to deliver him to the Keeper thereof, and requiring the Keeper to receive the Defendant into such gaol or prison, and there to imprison him, or to imprison him and keep him to hard labour, in the manner and for the time directed by the Act or Law on which the conviction or order mentioned in the warrant of distress is founded, unless the sum or sums adjudged to be paid, and all costs and charges of the distress, and also the costs and charges of the commitment and conveying of the Defendant to prison, if such Justice thinks fit so to order (the amount thereof being ascertained and stated in such commitment), be sooner paid; but if no term of imprisonment be specified in the Act or Law, the period for which the Justice shall order the Defendant to be so imprisoned shall not exceed three months.

63. Where a Justice or Justices of the Peace, upon any information or

complaint adjudges or adjudge the Defendant to be imprisoned, and the Defendant is then in prison undergoing imprisonment upon conviction for any other offence, the warrant of commitment for the subsequent offence shall be forthwith delivered to the gaoler or other officer to whom it is directed, and the Justice or Justices who issued the same, if he or they think fit, may award and order therein, that the imprisonment for the subsequent offence shall commence at the expiration of the imprisonment to which the Defendant was previously sentenced.

Where the defendant is summarily convicted at one time of several offences, the Justice has power under this section to award that the imprisonment under one or more of the convictions, shall commence at the expiration of the sentence previously pronounced. *R.* v. *Cutbush*, L. R., 2 Q. B., 379.

This section refers solely to those cases in which the defendant is already in the gaol of the territorial division, for which the magistrate acts. Should the defendant be in prison, however, in another division on another conviction, this section does not apply, and on his liberation therefrom, he should be arrested on the commitment indorsed, as provided by section 11 of this Act, and committed to the custody of the gaoler of the division within which the conviction or order was made. When a Justice convicts a defendon the same day, of two or more offences, the conviction and commitment in one of the cases should adjudge, and order the imprisonment to commence at the expiration of the imprisonment adjudged and ordered in the other case. *R.* v. *Wilkes*, 4 Burr., 2577 ; *R.* v. *Cutbush*, L. R., 2 Q. B., 379.

64. When any information or complaint is dismissed with costs, the sum awarded for costs in the Order for Dismissal may be levied by distress (Q 1) on the goods and chattels of the Prosecutor or Complainant in the manner aforesaid ; and in default of distress or payment, the Prosecutor or Complainant may be committed (Q 2) to the common gaol or other prison, in manner aforesaid, for any time not exceeding one month, unless such sum, and all costs and charges of the distress, and of the commitment and conveying of the Prosecutor or Complainant to prison (the amount thereof being ascertained and stated in the commitment), be sooner paid.

65. Unless it be otherwise provided in any special Act under which a conviction takes place, or an order is made by a Justice or Justices of the Peace, or unless some other Court of Appeal having jurisdiction in the premises, is

provided by an Act of the Legislature of the Province within which such conviction takes place or such order is made; any person who thinks himself aggrieved by any such conviction or order may appeal in the Province of Quebec to the Court of Queen's Bench, Crown side; in the Province of Ontario, to the Court of General or Quarter Sessions of the Peace; in the Province of Nova Scotia, to the County Court of the district where the cause of the information or complaint arose; in the Province of New Brunswick, to the County Court of the district where the cause of the information or complaint arose; in the Province of Manitoba, to the County Court of the County where the cause of the information or complaint arose; and in the Province of British Columbia, to the County or District Court at the sitting thereof, which shall be held nearest to the place where the cause of the information or complaint arose; in case some other Court of Appeal be provided in any Province as aforesaid, the appeal shall be to such Court; every right of appeal shall, unless it be otherwise provided in any special Act, be subject to the conditions following:

1. If the conviction or order be made more than twelve days before the sittings of the Court to which the appeal is given, such appeal shall be made to the then next sittings of such Court, but if the conviction or order be made within twelve days of the sittings of such Court, then to the second sittings next after such conviction or order.

2. The person aggrieved shall give to the prosecutor or complainant, or to the convicting Justice, or one of the convicting Justices for him a notice in writing of such appeal, within four days after such conviction or order.

3. The person aggrieved shall either remain in custody until the holding of the Court to which the appeal is given, or shall enter into a recognizance with two sufficient sureties, before a Justice or Justices of the Peace, conditioned personally to appear at the said Court and to try such appeal, and to abide the judgment of the Court thereupon, and to pay such costs as shall be by the Court awarded; or if the appeal be against any conviction or order whereby only a penalty or sum of money is adjudged to be paid, the person aggrieved may, although the order direct imprisonment in default of payment instead of remaining in custody as aforesaid, or giving such recognizance as aforesaid deposit with the Justice or Justices convicting or making the order such sum of money as such Justice or Justices deem sufficient to cover the sum so adjudged to be paid, together with the costs of the conviction or order and the costs of the appeal; and upon such recognizance being given or such deposit made, the Justice or Justices before whom such recognizance is entered into, or deposit made, shall liberate such person, if in custody, and the Court to which such appeal is made, shall thereupon hear and determine the matter of appeal, and make such order therein, with or without costs to either party, including costs of the Court below, as to the Court seems meet; and in

case of the dismissal of the appeal, or the affirmance of the conviction or order, shall order and adjudge the offender to be punished according to the conviction, or the defendant to pay the amount adjudged by the said order and to pay such costs as may be awarded, and shall if necessary, issue process for enforcing the judgment of the Court, and in any case where, after any such deposit has been made as aforesaid, the conviction or order is affirmed, the Court may order the sum thereby adjudged to be paid, together with the costs of the conviction or order, and the costs of the appeal, to be paid out of the money deposited, and the residue if any, to be repaid to the defendant; and in any case where, after any such deposit, the conviction or order is quashed, the Court shall order the money to be repaid to the defendant, and the said Court shall have power, if necessary, from time to time by order endorsed on the conviction or order to adjourn the hearing of the appeal from one sittings to another or others of the said Court; in every case where any conviction or order is quashed on appeal as aforesaid, the Clerk of the Peace or other proper officer shall forthwith endorse on the conviction or order a memorandum that the same has been quashed; and whenever any copy or certificate of such conviction or order is made, a copy of such memorandum shall be added thereto, and shall when certified under the hand of the Clerk of the Peace, or of the proper officer having the custody of the same, be sufficient evidence in all Courts, and for all purposes that the conviction or order has been quashed.

See 33 Vic., chap. 27, s. 1; 40 Vic., chap. 27, ss. 1 & 2.

In Prince Edward Island the appeal lies to the Supreme Court at the sitting thereof held next after ths expiration of twelve days from the time when such conviction was had or such order made the proceedings prior to the appeal being governed by the Act 32 & 33Vic., chap. 31, s 65 as amended by the 33 Vic., chap. 27. This provision is contained in the 40 Vic., chap. 4, s. 6 which takes effect on the 1st of April, 1878.

The 40 Vic., chap. 27, s. 3 also provides that whenever in the Act any duty in relation to an appeal is imposed on any officer by the term "clerk of the peace," the said term shall include the proper officer of the court having jurisdiction in appeal under the said Act and the Acts amending the same, including this Act.

The amendments introduced by the 33 Vic., chap. 27 were extended to Prince Edward Island by the 40 Vic., chap 4. Although the Act applies, as we have already seen, to the District of Keewatin and to the Northwest Territories, yet so much of the Act or of any Act amending it as gives any appeal from any conviction or order adjudged or made under it is not in force in the said District or Territories, (see 39 Vic., chap. 21, sched. 31 ; 38 Vic., chap. 49 sched. B.

This section applies to all convictions and orders founded upon statutes which do not give an appeal either to the prosecutor or to the defendant. It does not apply to any conviction or order founded upon a statute by which the right of appeal from such conviction or order is denied. It does not apply to any conviction or order founded upon a statute by which special provisions differing from those in the present section contained have been or may be made regulating appeals from convictions or orders made under it. Kerr's Acts, 223.

Under the former Acts the right of appeal was given only when the sum adjudged to be paid exceeded ten dollars, or the imprisonment exceeded one month, or the proceedings were before one Justice only. These restrictions are now removed, but if a Court of Appeal having jurisdiction in the premises is provided by an Act of the Legislature of the Province within which the conviction takes place, the appeal must be to such court and not the court named in the present Act. An appeal lies to the Supreme Court of Nova Scotia from a conviction for penalties under "The Fisheries Act," 31 Vic., chap. 60, section 23 providing that the laws relating to summary convictions and orders shall apply to cases under said Act. *R.* v. *Todd*, 1 Russell & Chesley Reps., N. S., 62.

It is not essential that the notice of appeal under the 33 Vic., chap. 27, should be signed by the party appealing, nor need the notice set forth the grounds of appeal. Under the 96th section of this Act (32 & 33 Vic., chap. 31,) the several forms in the schedule to the Act contained or forms to the like effect are deemed good, valid and sufficient in law. A notice therefore following the form given in the 33 Vic., chap. 27, but not signed by the appellants is sufficient. *R.* v. *Nichol* 40 Q. B., (Ont.), 46.

The notice may be signed by the attorney's clerk for the appellant. *R.* v. *Kent*, L. R. 8, Q. B., 305. Where there are several appellants they may either join in one notice or each of them may give a separate notice. *R.* v. *Oxford*, 4 Q. B., 177.

No practice of the sessions can do away with the notice of

appeal. *R.* v. *Lincolnshire*, 3 B. & C., 548; *R.* v. *West*, 4 B. & Ad., 685. Nor can the sessions diminish the time allowed for the notice of appeal, or add a new condition. *R.* v. *Staffordshire*, 4 A. & E., 842. It is not necessary that this notice should be personally served, if it be left for the party at his dwelling house it will be sufficient. *R.* v. *York*, 7 Q. B., 154. But it is not sufficient service to send the notice by post. *R.* v. *Leominster*, 2 B & S., 391.

Service of notice of appeal in Court, upon the clerk to Justices, in their presence, is good service. *R.* v. *Eaves*, L. R. 5 Ex., 75.

If the notice is given in time, the recognizance may be entered into at any time before the case is stated and delivered. *Stanhope* v. *Thorsby*, L. R., 1, C. P., 423.

The time of entering into recognizances is when the appellant appears before the Justice and verbally acknowledges them, though they are not drawn up until afterwards. *R.* v. *St. Albans*, 8 A. & E., 932.

When recognizances are tendered the Justice is bound to receive them, and cannot refuse them because he thinks the notice bad. *R.* v. *Carter*, 24 L. J., M. C., 72.

One member of a corporation cannot enter into a recognizance to bind the rest. *R.* v. *Manchester*, 7 E. & B., 453.

When, in the recognizance, the appellant, instead of being bound to appear and try the appeal, as required by the Act, was bound to appear at the sessions to answer any charge that might be made against him, the appeal was dismissed and the recognizance was not allowed to be taken in Court, for although it need not be entered into within four days, it must be entered into and filed before the sittings of the Court of Quarter Sessions, to which the appeal is made. *Kent* v. *Olds*, 7 U. C., L. J., 21.

It was held under the former statutes that the form of recognizance to try an appeal, given in the schedule to the Con. Stats. Can. chap. 103, p. 1,130 was sufficient, though the condition differed in form from that provided for by chap. 99, section 117. *Re Wilson*, 23 Q. B. (Ont.), 301.

The notice of appeal, given by the statute, was also held sufficiently particular to allow all objections being raised which were apparent on the face of the conviction, or order. *Helps and Eno*, 9 U. C., L. J., 302. It is not now necessary to state any grounds of appeal in the notice (see 33 Vic., chap. 27, s. 4), so that it is apprehended the appellant is not limited as to his objections.

If the conviction is made within twelve days of the sittings of the Court, and a notice of appeal is given to the sittings *then next ensuing*, instead of the second sittings next after such conviction, the notice will be void, and will not prevent a proper notice being afterwards given (if given within four days after the conviction) for the second sittings thereafter. *R.* v. *Caswell*, 33 Q. B. (Ont.), 303.

The words, within four days after conviction, exclude the day of conviction. *Scott* v. *Dickson*, 1 P. R. (Ont.), 366. If the last of the four days limited for notice fall on a Sunday, notice given on the Monday following is too late. It should be given on the Saturday preceding. *R.* v. *Middlesex*, 2 Dowl., N. S., 719; *Peacock* v. *R.*, 4 C. B., N. S., 264.

It appears to be the established practice for the sessions to hear appeals on the first day, but there is no law compelling them to do so. *Re Meyers*, 23 Q. B. (Ont.), 614.

The Court has no power to award costs on discharging an appeal, for want of proper notice of appeal, for the words, "shall hear and determine the matter of appeal," mean deciding it upon the merits. *Re Madden*, 31 Q. B. (Ont.), 333.

If the appeal is within a time after order made, the making of the order, or verbal decision, and not the service or formal drawing up of it is meant. *R.* v. *Derbyshire*, 7 Q. B., 193; *Ex parte Johnson*, 3 B. & S., 947. Sunday is usually included in the number of days. *Ex parte Simkin*, 2 E. & E., 392.

Where the right to appeal is given, under conditions such as entering into recognizance and giving notice, &c., as in the statute, all these conditions must be strictly complied with. *R.* v. *Lincolnshire*, 3 B. & C., 548. The person appealing must, not only give notice within the proper time, but he must also either remain in custody or enter into the proper recognizance. *Kent* v. *Olds*, 7 U. C., L. J., 21; Arch., J. P., 37. A failure to comply with these conditions will not be waived by the respondent asking for a postponement after the appellant has proved his notice of appeal on the first day of the Court. *Re Meyers*, 23 Q. B. (Ont.), 611.

If, by the death of the respondent, the giving of notice has become impossible, the appeal may be heard without it. *R.* v. *Lancashire*, 15 Q. B., 88.

The Court of Quarter Sessions has power to adjourn the hearing of a part heard appeal to a subsequent session. *R.* v. *Guardian C. Union*, 7 U. C., L. J. 331. The statute, as we have seen, also expressly confers the power of adjournment. An adjournment of the sessions is a continuance of the same sessions or sittings. *Rawnsley* v. *Hutchinson*, L. R. 6 Q. B., 305. An appeal dismissed for want of prosecution may, at the instance of the appellant and satisfactoilry accounting for his non-appearance, be reinstated. *Re Smith*, 10 U. C., L. J., 20.

There had been a conviction before two magistrates for a breach of the licence law. The counsel for the defendant then demanded an appeal—one of the magistrates asked him to prepare the bond and he himself would see the other necessary papers filed. The defendant's counsel thereupon had the bond prepared, sent it to the defendant and told her that the magistrates would instruct her what else was necessary. The defendant thereupon got the bond executed and gave it to the magistrate, who said "it was all right." There was no affidavit filed on the appeal as required by Rev. Stat. N. S., chap. 22, s. 28, on application to set aside the appeal, it was held that the appeal must be allowed, the appellant having been misled by the conduct of the magistrate. *McKay* v. *McKay*, Thomson, 75.

An appeal under the Con. Stat. U. C., chap. 114, was held not to be waived by the appellant, paying the fine and costs. *Re Justices York*, 13 C. P. (Ont.) 159.

There can be no doubt that, where the notice of appeal and the recognizances are duly given, execution is suspended for the Justice in the section now under consideration is directed to liberate the appellant if in custody in such case, and the same effect is given to the making of the deposit after notice of appeal, but there is no provision in the section to meet the circumstances when the would-be appellant elects to remain in custody, in lieu of giving a recognizance or making a deposit. *Kerr's Acts*, 226-7.

As to the evidence no witness is to be examined who was not examined before the Justice on the hearing of the case. See s. 66.

The appeal is also to be heard on its merits, and formal objections not taken before the Justice cannot be raised. See sections 67 and 68.

66. When an appeal has been lodged in due form, and in compliance with the requirements of this Act, against any summary conviction or decision, the Court of General or Quarter Sessions of the Peace or Court appealed to, may at the request of either appellant or respondent, empannel a Jury to try the facts of the case, and shall administer to such Jury the following oath:

"You shall well and truly try the facts in dispute in the matter of A. B. (*the informant*), against C. D. (*the defendant*), and a true verdict give according to the evidence: So help you God."

And the Court, on the finding of the Jury, shall give such judgment as the law requires; and if a Jury be not so demanded, the Court shall try and be the absolute judges as well of the facts as of the law in respect to such conviction or decision; but no witness shall in either case be examined who was not examined before the Justice or Justices at the hearing of the case.

The 36 Vic., chap. 58, s. 2, provides, and for the avoidance of doubt it is hereby declared and enacted, that the Court of General or Quarter Sessions of the Peace appealed to may grant or refuse, in its discretion, the request of the appellant or respondent to have a jury empanelled to try the facts of the case under this section.

Under the former statutes, the appellant could not of right demand that a jury be empanelled to try the appeal. It was discretionary with the court to try the appeal or to grant a Jury. *Gilchen* v. *Eaton*, 13 L. C. R. 471; 10 U. C., L. J., 81. A trial by jury was warranted by the 13 & 14 Vic., chap. 54. *Hespler and Shaw*, 16 Q. B. (Ont.), 104.

Under the Act as at present framed, the court may grant a jury at the request of either the appellant or respondent, and if a jury is not demanded, the court must try it.

Where neither party demands a jury, the court has authority to try the appeal without one, and a party who insists upon the trial without a jury, cannot afterwards have a trial by jury. *R. v. Bradshaw*, 38 Q. B. (Ont.), 564.

67. No judgment shall be given in favour of the appellant if the appeal is based on an objection to any information, complaint, or summons, or to any warrant to apprehend a defendant, issued upon any such information, complaint, or summons, for any alleged defect therein in substance or in form, or for any variance between such information, complaint, summons or warrant, and the evidence adduced in support thereof at the hearing of such information or complaint,—unless it shall be proved before the Court hearing the appeal that such objection was made before the Justice or Justices of the Peace before whom the case was tried, and by whom such conviction, judgment, or decision was given,—nor unless it is proved that notwithstanding it was shown to such Justice or Justices of the Peace that by such variance the person summoned and appearing or apprehended, had been deceived or misled, such Justice or Justices refused to adjourn the hearing of the case to some further day, as provided by this Act.

68. In all cases of appeal from any summary conviction or order had or made before any Justice or Justices of the Peace, the Court to which such appeal is made shall hear and determine the charge or complaint on which such conviction or order has been had or made upon the merits, notwithstanding any defect of form or otherwise in such conviction or order; and if the person charged or complained against is found guilty, the conviction or order shall be affirmed, and the court shall amend the same if necessary, and any conviction or order so affirmed, or affirmed and amended shall be enforced in the same manner as convictions or orders affirmed in appeal.

69. And for the more effectual prevention of frivolous appeals, the Court of General or Quarter Sessions of the Peace, or other Court or Judge to whom an appeal is made, upon proof of notice of the appeal to such Court having been given to the person entitled to receive the same, though such appeal was not afterwards prosecuted or entered, may, if such appeal has not been abandoned according to law, at the same Court for which such notice was given, order to the party or parties receiving the same, such costs and charges as by the said Court or Judge may be thought reasonable and just, to be paid by the party or parties giving such notice, such costs to be recoverable in the manner provided by this Act for the recovery of costs upon an appeal against an order or conviction.

An indictment will not lie to enforce an order of sessions directing payment of the costs of an appeal. *R.* v. *Orr*, 12 Q.B. (Ont.), 57.

Where the notice of appeal has been given and might have been acted on, the court to which the notice referred can give costs (*R.* v. *Leeds*, 3 E. & E., 561, *R.* v. *Liverpool*, 15 Q. B., 1070); and a notice for the wrong sessions cannot be treated as a notice for the right sessions. *R.* v. *Salop*, 4 E. & B., 257.

The court must exercise its discretion in each case as to costs, and cannot lay down a general rule applicable to all cases. *R.* v. *Merioneth*, 6 Q. B., 163.

The order for costs should direct payment to the Clerk of the Peace. *Gay* v. *Mathews*, 4 B. & S., 425; see sec. 74 of the Act.

The taxation of costs is a judicial act and must either be done by the court or they must adopt the act of the Clerk of the Peace, and insert the amount of costs in the order (*Selwood* v. *Mount*, 1 Q. B., 726) during the sitting of the court. *Freeman* v. *Reid*, 9 C. B., N. S., 301. If the sessions is adjourned to a future day the costs may be finally settled at the adjourned sessions. *R.* v. *Hants*, 33 L. J., M. C., 184. If there has been no adjournment, and nothing said about costs, they cannot be granted at the next subsequent sessions. *R.* v. *Staffordshire*, 7 E. & B., 935. If, however, the parties consent to have the costs taxed out of court this may be done, and the party enter the judgment *nunc pro tunc*. *Freeman* v. *Reid*, *supra*. Or the objection may be waived. *Ex parte Watkins*, 26 J. P., 71.

70. In case an appeal against any conviction or order be decided in favour of the Respondents, the Justice or Justices who made the conviction or order, or any other Justice of the Peace for the same Territorial Division, may issue the warrant of distress, or commitment for execution of the same, as if no appeal had been brought.

71. No conviction or order, affirmed or affirmed and amended, in appeal shall be quashed for want of form, or be removed by *certiorari* into any of Her Majesty's Superior Courts of Record; and no warrant or commitment shall be held void by reason of any defect therein, provided it be therein alleged that the party has been convicted and there be a good and valid conviction to sustain the same. (33 Vic., chap. 27, s. 2.)

In England it has been held that an enactment similar to this precluded the issuing of a *certiorari* for the purpose of bringing up a case stated by Justices in Quarter Sessions for the opinion of the court. *R.* v. *Chantrell*, L. R., 10 Q. B., 587.

This section does not prevent the issue of a *certiorari* when the notice of appeal to the sessions is void, and the appeal is dismissed. For instance, if the notice is for the next sittings of the court, where the conviction is *within* twelve days of such sittings. In such case it cannot be said that there is an appeal, or that the conviction is "affirmed or affirmed and amended in appeal" under the statute. *R.* v. *Caswell*, 33 Q. B. (Ont.), 303.

This section, it would seem, does not prevent the issue of the writ at the suit of the prosecutor, *R.* v. *Allen*, 15 East, 333; nor where there is a plain excess of jurisdiction by the Justice. *Hespeler and Shaw*, 16 Q. B. (Ont.), 104. So a *certiorari* would lie where there is an absence of jurisdiction in the convicting Justice, or a conviction on its face defective in substance. *Re Watts*, 5 P. R. (Ont.), 267; see also *Re Holland*, 37 Q. B. (Ont.), 214 (and cases cited), where an opinion was expressed that the (Ont.) 36 Vic., chap. 43, s. 35, did not take away the right to a *certiorari* when the conviction was entirely without jurisdiction.

But subject to these limitations, the section not only applies to cases where an adjudication has taken place, but even where the appeal has gone off on a preliminary objection to the right of entering it, and consequently a *certiorari* will not be granted by the Superior Court, even when the appeal to the sessions has not been decided on the merits. *R.* v. *Firmin*, 6 P. R. (Ont.), 67.

72. Every Justice of the Peace before whom any person shall be summarily convicted of any offence by virtue of this Act, shall transmit the conviction to the Court of General or Quarter Sessions or to the Court discharging the functions of the Court of General or Quarter Sessions as aforesaid, or to any other Court or Judge to which the right of appeal is given by section sixty-five of this Act, as the case may be, in and for the District, County or place wherein the offence has been committed, before the time when an appeal from such conviction could be heard, there to be kept by the proper officer among the records of the Court; and if such conviction has been appealed against, and a deposit of money made, shall return the deposit into the said Court and upon any indictment or information against any person for a subsequent offence, a copy of such conviction, certified by the proper officer of the Court, or proved to be a true copy, shall be sufficient evidence to prove a conviction for the former offence, and the conviction shall be presumed to have been unappealed against, until the contrary be shown.

Although this section does not mention orders, but appears to relate to convictions only, it is conceived the Justice should deal with orders in the same manner as convictions. Kerr's Acts, 228.

Where a party is sought to be convicted as for a second offence, he must be charged in the information with the commission of a second offence, and it must also be proved that at the time of the information he had been previously convicted. *R.* v. *Justices, &c.*, 2 Pugsley, 485.

73. In all cases where it appears by the conviction, that the defendant has appeared and pleaded, and the merits have been tried, and that the defendant has not appealed against the conviction where an appeal is allowed, or if appealed against, the conviction has been affirmed, such conviction shall not afterwards be set aside or vacated in consequence of any defect of form whatever, but the construction shall be such a fair and liberal construction as will be agreeable to the justice of the case.

Where the conviction shews that the defendant has appeared and pleaded, the construction must be such a fair and liberal construction as will be agreeable to the justice of the case. *R.* v. *Caswell*, 33 Q. B. (Ont.), 303, 310.

74. If upon any Appeal the Court trying the Appeal orders either party to pay costs, the order shall direct the costs to be paid to the Clerk of the Peace or other proper officer of the Court, to be by him paid over to the party entitled to the same, and shall state within what time the costs shall be paid.

Where the order of sessions, by mistake, ordered the costs to be paid to the party instead of to the clerk of the peace, it was holden that it did not affect the validity of the order, but was merely an erroneous procedure, and upon application for a *certiorari* to remove it, in order to its being quashed, on the ground that the Justices had no jurisdiction to make it (the *certiorari* being taken away), the court refused it. *R.* v. *Binney*, 22 L. J., M. C., 127.

75. If the same be not paid within the time so limited, and the party ordered to pay the same has not been bound by any recognizance conditioned to

pay such costs, the Clerk of the Peace or his Deputy, on application of the party entitled to the costs, or of any person on his behalf, and on payment of any fee to which he may be entitled, shall grant to the party so applying, a Certificate [R] that the costs have not been paid, and upon production of the Certificate to any Justice or Justices of the Peace for the same Territorial Division, he or they may enforce the payment of the costs by Warrant of Distress [S 1] in manner aforesaid, and in default of distress he or they may commit [S 2] the party against whom the Warrant has issued in manner hereinbefore mentioned, for any time not exceeding two months, unless the amount of the costs and all costs and charges of the distress and also the costs of the commitment and conveying of the party to prison, if the Justice or Justices think fit so to order (the amount thereof being ascertained and stated in the commitment), be sooner paid.

The issuing of a warrant of commitment under this section is discretionary, not compulsory, upon a Justice of the Peace, and the court will therefore, on this ground, as well as upon the ground that the party sought to be committed has not been made a party to the application, refuse a *mandamus* against the Justice to compel the issue of the warrant. The proper course, where Justices refuse to act according to the duties of their office, is to proceed under the Rev. Stat. (Ont.), chap. 73, s. 6. *Re Delaney* v. *Mac Nab*, 21 C. P. (Ont.), 563.

A Justice of the Peace who convicts, and issues a warrant regularly by virtue of a statute then in force, cannot be held liable by reason of the *execution* of the Warrant after the Act is disallowed by Her Majesty and has ceased to be in force. *Clapp* v. *Lawrason*, 6, O. S. 319. The statute law would seem to protect a Justice in a case of this kind. See 31 Vic., chap. 1, s. 7, thirty-fifthly, sixthly and seventhly.

76. Every Justice of the Peace shall make a return in writing under his hand of all convictions made by him to the next ensuing General or Quarter Sessions of the Peace, or to the next term or sitting of any Court having jurisdiction in appeal as hereinbefore provided, at which, in either case, the appeal can be heard, for the District or County or place in which such conviction takes place, and of the receipt and application by him of the moneys received from the Defendants (and in case of any convictions before two or more Justices, such Justices being present and joining therein, shall make a joint Return thereof,) in the following form :—

RETURN of Convictions made by me (*or* us, *as the case may be*) in the month of 18 .

Name of the Prosecutor.	Name of the Defendant.	Nature of the charge.	Date of Conviction.	Name of Convicting Justice.	Amount of Penalty, fine or damage.	Time when paid or to be paid to said Justice.	To whom paid over by said Justice.	If not paid, why not, and general observations, if any

A. B., Convicting Justice,

or

A. B. and C. D., Convicting Justices (*as the case may be*).

The returns required by this section of the Act shall be made by every Justice of the Peace, quarterly, on or before the second Tuesday in each of the months of March, June, September and December, in each year, to the Clerk of the Peace or other proper officer for receiving the same, under the said Act, notwithstanding the General or Quarter Sessions of the Peace of the county, in which such conviction was had, may not be held in the months or at the times aforesaid, and every such return shall include all convictions and other matters mentioned in the said section, seventy-six, and not included in some previous return, and shall, by the Clerk of the Peace or other proper officer receiving it, be fixed up and published, and a copy thereof shall be transmitted to the

Minister of Finance in the manner required by the eightieth and eighty-first sections of the said Act, and the provisions of the seventy-eighth section of the said Act, and the penalties thereby imposed, and all the other provisions of the said Act shall hereafter apply to the returns hereby required, and to any offence or neglect committed with respect to the making thereof, as if the periods hereby appointed for making the said returns had been mentioned in the said Act instead of the periods thereby appointed for the same. 33 Vic., chap. 27, s. 3.

In Prince Edward Island, the returns are to be made to the clerk of the court of assize for the county, at and up to the twelfth day next before the sitting of the said court next after such convictions respectively, and shall be dealt with by the said clerk of assize in the manner provided by the eightieth and eighty-first sections of this Act. See 40 Vic., chap. 4, s. 7.

The Clerk of the Peace is the clerk of all magistrates, and it is no objection that a conviction is not in the magistrate's office, but in that of the Clerk of the Peace. *R.* v. *Yeomans*, 6 P. R. (Ont.), 66.

The fact of the conviction being appealed from, does not relieve the Justices from the penalty on non-return of the conviction, under the Rev. Stat. (Ont.), chap. 76. *Murphy q. t.* v. *Harvey*, 9 C. P. (Ont.), 528; see also *Kelly q. t.* v. *Cowan*, 18 Q. B. (Ont.), 104.

And it seems that notice of appeal against the conviction or subsequent notice of abandonment thereof, given by the defendant, does not affect the duty of the Justice in making the return. *McLennan q. t.* v. *McIntyre*, 12 C. P. (Ont.), 546.

So the question as to the conviction being right or wrong is immaterial, and where a magistrate has actually convicted and imposed a fine, it is no defence that he had no jurisdiction to convict. *Bagley q. t.* v. *Curtis*, 15 C. P. (Ont.), 366; *O'Reilly q. t.* v. *Allan*, 11 Q. B. (Ont.), 411.

The illegality of a conviction is no excuse for not returning it, but if on that account the fine has not been levied, a return should be made explaining the circumstances (*O'Reilly q. t.* v. *Allan*, 11 Q. B. (Ont.), 411); see, however, *Spillane* v. *Wilton*, 4 C. P. (Ont.),

236, 242. Under the former statute, a Justice of the Peace was liable to a separate penalty of £20, for each conviction of which a return was not properly made to the sessions, and an action for the penalty would lie on proof of the conviction and fine imposed although no record thereof had been made by the Justice. *Donogh q. t.* v. *Longworth*, 8 C. P. (Ont.), 437.

So as the law now stands, the neglect of the Justice to return the convictions made by him as prescribed, renders him liable under this statute to a separate penalty for *each* conviction not returned, and not merely to one penalty for not making a general return of such convictions. *Darragh q. t.* v. *Paterson*, 25 C. P. (Ont.), 529.

Justices of the Peace must therefore now return all convictions made by them to the Clerk of the Peace, on or before the second Tuesday in March, June, September and December respectively following the date of the conviction. *Corsant q. t.* v. *Taylor*, 23 C P. (Ont.), 607; 33 Vic., chap, 27, s. 3; see also *Ollard q. t.* v. *Owens* 29 Q. B. (Ont.), 515.

The Rev. Stats. (Ont.), chap. 76, are now in force as to all convictions over which Ontario has jurisdiction. Under the former statute in Ontario, the penalty attached on *each* Justice making default in the return. *Metcalf q. t.* v. *Reeve*, 9 Q. B. (Ont.), 263.

The Dominion Legislature in the 32 & 33 Vic., chap. 31, has made a single penalty of $80, the maximum fine for any default, whether it be committed by a single Justice or by two or more, and if two or more Justices act and are in default, the penalty on all is single, only $80, and it seems that all the Justices might be sued together, or any one of them, at the election of the plaintiff *Drake q. t.* v. *Preston*, 34 Q. B. (Ont.), 257.

It is conceived that the Rev. Stat. (Ont.), chap. 76, s. 3, assimilates the law in Ontario, to that prevailing under the Dominion Act, and that there is not now in Ontario a separate penalty on *each* of several Justices joining in a conviction.

An action brought against a Justice for non-return by fraud and collusion, in order to prevent the Justice being liable to pay the penalty to others, will not bar a subsequent action brought in good faith for the penalty. *Kelly q.t.* v. *Cowan*, 18 Q.B. (Ont.), 104.

A Justice committed and fined the plaintiff for carrying away some cordwood, after notice of appeal the prosecutor finding that the conviction was improper went to the Justice who drew for him a notice of discontinuance which was served on the person acting as Attorney for the plaintiff before the meeting of the next Quarter Sessions. The Justice sent a general return to that court including this and another conviction, but ran his pen through the entry of this conviction, leaving the writing however quite legible, and wrote at the end of it "this case withdrawn by the plaintiff." This was held a sufficient return within the 4 & 5 Vic., chap. 12; *Bull q.t.* v. *Fraser*, 18 Q. B. (Ont.), 100.

It has been held that if one Justice of several who convict, makes the return and signs the name of the other convicting Justices to it by their direction or express authority it is sufficient. *McLellan q.t.* v. *Brown*, 12 C.P. (Ont.), 542.

It seems that there must be a return of the conviction in the form given by the Statute, and transmitting the conviction itself is not the same thing as making a return of it though one return may include several convictions. The conviction and the return of it are separate instruments and both should be returned by the Justice. See *McLennan q.t.* v. *McIntyre*, 12 C.P. (Ont.), 546; *Donogh q.t.* v. *Longworth*. 8 C.P. (Ont.), 437.

In an action for the penalty the plaintiff may sue for himself only, and need not sue *qui tam*. *Drake q.t.* v. *Preston*, 34 Q. B. (Ont.), 257; but the declaration must allege the defendant's neglect to have been contrary to the statutes, not merely the statute, there being two statutes upon the subject, each requiring a different return. *Ib.*

In an action against a Justice of the Peace for a penalty in not returning a conviction, it is no objection to the declaration that the plaintiff sues for the Receiver-General, and not for Her Majesty the Queen; inasmuch as suing for a penalty for the Receiver-General for the public uses of the Province, is in fact suing for the Queen. *Bagley q.t.* v. *Curtis*, 15 C.P. (Ont.), 366.

A conviction made by an alderman in a city must be returned to the next ensuing general sessions of the peace for the county, and not to the Recorder's Court for such city. *Keenahan q.t.* v.

Egleson, 22 Q.B. (Ont.), 626; see *Metcalfe q.t.* v. *Reeve*, 9 Q.B. (Ont.), 263.

An order for the payment of money under the Master and Servants Act, Con. Stat. U.C., chap. 75, is not a conviction which it is necessary to return to the sessions. *Ranney q.t.* v. *Jones*, 21 Q.B. (Ont.), 370.

The county courts have now jurisdiction to try an action for a penalty against a Justice of the Peace where the penalty claimed does not exceed $80. *Brush q.t.* v. *Taggart*, 16 C. P. (Ont.), 415. This case does not over-rule *O'Reilly q.t.* v. *Allan*, 11 Q.B. (Ont.), 526, there having been changes in the jurisdiction of the county courts since it was decided. See also *Medcalfe* v. *Widdefield*, 12 C.P. (Ont.), 411.

A plaintiff suing a Justice of the Peace for the penalty of $80 under the Rev. Stat. (Ont.), chap. 76, s. 3, for not returning a conviction, is entitled to full costs without a certificate. *Stinson q.t.* v. *Guess*, 1 U.C.,L.J., N.S., 19, following *OReilly q.t.* v. *Allan*, 11 Q.B. (Ont.), 526.

A penal action for not returning a conviction is founded on tort and for that reason cannot be brought in a division court. *Corsant q.t.* v. *Taylor*, 10 C.L.J., N.S., 320.

It would seem that the right to legislate on returns of convictions and fines for criminal offences, belongs to the Dominion and not the Provincial legislature. *Clemens q.t.* v. *Bemer*, 7 C.L.J., N.S., 126.

77. And any Justice or Justices to whom any such moneys may be afterwards paid, shall make a return of the receipts and application thereof, to the next General or Quarter Sessions of the Peace, or other Court as aforesaid, which return shall be filed by the Clerk of the Peace, with the records of his office.

78. In case the Justice or Justices, before whom any such conviction takes place or who receives any such moneys, neglect or refuse to make such return thereof, or in case any such Justice or Justices wilfully make a false, partial or incorrect return, or wilfully receive a larger amount of fees than by law they are authorized to receive, such Justice or Justices, so neglecting, or refusing, or wilfully making such false, partial or incorrect return, or wilfully receiving a larger amount of fees as aforesaid, shall forfeit and pay the sum of eighty dollars, together with full costs of suit, to be recovered by any per-

son suing for the same by action of debt or information in any Court of Record in the Province in which such return ought to have been or is made, one moiety whereof shall be paid to the party suing, and the other moiety into the hands of Her Majesty's Receiver General to and for the public uses of the Dominion.

79. All prosecutions for penalties arising under the provisions of the next preceding section shall be commenced within six months next after the cause of action accrues, and the same shall be tried in the District, County or place wherein such penalties have been incurred, and if a verdict or judgment passes for the defendant, or the plaintiff becomes non-suit, or discontinues the action after issue joined, or if upon demurrer, or otherwise, judgment be given against the plaintiff, the defendant shall recover his full costs of suit, as between Attorney and Client, and shall have the like remedy for the same, as any defendant hath by law in other cases.

80. The Clerk of the Peace of the District or County in which any such returns are made, or the proper officer, other than the Clerk of the Peace to whom such returns are made, shall, within seven days after the adjournment of the next ensuing General or Quarter Sessions, or of the term or sitting of such other court as aforesaid, cause the said returns to be published in one public newspaper in the District or County, or if there be no such newspaper, then in a newspaper of an adjoining District or County, and shall also fix up in the Court House of the District or County, and also in a conspicuous place in the office of such Clerk of the Peace, for public inspection, a schedule of the returns so made by such Justices ; and the same shall continue to be so fixed up and exhibited, until the end of the next ensuing General or Quarter Sessions of the Peace, or of the term or sitting of such other Court as aforesaid, and for every schedule so made and exhibited by the said Clerk of the Peace, he shall be allowed the expense of publication, and such fee as may be fixed by competent authority.

81. The Clerk of the Peace or other officer as last aforesaid of each District or County, within twenty days after the end of each General or Quarter Sessions of the Peace, or the sitting of such Court as aforesaid, shall transmit to the Minister of Finance a true copy of all such returns made within his District or County.

Under the 39 Vic., chap. 13, s. 2, the officers named must, before the end of October in each year, transmit to the Minister of Agriculture, or other minister named in the Act, true copies of all such returns for the year ending the thirtieth day of September preceding, instead of transmitting the same at the times required by this section of the Act.

82. Nothing in the six next preceding sections shall have the effect of preventing any person aggrieved, from prosecuting by indictment, a Justice of the Peace, for any offence, the commission of which would subject him to indictment at the time of the coming into force of this Act.

83. In all cases where a Warrant of Distress has issued against any person, and such person pays or tenders to the Constable having the execution of the same, the sum or sums in the warrant mentioned, together with the amount of the expenses of the distress up to the time of payment or tender, the Constable shall cease to execute the same.

84. In all cases in which any person is imprisoned for non-payment of any penalty or other sum, he may pay or cause to be paid to the keeper of the prison in which he is imprisoned, the sum in the Warrant of Commitment mentioned, together with the amount of the costs, charges and expenses (if any) therein also mentioned, and the keeper shall receive the same, and shall thereupon discharge the person, if he be in his custody for no other matter.

85. In all cases of summary proceedings before a Justice or Justices of the Peace out of Sessions, upon any information or complaint, one Justice may receive the information or complaint, and grant a summons or warrant thereon, and issue his summons or warrant to compel the attendance of any witnesses for either party, and do all other acts and matters necessary, preliminary to the hearing, even in cases where by the statute in that behalf the information or complaint must be heard and determined by two or more Justices.

An information to be *tried* before two Justices of the Peace is good though only signed by one. *Falconbridge q. t.* v. *Tourangeau*, Rob. Dig., 260.

Under this statute, one Justice may receive the complaint and grant the summons, even where the information and complaint must be heard and determined by two or more Justices. *R.* v. *Simmons*, 1 Pugsley, 158.

In the event of the case being heard before two Justices, and of their being divided in opinion, they cannot call in a third Justice to submit the notes of the evidence to him, and thereupon with him determine the case, he being a party to the conviction or order as one of the Justices having heard the case. Kerr's Acts, 173.

The special authority given to Justices must be exactly pursued according to the letter of the Act by which it is created, or their acts will not be good.

When two Justices of the Peace are appointed by statute to adjudicate upon complaints, more or less than two does not meet the requirement. *R.* v. *Lougee*, 10 C. L. J., N. S., 135.

And where a statute empowers two Justices of the Peace to convict, a conviction by one only is not sufficient. *Re Crow*, 1 U. C. L. J., N. S., 302.

If one Justice make a conviction where, by statute, two are required to convict, he is liable in trespass. *Graham* v. *McArthur*, 25 Q. B. (Ont.), 478.

When the statute under which the information is laid or the complaint made, requires expressly that it shall be laid or made before two Justices, this section does not apply. *R.* v. *Griffin*, 9 Q. B., 155; *R.* v. *Russell*, 13 Q. B., 237.

In a case heard before three Justices of the Peace, judgment may be rendered by two, where, by the statute, one Justice might have heard and determined the case. *Ex parte Trowley*, 9 L. C. J., 169.

Where a case is heard before two Justices of the Peace, and taken *en deliberé*, it is incompetent for one Justice to render judgment alone. *Ex parte Brodeur*, 2 L. C. J., 97. See also *St. Gemmes* v. *Cherrier*, 9 L. C. J., 22.

Where authority is given to two Justices to do a judicial act, they must be together at the time they do it, in order that they may consult together upon the judgment. *Penny* v. *Slade*, 5 Bing. N. C., 319; *R.* v. *Colin*, Burr. S. C., 136. See also section 88.

When Justices are called upon to do an act within their jurisdiction, and they do it, they are *functi officio* with respect to that act, and cannot treat it as a nullity and do it over again, nor can any other Justice do so; it must be quashed first either on appeal or upon *certiorari* before they or others again exercise their jurisdiction in respect of it.

86. After a case has been heard and determined, one Justice may issue all warrants of distress or commitment thereon.

But it would seem that it is not necessary that the magistrate who convicts should also issue the warrant of distress or commitment under this section. The warrant of commitment should, however, shew before whom the conviction was had. *Re Crow*, 1 U.C., L. J. N. S., 302.

87. It shall not be necessary that the Justice who acts before or after the hearing, be the Justice or one of the Justices by whom the case is or was heard and determined.

A case may be returned before one magistrate and adjourned from day to day by one or more, and the trial and conviction may be before a different magistrate, the jurisdiction not belonging exclusively to the one first having cognizance of it. *Ex parte Carignan*, 5 L. C. R., 479 ; see also *R.* v. *Milne*, 25 C. P. (Ont.), 94.

88. In all cases where by any Act or Law it is required that an information or complaint shall be heard and determined by two or more Justices, or that a conviction or order shall be made by two or more Justices, such Justices must be present and acting together during the whole of the hearing and determination of the case.

See also 31 Vic., chap. 1, s. 7, twenty-fifthly.

89. When several persons join in the commission of the same offence and upon conviction thereof, each is adjudged to forfeit a sum equivalent to the value of the property, or to the amount of the injury done, no further sum shall be paid to the party aggrieved than the amount forfeited by one of such offenders only, and the corresponding sum, forfeited by the other offender, shall be applied in the same manner as other penalties imposed by a Justice or Justices of the Peace are directed to be applied.

90. The evidence of the party aggrieved and also the evidence of any inhabitant of the District, County or place in which any offence has been committed shall be admitted in proof of the offence notwithstanding that any forfeiture or penalty incurred by the offence may be payable to any public fund of such District, County or place.

91. Any one Judge of Sessions of the Peace, Recorder, Police Magistrate, District Magistrate, or Stipendiary Magistrate, appointed for any District, County, City, Borough, Town or Place and sitting at a Police Court or other place appointed in that behalf, shall have full power to do alone whatever is

authorized by this Act to be done by two or more Justices of the Peace : and the several forms hereinafter contained may be varied so far as it may be necessary to render them applicable to Police Courts, or to the Court or other place of sitting of such functionary as aforesaid.

92. Any Judge of Sessions of the Peace, Police Magistrate, District Magistrate or Stipendiary Magistrate, sitting at any Police Court or other place appointed in that behalf, shall have such and like powers and authority to preserve order in the said Courts during the holding thereof, and by the like ways and means as now by law are or may be exercised and used in like cases and for the like purposes by any Courts of Law in Canada, or by the Judges thereof respectively, during the sittings thereof.

93. Any Judge of the Sessions of the Peace, Police Magistrate, District Magistrate, or Stipendiary Magistrate, in all cases where any resistance is offered to the execution of any Summons, Warrant of Execution or other Process issued by him, may enforce the due execution of the same by the means provided by the law for enforcing the execution of the Process of other Courts in like cases.

94. The expression "Territorial Division" whenever used in this Act, shall mean—District, County, Union of Counties, Township, City, Town, Parish or other judicial division or place to which the context may apply ; and the words "District or County" shall include any territorial or judicial division or place, in and for which there is such Judge, Justice, Justice's Court, officer or prison, as is mentioned in the context and to which the context may apply.

95. The words "Common Gaol" or "Prison," whenever they occur in this Act, shall be held to mean any place other than a Penitentiary, where parties charged with offences against the law are usually kept and detained in custody.

96. The several forms in the Schedule to this Act contained, varied to suit the case, or forms to the like effect, shall be deemed good, valid and sufficient in law.

See *R.* v. *Nichol*, 40 Q. B. (Ont), 76.

97. This Act shall commence and take effect on the first day of January, in the year of our Lord, one thousand eight hundred and seventy.

SCHEDULE.

(A) *See* s. 1.

SUMMONS TO THE DEFENDANT UPON AN INFORMATION OR COMPLAINT.

Canada,
Province of ,
District (*or* County,
United Counties, *or*
as the case may be),
of ,

To A. B., of (*labourer*) :

Whereas information hath this day been laid (*or* complaint hath this day been made) before the undersigned (one) of Her Majesty's Justices of the Peace in and for the said District (*or* County, United Counties, City, Town, &c., *as the case may be*), of , (for that you, *here state shortly the matter of the information or complaint*) : These are therefore to command you, in Her Majesty's name, to be and appear on , at o'clock in the forenoon, at , before me, or such Justice or Justices of the Peace for the said District (*or* County, United Counties, *or as the case may be*), as may then be there, to answer to the said information (*or* complaint), and to be further dealt with according to law.

Given under (*my*) hand and seal, this day of , in the year of our Lord , at , in the District (*or* County, *or as the case may be*) aforesaid.

J. S. [L. S.]

(B) *See* s. 6.

WARRANT WHEN THE SUMMONS IS DISOBEYED.

Canada,
Province of ,
District (*or* County,
United Counties, *or*
as the case may be),
of ,

To all or any of the Constables or other Peace Officers in the District (*or* County, United Counties, *or as the case may be*) of :

Whereas on last past, information was laid (*or* complaint was made) before , (one) of Her Majesty's Justices of the Peace in and for the said District (*or* County, United Counties, *or as the case may be*), of , for that A. B., (&c., *as in the Summons*): And whereas (I) the said Justice of the Peace then issued (my) Summons unto the said A. B., commanding him, in Her Majesty's name, to be and appear on , at , o'clock in the (*fore*) noon, at , before (me) or such Justice or Justices of the Peace as might then be there, to answer unto the said information (*or* complaint), and to be further dealt with according to law; And whereas the said A. B. hath neglected to be and appear at the time and place so appointed in and by the said Summons, although it hath now been proved to me upon oath that the said Summons hath been duly served upon the said A. B.: These are therefore to command you, in Her Majesty's name, forthwith to apprehend the said A. B., and to bring him before (me) or some one or more of Her Majesty's Justices of the Peace, in and for the said District (*or* County, United Counties, *or as the case may be*), to answer to the said information (*or* complaint); and to be further dealt with according to law.

Given under my hand and seal, this day of , in the year of our Lord at , in the District (*or* County, United Counties, *or as the case may be*) aforesaid.

J. S. [L. S.]

(C) *See* s. 6.

WARRANT IN THE FIRST INSTANCE.

Canada,
Province of ,
District (*or* County,
United Counties, *or*
as the case may be,)
of ,

To all or any of the Constables or other Peace Officers in the said District (*or* County, United Counties, *or as the case may be,*) of

Whereas information hath this day been laid before the undersigned, (*one*) of Her Majesty's Justices of the Peace in and for the said District (*or* County, United Counties, *or as the case may be,*) of for that A. B. (*here state shortly the matter of information*); and oath being now made before me substantiating the matter of such information: These are therefore to command you, in Her Majesty's name, forthwith to apprehend the said A. B. and to bring him before (me) or some one or more of Her Majesty's Justices of the Peace in and for the said District, (*or* County, United Counties, *or as the case may be,*) to answer to the said information, and to be further dealt with according to law.

Given under my Hand and Seal, this day of in the year of our Lord , at , in the District (County, &c., *as the case may be)* aforesaid.

J. S. [L. S.]

(D) *See* ss. 12, 22, 34, 46.

WARRANT OF COMMITTAL FOR SAFE CUSTODY DURING AN ADJOURNMENT OF THE HEARING.

Canada,
Province of
District (*or* County, United Counties, *or as the case may be,*) of

To all or any of the Constables or Peace Officers in the District (*or* County, United Counties, *or as the case may be*) of , and to the Keeper of the Common Gaol (*or* Lock-up House) at :

Whereas on last past, information was laid (*or* complaint made) before , (one) of Her Majesty's Justices of the Peace in and for the said District (*or* County, United Counties, *or as the case may be*) of , for that (*&c., as in the Summons*) ; And whereas the hearing of the same is adjourned to the of (*instant,*) at o'clock in the (*fore*) noon, at , and it is necessary that the said A. B. should in the meantime be kept in safe custody : These are therefore to command you, or any one of the said Constables or Peace Officers, in Her Majesty's name, forthwith to convey the said A. B. to the Common Gaol (*or* Lock-up House,) at , and there deliver him into the custody of the Keeper thereof, together with this Precept ; And I hereby require you, the said Keeper, to receive the said A. B. into your custody in the said Common Gaol (*or* Lock-up House) and there safely keep him until the day of , (*instant*) when you are hereby required to convey and have him, the said A. B., at the time and place to which the said hearing is so adjourned as aforesaid, before such Justices of the Peace for the said District (*or* County, United Counties, *as the case may be*) as may then be there, to answer further to the said information (*or* complaint), and to be further dealt with according to law.

Given under my Hand and Seal, this day of in the year of our Lord , at , in the District (*or* County, &c., *as the case may be*) aforesaid.

J. S. [L. S.]

(E) *See* ss. 12, 22, 34, 46.

RECOGNIZANCE FOR THE APPEARANCE OF THE DEFENDANT WHEN THE CASE IS ADJOURNED, OR NOT AT ONCE PROCEEDED WITH.

Canada,
Province of ,
District (*or* County,
United Counties, *or*
as the case may be)
of .

Be it remembered, That on , A. B. of (*labourer*), and L. M. of , (*grocer*), and O. P. of (*yeoman*), personally came and appeared before the undersigned, (*one*) of Her Majesty's Justices of the Peace in and for the said District (*or* County, United Counties, *or as the case may be*) of , and severally acknowledged themselves to owe to our Sovereign Lady the Queen the several sums following, that is to say: the said A. B. the sum of and the said L. M. and O. P. the sum of , each, of good and lawful current money of Canada, to be made and levied of their several goods and chattels, lands and tenements respectively, to the use of our said Lady the Queen, Her Heirs and Successors, if he the said A. B. shall fail in the condition endorsed (*or* hereunder written).

Taken and acknowledged the day and year first above mentioned at before me.

J. S. [L. S.]

The condition of the within (*or* the above) written recognizance is such that if the said A. B. shall personally appear on the day of , (*instant*,) at o'clock in the (*fore*) noon, at , before me or such Justices of the Peace for the said District (*or* County, United Counties, *or as the case may be*) as may then be there, to answer further to the information (*or* complaint) of C. D. exhibited against the said A. B. and to be further dealt with according to law, then the said recognizance to be void, or else to stand in full force and virtue.

NOTICE OF SUCH RECOGNIZANCE TO BE GIVEN TO THE DEFENDANT AND HIS SURETIES.

Take notice that you A. B., are bound in the sum of and you L. M. and O. P., in the sum of , each, that you A. B., appear personally on at o'clock in the (*fore*) noon at , before me or such Justices of the Peace for the District (*or* County, United Counties, *or as the case may be*) of as shall then be there, to answer further to a certain information (*or* complaint) of C. D. the further hearing of which was adjourned to the said time and place, and unless you appear accordingly, the recognizance entered into by you, A. B., and by L. M. and O. P. as your sureties, will forthwith be levied on you and them.

Dated this day of , one thousand eight hundred and .

J. S. [L. S.]

(F) *See* ss. 13, 23, 35, 49, 61.

CERTIFICATE OF NON-APPEARANCE TO BE ENDORSED ON THE DEFENDANT'S RECOGNIZANCE.

I hereby certify, that the said A. B. hath not appeared at the time and place in the said condition mentioned, but therein hath made default, by reason whereof the within written recognizance is forfeited.

J. S. [L. S.]

(G 1) *See* s. 16.

SUMMONS TO A WITNESS.

Canada,
Province of ,
District (*or* County,
United Counties, *or*
as the case may be),
of , .

To E. F. of , in the said District (*or* County, United Counties, *or as the case may be*) of .

Whereas information was laid (*or* complaint was made) before (*one*) of Her Majesty's Justices of the Peace in and for the said District (*or* County, United Counties, *or as the case may be*) of , for that (&c., *as in the*

Summons,) and it hath been made to appear to me upon *(oath)* that you are likely to give material evidence on behalf of the prosecutor (*or* complainant *or* defendant) in this behalf; These are therefore to require you to be and appear on , at o'clock in the (*fore*) noon, at before me or such Justice or Justices of the Peace for the said District (*or* County, United Counties, *or as the case may be*,) as may then be there, to testify what you shall know concerning the matter of the said information (*or* complaint).

Given under my hand and seal, this day of in the year of our Lord , at in the District (*or* County, *or as the case may be*) aforesaid.

J. S. [L. S.]

(G 2) *See* s. 17.

WARRANT WHERE A WITNESS HAS NOT OBEYED A SUMMONS.

Canada,
Province of ,
District (*or* County,
United Counties, *or*
as the case may be),
of

To all or any of the Constables and other Peace Officers in the said District (*or* County, United Counties, *or as the case may be*), of

Whereas information was laid (*or* complaint was made) before (*one*) of Her Majesty's Justices of the Peace in and for the said District (*or* County, United Counties, *or as the case may be*) of , for that (*&c.*, *as in the Summons*), and it having been made to appear to (*me*) upon oath, that E. F., of , in the said District (*or* County, United Counties, *or as the case may be*), (*labourer*) was likely to give material evidence on behalf of the Prosecutor, *or as the case may be*) (*I*) did duly issue (*my*) Summons to the said E.F., requiring him to be and appear on , at o'clock in the (*fore*) noon of the same day, at , before me or such Justice or Justices of the Peace for the said District (*or* County, United Counties, *or as the case may be*) as might then be there, to testify what he should know concerning the said A. B., or the matter of the said information (*or* complaint): And whereas proof hath this day been made before me, upon oath, of such Summons having been duly served upon the said E.F.; And whereas the said E.F. hath neglected to appear at the time and place appointed by the said Summons, and no just excuse has been offered for such neglect; These are therefore to command you to take the said E. F., and to bring and have him on , at o'clock in the noon, at , before me or such Justice or Justices of the Peace for the District (*or* County, United Counties, *or as the case may be*) as may then be there, to testify what he shall know concerning the said information (*or* complaint).

Given under my hand and seal, this day of , in the year of our Lord , at , in the District (*or* County, *or as the case may be*) aforesaid.

J. S. [L.S.]

[G 3] *See* s. 18.

WARRANT FOR A WITNESS IN THE FIRST INSTANCE.

Canada,
Province of ,
District [*or* County,
United Counties, *or*
as the case may be],
of

To all or any of the Constables, or other Peace Officers in the said District [*or* County, United Counties, *or as the case may be*] of

Whereas information was laid [*or* complaint was made] before the undersigned [*one*] of Her Majesty's Justices of the Peace in and for the said District [*or* County, United Counties, *or as the case may be*] of , for that [&c., *as in the Summons*], and it being made to appear before me upon oath, that E. F., of [*labourer*], is likely to give material evidence on behalf of the [prosecutor, *or as the case may be*], in this matter, and it is probable that the said E. F, will not attend to give evidence without being compelled so to do: These are therefore to command you to bring and have the said E.F., on , at o'clock in the [*fore*] noon, at , before me or such other Justice or Justices of the Peace for the District [*or* County, United Counties, *or as the case may be*] as may then be there, to testify what he shall know concerning the matter of the said information [*or* complaint].

Given under [*my*] hand and seal, this day of , in the year of our Lord , at , in the District [*or* County, *or as the case may be*], aforesaid.

J. S. [L.S.]

[G 4] *See* s. 19.

COMMITMENT OF A WITNESS FOR REFUSING TO BE SWORN OR GIVE EVIDENCE.

Canada,
Province of ,
District [*or* County,
United Counties, *or*
as the case may be],
of

To all or any of the Constables or other Peace Officers in the said District [*or* County, United Counties, *or as the case may be*] of , and to the Keeper of the Common Gaol of the said District [*or* County, United Counties, *or as the case may be*] at

Whereas information was laid [*or* complaint was made] before [*me*] [*one*] of Her Majesty's Justices of the Peace in and for the said District [*or* County, United Counties, *or as the case may be*] of , for that [&c., *as in the Summons*], and one E.F., now appearing before me such Justice as afore said, on , at , and being required by me to make oath [*or* affirmation] as a witness in that behalf, hath now refused so to do, [*or* being now here duly sworn as a witness in the matter of the said information *or* complaint] doth refuse to answer a certain question concerning the premises which is now here put to him, and more particularly the following question [*here insert the exact words of the question*], without offering any just excuse for such his refusal : These are therefore to command you, or any one of the said Constables or Peace Officers to take the said E.F., and him safely to convey to the said Common Gaol at aforesaid, and there deliver him to the said Keeper thereof, together with this precept ; and I do hereby command you the said Keeper of the said Common Gaol, to receive the said E.F. into your custody in the said Common Gaol, and there imprison him for such his contempt for the space of days, unless he shall in the meantime consent to be examined and to answer concerning the premises, and for so doing this shall be your sufficient warrant.

Given under my hand and seal, this day of in the year of our Lord , at , in the District (*or* County, *or as the case may be*) aforesaid.

J. S. [L. S.]

(H) *See* s. 33.

WARRANT TO REMAND A DEFENDANT WHEN APPREHENDED.

Canada,
Province of ,
District (*or* County,
United Counties, *or*
as the case may be,)
of ,

To all or any of the Constables, or other Peace Officers in the said District (*or* County, United Counties, *or as the case may be*) of , and to the Keeper of the Common Gaol (*or* Lock-up House) at

Whereas information was laid (*or* complaint was made) before (*one*) of Her Majesty's Justices of the Peace in and for the District (*or* County, United Counties, *or as the case may be*) of for that (*&c., as in the Summons or Warrant*) ; And whereas the said A. B. hath been apprehended under and by virtue of a Warrant, upon such information (*or* complaint) and is now brought before me as such Justice as aforesaid : These are therefore to command you, or any one of the said Constables, or Peace Officers, in Her Majesty's name, forthwith to convey the said A. B. to the Common Gaol (*or* Lock-up House) at , and there to deliver him to the said Keeper thereof, together with this Precept ; And I do hereby command you the said Keeper to receive the said A. B. into your custody in the said Common Gaol (*or* Lock-up House) and there safely keep him until next, the day of (*instant*), when you are hereby commanded to convey and have him at , at o'clock in the noon of the same day, before me, or such Justice or Justices of the Peace of the said District (*or* County, United Counties, *or as the case may be*) as may then be there, to answer to the said information (*or* complaint,) and to be further dealt with according to law.

Given under my hand and seal, this day of , in the year of our Lord , at , in the District (*or* County, *as the case may be*) aforesaid.

J. S. [L. S.]

(I 1) *See* ss. 42, 50.

CONVICTION FOR A PENALTY TO BE LEVIED BY DISTRESS, AND IN DEFAULT OF SUFFICIENT DISTRESS, BY IMPRISONMENT.

Canada,
Province of ,
District [*or* County,
United Counties, *or*
as the case may be,]
of

Be it remembered, That on the day of , in the year of our Lord, , at in the said District [*or* County, United Counties, *or as the case may be*], A. B. is convicted before the undersigned, [*one*] of Her Majesty's Justices of the Peace for the said District [*or* County, United Counties, *or as the case may be,*] for that the said A. B. *&c, stating the offence and the time and place when and where committed,*] and I adjudge the said A. B. for his said offence to forfeit and pay the sum of [*stating the penalty, and also the compensation, if any,*] to be paid and applied according to law, and also to pay to the said C. D. the sum of , for his costs in this behalf; and if the said several sums be not paid forthwith [*or* on or before the of next,] * I order that the same be levied by distress and sale of the goods and chattels of the said A. B., and in default of sufficient distress, * I adjudge the said A. B., to be imprisoned in the Common Gaol of the said District [*or* County, United Counties,*or as the case may be,*] at in the said District [*or* County] of [there to be kept at hard labour if such be the sentence] for the space of unless the said several sums and all costs and charges of the said distress [and of the commitment and conveying of the said A. B. to the said Gaol] be sooner paid.

Given under [my] hand and seal, the day and year first above mentioned, at in the District [*or* County, United Counties, *or as the case may be*] aforesaid.

J. S. [L. S.]

* *Or when the issuing of a Distress Warrant would be ruinous to the Defendant or his family, or it appears he has no goods whereon to levy a distress, then instead of the words between the asterisks * * say,* "inasmuch as it hath now been made to appear to me that the issuing of a Warrant of Distress in this behalf would be ruinous to the said A. B. or his family," [*or,* "that the said A. B. hath no goods or chattels whereon to levy the said sums by distress."] I adjudge, &c., [*as above to the end.*]

(I 2) *See* ss. 42, 50.

CONVICTION FOR A PENALTY, AND IN DEFAULT OF PAYMENT, IMPRISONMENT.

Canada,
Province of
District (or County,
United Counties, *or*
as the case may be,)
of

Be it remembered, that on the day of , in the year of our Lord, , at , in the said District (*or* County, United Counties, *or as the case may be,)* A. B., is convicted before the undersigned, (*one*) of Her Majesty's Justices of the Peace for the said District, *or* County, United Counties, *or as the case may be,)* for that he the said A. B., (*&c., stating the offence, and the time and place when and where it was committed,)* and I adjudge the said A. B. for his said offence to forfeit and pay the sum of (*stating the penalty and the compensation, if any,)* to be paid and applied according to law ; and also to pay to the said C. D. the sum of for his costs in this behalf ; and if the said several sums be not paid forthwith, (*or*, on or before next,) I adjudge the said A. B. to be imprisoned in the Common Gaol of the said District, (*or* County, United Counties, *or as the case may be,)* at in the said District (*or* County) of (*and there to be kept at hard labour*) for the space of , unless the said sums and the costs and charges of conveying the said A. B. to the said Common Gaol, shall be sooner paid.

Given under my hand and seal, the day and year first above mentioned, at in the District (*or* County, United Counties, *or as the case may be,)* aforesaid.

J. S. [L. S.]

(I 3) *See* ss. 42, 50.

CONVICTION WHEN THE PUNISHMENT IS BY IMPRISONMENT, &c.

Canada,
Province of
District (*or* County,
United Counties, *or*
as the case may be,)
of

Be it remembered, That on the day of , in the year of our Lord , in the said District (*or* County, United Counties, *or as the case may be,*) A. B. is convicted before the undersigned (*one*) of Her Majesty's Justices of the Peace in and for the said District (*or* County, United Counties, *or as the case may be,*) for that he the said A. B. (*&c., stating the offence and the time and place when and where it was committed*); and I adjudge the said A. B. for his said offence to be imprisoned in the Common Gaol of the said District (*or* County, United Counties, *or as the case may be,*) at in the County of (and there to be kept at hard labour) for the space of ; and I also adjudge the said A. B. to pay to the said C. D. the sum of for his costs in this behalf, and if the said sum for costs be not paid forthwith, (*or* on or before next,) then * I order that the said sum be levied by distress and sale of the goods and chattels of the said A. B.; and in default of sufficient distress in that behalf, * I adjudge the said A. B. to be imprisoned in the said Common Gaol, (and kept there at hard labour) for the space of , to commence at and from the term of his imprisonment aforesaid, unless the said sum for costs shall be sooner paid.

Given under my hand and seal, the day and year first above mentionet, at in the District (*or* County, United Counties, *or as the case may be.*) aforesaid.

J. S. [L. S.]

* *Or, when the issuing of a distress warrant would be ruinous to the Defendant and his family, or it appears that he has no goods whereon to levy a distress, then, instead of the words between the asterisks* * * say, "inasmuch as it hath now been made to appear to me that the issuing of a warrant of distress in this behalf would be ruinous to the said A. B., and his family," (*or,* "that the said A. B. hath no goods or chattels whereon to levy the said sum for costs by distress ") I adjudge, &c.

(K 1) *See* ss. 42, 51.

ORDER FOR PAYMENT OF MONEY TO BE LEVIED BY DISTRESS, AND IN DEFAULT OF DISTRESS, IMPRISONMENT.

Canada,
Province of
District (*or* County,
United Counties, *or*
as the case may be,)
of

Be it remembered, That on complaint was made before the undersigned, (*one*) of Her Majesty's Justices of the Peace in and for the said District (*or* County, United Counties, *or as the case may be*) of for that (*stating the facts entitling the Complainant to the order, with the time and place when and where they occurred,*) and now at this day, to wit, on , at , the parties aforesaid appear before me the said Justice (*or*, the said C. D. appears before me the said Justice, but the said A. B. although duly called, doth not appear by himself, his Counsel or Attorney, and it is now satisfactorily proved to me on oath that the said A. B. has been duly served with the Summons in this behalf, which required him to be and appear here on this day before me or such Justice or Justices of the Peace for the said District (*or* County, United Counties, *or as the case may be*) as should now be here to answer the said complaint, and to be further dealt with according to law) ; and now having heard the matter of the said complaint, I do adjudge the said A. B. (to pay to the said C. D. the said sum of forthwith (*or* on or before next, *or as the Act or Law may require*), and also to pay to the said C. D., the sum of for hiscosts in this behalf ; and if the said several sums be not paid forthwith (*or* on or before next) then,* I hereby order that the same be levied by distress, and sale of the goods and chattels of the said A. B.) and in default of sufficient distress in that behalf,* I adjudge the said A. B. to be imprisoned in the Common Gaol of the said District (*or* County, United Counties, *or as the case may be*) at in the said District (*or* County) of , (and there kept to hard labour) for the space of unless the said several sums and all costs and charges of the said distress (and of the commitment and conveying of the said A. B. to the said Common Gaol) shall be sooner paid.

Given under my hand and seal, this day of in the year of Our Lord , at in the District (*or* County *or as the case may be,*) aforesaid.

J. S. [L. S.]

* *Or, when the issuing of a distress warrant would be ruinous to the Defendant or his family, or it appears he has no goods whereon to levy a distress, then, instead of the words between the asterisks * * say,* "inasmuch as it hath now been made to appear to me that the issuing of a warrant of distress in this behalf would be ruinous to the said A. B., and his family," (*or*, "that the said A. B. hath no goods or chattels whereon to levy the said sums by distress.")

(K 2) *See* ss. 42, 51.

ORDER FOR PAYMENT OF MONEY, AND IN DEFAULT OF PAYMENT, IMPRISONMENT.

Canada,
Province of ,
District (*or* County,
United Counties, *or*
as the case may be,)
of

Be it remembered, That on complaint was made before the undersigned [*one*] of Her Majesty's Justices of the Peace in and for the said District (*or* County, United Counties, *or as the case may be*,) of , for that (*stating the facts entitling the complainant to the order with the time and place when and where they occurred*,) and now on this day, to wit, on , at , the parties aforesaid appear before me the said Justice, (*or* the said C. D. appears before me the said Justice, but the said A. B. although duly called doth not appear by himself, his Counsel or Attorney, and it is now satisfactorily proved to me upon oath that the said A. B. has been duly served with the summons in this behalf, which required him to be and appear here this day before me, or such Justice or Justices of the Peace for the said District (*or* County, United Counties, *or as the case may be*,) as should now be here, to answer to the said complaint, and to be further dealt with according to law,) and now having heard the matter of the said complaint, I do adjudge the said A. B. (to pay to the said C. D. the sum of forthwith, (*or* on or before next, *or as the Act or Law may require*,) and also to pay to the said C. D. the sum of for his costs in this behalf; and if the said several sums be not paid forthwith, (*or* on *or* before next), then I adjudge the said A. B. to be imprisoned in the Common Gaol of the said District (*or* County, United Counties, *or as the case may be*,) at , in the said District (*or* County of (there to be kept at hard labour *if the Act or Law authorizes this*) for the space of , unless the said several sums, and costs (and charges of commitment and conveying the said A. B. to the said Common Gaol) shall be sooner paid.

Given under (*my*) Hand and Seal, this day of , in the year of our Lord , at , in the District (*or* County, United Counties, *or as the case may be*,) aforesaid.

J. S. [L. S.]

(K 3) *See* ss. 42, 51.

ORDER FOR ANY OTHER MATTER WHERE THE DISOBEYING OF IT IS PUNISHABLE WITH IMPRISONMENT.

Canada,
Province of
District [*or* County, United Counties, *or as the case may be,*] of

Be it remembered, That on complaint was made before the undersigned, (*one*) of Her Majesty's Justices of the Peace in and for the said District (*or* County, United Counties, *or as the case may be,*) of , for that *stating the facts entitling the Complainant to the order, with the time and place where and when they occurred*) and now on this day, to wit, on ; at , the parties aforesaid appear before me the said Justice, (*or* the said C. D. appears before me the said Justice, but the said A. B. although duly called doth not appear by himself, his Counsel or Attorney, and it is now satisfactorily proved to me upon oath that the said A. B. has been duly served with the summons in this behalf, which required him to be and appear here this day before me, or such Justice or Justices of the Peace for the said District (*or* County, United Counties, *or as the case may be,*) as should now be here, to answer to the said complaint, and to be further dealt with according to law,) and now having heard the matter of the said complaint, I do therefore adjudge the said A. B. to (*here state the matter required to be done,*) and if upon a copy of the Minute of this Order being served upon the said A. B. either personally or by leaving the same for him at his last or most usual place of abode, he shall neglect or refuse to obey the same, in that case I adjudge the said A. B. for such his disobedience to be imprisoned in the Common Gaol of the said District (*or* County, United Counties, *or as the case may be,*) at in the said County of (there to be kept at hard labour *if the Statute authorize this*), for the space of unless the said order be sooner obeyed, and I do also adjudge the said A. B. to pay to the said C. D. the sum of for his costs in this behalf, and if the said sum for costs be not paid forthwith, (*or* on or before next,) I order the same to be levied by distress and sale of the goods and chattels of the said A. B., and in default of sufficient distress in that behalf, I adjudge the said A. B. to be imprisoned in the said Common Gaol (there to be kept at hard labour) for the space of to commence at and from the termination of his imprisonment aforesaid, unless the said sum for costs shall be sooner paid.

Given under (*my*) hand and seal, this day of in

the year of our Lord , at , in the District (*or* County, United Counties, *or as the case may be*) aforesaid.

J. S. [L. S.]

(L) *See* s. 43.

ORDER OF DISMISSAL OF AN INFORMATION OR COMPLAINT.

Canada,
Province of ,
District (*or* County, United Counties, *or as the case may be*), of

Be it remembered, That on information was laid (*or* complaint was made) before the undersigned, [*one*] of Her Majesty's Justices of the Peace in and for the said District [*or* County, United Counties, *or as the case may be*] of , for that [*&c., as in the Summons to the Defendant,* and now at this day, to wit, on , at , both the said parties appear before me in order that I should hear and determine the said information [*or* complaint] [*or* the said A. B. appeareth before me, but the said C. D. although duly called doth not appear,*] whereupon the matter of the said information [*or* complaint] being by me duly considered [it manifestly appears to me that the said information [*or* complaint] is not proved,] I do therefore dismiss the same, and do adjudge that the said C. D. do pay to the said A. B. the sum of for his costs incurred by him in his defence in this behalf : and if the said sum for costs be not paid forthwith, *or* on or before ,] I order that the same be levied by distress and sale of the goods and chattels of the said C. D., and in default of sufficient distress in that behalf, I adjudge the said C. D. to be imprisoned in the Common Gaol of the said District [*or* County, United Counties, *or as the case may be*] at in the said County of [and there to be kept at hard labour] for the space of , unless the said sum for costs and all costs and charges of the said distress [and of the commitment of the said C. D. to the said Common Gaol,] shall be sooner paid.

Given under my hand and seal, this day of in the year of our Lord , at , in the District [*or* County, United Counties, *or as the case may be*] aforesaid.

J. S. [L. S.]

* *If the Informant* [or *Complainant*] *do not appear, these words may be omitted.*

(M) *See* s. 43.

CERTIFICATE OF DISMISSAL.

I hereby certify that an information [*or* complaint preferred by C. D. against A. B. for that [*or as in the summons,*] was this day considered by me, one of Her Majesty's Justices of the Peace in and for the District (*or* County, United Counties, *or as the case may be*) of , and was by (me) dismissed [*with costs.*]

Dated this day of , one thousand eight hundred and

, J. S. [L. S.]

(N 1) *See* s. 57.

WARRANT OF DISTRESS UPON A CONVICTION FOR A PENALTY.

Canada,
Province of,
District [*or* County,
United Counties, or
as the case may be]
of

To all or any of the Constables, or other Peace Officers in the said District [*or* County, United Counties, *as the case may be* of

Whereas A. B., late of , (*labourer*) was on this day (*or* on last past) duly convicted before (*one*) of Her Majesty's Justices of the Peace, in and for the said District (*or* County, United Counties, *or as the case may be*) of for that (*stating the offence as in the conviction*) and it was thereby adjudged that the said A. B., should for such his offence forfeit and pay, [*&c., as in the conviction*], and should also pay to the said C. D. the sum of for his costs in that behalf; and it was thereby ordered that if the said several sums should not be paid [*forthwith*] the same should be levied by distress and sale of the goods and chattels of the said A. B.; and it was thereby also adjudged that the said A. B., in default of sufficient distress, should be imprisoned in the Common Gaol of the said District [*or* County, United Counties, *or as the case may be*] at in the said County of [*and there to be kept at hard labour*] for the space of unless the said several sums and all costs and charges of the said distress, and of the commitment and conveying of the said A. B., to the said Common Gaol should be sooner paid; * And whereas the said A. B., being so convicted as aforesaid, and being [*now*] required to pay the said sums of and hath not paid the same or any part thereof, but therein hath made defaults; These are therefore to command you, in Her Majesty's name, forthwith to make distress of the goods and chattels of the said A. B.; and if within days next after the making of such distress, the said sums, together with the reasonable charges of taking and keeping the distress, shall not be paid, then you do sell the said goods and chattels so by you distrained, and do pay the money arising from such sale unto me [*the convicting Justice* or *one of the convicting Justices*] that I may pay and apply the same as by law is directed, and may render the overplus, if any, on demand, to the said A. B.; and if no such distress can be found, then that you certify the same unto me, to the end that such further proceedings may be had thereon as to law doth appertain.

Given under my hand and seal, this day of in the year of our Lord , at in the District [*or* County, *or as the case may be*] aforesaid.

J. S. [L. S.]

(N 2) *See* s. 57.

WARRANT OF DISTRESS UPON AN ORDER FOR THE PAYMENT OF MONEY.

Canada,
Province of ,
District (*or* County,
United Counties, *or*
as the case may be,)
of

To all or any of the Constables, or other Peace Officers, in the said District (*or* County, United Counties, *or as the case may be*) of

Whereas on last past, a complaint was made before (*one*) of Her Majesty's Justices of the Peace in and for the said District (*or* County, United Counties, *or as the case may be*) for that [*&c., as in the order*,] and afterwards, to wit, on , at the said parties appeared before (*as in the order*,) and thereupon the matter of the said complaint having been considered, the said A. B. was adjudged [to pay to the said C. D. the sum of on or before then next,] and also to pay to the said C. D. the sum of for his costs in that behalf; and it was ordered that if the said several sums should not be paid on or before the said then next, the same should be levied by distress and sale of the goods and chattels of the said A. B.; and it was adjudged that in default of sufficient distress in that behalf, the said A. B., should be imprisoned in the Common Gaol of the said District [*or* County, or United Counties, *or as the case may be*] at , in the said County of (and there kept at hard labour) for the space of , unless the said several sums and all costs and charges of the distress (and of the commitment and conveying of the said A. B. to the said Common Gaol) should be sooner paid; * And whereas the time in and by the said order appointed for the payment of the said several sums of and hath elapsed, but the said A. B. hath not paid the same, or any part thereof, but herein hath made default; These are therefore to command you, in Her Majesty's name, forthwith to make distress of the goods and chattels of the said A. B.; and if within the space of days after the making of such distress, the said last mentioned sums, together with the reasonable charges of taking and keeping the said distress, shall not be paid, that then you do sell the said goods and chattels so by you distrained, and to pay the money arising from such sale unto me, [*or some other of the convicting Justices as the case may be*] that I [*or* he] may pay and apply the same as by law directed, and may render the overplus, if any, on demand to the said A. B.; and if no such distress can be found, then that you certify the same unto me, to the end that such proceedings may be had therein, as to law doth appertain.

Given under my hand and seal, this day of in the year of our Lord , at , in the District [*or* County, *or as the case may be*] aforesaid.

J. S. [L. S.]

(N 3) *See* s. 58.

ENDORSEMENT IN BACKING A WARRANT OF DISTRESS.

Canada,
Province of ,
District (*or* County,
United Counties, *or*
as the case may be,)
of

Whereas proof upon oath hath this day been made before me, one of Her Majesty's Justices of the Peace in and for the said District (*or* County, United Counties, *or as the case may be*) that the name of J. S. to the within Warrant subscribed, is of the hand-writing of the Justice of the Peace within mentioned, I do therefore authorize U. T. who bringeth me this Warrant, and all other persons to whom this Warrant was originally directed, or by whom the same may be lawfully executed, and also all Constables and other Peace Officers in the said District (*or* County, United Counties, *or as the case may be,*) of to execute the same within the said District (*or* County, United Counties, *or as the case may be*)

Given under my hand, this day of , one thousand eight hundred and O. K.

(N 4) *See* s. 62.

CONSTABLE'S RETURN TO A WARRANT OF DISTRESS.

I, W. T., Constable of , in the District [*or* County, United Counties, *or as the case may be*] of , hereby certify to J. S., Esquire, one of Her Majesty's Justices of the Peace for the District [*or* County, United Counties, *or as the case may be*] that by virtue of this Warrant, I have made diligent search for the goods and chattels of the within mentioned A. B., and that I can find no sufficient goods or chattels of the said A. B. whereon to levy the sums within mentioned.

Witness my hand, this day of , one thousand eight hundred and

J. S. [L. S.]

(N 5) *See s.* 62.

WARRANT OF COMMITMENT FOR WANT OF DISTRESS.

Canada,
Province of ,
District [*or* County,
United Counties, *or as the case may be,*]
of

To all or any of the Constables and other Peace Officers in the District [*or* County, United Counties, *or as the oase may be,*] of , and to the Keeper of the Common Gaol of the said District [*or* County, United Counties, *or as the case may be,*] of at , in the said District [*or* County of

Whereas [*&c., as in either of the foregoing distress warrants, N.* 1, 2, *to the asterisks,* and then thus*]; And whereas afterwards on the day of , in the year aforesaid, I, the said Justice, issued a Warrant to all or any of the Constables or other Peace Officers of the District [*or* County, United Counties, *or as the case may be,*] of commanding them, or any of them, to levy the said sums of and by distress and sale of the goods and chattels of the said A. B.; And whereas it appears to me, as well by the return to the said warrant of distress, by the Constable who had the execution of the same, as otherwise, that the said Constable hath made diligent search for the goods and chattels of the said A. B., but that no sufficient distress whereon to levy the sums above mentioned could be found: These are therefore to command you, the said Constables or Peace Officers, or any one of you, to take the said A. B., and him safely to convey to the Common Gaol at aforesaid, and there deliver him to the said Keeper, together with this Precept; And I do hereby command you, the said Keeper of the said Common Gaol, to receive the said A. B. into your custody, in the said Common Gaol, there to imprison him [and keep him at hard labour] for the space of , unless the said several sums, and all the costs and charges of the said distress, [and of the commitment and conveying of the said A. B. to the said Common Gaol] amounting to the further sum of , shall be sooner paid unto you, the said Keeper; and for so doing, this shall be your sufficient warrant.

Given under my Hand and Seal, this day of in the year of Our Lord , at in the District [*or* County, *or as the case may be*,] aforesaid.

J. S. [L. S.]

(O 1) *See* s. 59.

WARRANT OF COMMITMENT UPON A CONVICTION FOR A PENALTY IN THE FIRST INSTANCE.

Canada,
Province of ,
District (*or* County, United Counties, *or as the case may be*) of

To all or any of the Constables, and other Peace Officers, in the said District (*or* County, United Counties, *or as the case may be*) of , and to the Keeper of the Common Gaol of the said District (*or* County, United Counties, *or as the case may be*) of at , in the said District *or* County of

Whereas A. B. late of [*labourer*,] was on this day convicted before the undersigned, [*one*] of Her Majesty's Justices of the Peace, in and for the said District [*or* County, United Counties, *or as the case may be*] for that [*stating the offence as in the conviction*], and it was thereby adjudged that the said A. B., for his offence should forfeit and pay the sum of [*&c., as in the conviction*], and should pay to the said C. D. the sum of for his costs in that behalf; and it was thereby further adjudged that if the said several sums should not be paid [*forthwith*] the said A. B. should be imprisoned in the Common Gaol of the said District [*or* County, United Counties, *or as the case may be*] at in the said District [*or* County] of and there kept at hard labour] for the space of , unless the said several sums and the costs and charges of conveying the said A. B. to the said Common Gaol] should be sooner paid; And whereas the time in and by the said conviction appointed for the payment of the said several sums hath elapsed, but the said A. B. hath not paid the same or any part thereof, but therein hath made default; These are therefore to command you, the said Constables or Peace Officers, or any one of you, to take the said A. B., and him safely to convey to the Common Gaol at aforesaid, and there to deliver him to the said Keeper thereof, together with this Precept; and I do hereby command you, the said Keeper of the said Common Gaol, to receive the said A. B. into your custody in the said Common Gaol, there to imprison him [and keep him at hard labour] for the space of , unless the said several sums [and costs and charges of carrying him to the said Common Gaol, amounting to the further sum of], shall be sooner paid unto you, the said Keeper; and for your so doing, this shall be your sufficient warrant.

Given under [*my*] hand and seal, this day of in the year of our Lord , at , in the District [*or* County, *or as the case may be*] aforesaid.

J. S. [L. S.]

[O 2] *See* s. 59.

WARRANT OF COMMITMENT ON AN ORDER IN THE FIRST INSTANCE.

Canada,
Province of ,
District [*or* County,
United Counties, *or*
as the case may be]
of .

To all or any of the Constables and other Peace Officers in the said District, [*or* County, United Counties, *or as the case may be*] of , and to the Keeper of the Common Gaol of the District *or* County, United Counties, *or as the case may be*] of at in the said District [*or* County] of

Whereas on last past, complaint was made before the undersigned, [*one*] of Her Majesty's Justices of the Peace in and for the said District [*or* County, United Counties *or as the case may be*] of or that [*&c., as in the order*], and afterwards, to wit, on the day of , at the parties appeared before me, the said Justice [*or as it may be in the order*], and thereupon having considered the matter of the complaint, I adjudged the said A. B. to pay the said C. D. the sum of , on or before the day of then next, and also to pay to the said C. D. the sum of for his costs in that behalf; and I also thereby abjudged that if the said several sums should not be paid on or before the day of then next, the said A. B. should be imprisoned in the Common Gaol of the District [*or* County, United Counties, *or as the case may be*] of at in the said County of [and there be kept at hard labour] for the space of unless the said several sums [and the costs and charges of conveying, the said A. B. to the said Common Gaol, *as the case may be*] should be sooner paid; And whereas the time in and by the said order appointed for the payment of the said several sums of money hath elapsed, but the said A. B. hath not paid the same or any part thereof, but therein hath made default; These are therefore to command you, the said Constables and Peace Officers, or any of you, to take the said A. B. and him safely to convey to the said Common Gaol, at aforesaid, and there to deliver him to the Keeper thereof, together with this Precept; and I do hereby command you, the said Keeper of the said Common Gaol, to receive the said A. B. into your custody in the said Common Gaol, there to imprison him [*and keep him at hard labour*] for the space of , unless the said several sums [and the costs and charges of conveying him to the said Common Gaol, amounting to the further sum of ,] shall be sooner paid unto you the said Keeper; and for your so doing, this shall be your sufficient warrant.

Given under [*my*] Hand and Seal, this day of , in the year of Our Lord , at , in the District [*or* County, *or as the case may be*] aforesaid.

J.S. [L. S.]

(Q 1)—*See* s. 64.

WARRANT OF DISTRESS FOR COSTS UPON AN ORDER FOR DISMISSAL OF AN INFORMATION OR COMPLAINT.

Canada,
Province of ,
District (*or* County,
United Counties, *or*
as the case may be),
of .

To all or any of the Constables or other Peace Officers in the said District (*or* County, United Counties, *or as the case may be*), of :

Whereas on last past, information was laid (*or* complaint made before (*one*) of Her Majesty's Justices of the Peace, in and for the said District (*or* County, United Counties, *or as the case may be*) of for that (*&c., as in the order of dismissal*), and afterwards, to wit, on at , both parties appearing before in order that *(I)* should hear and determine the same, and the several proofs adduced to *(me)* in that behalf being by (*me*) duly heard and considered, and it manifestly appearing to (*me*) that the said information (*or* complaint) was not proved, (*I*) therefore dismissed the same and adjudged that the said C. D. should pay to the said A. B., the sum of for his costs incurred by him in his defence in that behalf; and (*I*) ordered that if the said sum for costs should not be paid (*forthwith*), the same should be levied on the goods and chattels of the said C. D., and (*I*) adjudged that in default of sufficient distress in that behalf the said C. D. should be imprisoned in the Common Gaol of the said District (*or* County, United Counties, *or as the case may be*) of at , in the said District *or* County of (and there kept at hard labour) for the space of , unless the said sum for costs, and all costs and charges of the said distress, and of the commitment and conveying of the said A. B. to the said Common Gaol should be sooner paid ;* And whereas the said C. D., being now required to pay to the said A. B., the said sum for costs, hath not paid the same, or any part thereof, but therein hath made default: These are therefore to command you, in Her Majesty's name, forthwith to make distress of the goods and chattels of the said C. D., and if within the space of days next after the making of such distress, the said last mentioned sum, together with the reasonable charges of taking and keeping the said distress, shall not be paid, then that you do sell the said goods and chattels so by you distrained, and do pay the money arising from such sale to me (*the Justice who made such order or dismissal as the case may be*) that *(I)* may pay and apply the same as by law directed, and may render the overplus (if any) on demand to the said C. D., and if no such distress can be found, then that you certify the same unto me, (*or* to any other Justice of the Peace for the same District (*or* County, United Counties, *or as the case may be*), to the end that such proceedings may be had therein as to law doth appertain.

Given under (*my*) Hand and Seal, this day of , in the year of our Lord , at , in the District (*or* County, *or as case may be*) aforesaid.

J. S. [L. S.]

(Q 2) *See* s. 64.

WARRANT OF COMMITMENT FOR WANT OF DISTRESS IN THE LAST CASE.

Canada,
Province of ,
District (*or* County,
United Counties *or*
as the case may be)
of

To all or any of the Constables or Peace Officers in the said District (*or* County, United Counties, *or as the case may be*) of , and to the Keeper of the Common Gaol of the said District (*or* County, United Counties, *or as the case may be*) of , at , in the said District (*or* County) of :

Whereas (*&c., as in the last form, to the asterisk,* and then thus*): And whereas afterwards, on the day of , in the year aforesaid, I, the said Justice, issued a warrant to all or any of the Constables or other Peace Officers of the said District (*or* County, United Counties, *or as the case may be*) commanding them, or any one of them to levy the said sum of for costs, by distress and sale of the goods and chattels of the said C. D.; And whereas it appears to me, as well by the return to the said warrant of distress of the Constable (*or* Peace Officer) charged with the execution of the same, as otherwise, that the said Constable hath made diligent search for the goods and chattels of the said C. D., but that no sufficient distress whereon to levy the sum above mentioned could be found; These are therefore to command you, the said Constables and Peace Officers, or any one of you, to take the said C. D., and him safely convey to the Common Gaol of the said District (*or* County, United Counties, *or as the case may be*), at aforesaid, and there deliver him to the Keeper thereof, together with this Precept; and I hereby command you, the said Keeper of the said Common Gaol, to receive the said C. D. into your custody in the said Common Gaol, there to imprison him (and keep him at hard labour) for the space of , unless the said sum, and all the costs and charges of the said distress (and of the commitment and conveying of the said C. D. to the said Common Gaol, amounting to the further sum of), shall be sooner paid up unto you the said Keeper; and for your so doing, this shall be your sufficient warrant.

Given under my hand and seal, this day of , in the year of our Lord , at , in the District (*or* County, *or as the case may be*) aforesaid.

J. S. [L. S.]

(R) *See* s. 75.

CERTIFICATE OF CLERK OF THE PEACE THAT THE COSTS OF AN APPEAL ARE NOT PAID.

Office of the Clerk of the Peace for the District (*or* County, United Counties, *or as the case may be*) of

TITLE OF THE APPEAL.

I hereby certify that at a Court of General *or* Quarter Sessions of the Peace (*or other Court discharging the functions of the Court of General or Quarter Sessions, as the case may be*), holden at , in and for the said District (*or* County, United Counties, *or as the case may be*) on last past, an appeal by A.B. against a conviction (*or* order) of J.S., Esquire, one of Her Majesty's Justices of the Peace in and for the said District (*or* County, United Counties, *or as the case may be*), came on to be tried, and was there heard and determined, and the said Court of General *or* Quarter Sessions (*or other Court, as the case may be*), thereupon ordered that the said conviction (*or* order) should be confirmed (*or* quashed), and that the said (*Appellant*) should pay to the said (*Respondent*) the sum of for his costs incurred by him in the said appeal, and which sum was thereby ordered to be paid to the Clerk of the Peace for the said District (*or* County, United Counties, *or as the case may be*), on or before tho day of instant, to be by him handed over to the said (*Respondent*), and I further certify that the said sum for costs has not, nor has any part thereof, been paid in obedience to the said order.

Dated this day of , one thousand eight hundred and

G. H.
Clerk of the Peace.

(S 1) *See* s. 75.

WARRANT OF DISTRESS FOR COSTS OF AN APPEAL AGAINST A CONVICTION OR ORDER.

Canada,
Province of ,
District (*or* County,
United Counties, *or*
as the case may be),
of

To all or any of the Constables or other Peace Officers in the said District (*or* County, United Counties, *or as the case may be*) of

Whereas (*&c., as in the warrants of distress, N°* 1, 2, *ante, and to the end of* *the statement of the Conviction or Order, and then thus*): And whereas the said A. B. appealed to the Court of General Quarter Sessions of the Peace (*or other Court discharging the functions of the Court of General or Quarter Sessions, as the case may be*) for the said District (*or* County, United Counties, *or as the case may be*), against the said Conviction or Order, in which appeal the said A. B. was the Appellant, and the said C. D. (*or* J. S., Esquire, the Justice of the Peace who made the said Conviction *or* Order) was the Respondent, and which said appeal came on to be tried, and was heard and determined at the last General Quarter Sessions of the Peace (*or other Court, as the case may be*), for the said District (*or* County, United Counties, *or as the case may be*), holden at , on , and the said Court thereupon ordered that the said conviction (*or* Order), should be confirmed (*or* quashed), and that the said (*Appellant*) should pay to the said (*Respondent*) the sum of for his costs incurred by him in the said appeal, which said sum was to be paid to the Clerk of the Peace for the said District (*or* County, United Counties, *or as the case may be*), on or before the day of , one thousand eight hundred and , to be by him handed over to the said C. D.; and whereas the Clerk of the Peace of the said District (*or* County, United Counties, *or as the case may be*), hath, on the day of instant, duly certified that the said sum for costs had not been paid;* These are therefore to command you, in Her Majesty's name, forthwith to make distress of the goods and chattels of the said A.B., and if within the space of . days next after the making of such distress, the said last-mentioned sum, together with the reasonable charges of taking and keeping the said distress, shall not be paid, that then you do sell the said goods and chattels so by you distrained, and do pay the money arising from such sale to the Clerk of the Peace for the said District (*or* County, United Counties, *or as the case may be*) of , that he may pay and apply the same as by law directed; and if no such distress can be found, then that you certify the same unto me or any other Justice of the Peace for the same District (*or* County, United Counties, *or as the case may be*), to the end that such proceedings may be had therein as to law doth appertain.

Given under my Hand and Seal, this day of , in the year of Our Lord , at , in the District (*or* County, *or as the case may be*), aforesaid.

O. K. [L.S.]

(S 2) *See* s. 75.

WARRANT OF COMMITMENT FOR WANT OF DISTRESS IN THE LAST CASE.

Canada,
Province of
District (*or* County,
United Counties, *or*
as the case may be)
of

To all or any of the Constables, or other Peace Officers, in the said District [*or* County, United Counties, *or as the case may be*] of and to the Keeper of the Common Gaol of the said District [*or* County, United Counties, *or as the case may be*] of , at , in the said County of :

Whereas [*&c, as in the last form to the asterisk,* * *and then thus:* And whereas, afterwards, on the day of , in the year aforesaid, I, the undersigned, issued a warrant to all or any of the Constables and other Peace Officers in the said District [*or* County, United Counties, *or as the case may be*] of , commanding them, or any of them, to levy the said sum of , for costs, by distress and sale of the goods and chattels of the said A. B.; And whereas it appears to me, as well by the return to the said Warrant of Distress to the Constable [*or* Peace Officer], who was charged with the execution of the same, as otherwise, that the said Constable hath made diligent search for the goods and chattels of the said A. B., but that no sufficient distress whereon to levy the said sum above mentioned could be found; These are therefore to command you, the said Constables or Peace Officers, or any one of you, to take the said A. B., and him safely to convey to the Common Gaol of the said District (*or* County, United Counties of *as the case may be*], at aforesaid, and there deliver him to the said keeper thereof, together with this Precept; and I do hereby command you, the said Keeper of the said Common Gaol, to receive the said A. B. into your custody in the said Common Gaol, there to imprison him [*and keep him at hard labour*] for the space of , unless the same sum and all costs and charges of the said distress [and for the commitment and conveying of the said A. B. to the said Common Gaol, amounting to the further sum of ,] shall be sooner paid unto you, the said Keeper, and for so doing, this shall be your sufficient warrant.

Given under my hand and seal, this day of , in the year of Our Lord , at , in the District [*County, United Counties, or as the case may be,*] afoesaid.

J. N. [L. S.]

(T.)

GENERAL FORM OF INFORMATION OR OF COMPLAINT ON OATH.

Canada,
Province of ,
District *(or* County,
United Counties, *or*
as the case may be,)
of

The information [*or* complaint] of C. D., of the Township of in the said District [*or* County, United Counties, *or as the case may be,*] of [*labourer*]. [*If preferred by an Attorney or Agent, say:*] "D. E.] his duly authorized Agent [*or Attorney*], in this behalf, taken upon oath, before me, the undersigned, one of Her Majesty's Justices of the Peace, in and for the said District [*or* County, United Counties, *or as the case may be*] of , at N., in the said District [County, *or as the case may be*], of this day of , in the year of our Lord, one thousand eight hundred and , who saith* that [he hath just cause to suspect and believe, and doth suspect and believe that] A. B., of the [*township*] of , in the said District [*or* County, *as the case may be*] of , within the space of , [*the time within which the information* [*or complaint*] *must be laid*] last past, to wit, on the day of instant, at the [*township*] of in the District [*County, or as the case may be*] aforesaid, did [*here set out the offence &c.,*] contrary to the form of Statute in such case made and provided.

C. D. [*or* D. E.]

Taken and sworn before me, the day and year and at the place above mentioned.

J. S.

FORM OF ORDER OF DISMISSAL OF AN INFORMATION OR COMPLAINT.

Canada,
Province of ,
District (*or* County,
United Counties, *or*
as the case may be,)
of

Be it remembered, that on , information was laid (*or* complaint was made) before the undersigned, (*one*) of Her Majesty's Justices of the Peace in and for the said District, (*or* County, United Counties, *or as the case may be*) of , for that (*&c., as in the Summons of the Defendant*) and now at this day, to wit, on , at , (*if at any adjournment insert here :*) "To which day the hearing of this case hath been duly adjourned, of which the said C. D. had due notice," both the said parties appear before me in order that I should hear and determine the said information, (*or* complaint) (or the said A. B. appeareth before me, but the said C. D., although duly called, doth not appear) ; whereupon the matter of the said information (*or* complaint) being by me duly considered,(it manifestly appears to me that the said information (*or* complaint) is not proved, and (*If the Informant* (*or Complainant*) *do not appear these words may be omitted*) I do therefore dismiss the same, and do adjudge that the said C. D. do pay to the said A. B. the sum of for his costs incurred by him in defence in his behalf ; and if the said sum for costs be not paid forthwith (*or* on or before), I order that the same be levied by distress and sale of the goods and chattels of the said C. D. and in default of sufficient distress in that behalf, I adjudge the said C. D. to be imprisoned in the Common Gaol of the said District (or County, United Counties, *as the case may be*) of at in the said (*County*) of (*and there kept at hard labour* for the space of , unless the said sum for costs, and all costs and charges of the said distress (and of the commitment and conveying of the said C. D. to the said Common Gaol) shall be sooner paid.

Given under my Hand and Seal, this day of in the year of our Lord, at in the District (*or* County, *or as the case may be*) aforesaid.

J. S. [L. S.]

FORM OF CERTIFICATE OF DISMISSAL.

I hereby certify, that an information (*or* complaint) preferred by C. D. against A. B. for that (*&c., as in the Summons*) was this day considered by me, one of Her Majesty's Justices of the Peace in and for the said District (*or* County, United Counties, *or as the case may be*) of , and was by me dismissed (with costs).

Dated this day of , one thousand

J. S.

GENERAL FORM OF NOTICE OF APPEAL AGAINST A CONVICTION OR ORDER.

To C. D. of, &c., and (*the names and additions of the parties to whom the notice of appeal is required to be given.*)

Take notice, that I, the undersigned A. B., of &c., do intend to enter and prosecute an appeal at the next General Quarter Sessions of the Peace, (*or other Court, as the case may be,*) to be holden at , in and for the District (*or* County, United Counties, *or as the case may be,*) of , against a certain conviction (or order) bearing date on or about the day of instant, and made by (you) C. D., Esquire, (*one*) of Her Majesty's Justices of the Peace for the said District (*or* County, United Counties, *or as the case may be,*) of , whereby the said A. B. was convicted of having (or was ordered to pay (*here state the offence as in the conviction, information or summons, or the amount adjudged to be paid as in the order, as correctly as possible.*

Dated this day of , one thousand eight hundred and

A. B.

MEM.—*If this notice be given by several Defendants, or by an Attorney, it can easily be adapted, 33 Vic., chap. 27, s. 4.*

FORM OF RECOGNIZANCE TO TRY THE APPEAL, &C.

Be it remembered, that on , A. B. of (*labourer,*) and L. M., of (*grocer*) and N. O., of (*yeoman,*) personally came before the undersigned, (*one*) of Her Majesty's Justices of the Peace in and for the said District (*or* County, United Counties, *or as the case may be,*) of , and severally acknowledged themselves to owe to our Sovereign Lady the Queen, the several sums following, that is to say, the said A. B. the sum of , and the said L: M. and N. O. the sum of , each, of good and lawful money of Canada, to be made and levied of their several goods and chattels, lands and tenements respectively, to the use of our said Lady the Queen, Her Heirs and Successors, if he the said A.B. shall fail in the condition endorsed:

Taken and acknowledged the day and year first mentioned at , before me

J. S.

The condition of the within written Recognizance is such, that if the said A. B. shall at the (*next*) General or Quarter Sessions of the Peace (*or other Court discharging the functions of the Court of General or Quarter Sessions, as the case may be*) to be holden at , on the day of next, in and for the said District (*or* County, United Counties, *or as the case may be,*) of , enter and prosecute an appeal against a certain conviction bearing date the day of instant, and made by (me) the said Justice, whereby he the said A. B. was convicted, for that he the said A. B. did on the day of , at the township of , in the said District (*or* County, United Counties, *or as the case may be,*) of , *(here set out the offence as stated in the conviction)* ; And further, that if the said A. B. shall abide by and duly perform the order of the Court to be made upon the trial of such appeal, then the said Recognizance to be void, or else to remain in full force and virtue.

FORM OF NOTICE OF SUCH RECOGNIZANCE TO BE GIVEN TO THE DEFENDANT (APPELLANT) AND HIS SURETIES.

Take notice, that you A. B. are bound in the sum of , and you, L. M., and N. O. in the sum of each, that you the said A. B., at the next General or Quarter Sessions of the Peace to be holden at , in and for the said District (*or* County, United Counties, *or as the case may be,*) of , enter and prosecute an Appeal against a conviction (*or* order) dated the day of (*instant,*) whereby you, A. B., were convicted of (*or* order, &c.,) *stating offence or the subject of the order shortly*), and abide by and perform the Order of the Court to be made upon the trial of such Appeal ; and unless you, the said A. B., prosecute such Appeal accordingly, the Recognizance entered into by you will forthwith be levied on you, and each of you.

Dated this day of one thousand eight hundred and

SURETIES.

COMPLAINT BY THE PARTY THREATENED, FOR SURETIES FOR THE PEACE.

Proceed as in the Form (T) *to the asterisk* *, *then :* that A. B. of the (*Township*) of , in the District (County, *or as the case may be*) of , did, on the day of (instant or last past, *as the case may be*), threaten the said C. D. in the words or to the effect following, that is to say, (*set them out, with the circumstances under which they were used :*) and that from the above and other threats used by the said A. B. towards the said C. D., he the said C. D. is afraid that the said A. B. will do him some bodily injury, and therefore prays that the said A. B. may be required to find sufficient Sureties to keep the peace and be of good behaviour towards him the said C. D.; and the said C. D. also saith that he doth not make this complaint against nor require such Sureties from the said A. B. from any malice or illwill, but merely for the preservation of his person from injury.

FORM OF RECOGNIZANCE FOR THE SESSIONS.

Be it remembered, that on the day of , in the year of our Lord , A. B. of (*labourer*), L. M. of (*grocer*), and N. O. of (*butcher*), personally came before (*us*) the undersigned, (*two*) of Her Majesty's Justices of the Peace for the said District (*or* County, United Counties, *or as the case may be*,) of and severally acknowledged themselves to owe to our Lady the Queen the several sums following, that is to say : the said A. B. the sum of , and the said L. M. and N. O. the sum of , each, of good and lawful money of Canada, to be made and levied of their goods and chattels, lands and tenements respectively, to the use of our said Lady the Queen, Her Heirs and Successors, if he the said A. B. fail in the condition endorsed.

Taken and acknowledged the day and year first above mentioned, at , before us.

J. S.
J. T.

The condition of the within written Recognizance is such, that if the within bounded A. B. (of, &c.,) shall appear at the next Court of General or Quarter Sessions of the Peace (*or other Court discharging the functions of the Court of General Quarter Sessions, as the case may be*,) to be holden in and for the said District (*or* County, United Counties, *or as the case may be*) of , to do and receive what shall be then and there enjoined him by the Court, and in the meantime shall keep the peace and be of good behaviour towards Her Majesty and all Her liege people, and specially towards C. D. (of &c.) for the term of now next ensuing, then the said Recognizance to be void, or else to stand in full force and virtue.

FORM OF COMMITMENT IN DEFAULT OF SURETIES.

Canada,
Province of
District (*or* County,
United Counties, *or as the case may be*),
of

To all or any of the Constables or other Peace officers in the District (*or* County) (*or* one of the United Counties, *or as the case may be*) of and to the Keeper of the Common Gaol of the said District, (County *or* United Counties, *or as the case may be*) at , in the said District (or County, &c.,)

Whereas on the day of instant, complaint on oath

was made before the undersigned *(or* J. L., Esquire,*)* (*one*) of Her Majesty's Justices of the Peace in and for the said District *(or* County, United Counties, *or as the case may be)* of , by C. D. of the township of in the said District (County, *or as the case may be*) *(labourer,)* that A. B. of, &c., on the day of , at the township of aforesaid, did threaten (*&c., follow to end of complaint, as in form above, in the past tense, then*) : And whereas the said A. B. was this day brought and appeared before the said Justice (*or* J. L., Esquire, one of Her Majesty's Justices of the Peace in and for the said District *(or* County, United Counties, *or as the case may be)* of , to answer unto the said complaint : And * having been required by me to enter into his own Recognizance in the sum of with two sufficient sureties in the sum of each, as well for his appearance at the next General or Quarter Sessions of the Peace, (*or other Court discharging the functions of the Court of General or Quarter Sessions, as the case may be*,) to be held in and for the said District (*or* County, United Counties, *or as the case may be*,) of , to do what shall be then and there enjoined him by the Court, as also in the meantime to keep the Peace and be of good behaviour towards Her Majesty and Her liege people, and especially towards the said C. D., hath refused and neglected, and still refuses and neglects to find such sureties) ; These are therefore to command you and each of you to take the said A. B., and him safely to convey to the (*Common Gaol*) at aforesaid, and there to deliver him to the Keeper thereof, together with this Precept ; And I do hereby command you the said Keeper of the (*Common Gaol*) to receive the said A. B. into your custody, in the said (*Common Gaol*,) there to imprison him until the said next General or Quarter Sessions of the Peace (or the next term or sitting of the said Court discharging the functions of the Court of General or Quarter Sessions, (*as the case may be*,) unless he in the meantime find sufficient sureties as well for his appearance at the said Sessions (*or Court*) as in the meantime to keep the Peace as aforesaid.

Given under (*my*) Hand and Seal, this day of , in the year of Our Lord , at , in the District (*or* County, *or as the case may be*) aforesaid.

J. S. [L.S.]

---

32 & 33 VIC., CHAP. XXXII.

An Act respecting the prompt and summary administration of Criminal Justice in certain cases.

[*Assented to 22nd June*, 1869.]

HER MAJESTY, by and with the advice and consent of the Senate and House of Commons of Canada, enacts as follows :

1. In this Act the expression "a competent Magistrate" shall, as respects the Province of Quebec and the Province of Ontario, mean and include any Recorder, Judge of a County Court, being a Justice of the Peace, Commissioner of Police, Judge of the Sessions of the Peace, Police Magistrate, District Magistrate or other functionary or tribunal invested at the time of the passing of this Act with the powers vested in a Recorder by chapter one hundred and five of the Consolidated Statutes of Canada, intituled "*An Act respecting the prompt and summary administration of Criminal Justice in certain cases*," and acting within the local limits of his or of its jurisdiction, and any functionary or tribunal invested by the proper legislative authority with power to do alone such acts as are usually required to be done by two or more Justices of the Peace ; and as respects the Province of Nova Scotia or the Province of New Brunswick, the said expression shall mean and include a Commissioner of Police and any functionary, tribunal or person invested or to be invested by the proper legislative authority with power to do alone such acts as are usually required to be done by two or more Justices of the Peace, and the expression, "the Magistrate" shall mean a competent Magistrate as above defined.

The 37 Vic., chap. 40, provides that the expression, "a competent magistrate" in the Act shall, as respects the Province of Nova Scotia, or the Province of New Brunswick, mean and include any Recorder, Judge of the County Court, Stipendiary Magistrate, or Police Magistrate acting within the local limits of his jurisdiction, as well as any functionary included by the said expression as respects either of the said Provinces, under the terms of the said Act, and the expression, "the magistrate" in the said Act shall, as respects either of the said Provinces, mean a competent magistrate as above defined, and the said Act shall, from and after the passing of this Act, be construed and have effect accordingly. In applying this Act to British Columbia, or to the District of Keewatin, or to Prince Edward Island, the expression " competent magistrate " shall be construed as meaning any two Justices of the Peace sitting together, as well as any functionary or tribunal having the powers of two Justices of the Peace, and the jurisdiction shall be absolute, without the consent of the parties charged. See 37 Vic., chap. 42, sched. A., and 39 Vic., chap. 21 ; also 40 Vic., chap. 4.

With regard to the Province of Manitoba, the expression " a competent magistrate," and the expression " the magistrate " shall have the same meaning and include the like functionaries and tribunals as with respect to the Provinces of Quebec and Ontario. 37 Vic., chap. 39, s. 3.

And the expression " the Common Gaol or other place of confinement," shall in the case of any offender whose age at the time of his conviction does not in the opinion of the Magistrate exceed sixteen years, include any Reformatory Prison provided for the reception of juvenile offenders in the Province in which the conviction referred to takes place, and to which by the law of that Province the offender can be sent.

In Manitoba the above expression has the same meaning as in the other Provinces mentioned in the Act. 37 Vic., chap. 39, s. 3.

This Act was extended to Manitoba by the 37 Vic., chap. 39 ; to Prince Edward Island by the 40 Vic., chap. 4.; to the District of Keewatin by the 39 Vic., chap. 21 ; and to British Columbia by the 37 Vic., chap. 42.

Violations of the Act making provision against the improper use of fire arms (40 Vic., chap. 30) are to be tried and dealt with according to the provisions of this Act. See 40 Vic., chap. 30, s. 5 ; also 32 & 33 Vic., chap. 20, ss. 74, 75, 76.

This Act also applies to the offence of a person playing or looking on while any other person is playing in a common gaming house. See 40 Vic., chap. 33, ss. 4 & 5.

2. Where any person is charged before a competent Magistrate with having committed—

1. Simple larceny, larceny from the person, embezzlement, or obtaining

money or property by false pretences, or feloniously receiving stolen property, and the value of the whole of the property alleged to have been stolen, embezzled, obtained, or received does not in the judgment of the Magistrate exceed ten dollars ; or

2. With having attempted to commit larceny from the person or simple larceny ; or,

3. With having committed an aggravated assault, by unlawfully and maliciously inflicting upon any other person, either with or without a weapon or instrument, any grievous bodily harm, or by unlawfully and maliciously cutting, stabbing or wounding any other person ; or,

4. With having committed an assault upon any female whatever, or upon any male child whose age does not in the opinion of the Magistrate exceed fourteen years, such assault being of a nature which cannot in the opinion of the Magistrate be sufficiently punished by a summary conviction before him under any other Act, and such assault, if upon a female, not amounting in his opinion to an assault with intent to commit a rape ; or,

5. With having assaulted, obstructed, molested or hindered any magistrate, bailiff, or constable, or officer of customs or excise or other officer in the lawful performance of his duty, or with intent to prevent the performance thereof ; or,

6. With keeping or being an inmate, or habitual frequenter of any disorderly house, house of ill-fame or bawdy house ;

7. With having committed a misdemeanor under the Act passed in the fortieth year of Her Majesty's reign, intituled, "An Act for the repression of betting and pool selling." 40 Vic., chap. 31, s. 3.

The Magistrate may, subject to the provisions hereinafter made, hear and determine the charge in a summary way.

The prisoner was convicted by the Police Magistrate for the City of Toronto, for that she "did on," etc., "at the said City of Toronto, keep a common, disorderly, bawdy-house on Queen Street, in the said city," etc., and committed to Gaol at hard labour for six months. A *habeas corpus* and *certiorari* issued; in return, to which the commitment, conviction, information, and depositions, were brought up. On application for her discharge, no motion being made to quash the conviction, it was held,—

(1) No objection that the commitment stated the offence to have been committed on the 11th August instead of the 10th, as

in the conviction the variance not being material to the merits, and the Court not being able to go behind the return and commitment which was set forth.

(2) Nor that the commitment charged that the prisoner "was the keeper of," and the conviction that "she did keep," both differing from the statute which designates the offence as "keeping any disorderly house," etc.; for it would seem the Court could not go behind the commitment, and all these expressions conveyed but one idea.

(3) Nor that the commitment did not show that the offence was committed within the "police limits" of the city, the words used in the Act; for the limits of the City of Toronto were assigned by a public statute and the Municipal Institutions Act, creating the Police Court and Magistrate, and the whole body of police, contained nothing to show that there were any police limits differing from the ordinary city limits.

(4) Nor that the commitment did not follow the form of conviction given in the statute, in showing that the party was charged before the convicting magistrate, *i.e.*, charged as the statute required, namely, put upon her trial and asked whether she was guilty or not guilty, nor whether she pleaded to the charge or confessed it. It might, and probably would be, a defect in the conviction, if it did not pursue the statutory form in shewing that the party was charged, more especially as by the second section of the Act the jurisdiction is made to depend upon the fact of the party being charged before the convicting Justice. That point, however, was not decided; the Court merely intimating that it might or might not be a defect in the conviction. Unless the commitment must contain all that the conviction does or ought to contain, it is unnecessary to state the information in it; and more especially as by the form given by the statute it does not appear necessary that the information should be set out in the conviction.

(5) Nor that the conviction was not sustained by the information, the latter being that defendant was the keeper of a well-known disorderly house; and the former that the prisoner did keep a common, disorderly bawdy-house, for the commitment would not be void on the face of it because of a variance between the original

information and the conviction made after hearing evidence. But if the prisoner had been charged with the information, and on being called on to answer had confessed the information, and then had been convicted of matter not contained in the information, no doubt the conviction could be quashed; but even in that case while it stood unreversed it would warrant a commitment following its terms.

(6) Nor that no notice had been put up as required by s. 26 of the same Act, to show that the Court was that of a Police Magistrate, not of an ordinary Justice of the Peace; for the jurisdiction, in the absence of express enactment, could not be made to depend on the omission of the Clerk to post up such notice.

(7) Nor that the evidence was unsatisfactory and insufficient to warrant the conviction; for when a proper commitment is returned to a *Habeas Corpus*, and there was evidence, the Court will never enter into the question whether the magistrate has drawn the right conclusion from it.

(8) Nor that the offence of " keeping a common disorderly bawdy-house," was not sufficiently certain; for the legal meaning of the last two words is clear, and a house will not be less a public nuisance because it is found to be disorderly as well as bawdy; and if keeping a disorderly house be no offence the term becomes mere surplusage, and would not vitiate an otherwise sufficient statement. But the statute does give jurisdiction over persons charged with keeping any disorderly house, house of ill-fame, or bawdy-house. *R* v. *Munro*, 24 Q.B. (Ont.), 44.

It is to be observed that the jurisdiction of the magistrate in cases of this kind is absolute, and does not depend on the consent of the party charged to be tried by such magistrate. See section 15.

A conviction under this statute for keeping a house of ill fame, or being an inmate of such a house, adjudicating that the accused should pay a fine of $50 forthwith, and be imprisoned for three months unless the fine be sooner paid, is not warranted by section 17 of the statute, for imprisonment is only authorized by the Act when it has been awarded as a substantive punishment. *Re Slater*, 9 U. C., L. J., 21.

It would seem that though a magistrate may have a general

jurisdiction to hear any complaint against a disorderly inn or house, he has no right to issue a warrant to arrest a casual guest visiting a licensed tavern as a guest at a time subsequent to the charge, and in no way present at or assisting in any disturbance or disorder. *Cleland* v. *Robinson*, 11 C. P. (Ont.), 421.

The owner of a house letting it to several young women for the purpose of prostitution cannot be indicted for keeping a disorderly house. *R.* v. *Stannard*, 9 Cox. C. C., 405 ; *R.* v. *Barrett*, (*ib.*), 255.

It is not necessary that the disorderly conduct should be visible from the exterior of the house. *R.* v. *Rice*, L. R., 1 C. C. R., 21. See also vagrancy, *post*.

In case any person is charged in Ontario before a Police Magistrate or before a Stipendiary Magistrate, in any County, District or Provisional County in Ontario, with having committed any offence for which he may be tried at a Court of General Sessions of the Peace, or in case any person is committed to a gaol in the County, District or Provisional County, under the the warrant of any Justice of the Peace for trial on a charge of being guilty of any such offence, such person may, with his own consent, be tried before such magistrate, and may, if found guilty, be sentenced by the magistrate to the same punishment as he would have been liable to if he had been tried before the Court of General Sessions. 38 Vic., chap. 47, s. 1.

The proceedings upon and subsequent to such trial, shall be as nearly as may be the same as upon a trial under the Act of the Parliament of Canada, passed in the Session held in the thirty-second and thirty-third years of Her Majesty's reign, intituled, "An Act respecting the prompt and summary Administration of Criminal Justice in certain cases." *Ib.* s. 2.

Every conviction under this Act shall have the same effect as a conviction upon indictment for the same offence would have had, save that no conviction under this Act shall be attended with forfeiture beyond the penalty (if any) imposed in the case. *Ib.* s. 3.

Every person who obtains a certificate of dismissal, or is convicted under this Act, shall be released from all further or other criminal proceedings for the same cause. *Ib.* s. 4.

No conviction, sentence, or proceeding under this Act shall be quashed for want of form ; and no warrant of commitment upon a conviction shall be held void by reason of any defect therein, if it be therein alleged that the offender has been convicted, and there be a good and valid conviction to sus tain the same. *Ib.* s. 5.

If any person has under this Act or under the said Act passed in the session held in the thirty-second and thirty-third years of Her Majesty's reign, chaptered thirty-two, or under any other Act giving such election, been asked to elect whether he should be tried by the magistrate or before a jury, and has elected to be tried before a jury, then in case such election is stated in the warrant of committal for trial, or upon the depositions, the Sheriff or the County Judge or junior or Deputy Judge, shall not be required to take the proceedings directed by the Act passed in the said session, and chaptered thirty-five, intituled, " An Act for the more speedy trial in certain cases of persons charged with Felonies and Misdemeanors in the Provinces of Ontario and Quebec," and in all such cases it shall be the duty of the committing magistrate to state in the warrant the fact of such election having been made. *Ib.* s. 6.

If the magistrate is of opinion from any circumstances appearing in the case that the charge cannot be properly disposed of before him, he may at any time before the person charged has made his defence, decide not to adjudicate summarily thereon, and may thereupon deal with the same as if this Act had not been passed; and in such case such prisoner may be afterwards tried summarily by his own consent at the County Judge's Criminal Court. *Ib.* s. 7.

3. Whenever the magistrate before whom any person is charged as aforesaid, proposes to dispose of the case summarily under the provisions of this Act, such magistrate, after ascertaining the nature and extent of the charge, but before the formal examination of the witnesses for the prosecution, and before calling on the party charged for any statement which he may wish to make, shall state to such person the substance of the charge against him, and (if the charge is not one that can be tried summarily without the consent of the accused) shall then say to him, these words, or words to the like effect: " Do you consent that the charge against you shall be tried by me, or do you desire that it shall be sent for trial by a jury at the (*naming the Court at which it could soonest be tried*);" and if the person charged consents to the charge being summarily tried and determined as aforesaid, or if the power of the magistrate to try it does not depend on the consent of the accused, the magistrate shall reduce the charge into writing, and read the same to such person, and shall then ask him whether he is guilty or not of such charge.

See sections 15 and 16 as to the cases in which consent is not necessary.

4. If the person charged confesses the charge, the magistrate shall then proceed to pass such sentence upon him as may by law be passed (subject to the provisions of this Act,) in respect to such offence; but if the person charged says that he is not guilty, the magistrate shall then examine the

witnesses for the prosecution, and when the examination has been completed, the magistrate shall inquire of the person charged whether he has any defence to make to such charge, and if he states that he has a defence, the magistrate shall hear such defence, and shall then proceed to dispose of the case summarily.

Under this Act, the magistrate may, before any formal examination of witnesses, ascertain the nature and extent of the charge, and if the party consents to be tried summarily, may reduce it into writing. It would seem that the magistrate may then (that is when a person is charged before him prior to the formal examination of witnesses) reduce the charge into writing, and try the party upon the charge thus reduced to writing, and if this is the meaning of the statute, it would not signify whether the original information and warrant to apprehend did or did not state a charge in the precise language of the Act. But the magistrate must either, by the original information, or by the charge which he makes when the party is before him, have the charge in writing, and must read it to the prisoner, and ask him whether he is guilty or not. It appeared on an application for a *habeas corpus*, that the information laid before a police magistrate, and warrant to apprehend, were for an assault and beating, but it was disputed whether upon the examination and trial this was all the charge made, or whether he was not then charged with an aggravated assault under Con. Stat. Can., chap. 105, s. 1, s.-s. 4, and whether when he pleaded guilty, he did so under the former or latter charge. The information seemed to be laid under Con. Stat. Can., chap. 91, ss. 37, 38, for an assault and beating, while the conviction purported to be under Con. Stat. Can., chap. 105, and imposed the punishment prescribed by the latter statute.

Numerous contradictory affidavits were filed, the Justice alleging that the defendant was charged with an aggravated assault, and, with full knowledge of the fact, consented to the charge being summarily disposed of by the Justice according to the statute, while the defendant contradicted this and alleged that he would not have pleaded guilty if he had known the charge was of aggravated assault. Four several warrants of commitment were in the gaoler's hands, upon one at least of which the prisoner was detained in custody. They were all for the same offence, one having been from time to time substituted for the other. It was held that a charge of an assault and beating is not a charge of aggravated assault, and a complaint of the former will not sustain a conviction of the latter under the statute, though when the party is before the magistrate, the charge of aggravated assault may be made in writing and followed by a conviction therefor. *Re McKinnon*, 2 U. C. L. J., N. S., 327.

5. In the case of larceny, feloniously receiving stolen property or attempt to commit larceny from the person, or simple larceny, charged under the first or second sub-sections of the second section of this Act, if the Magistrate after hearing the whole case for the prosecution and for the defence, finds the charge proved, then he shall convict the person charged and commit him to the Common Gaol or other place of confinement, there to be imprisoned, with or without hard labour, for any period not exceeding six months.

6. If in any case the Magistrate finds the offence not proved, he shall dismiss the charge, and make out and deliver to the person charged a certificate under his hand stating the fact of such dismissal.

7. Every such conviction and certificate respectively may be in the forms A and B, in this Act, or to the like effect.

8. If (when his consent is necessary) the person charged does not consent to have the case heard and determined by the Magistrate, or in any case if it appears to the Magistrate that the offence is one which, owing to a previous conviction of the person charged, or from any other circumstance, ought to be made the subject of prosecution by indictment rather than to be disposed of summarily, such Magistrate shall deal with the case in all respects as if this Act had not been passed ; but a previous conviction shall not prevent the Magistrate from trying the offender summarily, if he thinks fit so to do.

9. If upon the hearing of the charge the Magistrate is of opinion that there are circumstances in the case which render it inexpedient to inflict any punishment, he may dismiss the person charged without proceeding to a conviction.

10. Where any person is charged before a competent Magistrate with simple larceny, or with having obtained property by false pretences, or with having embezzled or having feloniously received stolen property, or with committing larceny from the person, or with larceny as a clerk or servant, and the value of the property stolen, obtained, embezzled, or received exceeds ten dollars, and the evidence in support of the prosecution is in the opinion of the Magistrate sufficient to put the person on his trial for the offence charged, such

Magistrate, if the case appear to him to be one which may properly be disposed of in a summary way, and may be adequately punished by virtue of the powers of this Act, shall reduce the charge into writing and shall read it to the said person, and (unless such person is one who can be tried summarily without his consent) shall then put to him the question mentioned in section three, and shall explain to him that he is not obliged to plead or answer before such Magistrate at all; and that if he do not plead or answer before him, he will be committed for trial in the usual course.

11. If the person so charged consents to be tried by the Magistrate, the Magistrate shall then ask him whether he is guilty or not of the charge, and if such person says that he is guilty, the Magistrate shall thereupon cause a plea of guilty to be entered upon the proceedings, and shall convict him of the offence, and commit him to the Common Gaol or other place of confinement, there to be imprisoned, with or without hard labour, for any term not exceeding twelve months, and every such conviction may be in the form C, or to the like effect.

12. In every case of summary proceedings under this Act, the person accused shall be allowed to make his full answer and defence, and to have all witnesses examined and cross-examined, by counsel or attorney.

13. The Magistrate before whom any person is charged under this Act, may by summons require the attendance of any person as a witness upon the hearing of the case at a time and place to be named in such summons, and such Magistrate may bind by recognizance all persons whom he may consider necessary to be examined touching the matter of such charge, to attend at the time and place to be appointed by him, and then and there to give evidence upon the hearing of such charge; and in case any person so summoned or required or bound as aforesaid, neglects or refuses to attend in pursuance of such summons or recognizance, then upon proof being first made of such person's having been duly summoned as hereinafter mentioned, or bound by recognizance as aforesaid, the Magistrate before whom such person ought to have attended may issue a warrant to compel his appearance as a witness.

14. Every summons issued under this Act may be served by delivering a copy of the summons to the party summoned, or by delivering a copy of the summons to some inmate of such party's usual place of abode; and every person so required by any writing under the hand of any competent Magistrate to attend and give evidence as aforesaid, shall be deemed to have been duly summoned.

15. The jurisdiction of the Magistrate in the case of any person charged within the Police limits of any City in Canada, with therein keeping or being an inmate or an habitual frequenter of any disorderly house, house of ill-

fame or bawdy house, shall be absolute, and shall not depend on the consent of the party charged to be tried by such Magistrate, nor shall such party be asked whether he consents to be so tried ; nor shall this Act affect the absolute summary jurisdiction given to any Justice or Justices of the Peace in any case, by any other Act.

16. The jurisdiction of the Magistrate shall also be absolute in the case of any person, being a sea-faring person and only transiently in Canada, and having no permanent domicile therein, charged, either within the City of Quebec as limited for the purpose of the Police Ordinance, or within the City of Montreal as so limited, or in any other Seaport, City or Town in Canada, where there is a competent Magistrate, with the commission therein of any of the offences mentioned in the second section of this Act, and also in the case of any other person charged with any such offence on the complaint of any such sea-faring person whose testimony is essential to the proof of the offence, and such jurisdiction shall not depend on the consent of any such party to be tried by the Magistrate, nor shall such party be asked whether he consents to be so tried.

17. In any case summarily tried under the third, fourth, fifth, or sixth sub-section of the second section of this Act, if the Magistrate finds the charge proved, he may convict the person charged and commit him to the Common Gaol or other place of confinement, there to be imprisoned with or without hard labour for any period not exceeding six months, or may condemn him to pay a fine not exceeding, with the costs in the case, one hundred dollars, or to both fine and imprisonment, not exceeding the said period and sum ; and such fine may be levied by Warrant of Distress under the hand and seal of the Magistrate, or the party convicted may be condemned (in addition to any other imprisonment on the same conviction) to be committed to the Common Gaol or other place of confinement, for a further period not exceeding six months, unless such fine be sooner paid.

In Prince Edward Island, fines collected under this Act are to be paid over to the Provincial Secretary and Treasurer, 40 Vic., chap. 4, s. 8.

18. Whenever the nature of the case requires it, the forms given at the end of this Act shall be altered by omitting the words stating the consent of the party to be tried before the Magistrate, and by adding the requisite words stating the fine imposed (if any) and the imprisonment (if any) to which the party convicted is to be subjected if the fine be not sooner paid.

19. Where any person is charged before any Justice or Justices of the Peace, with any offence mentioned in this Act, and in the opinion of such Justice or Justices, the case is proper to be disposed of by a competent Ma-

gistrate, as herein provided, the Justice or Justices before whom such person is so charged may, if he or they see fit, remand such person for further examination before the nearest competent Magistrate, in like manner in all respects as a Justice or Justices are authorized to remand a party accused for trial at any Court, under any general Act respecting the duties of Justices of the Peace out of Sessions, in like cases.

20. No Justice or Justices of the Peace in any Province shall so remand any person for further examination or trial before any such Magistrate in any other Province.

21. Any person so remanded for further examination before a competent Magistrate in any City may be examined and dealt with by any other competent Magistrate in the same City.

22. If any person suffered to go at large upon entering into such Recognizance as the Justice or Justices are authorized under any such Act as last mentioned to take, on the remand of a party accused, conditioned for his appearance before a competent Magistrate under the preceding sections of this Act, does not afterwards appear pursuant to such Recognizance, then the Magistrate before whom he ought to have appeared shall certify (under his hand on the back of the Recognizance,) to the Clerk of the Peace of the District, County or place (as the case may be) the fact of such non-appearance, and such Recognizance shall be proceeded upon in like manner as other Recognizances, and such certificate shall be deemed sufficient *prima facie* evidence of such non-appearance.

23. The Magistrate adjudicating under this Act shall transmit the conviction, or a duplicate of a certificate of dismissal with the written charge, the depositions of witnesses for the prosecution and for the defence, and the statement of the accused, to the next Court of General or Quarter Sessions of the Peace, or to the Court discharging the functions of a Court of General or Quarter Sessions of the Peace, for the District, County or Place, there to be kept by the proper Officer among the records of the Court.

24. A copy of such conviction, or of such certificate of dismissal, certified by the proper Officer of the Court, or proved to be a true copy, shall be sufficient evidence to prove a conviction or dismissal for the offence mentioned therein, in any legal proceedings whatever.

25. The Magistrate, by whom any person has been convicted under this Act may order restitution of the property stolen, or taken or obtained by false pretences, in those cases in which the Court before whom the person convicted would have been tried but for this Act, might by law order restitution.

As to restitution of stolen property, see 32 & 33 Vic., chap. 21, s. 113.

26. Every Court held by a competent Magistrate for the purposes of this Act, shall be an open public Court, and a written or printed notice of the day and hour for holding such Court, shall be posted or affixed by the Clerk of the Court upon the outside of some conspicuous part of the building or place where the same is held.

27. The provisions of the *Act respecting the duties of Justices of the Peace out of Sessions, in relation to summary convictions and orders*, and the provisions of the *Act respecting the duties of Justices of the Peace out of Sessions in relation to persons charged with indictable offences* shall not be construed as applying to any proceedings under this Act except as mentioned in section nineteen.

28. Every conviction by a competent Magistrate under this Act shall have the same effect as a conviction upon indictment for the same offence would have had, save that no conviction under this Act shall be attended with forfeiture beyond the penalty (if any) imposed in the case.

29. Every person who obtains a certificate of dismissal or is convicted under this Act, shall be released from all further or other criminal proceedings for the same cause.

See 32 & 33 Vic., chap. 20, s. 45, and notes thereon, *post*, title "Assault."

30. No conviction, sentence or proceeding under this Act shall be quashed for want of form ; and no warrant of commitment upon a conviction shall be held void by reason of any defect therein, if it be therein alleged that the offender has been convicted, and there be a good and valid conviction to sustain the same.

31. Nothing in this Act shall affect the provisions of the *Act respecting the Trial and Punishment of Juvenile Offenders* ; and this Act shall not extend to persons punishable under that Act, so far as regards offences for which such persons may be punished thereunder.

32. Every fine imposed under the authority of this Act shall be paid to the Magistrate, who has imposed the same, or to the Clerk of the Court or Clerk of the Peace, as the case may be, and shall be by him paid over to the County Treasurer for County purposes if it has been imposed in the Province of Ontario,—and if it has been imposed in any new district in the Province of Quebec, constituted by any Act of the Legislature of the Late Province of Canada passed in or after the year one thousand eight hundred and fifty-

seven, then to the Sheriff of such District as Treasurer of the Building and Jury Fund for such District to form part of the said Fund,—and if it has been imposed in any other District in the said Province, then to the Prothonotary of such District, to be by him applied under the direction of the Lieutenant-Governor in Council, towards the keeping in repair of the Court House in such District, or to be by him added to the moneys and fees collected by him for the erection of a Court House and Gaol in such District, so long as such fees shall be collected to defray the cost of such erection ; and in the Province of Nova Scotia to the County Treasurer for County purposes, and in the Province of New Brunswick to the County Treasurer for County purposes.

33. In the interpretation of this Act the word " property " shall be construed to include everything included under the same word or the expression "valuable security," as used in the *Act respecting Larceny and other similar offences*; and in the case of any "valuable security," the value thereof shall be reckoned in the manner prescribed in the said Act.

34. The Act cited in the first section of this Act chapter one hundred and five of the Consolidated Statutes of Canada is hereby repealed, except as to cases pending under it at the time of the coming into force of this Act and as to all sentences pronounced and punishments awarded under it, as regards all which this Act shall be construed as a re-enactment of the said Aet, with amendments, and not as a new law.

35. This Act shall commence and take effect on the first day of January, in the year of our Lord one thousand eight hundred and seventy.

FORM A. *See* s. 7.

CONVICTION.

Province of , City *or* ,
as the case may be of, to wit :

Be it remembered that on the day of , in the year of our Lord , at , A. B., being charged before me the undersigned , of the said (City), (and consenting to my deciding upon the charge summarily), is convicted before me, for that he the said A.B. &c. (*stating the offence, and the time and place when and where committed*), and I adjudge the said A. B., for his said offence, to be imprisoned in the (and there kept to hard labour), for the space of .

Given under my hand and seal, the day and year first above mentioned, at aforesaid.

J. S. [L. S.

FORM B. *See* s. 7.

CERTIFICATE OF DISMISSAL.

Province of City *or*
as the case may be of, to wit :

I, the undersigned, , of the City *or as the case may be*, of , certify that on the day of , in the year of our Lord , at aforesaid, A.B., being charged before me (and consenting to my deciding upon the charge summarily), for that he the said A.B., &c. (*stating the offence charged, and the time and place when and where alleged to have been committed*), I did, after having summarily adjudicated thereon, dismiss the said charge.

Given under my hand and seal, this , day of , at aforesaid.

J. S. [L.S.]

FORM C. *See* s. 11.

CONVICTION UPON A PLEA OF GUILTY.

Province of City *or*
as the case may be of, to wit :

Be it remembered that on the day of , in the year of our Lord , at , A. B., being charged before me the undersigned , of the said City (and consenting to my deciding upon the charge summarily), for that he the said A. B., &c. (*stating the offence, and the time and place when and where committed*), and pleading guilty to such charge, he is thereupon convicted before me of the said offence ; and I adjudge him the said A. B. for his said offence, to be imprisoned in the (and there kept to hard labour) for the space of

Given under my hand and seal, the day and year first above-mentioned, at aforesaid.

J. S. [L.S.]

32 & 33 VIC., CHAP. XXXIII.

An Act respecting the trial and punishment of Juvenile Offenders.

[*Assented to, 22nd June*, 1869.]

HER MAJESTY, by and with the advice and consent of the Senate and House of Commons of Canada, enacts as follows:

1. In this Act the expression "any two or more Justices," shall, as respects the Province of Quebec, include any two or more Justices of the Peace, the Sheriff of any District except Montreal and Quebec, the Deputy Sheriff of Gaspé, and any Recorder, Judge of the Sessions of the Peace, Police Magistrate, District Magistrate or Stipendiary Magistrate acting within the limits of their respective jurisdictions;—and as respects the Province of Ontario, any Judge of the County Court, being a Justice of the Peace, Police Magistrate or Stipendiary Magistrate, or any two Justices of the Peace acting within their respective jurisdictions;—and as respects the Province of Nova Scotia or the Province of New Brunswick, the said expression shall mean and include any functionary or tribunal invested or to be invested by the proper legislative authority with power to do acts usually required to be done by two or more Justices of the Peace;—and the expression "the Justices" shall have the same meaning as the expression "two or more Justices of the Peace" as above defined;—and the expression "the Common Gaol or other place of confinement" shall include any Reformatory Prison provided for the reception of juvenile offenders in the Province in which the conviction referred to takes place, and to which by the law of that Province the offender can be sent.

This Act was extended to Manitoba by the 37 Vic., chap. 39, to the District of Keewatin by the 39 Vic., chap. 21, and to British Columbia by the 37 Vic., chap. 42. The expression "any two or more Justices" and the expression "the Justices" shall, with respect to the Province of Manitoba, have the same meaning and include the like functionaries and tribunals as with respect to the said Provinces of Quebec and Ontario, and the expression "the Common Gaol or other place of confinement" in either of the said Acts shall have the same meaning with respect to the said Province of Manitoba, as with respect to the other Provinces mentioned in the said Act. 37 Vic., chap. 39, s. 3. In applying the Act to the District of Keewatin and to British Columbia, the expression "any two or more Justices" shall be construed as including any magistrate having the powers of two Justices of the Peace. The Act shall not apply to any offence punishable by imprisonment for two years and upwards, and it shall not be necessary that the recognizance be transmitted to any Clerk of the Peace. 37 Vic., chap. 42, schedule A.; 39 Vic., chap. 21. The Act was also extended to Prince Edward Island by the 40 Vic., chap. 4, but in this Province the expression "any two or more Justices" shall be construed as including any magistrate having the powers of two Justices of the Peace, and the Act shall not apply to any offence punishable by imprisonment for two years and upwards, and it shall not be necessary that the recognizance be transmitted to any Clerk of the Peace. The fines collected under the Act are, in Prince Edward Island, to be paid over to the Provincial Secretary and Treasurer. 40 Vic., chap. 4, s. 8.

2. Every person charged with having committed or having attempted to commit, or with having been an aider, abettor, counsellor or procurer in the commission of any offence which is simple larceny, or punishable as simple larceny, and whose age at the period of the commission or attempted commission of such offence does not, in the opinion of the Justice before whom he is brought or appears as mentioned in section seven, exceed the age of sixteen years, shall upon conviction thereof, in open Court, upon his own confession or upon proof, before any two or more Justices, be committed to the Common Gaol or other place of confinement within the jurisdiction of such Justices, there to be imprisoned with or without hard labour, for any term not exceeding three months, or, in the discretion of such Justices, shall forfeit and pay such sum, not exceeding twenty dollars, as the said Justices may adjudge.

3. The Justices before whom any person is charged and proceeded against under this Act, before such person is asked whether he has any cause to show why he should not be convicted, shall say to the person so charged, these words, or words to the like effect :—

"We shall have to hear what you wish to say in answer to the charge "against you; but if you wish to be tried by a Jury, you must object now "to our deciding upon it at once:"

And if such person, or a parent or guardian of such person, then objects, such person shall be dealt with as if this Act had not been passed ; but nothing in this Act shall prevent the summary conviction of any such person before one or more Justices of the Peace, for any offence for which he is liable to be so convicted under any other Act.

4. If the Justices, upon the hearing of any such case, deem the offence not proved, or that it is not expedient to inflict any punishment, they shall dismiss the party charged, in the latter case on his finding sureties for his future good behaviour, and in the former case without sureties, and then make out and deliver to the party charged, a certificate under the hands of such Justices stating the fact of such dismissal.

Such certificate shall be in the form or to the effect set forth in the form following :—

, } To wit : We , of Her Majesty's Justices of the Peace for the of , (*or, if a Recorder, &c.*, I, a , of the of , *as the case may be*) do hereby certify, that on the day of , in the year of our Lord, , at , in the said of , M. N., was brought before us the said Justices (*or* me the said) charged with the following offence, that is to say (*here state briefly the particulars of the charge*,) and that we the said Justices (*or* I the said) thereupon dismissed the said charge.

Given under our hands (*or* my hand) this day of

5. If the Justices are of opinion, before the person charged has made his defence, that the charge is from any circumstance a fit subject for prosecution by indictment, or if the person charged, upon being called upon to answer the charge, objects to the case being summarily disposed of under the provisions of this Act, such Justices shall, instead of summarily adjudicating thereupon, deal with the case in all respects as if this Act had not been passed ; but this shall not prevent his being afterwards tried summarily by his own consent by a Judge of a County Court in the Province of Ontario, under any Act then in force for that purpose.

6. Every person obtaining such certificate of dismissal as aforesaid, and every person convicted under the authority of this Act, shall be released from all further or other criminal proceedings for the same cause.

7. In case any person whose age is alleged not to exceed sixteen years be charged with any offence mentioned in section two, on the oath of a credible witness before any Justice of the Peace, such Justice may issue his summons or warrant, to summon or to apprehend the person so charged, to appear be-

fore any two Justices of the Peace, at a time and place to be named in such summons or warrant.

8. Any Justice or Justices of the Peace, if he or they think fit, may remand for further examination or for trial, or suffer to go at large upon his finding sufficient sureties, any such person charged before him or them with any such offence as aforesaid.

9. Every such surety shall be bound by recognizance to be conditioned for the appearance of such person before the same or some other Justice or Justices of the Peace for further examination, or for trial before two or more Justices of the Peace as aforesaid, or for trial by indictment at the proper Court of Criminal Jurisdiction, as the case may be.

10. Every such recognizance may be enlarged from time to time by any such Justice or Justices or Court to such further time as he or they appoint; and every such recognizance not so enlarged shall be discharged without fee or reward when the party has appeared according to the condition thereof.

11. Any Justice of the Peace may, by summons, require the attendance of any person as a witness upon the hearing of any case before two Justices under the authority of this Act, at a time and place to be named in such summons.

12. Any such Justice may require and bind by recognizance all persons whom he considers necessary to be examined touching the matter of such charge, to attend at the time and place appointed by him, and then and there to give evidence upon the hearing of such charge.

13. In case any person so summoned or required or bound as aforesaid, neglects or refuses to attend in pursuance of such summons or recognizance, then upon proof being first given of such person having been duly summoned as hereinafter mentioned, or bound by recognizance as aforesaid, either of the Justices before whom any such person ought to have attended, may issue a warrant to compel his appearance as a witness.

14. Every summons issued under the authority of this Act, may be served by delivering a copy thereof to the party, or to some inmate at such party's usual place of abode, and every person so required by any writing under the hand or hands of any Justice or Justices to attend and give evidence as aforesaid, shall be deemed to have been duly summoned.

15. The Justices before whom any person is summarily convicted of any such offence as hereinbefore mentioned, may cause the conviction to be drawn up in the following form, or in any other form of words to the same effect, (varying the wording to suit the case,) that is to say :

, } To wit : } Be it remembered, that on the day of , in the year of our Lord one thousand eight hundred and , at , in the District of , (County *or* United Counties, &c., *or as the case may be*) A. O. is convicted before us J. P. and J. R., two of Her Majesty's Justices of the Peace for the said District (*or* City, &c.,) *or* me, S. J., *Recorder*, &c., , of the of , *or as the case may be*) for that he the said A. O. did (*specify the offence and the time and place when and where the same was committed, as the case may be, but without setting forth the evidence*), and we the said J. P. and J. R. (*or* I the said S. J.) adjudge the said A. O. for his said offence to be imprisoned in the (*or* to be imprisoned in the and there kept at hard labour, for the space of , (*or* we (*or* I) adjudge the said A. O. for his said offence to forfeit and pay , (*here state the penalty actually imposed*,) and in default of immediate payment of the said sum, to be imprisoned in the (*or* to be imprisoned in the , and kept to hard labour) for the space of , unless the said sum shall be sooner paid.

Given under our hands and seals (*or* my hand and seal) the day and year first above mentioned.

And the conviction shall be good and effectual to all intents and purposes.

16. No such conviction shall be quashed for want of form, or be removed by *certiorari* or otherwise, into any of Her Majesty's Superior Courts of Record ; and no warrant of commitment shall be held void by reason of any defect therein, provided it be therein alleged that the party has been convicted, and there is a good and valid conviction to sustain the same.

See 32 & 33 Vic., chap. 31, s. 71, and notes thereon, *ante*, p. 146.

17. The Justices before whom any person is convicted under the provisions of this Act, shall forthwith transmit the conviction and recognizances to the Clerk of the Peace for the district, city, county or union of counties wherein the offence was committed, there to be kept by the proper officer among the records of the Court of General or Quarter Sessions of the Peace, or of any other Court discharging the functions of a Court of General or Quarter Sessions of the Peace.

18. Each such Clerk of the Peace shall transmit to the Secretary of State of Canada, a quarterly return of the names, offences and punishments mentioned in the convictions, with such other particulars as may from time to time be required.

19. No conviction under the authority of this Act shall be attended with any forfeiture, except such penalty as may be imposed by the sentence, but whenever any person is adjudged guilty under the provisions of this Act, the presiding Justice may order restitution of the property in respect of which the offence was committed, to the owner thereof or his representatives.

20. If such property be not then forthcoming, the Justices, whether they award punishment or dismiss the complaint, may inquire into and ascertain the value thereof in money, and if they think proper, order payment of such sum of money to the true owner, by the person convicted, either at one time or by instalments, at such periods as the Court deems reasonable.

21. The party so ordered to pay may be sued for the same as a debt in any Court in which debts of the like amount may be by law recovered, with costs of suit, according to the practice of such Court.

22. Whenever the Justices adjudge any offender to forfeit and pay a pecuniary penalty under the authority of this Act, and such penalty is not forthwith paid, they may if they deem it expedient, appoint some future day for the payment thereof, and order the offender to be detained in safe custody until the day so to be appointed, unless such offender gives security to the satisfaction of the Justices for his appearance on such day, and the Justices may take such security by way of recognizance or otherwise at their discretion.

23. If at any time so appointed such penalty has not been paid, the same or any other Justices of the Peace may, by Warrant under their hands and seals, commit the offender to the Common Gaol or other place of confinement within their jurisdiction, there to remain for any time not exceeding three months, reckoned from the day of such adjudication ; such imprisonment to cease on payment of the said penalty.

24. The Justices before whom any person is prosecuted or tried for any offence cognizable under this Act, may, in their discretion, at the request of the prosecutor or of any other person who appears on recognizance or summons to prosecute or give evidence against such person, order payment to the prosecutor and witnesses for the prosecution, of such sums of money as to them seem reasonable and sufficient, to reimburse such prosecutor and witnesses for the expenses they have severally incurred in attending before them, and in otherwise carrying on such prosecution, and also to compensate them for their trouble and loss of time therein, and may order payment to the Constables and other Peace Officers for the apprehension and detention of any person so charged.

25. And although no conviction takes place, the said Justices may order

all or any of the payments aforesaid, when they are of opinion that the parties or any of them have acted *bona fide.*

26. Every fine imposed under the authority of this Act shall be paid to the Justices who impose the same or to the Clerk of the Recorder's Court, or the Clerk of the County Court, or the Clerk of the Peace, or other proper officer, as the case may be, and shall be by him or them paid over to the County Treasurer for County purposes, if the same was imposed in the Province of Ontario; and if it was imposed in any new district in the Province of Quebec, then to the Sheriff of such district as Treasurer of the Building and Jury Fund for such district, to form part of the said Fund, and if it was imposed in any other district in the Province of Quebec, then to the Prothonotary of such district, to be by him applied, under the direction of the Lieutenant-Governor in Council, towards the keeping in repair of the Court House in such district, or to be by him added to the moneys or fees collected by him, for the erection of a Court House or Gaol in such district, so long as such fees are collected to defray the cost of such erection, and if it was imposed in the Province of Nova Scotia it shall be paid over to the County Treasurer, for County purposes, and if it was imposed in the Province of New Brunswick, it shall be paid over to the County Treasurer, for County purposes.

See as to Prince Edward Island, 40 Vic., chap. 4, s. 8.

27. The amount of expenses of attending before the Justices and the compensation for trouble and loss of time therein, and the allowances to the Constables and other Peace Officers for the apprehension and detection of the offender, and the allowances to be paid to the prosecutor, witnesses, and constables for attending at the trial or examination of the offender, shall be ascertained by and certified under the hands of such Justices, but the amount of the costs, charges and expenses attending any such prosecution, to be allowed and paid as aforesaid, shall not in any one case exceed the sum of eight dollars.

28. Every such order of payment to any prosecutor or other person, after the amount thereof has been certified by the proper Justices of the Peace as aforesaid, shall be forthwith made out and delivered by the said Justices or one of them, or by the Clerk of the Recorder's Court, Clerk of the County Court or Clerk of the Peace, as the case may be, unto such prosecutor or other person, upon such Clerk being paid his lawful fee for the same, and shall be made upon the officer to whom fines imposed under the authority of this Act are required to be paid over in the district, city, county or union of counties in which the offence was committed, or was supposed to have been committed, who, upon sight of every such order, shall forthwith pay to the person named therein, or to any other person duly authorized to

receive the same on his behalf, out of any moneys received by him under this Act, the money in such order mentioned, and shall be allowed the same in his accounts of such moneys.

29. The Act chapter one hundred and six of the Consolidated Statutes of Canada is hereby repealed, except as to cases pending under it at the time of the coming into force of this Act, and as to all sentences pronounced and punishments awarded under it, as regards all which this Act shall be construed as a re-enactment of the said Act with the amendments hereby made and not as a new law.

30. This Act shall commence and take effect on the first day of January, in the year of Our Lord one thousand eight hundred and seventy.

---

32 & 33 VIC., CHAP. XXXV.

An Act for the more speedy trial, in certain cases, of persons charged with felonies and misdemeanors in the Provinces of Ontario and Quebec.

[*Assented to 22nd June,* 1869.]

HER MAJESTY, by and with the advice and consent of the Senate and House of Commons, enacts as follows :

1. Any person committed to a gaol for trial on a charge of being guilty of any offence for which he may be tried at a Court of General Sessions of the Peace, may, with his own consent, of which consent an entry shall then be made of record, and subject to the provisions hereinafter made, be tried out of Sessions, and if convicted may be sentenced by the Judge.

This Act was extended to Manitoba by the 38 Vic., chap. 54, and as respects the Province of Manitoba the expression, "a Court of General Sessions of the Peace" in the said Act, shall mean and include the Court of Queen's Bench of that Province ; and the expression, " the Judge," shall mean " the Chief Justice," or " a puisne Judge" of the said Court of Queen's Bench ; and the expression, " County-Attorney or Clerk of the Peace," shall mean the prothonotary of the said Court of Queen's Bench. It applies also in the District of Algoma. See 37 Vic., chap. 41.

2. It shall be the duty of every Sheriff within twenty-four hours after any prisoner charged as aforesaid is committed to gaol for trial, to notify the Judge in writing that such prisoner is so confined, stating his name and the nature of the charge preferred against him, whereupon, with as little delay as possible, such Judge shall cause the prisoner to be brought up before him.

3. Having obtained the depositions on which the prisoner was so committed, the Judge shall state to him,—

(1) That he is charged with the offence, describing it ;

(2) That the prisoner has his option to be forthwith tried before such Judge without the intervention of a Jury, or to remain untried until the next sitt-

ings of such sessions or of a Court of Oyer and Terminer, or, in Quebec, of any Court having criminal jurisdiction ;

(3) If the prisoner demands a trial by Jury, the Judge shall remand him to gaol ; but if he consents to be tried by the Judge without a Jury, the County Attorney or Clerk of the Peace shall draw up a record of the proceedings as nearly as may be in one of the forms in the Schedules A and B to this Act ; if upon being arraigned upon the charge the prisoner pleads guilty, such plea shall be entered in the Record, and the Judge shall pass the sentence of the law on such prisoner, which shall have the same force and effect as if passed at any Court of General Sessions of the Peace.

4. If the prisoner upon being so arraigned and consenting as aforesaid, pleads not guilty, the Judge shall appoint an early day, or the same day, for his trial, and it shall be the duty of the County Attorney or Clerk of the Peace to subpœna the witnesses named in the depositions, or such of them, and such other witnesses as he may think requisite to prove the charge, to attend at the time appointed for such trial, and the prisoner being ready, the Judge shall proceed to try him, and if he is found guilty, sentence shall be passed as in the last preceding section mentioned, but if he is found not guilty, the Judge shall immediately discharge him from custody so far as respects the charge in question.

Under this statute it is not necessary to have more than one record, in which shall be entered the proceedings from time to time taken, until the final determination of the matter.

After the prisoner has heard the charge read to him, and has elected to have it tried by the Judge and has pleaded to it, and has been tried, he cannot object to the record which has been made up against him, because it describes or lays the charge in different forms to meet the facts of the case, so long as it does not contain different distinct offences. The Judge's jurisdiction is not confined to the trial only of the charge as stated in the commitment. Where therefore a prisoner was committed to gaol for trial on a charge of kidnapping another person, with intent to cause such person to be secretly confined or imprisoned in Canada, which is made felony under the Statute 32 & 33 Vic., chap. 20, s. 69, and on being brought before the Judge under this statute (32 & 33 Vic., chap. 35), was charged and tried also for the other offence under the statute of, without lawful authority, forcibly seizing and confining any other person within Canada. It was held that this might be lawfully done, the prisoner being committed on a charge for which he might be tried at the Sessions. *Cornwall* v. *R.*, 33 Q. B. (Ont.), 106.

The purpose of the statute was not to compel the Judge to try the prisoner upon any charge he was confined upon, in the language of that charge, but to try him on that charge in any form in which the charge could properly be laid against him. But it was never intended that the prisoner, if he were committed on a charge of larceny, should be tried for manslaughter by the Judge, nor if he were in for an assault that he should be tried for larceny, nor if he were in for arson that he should be tried for burglary. But on the other hand, it was never intended that if the prisoner were committed for trial for stealing the goods of A, that the same goods should not be described in another count, if it were necessary to do so, as the goods of B, nor if he were in on a charge of larceny, that he should not also be tried for feloniously receiving the same goods, nor if he were in on a charge for unlawfully and maliciously wounding with intent to maim, that he should not be tried on another count for the same wounding with intent to do some grievous bodily harm. So it would seem also in those cases in which a jury could acquit of the felony and convict of a misdemeanor or of an assault, or could acquit of the offence charged, if it were not completed, and convict the prisoner of an attempt to commit it, the Judge might under the statute do the same thing. *Ib.* 119, 120.

The record will be properly framed, if it states the offence charged in such form as the depositions or evidence show, that it should have been laid, and the Judge is not to call for the warrant of commitment to find out what offence the prisoner is charged with, but he is to obtain "the depositions on which the prisoner was committed," and he is to state to the prisoner the offence with which he is there charged.

Where the Judge has appointed a day for trial under the 4th section, and the prisoner on being brought up before the Judge on the appointed day, declares his readiness to proceed, the Judge has nevertheless power on the application of the counsel for the Crown to adjourn the trial to a subsequent day, and the record is not objectionable in failing to mention the cause of adjournment. *Cornwall* v. *R.*, 33 Q. B. (Ont.), 106.

The Judge has also power to amend the record by changing the name of the prisoner; in the case in question, Rufus Bratton was changed to James Rufus Bratton (*ib.*).

A record which follows the form provided by the statute is sufficient, although the special jurisdiction conferred by the Act is not shewn. The notice from the sheriff under section 2 need only shew the nature of the charge against the prisoner, and need not charge the different offences of which the prisoner is tried as in the counts of an indictment (*ib.*).

5. The Judge sitting on any such trial for all the purposes thereof and proceedings connected therewith or relating thereto, is hereby constituted a Court of Record, and the record in any such case shall be filed among the records of the Court of General Sessions of the Peace, as indictments are, and as part of such records.

6. Any witness, whether on behalf of the prisoner or against him, duly summoned or subpœnaed to attend and give evidence before such Judge sitting on any such trial on the day appointed for the same, shall be bound to attend, and remain in attendance throughout the whole trial, and in case he fails so to attend he shall be held guilty of contempt of Court, and he may be proceeded against therefor accordingly.

7. Upon proof to the satisfaction of the Judge of the service of subpœna upon any witness who fails to attend before him as required by such subpœna, and such Judge being satisfied that the presence of such witness before him is indispensable to the ends of justice, he may by his warrant cause the said witness to be apprehended, and forthwith brought before him to give evidence as required by such subpœna, and to answer for his disregard of the same, and such witness may be detained on such warrant before the said Judge or in the Common Gaol, with a view to secure his presence as a witness; or in the discretion of the Judge, such witness may be released on recognizance with or without sureties conditioned for his appearance to give evidence as therein mentioned, and to answer for his default in not attending upon the said subpœna as for a contempt; the Judge may in a summary manner examine into and dispose of the charge of contempt against the said witness, who if found guilty thereof may be fined or imprisoned, or both, such fine not to exceed one hundred dollars, and such imprisonment to be in the Common Gaol, with or without hard labour, and not to exceed the term of ninety days; the said warrant may be in the Form "C," and the conviction for contempt in

the Form "D" to this Act, and shall be authority to the persons and officers therein required to act, to do as therein they are respectively directed.

8. All the powers and duties hereby conferred and imposed upon the Judge, shall be exercised and performed in the Province of Ontario by any County Judge, junior or Deputy Judge, authorized to act as Chairman of the General Sessions of the Peace; and in the Province of Quebec in any District wherein there is a Judge of the Sessions, by such Judge of Sessions, and in any District wherein there is no Judge of Sessions but wherein there is a District Magistrate, by such District Magistrate, and in any District wherein there is neither a Judge of Sessions nor a District Magistrate, by the Sheriff of such District.

9. This Act shall apply only to the Provinces of Ontario and Quebec.

This section does not prevent the application of the Act in the Province of Manitoba and the District of Algoma (see *ante*, p. 216), the Acts so extending it being subsequent to this Act.

Any Judge, Junior Judge, or Deputy Judge, trying any person under the said Act in the Province of Ontario may, in his discretion, reserve any question of law arising on such trial, for the consideration of the Justices of one of Her Majesty's Superior Courts of Common Law of the said Province, in the same manner and to the same extent as may be done by the Court of General Sessions of the Peace under chapter one hundred and twelve of the Consolidated Statutes for Upper Canada, and the said last named Act shall form and be taken and read as part of the said Act in the title to this Act mentioned. (38 Vic., chap. 45, s. 1.)

The powers conferred and imposed upon the Judge to be exercised and performed under the Act cited in the title to this Act, with and after the consent of the person charged, may be exercised and performed, notwithstanding that the court before which but for such consent the said person would be triable for the offence charged, or the Grand Jury thereof, may then be in session. *Ib.* s. 2.

If one of two or more prisoners charged with the same offence demands a trial by jury, and the other or others consent to be tried by the Judge without a jury, the Judge in his discretion may remand the said prisoners to gaol to await trial in all respects as if the Act cited in the title (32 & 33 Vic., chap. 35) had not been passed. *Ib.* s. 3.

SCHEDULE A.

Form of Record when the Prisoner pleads Not Guilty.

Province of
County *or* District of
To wit :

Be it remembered that A. B. being a prisoner in the Jail of the said County *or* District, committed for trial on a charge of having on day of 18 , feloniously stolen, &c., (*one cow, the property of C. D., or as the case may be, stating briefly the offence*), and being brought before me, (*describe the Judge*) on the day of 18 , and asked by me if he consented to be tried before me without the intervention of a jury, consented to be so tried ; and that upon the day of 18 , the said A. B., being again brought before me for trial, and declaring himself ready, was arraigned upon the said charge and pleaded not guilty ; and after hearing the evidence adduced as well in support of the said charge as for the prisoner's defence (*or as the case may be*) I find him to be guilty of the offence with which he is charged as aforesaid, and I accordingly sentence him to be (*here insert such sentence as the law allows and the Judge thinks right*) *or* I find him not guilty of the offence with which he is charged, and discharge him accordingly. Witness my hand at in the County (*or* District) of , this day of 18 .

O. K.
Signature of Judge.

SCHEDULE B.

Form of Record when the Prisoner pleads Guilty.

Province of
County (*or* District) of
To wit :

Be it remembered that A. B. being a prisoner in the Jail of the said County (*or* District), on a charge of having on the day of 18 , feloniously stolen, &c., (*one cow the property of, or as the case may be, stating briefly the offence,*) and being brought before me (*describe the Judge*) on the day of 18 , and asked by me if he consented to be tried before me without the intervention of a jury, consented to be so tried ; and that the said A. B, being then arraigned upon the said charge, he pleaded guilty thereof, whereupon I sentenced the said A. B. to be (*here insert such sentence as the law allows and the Judge thinks right.*) Witness my hand this day of 18 .

O. K.
Signature of Judge.

SCHEDULE C.

(L.S.) Canada Province of County (*or* District, as the case may be) of , To wit :	To all or any of the Constables or other Peace Officers in the said County (*or* District, *as the case may be*) of

Whereas it having been made to appear before me, that E. F., in the said County [*or* District, *or as the case may be*,] was like to give material evidence on behalf of the prosecution [*or* defence, *as the case may be*] on the trial of a certain charge of [as *larceny, or as the case may be*,] against A. B., and that the said E. F. was duly subpœnaed or bound under recognizances to appear on the day of 18 , at in the said [County *or* District, *as the case may be*,] at o'clock [forenoon *or* afternoon, *as the case may be*,] before me to testify what he should know concerning the said charge against the said E. F.

And whereas proof hath this day been made before me upon oath of such subpœna having been duly served upon the said E. F., or of the said E. F. having been duly bound in recognizance to appear before me [*as the case may be*]; And whereas the said E. F., hath neglected to appear at the trial and place appointed, and no just excuse has been offered for such neglect; These are therefore to command you to take the said E. F., and to bring and have him forthwith before me, to testify what he shall know concerning the said charge against the said A. B., and also to answer his contempt for such neglect.

Given under my hand this day of in the year of Our Lord 18

J. S.,
Judge.

SCHEDULE D.

(L.S.) Canada, Province of (County *or* District) To wit :	Be it remembered that on the day of in the year of our Lord 18 , in the (County *or* District *as the case may be*) of E. F. is convicted before me, for that he the said

E. F. did not attend before me to give evidence on the trial of a certain charge against one A. B. of larceny, (*or as the case may be*,) although duly subpœnaed or bound by recognizance to appear and give evidence in that behalf (*as the case may be*) but made default therein, and hath not shown before me any sufficient excuse for such default, and I adjudge the said E. F.

for his said offence to be imprisoned in the Common Gaol of the (County *or* District) of at for the space of there to be kept at hard labour (*and in case a fine is also intended to be imposed, then proceed*) And I also adjudge that the said E. F. do forthwith pay to and for the use of Her Majesty a fine of dollars, and in default of payment that the said fine with the costs of collection be levied by distress and sale of the goods and chattels of the said E. F. (*or in case a fine alone is imposed, then the clause for imprisonment will be omitted*).

Given under my hand at , in the said (County, *or* District) of the day and year first above mentioned.

J. S.,
Judge.

SCHEDULE E.

ACCUSATION. (Not in Statute.)

In the County Judge's Criminal Court for the County of Middlesex :

Province of Ontario, County of Middlesex, To wit: } The twenty-fourth day of June, A. D. 1872, at London, in the County of Middlesex, before William Elliot, Esquire, County Judge of the said County, exercising criminal jurisdiction under the provisions of the Act, entitled "An Act for the more speedy trial in certain cases of persons charged with felonies and misdemeanors in the Provinces of Ontario and Quebec," Isaac Bell Cornwall, who is committed for trial to the Common Gaol of the said County, and is now a prisoner in close custody therein, stands charged this day before the said Judge, sitting in public open Court assembled for the trial of the said Isaac Bell Cornwall. First count, for that he, the said Isaac Bell Cornwall, on the fourth day of June, in the year A. D. 1872, at the City of London, in the said County, did feloniously and without lawful authority, forcibly seize and confine one James Rufus Bratton within Canada, against the form of the Statute in such case made and provided, and against the peace of our Lady the Queen, Her Crown and Dignity. Second count, and for that he, the said Isaac Bell Cornwall, afterwards, to wit, on the day and year last aforesaid at the City and County aforesaid, without lawful authority, did feloniously kidnap one James Rufus Bratton, with intent to cause the said James Rufus Bratton to be unlawfully transported out of Canada against his will, against the form of the Statute in such case made and provided, and against the peace of our Lady the Queen, Her Crown and Dignity.

(Signed) CHARLES HUTCHINSON,
County Crown Attorney, County of Middlesex.

Isaac Bell Cornwall, within named, upon the within charge being read to him by the Judge in open Court, and being informed by the Judge that he has his option either of being forthwith tried without the intervention of a Jury upon the said charge, or of remaining untried until the next Court of Oyer and Terminer of this County, consents to be now tried upon the said charge, by the said Judge, without a Jury, and the prisoner pleads not guilty to the said charge.

Upon the accusation was endorsed the following order :—

"ORDER AMENDING ACCUSATION.

"*County Judge's Criminal Court, County of Middlesex.*

"*The Queen* v. *Cornwall.*

"It is ordered that the accusation be amended by the inserting the name James before the names *Rufus Bratton*.

"By the Court,

"(Signed) CHARLES HUTCHINSON,
"Clerk of the Peace."

SCHEDULE F.

SHERIFF'S NOTICE. (Not in Statute.)

To His Honour the County Judge of the
County of Middlesex.

Pursuant to the second section of the Act for the more speedy trial in certain cases of persons charged with felonies and misdemeanors in the Provinces of Ontario and Quebec.

I, William Glass, Sheriff of the said county, certify that the several persons whose names are mentioned in the first column of the Schedule hereunder written, were committed for trial to the Common Gaol of the said county, and were received by the Gaoler of the said Gaol on the days severally mentioned in the second column of the said Schedule, opposite the names of the said persons respectively, and were so committed to the said Gaol, and were received each severally, under and by virtue of a Warrant from L. Lawrason, P.M., on a charge of being guilty of an offence which may be tried at a General Sessions of the Peace, and that the nature of the charge against the said several persons respectively, as contained in the warrant of commitment, is set forth in the third column of the said Schedule, opposite the names of the said several persons respectively.

SCHEDULE ABOVE REFERRED TO.

NAME OF PRISONER.	TIME WHEN COMMITTED FOR TRIAL.	NATURE OF CHARGES AS CONTAINED IN THE WARRANT OF COMMITMENT.
Isaac Bell Cornwall, London, 15th June, 1872.	15th June, 1872.	For that he did unlawfully and forcibly kidnap and take one Rufus Bratton, without authority, with intent to transport him out of Canada against his will.

(Signed) W. G.,
Sheriff of the County of Middlesex.

REV. STAT. (ONT.), CHAP. 73.

An Act to protect Justices of the Peace and other Officers from vexatious actions.

HER MAJESTY, by and with the advice and consent of the Legislative Assembly of the Province of Ontario, enacts as follows:

Every action brought against any Justice of the Peace for any act done by him in the execution of his duty as such Justice, with respect to any matter within his jurisdiction as such Justice, or against any other officer or person fulfilling any public duty, for anything by him done in the performance of such public duty, whether any such duties arise out of the Common Law or are imposed by any Act, either of the Imperial or Dominion Parliament, or of the Legislature of this Province, shall be an action on the case as for a tort, and in the declaration it shall be expressly alleged that such act was done maliciously and without reasonable and probable cause, and if at the trial of any such action, upon the general issue pleaded, the plaintiff fails to prove such allegation, he shall be non-suited or a verdict shall be given for the defendant.

When the Justice has jurisdiction over the subject matter of complaint and over the person of the party, an action of trespass will not lie against the Justice unless there is malice or want of reasonable and probable cause (*Hallett* v. *Wilmot*, 40 Q.B. (Ont.), 263; *Birch* v. *Perkins*, 2 Pugsley, 327); but if the matter was one in which the magistrate had no jurisdiction at all, then he is a trespasser. *West* v. *Smallwood*, 3 M. & W., 418.

Whenever there is an arrest, and it can be said there was no jurisdiction, trespass is the proper form of action. See *Hunt* v. *McArthur*, 24 Q. B. (Ont.), 254. Whenever it can be said that there was jurisdiction, the remedy is an action on the case as for a tort, and it must be expressly alleged and proved that the act was done maliciously and without reasonable or probable cause. *Caudle* v. *Seymour*, 1 Q. B., 889; *Appleton* v. *Lepper*, 20 C. P. (Ont.), 138; *Crawford* v. *Beattie*, 39 Q. B. (Ont.), 13; *Stoness* v. *Lake*, 40 Q. B. (Ont.), 326.

When a magistrate has jurisdiction he never can be made liable in an action of trespass for an irregularity in procedure, mistake of law or erroneous conclusion from facts. *Mills* v. *Collett*, 6 Bing., 85; *Sprung* v. *Anderson*, 23 C. P. (Ont.), 152; *Col. Bk. of A.* v. *Willan*, L. R., 5 P. C. App., 417. See also *Dobbyn* v. *Decow*, 25 C. P. (Ont.), 18; *Gardner* v. *Burwell*, Taylor, 189.

When a Justice acts within his jurisdiction and without malice, he is free from damages. *Cartier* v. *Burland*, 2 Revue Critique, 475.

After a conviction by a magistrate is quashed, an action on the case will not lie against him unless the acts complained of be proved to have been committed by him without any reasonable or probable cause and maliciously, and the question of malice must be left to the jury. *Burney* v. *Gorham*, 1 C. P. (Ont), 358.

One A. went before the defendants, two Justices, and swore that from circumstances mentioned he was afraid that the plaintiff would destroy his property, and he, therefore, prayed that he might be bound over to keep the peace. Defendants thereupon, on plaintiff's refusal to find sureties, committed him to gaol. It was held that this Act clearly applied, and that, therefore, only a special action on the case could be maintained. *Fullarton* v. *Switzer*, 13 Q. B. (Ont.), 575.

The Justice is not deprived of the protection of this section by some irregularity in drawing up the conviction, such as signing the conviction leaving blanks for the amount of costs, *Bott* v. *Ackroyd*, 28 L. J., M. C., 207; and when supposing the facts alleged to be true, the magistrate has jurisdiction, his liability to be sued or his exemption from such liability on the ground of jurisdiction cannot be affected by the truth or falsehood of those facts or by the sufficiency or insufficiency of the evidence adduced for the purpose of establishing them. *Cave* v. *Mountain*, 1 M. & Gr., 257.

The falsity of the charge in an information cannot give a cause of action against a magistrate who acts upon the assumption and belief of its truth. Where an information contained every material averment necessary to give a magistrate jurisdiction to make an order upon the plaintiff to find sureties to keep the peace, but contained also additional matter which it was contended so qualified and explained these averments as to render them nugatory; it was held that this was a judicial question for the magistrate to decide, and therefore that in issuing his warrant for the appearance of the accused he was not acting without jurisdiction, even although a Superior Court might quash his order to find sureties. *Sprung* v. *Anderson*, 23 C. P. (Ont.), 152.

An action of trespass cannot be maintained against an officer who executes a writ issued upon a judgment rendered by an inferior Court in a matter over which they had jurisdiction. *Goudie* v. *Langlois Stuart*, 142; *Owens* v. *Taylor*, 19 C. P. (Ont.), 49. The Court would not in such case be responsible, and where the officer executing the writ of an inferior Court is sought to be made liable the want of jurisdiction in the Court from which it issued must be apparent on the face of the writ itself, and unless it be so, the officer cannot be considered as a trespasser. (*Goudie* v. *Langlois, supra.*)

2. For any act done by a Justice of the Peace in a matter in which by law he has not jurisdiction, or in which he has exceeded his jurisdiction, or for any act done under any conviction, or order made or warrant issued by such Justice in any such matter, any person injured thereby may maintain an action against such Justice in the same form and in the same case as he might have done before the passing of this Act without making any allegation in his declaration that the act complained of was done maliciously and without reasonable and probable cause.

This section must be read in connection with the first section of the Act, and therefore where, in the course of a matter transacted before a Justice, there has been an excess of jurisdiction, the second section does not apply unless the action in which it is sought to be applied is brought for an act done in respect of that part of the matter, or some part of it which was beyond the jurisdiction. *Barton* v. *Bricknell*, 13 Q. B., 393.

Where a conviction contained no adjudication as to costs, but the Justices issued a warrant of distress reciting the conviction as adjudicating costs, and the party's goods were seized as well for the costs as the penalty, this was holden to be an excess of jurisdiction, within the meaning of the above section, and that trespass lay for it. *Leary* v. *Patrick*, 19 L. J., M. C., 211. The meaning of the words, "exceeded his jurisdiction" in the above section, means assuming to do something which the statute, under which the Justice is proceeding, could by no possibility justify. *Ratt* v. *Parkinson*, 20 L. J., M. C., 208. And they apply only to cases where the act, in respect of which the action is brought against the Justices, is itself an excess of jurisdiction. *Barton* v. *Bricknell*, 13 Q. B., 393; *Somerville* v. *Mirehouse*, 1 B. & S., 652. So if an order be good in part and bad in part, a Justice may issue a warrant of distress to enforce so much of it as is good, without subjecting himself to an action. *R.* v. *Green*, 20 L. J., M. C., 168.

When magistrates commit a person upon a general charge of felony given upon oath, they will not be liable to an action of trespass, although the facts sworn to, in order to substantiate that charge, may not, in point of law, support it. *Gardner* v. *Burwell*, Taylor, 189.

If a magistrate cause a party to be wrongfully imprisoned without any reasonable cause until he give his note to obtain a discharge, the magistrate is liable in trespass. *Brennan* v. *Hatelie*, 6 O. S., 308.

A magistrate sued in trespass for an alleged illegal proceeding under the 4 & 5 Vic., chap. 26, may give in evidence a tender of amends, under the plea of the general issue. *Moore* v. *Holditch*, 7 Q. B. (Ont.), 207.

A Justice of the Peace who issues a warrant without jurisdiction, as on an insufficient information, is liable to an action of trespass for assault and false imprisonment, and the question of reasonable and probable cause cannot arise in such a case as this, but only in a case where the Justice has jurisdiction. *Whittier* v. *Diblee*, 2 Pugsley, 243.

In an action for malicious prosecution, it appeared that the defendant was a Justice of the Peace, and as such acquired his knowledge of the circumstances on which he preferred the charge against the defendant. The Court, however, held that this was clearly no ground for requiring that express malice should be proved against him. *Orr* v. *Spooner*, 19 Q, B. (Ont.), 601.

Defendant as a Justice issued a warrant against the plaintiff upon a complaint for detaining the clothes of one K. The plaintiff on being told by the constable that he had the warrant, went alone to defendant, heard the evidence, was allowed to go away without giving bail, and returned the next day when he was discharged. It was held that no imprisonment was proved, and that defendant having jurisdiction over the subject matter of the complaint was not liable in trespass, even if the information were insufficient in point of form. *Thorpe* v. *Oliver*, 20 Q. B. (Ont.), 264.

A magistrate has no jurisdiction to administer an oath and take examinations within the limits of a foreign country, and a commitment founded on such proceedings is void and affords no justification in an action of trespass against the magistrate. *Nary* v. *Owen*, Berton, N. B. Reps., 377.

It was laid down in a suit before a Justice for wages, in the Vice Admiralty Court of Quebec, that although Justices of the Peace exercising summary jurisdiction are the sole judges of the weight of the evidence given before them, and no other Court will examine whether they have formed the right conclusion from it, yet other Courts may and ought to examine whether the premises stated by the Justices are such as will warrant the conclusion in point of law. *The Scotia*, 1 Stuart, V. A. Reps., 160.

Justices cannot give themselves jurisdiction by finding that as a fact which is not a fact, and their warrant in such case will be no protection to the officer who acts under it. *The Haidee*, 2 Stuart, V. A. Reps., 25; 10 L. C. R., 101.

An action for false imprisonment was brought against the informant, the bailiff making the arrest, and the two committing Justices, and judgment was rendered against the four, jointly, but it was held that the two committing magistrates were alone liable in damages, and the judgment against the other two was set aside. *Bissonette & Bornais*, 2 L. C., L. J., 18.

Omitting to state the conviction of a defendant, in his warrant of commitment, will not subject a Justice of the Peace to an action for false imprisonment, provided the actual conviction is proved upon his defence. *Whelan* v. *Stevens*, Taylor, 245.

3. Where a conviction or order has been made by a Justice or Justices of the Peace and a warrant of distress or of commitment has been granted thereon by some other Justice of the Peace *bona fide*, and without collusion, no action shall be brought against the Justice who granted such warrant by reason of any defect in the conviction or order, or for any want of jurisdiction in the Justice or Justices who made the same, but the action (if any is brought) shall be against the Justice or Justices who made the conviction or order.

4. No such action shall be brought for anything done under such conviction or order until the conviction or order has been quashed either upon appeal or upon application to one of the Superior Courts of Common Law ; nor shall any such action be brought for anything done under any warrant issued by such Justice to procure the appearance of the party, and which has been followed by a conviction or order in the same matter until the conviction or order has been quashed as aforesaid.

An action of trespass will not now lie against a magistrate until the "conviction or order has been quashed," for the statute limits the form of action to case so long as the magistrate had jurisdiction over the matter adjudicated upon. *Haacke* v. *Adamson*, 14 C. P. (Ont.), 201.

A conviction not set aside protects a magistrate against an action of trespass. *Gates* v. *Devenish*, 6 Q. B. (Ont.), 260.

A conviction bad on the face of it, though not quashed, is no defence to an action of trespass. *Briggs* v. *Spilsbury*, Taylor, 245.

Where a conviction exists *de facto*, though it is unsustainable, it is necessary that the same be quashed before an action of trespass or trover is brought against the magistrate for the property disposed of by the conviction (*Jones* v. *Holden*, 13 C. L. J., N. S., 19 : *Graham* v. *McArthur*, 25 Q. B. (Ont.), 478) ; and under the Rev. Stat. (Ont.), chap. 73, even in cases where the magistrate has not jurisdiction or has exceeded his jurisdiction no action will lie against him for anything done under an order until the same has been quashed. *Sprung* v. *Anderson*, 23 C. P. (Ont.), 152.

But an order or conviction not under seal need not be quashed before action, *McDonald* v. *Stuckey*, 31 Q. B. (Ont.), 577 ; following *Haacke* v. *Adamson*, 14 C. P. (Ont.), 201 ; see further *Huard* v. *Dunn*, 1 Revue Critique, 247.

A conviction made by one magistrate in a matter in which

jurisdiction was given to two only must be quashed though wholly void. *Graham* v. *McArthur*, 25 Q. B. (Ont.), 478.

5. If such last mentioned warrant has not been followed by a conviction or order, or in case it is a warrant upon an information for an alleged indictable offence, if a summons was issued previously to such warrant, and such summons was served upon such person either personally or by leaving the same for him with some person at his last or most usual place of abode, and he did not appear according to the exigency of such summons, in such case no such action shall be maintained against the Justice for anything done under such warrant.

This section has been holden not to have reference to a case where the magistrate, having convicted a man summoned him to shew cause why he had not paid the penalty and costs, and because he did not attend personally, but merely by his counsel and attorney, and the magistrate issued his warrant to bring him up to shew cause, and he was apprehended upon it, for which he brought an action of trespass against the magistrate, the Court held that the action lay, for this section relates only to cases where the summons and warrant are before conviction and not to a summons and warrant after conviction. *Bessell* v. *Wilson*, 24 L. J., M. C., 94.

6. In all cases where a Justice or Justices of the Peace refuse to do any act relating to the duties of his or their office as such Justice or Justices, the party requiring such act to be done may, upon an affidavit of the facts, apply to either of the Superior Courts of Common Law, or to the Judge of the County Court of the County or United Counties in which such Justice or Justices reside, for a rule calling upon such Justice or Justices, and also the party to be affected by such act, to show cause why such act should not be done; and if, after due service of such rule, good cause is not shown against it, the said Court may make the same absolute, with or without or upon payment of costs, as may seem meet, and the Justice or Justices, upon being served with such rule absolute, shall obey the same, and shall do the act required; and no action or proceeding shall be commenced or prosecuted against such Justice or Justices for having obeyed the rule and done the act required as aforesaid.

Under this section, it is only where Justices would need protection, if they proceeded to do "any act relating to the duties of their office," that a rule calling upon them to shew cause why such act should not be done, can be granted.

Therefore, where Justices had refused to hear a summons against a person for having a board over his door, stating that he was licensed to retail beer, &c., he not being so licensed, contrary to the 35 & 36 Vic., chap. 74, s. 11; the court refused a rule against the Justices, under this section, but granted a rule nisi for a mandamus. *R.* v. *Percy,* L. R., 9 Q. B., 64.

Under this section, if a Justice refuse to do any act, either of the Superior Courts of Common Law may order him to do it. Although the court will thus interfere in cases where they think that the Justice ought to do the act, yet if they think that the Justice has acted rightly in refusing to do it, they will not compel him to do it (*R.* v. *Hartley,* 31 L. J., M. C., 232; *R.* v. *Deverell,* 3 E. & B., 372); and the court will not grant a rule merely to set the Justices in motion. *R.* v. *Kesteren,* 13 L. J., M. C., 78. The main object of the section is to protect the Justice and not the parties from an action (*R.* v. *Cotton,* 15 A. & E., 574); and it is not to settle points of jurisdiction generally, except where the ministerial act depends on it. *R.* v. *Collins,* 21 L. J., M. C., 73; *R.* v. *Dayman,* 7 E. & B. 328; *R.* v. *Brown,* 13 Q. B., 654.

As such a rule is a substitute for a *mandamus,* the Court will not grant it if the proper remedy was by appeal to the Quarter Sessions. *R.* v. *Oxfordshire,* 18 L. J., M. C., 222.

Where the magistrate has heard and adjudicated, the section does not apply. *R.* v. *Dayman, supra.*

So there must be a refusal to adjudicate before the Act can be invoked (*R.* v. *Paynter,* 26 L. J., M. C., 102); and this section does not apply at all where Justices have acted, though perhaps erroneously. *Re Clee,* 21 L. J., M. C., 112; *R.* v. *Blanshard,* 18 L. J., M. C., 110. Under the section, the unsuccessful party pays the costs. *R.* v. *Ingham,* 17 Q. B., 884. But the rule should ask for the costs. *Leamington* v. *Moultrie,* 7 D & L., 311. See also *Re Delaney* v. *MacNab,* 21 C. P. (Ont.), 563.

7. In case a Justice of the Peace has granted a warrant of distress or a warrant of commitment upon any conviction or order which, either before or after the granting of the warrant, has been confirmed upon appeal, no action

shall be brought against such Justice by reason of any defect in such conviction or order for anything done under the warrant.

8. In case any action is brought, where by this Act it is enacted that no such action shall be brought under the particular circumstances, a Judge of the Court in which the action is pending shall, upon application of the defendant, and upon an affidavit of facts, set aside the proceedings in such action, with or without costs, as to him seems meet.

A gold watch having been taken upon a search-warrant from a person who absconded, the plaintiff claimed title to it, and brought replevin therefor against a city Police Magistrate who applied to stay proceedings under this section.

It was held that replevin was not within the Act, and the application was dismissed. *Munson* v. *Gurnett*, 2 P. R. (Ont.). 389.

9. No action shall be brought against any Justice of the Peace for anything done by him in the execution of his office, unless the same is commenced within six months next after the act complained of was committed.

The day on which the act was done is not to be included in these six months, and therefore where a person committed by a Justice was discharged out of custody on the 14th December, and he commenced his action on the 14th of June, it was holden that the action was commenced in time. *Hardy* v. *Ryle*, 9 B. & C., 603.

Where the cause of action is a continued one by imprisonment, the action may be brought within six calendar months after the last day of the imprisonment (*ib. Massey* v. *Johnson*, 12 East., 67), provided that be within six months after the service of notice of action. *Watson* v. *Fournier*, 14 East., 491.

There may be a series of acts connected together, and yet each giving rise to a cause of action. *Collins* v. *Rose*, 5 M. & W., 194.

The word "month" in this section means a calendar month. Rev. Stat. (Ont.), chap. 1, s. 8, s.-s. 15.

10. No such action shall be commenced against any Justice of the Peace until one month at least after a notice in writing of the intended action has been delivered to him, or left for him at his usual place of abode, by the

party intending to commence the action, or by his attorney or agent, in which notice the cause of action, and the Court in which the same is intended to be brought, shall be clearly and explicitly stated; and upon the back thereof shall be endorsed the name and place of abode of the party intending to sue, and also the name and place of abode or of business of his attorney or agent, if the notice be served by such attorney or agent.

It would appear that the words, "one month at least," mean a clear month's notice, exclusive of the first and last days, or the day of giving notice and suing out the writ. *Dempsey* v. *Dougherty*, 7 Q. B. (Ont.), 313; *Young* v. *Higgon*, 9 L. J., M. C., 29; *R.* v. *Shropshire*, 8 A. & E., 173.

Where the notice was served on the 28th of March, and the writ sued out on the 29th of April, this was held sufficient as being at least one month's notice. *McIntosh* v. *Vansteenburgh*, 8 Q. B. (Ont.), 248.

A notice of action for false imprisonment was served on defendant, a Justice of the Peace, on the 19th of March, and a writ issued on 17th April. The plaintiff took out a rule to discontinue that suit and got an appointment to tax the costs on the 9th July. On the 7th of July a second notice of action was served on defendant, and a writ issued on Monday, the 9th of August. It was held that if the second notice was bad the plaintiff could avail himself of the first notice, notwithstanding the discontinuance of the suit commenced thereon, the object of the notice being to enable the party to tender amends, and the discontinuance of the first writ or giving the second notice in no way prevented this. It was also held that though the last day of the month's notice expired on Sunday, the defendant had not the whole of the following day to tender amends, and, therefore, the action was not commenced too soon. *Hatch* v. *Taylor*, 1 Pugsley, 39.

Where a Justice acts either wholly without jurisdiction, or entirely in excess of his jurisdiction, the notice of action need not contain an allegation of malice. *Ib.*

The effect of this section is to protect persons acting illegally, but in the supposed pursuance and with a *bona fide* intention of discharging a public duty. If the officer in the supposed discharge of duty had done nothing illegal he would not need the protection of any statute. See *Selmes* v. *Judge*, L. R., 6 Q. B., 724; *McDougall* v. *Peterson*, 40 Q. B. (Ont.), 98. When what is complained of is the negligent omission to do what the defendant was called upon to do in the discharge of the duty of his office, then no notice of action would be required; but where the party neglects to do an act, and in that way carrying out the law according to his erroneous idea of his duty, then he is entitled to notice of action. *McDougall* v. *Peterson, supra*, 101; *Moran* v. *Palmer*, 13 C. P. (Ont.), 528; *Harrison* v. *Brega*, 20 Q. B. (Ont.), 324; *Harrold* v. *Corporation Simcoe*, 16 C. P. (Ont.), 43.

A Justice of the Peace is entitled to notice of action whenever the act which is complained of is done by him in the honest belief that he was acting in the execution of his duty as a magistrate in the premises. *Sprung* v. *Anderson*, 23 C. P. (Ont.), 159; *Booth* v. *Clive*, 10 C. B., 827; *Cox* v. *Reid*, 13 Q. B., 558; *Read* v. *Coker*, 13 C. B., 850; *Friel* v. *Ferguson*, 15 C. P. (Ont.), 584. See further, *Pacaud* v. *Quesnel*, 10 L. C. J., 207; *Bettersworth* v. *Hough*, 10 L. C. J., 184; *Murphy* v. *Ellis*, 2 Hannay, 345; *Condell* v. *Price*, 1 Hannay, 333; *Pickett* v. *Perkins*. 1 Hannay, 131.

In an action for wrongful arrest, though the conviction made by defendant is void, he is entitled to notice of action if he was acting in his official capacity as a magistrate and had jurisdiction over the plaintiff and the subject matter. *Haacke* v. *Adamson*, 14 C. P. (Ont.), 201.

If it be doubtful whether defendant was acting in the execution of his duty, it should be left to the jury to say whether they believed he was acting as a magistrate or not, and if they find in his favour on that point, notice must be proved. *Carswell* v. *Huffman*, 1 Q. B. (Ont.), 381.

Under the 29 Vic., chap. 33, proceedings under the Master and Servant's Act (Con. Stats. U. C., chap. 75) must be taken within one month after the engagement has ceased. A magistrate having entertained a case under the Act, notwithstanding more than a month had elapsed since the termination of the engagement, and although he was told that he had no jurisdiction and was shown a professional opinion to that effect and referred to the statute, the court held in an action against the magistrate that the jury were warranted in finding that he did not *bona fide* believe that he was acting in the execution of his duty in a matter within his jurisdiction, and that he was, therefore, not entitled to notice of action. *Cummins* v. *Moore*, 37 Q. B. (Ont.), 130.

Defendant, a Justice of the Peace, commenced a trial, but being required as a witness in the cause, another Justice took up the trial during the examination, after which the defendant resumed it, and during the latter stage of the trial committed an assault on the plaintiff. It was held that, though the defendant, when he committed the assault, was acting without jurisdiction, having no right to resume the trial under the Rev. Stats. N. B., chap. 137, s. 28, still, if he had reasonable grounds to believe that he had jurisdiction to do so, he was entitled to notice of action, and that this question should have been left to the jury. *Sumner* v. *McMonagle*, Stephens Dig., N. B., 10.

Where the plaintiff's evidence shows that the defendant sued in trespass was acting *bona fide* as a Justice of the Peace, and the Jury so find, the plaintiff must prove notice of action, and this though defendant has pleaded only the general issue without adding "by Statute" in the margin. *Marsh* v. *Boulton*, 4 Q. B. (Ont.), 354.

A magistrate is entitled to notice though he has acted without jurisdiction. Where it was clear that defendant had acted as a Justice and there was no evidence of malice, except the want of jurisdiction, it was held not necessary to entitle him to notice to leave it to the jury to say whether he had acted in good faith. *Bross* v. *Huber*, 18 Q. B. (Ont.), 282.

Where a magistrate acts in direct contravention of the statute in issuing a warrant without the proper information under the statute, or without even a verbal charge having been laid against the plaintff, and there is no evidence of *bona fides* on his part, he is not entitled to notice of action. *Friel* v. *Ferguson*, 15 C. P. (Ont.), 584.

The Justice must honestly believe that he was acting in the execution of his duty as a magistrate with respect to some matter within his jurisdiction, or he must honestly believe he was acting in the execution of his office. He must believe in the existence of those facts, which, if they had existed, would have afforded him a justification under the statute, and honestly intended to put the law in force (*ib*).

In the above case the court expressed an opinion that the fact of a magistrate issuing a warrant without the limits of the county for which he acts, does not necessarily disentitle him to notice of action.

Where a magistrate acts clearly in excess of, or without jurisdiction, he is nevertheless entitled to notice, unless the *bona fides* of his conduct be disproved; but the plaintiff may require that question to be left to the jury, and if they find that he did not honestly believe he was acting as a magistrate, he has no claim to notice. *Neill* v. *McMillan*, 25 Q. B. (Ont.), 485.

The following notice of action :—" And also for that you on" &c., "at" &c., did cause the horse upon which the said J. U., was then riding, to be seized, taken, and led away, and the said J. U. to be obliged to dismount and give up the said horse, and converted and disposed of the said horse to your own use, and also for that you caused the saddle and bridle and halter then on the said horse to be seized, taken, and carried away, and to be converted and disposed of to your own use, and other wrongs to the said J. U., then and there did" &c., was held sufficient to enable the plaintiff to recover the value of the horse as being his property. *Upper* v. *McFarland*, 5 Q. B. (Ont.), 101.

So the following notice was held sufficient : " For that you (the defendant), on" &c., " at" &c., " seized and took away divers goods and chattels of the plaintiff," stating the value, "and converted and disposed thereof to your own use, and other wrongs to the said (the plaintiff), did to his great damage of £50, and against the peace of our Lady the Queen." *Gillespie* v. *Wright*, 14 Q. B. (Ont.), 52. See as to form of action, *Connolly* v. *Adams*, 11 Q. B. (Ont.), 327.

A notice of action was given to a Justice of the Peace in the following words :—" To John G. Bowes, of the City of Toronto, Esquire, I, Annie Armstrong, of the City of Toronto, in the Province of Canada, spinster, residing with my father, James Armstrong, at No. 148 Duchess Street, in the said City of Toronto, &c.," and was signed by the plaintiff, and endorsed "C. P., *Armstrong* v. *Bowes*. Notice of Annie Armstrong to John G. Bowes. The within named Annie Armstrong resides at No. 148 Duchess street, in the City of Toronto, Cameron & McMichael for the plaintiff." It was held that this notice did not conform to the provisions of the 10th section of the statute, not having the place of abode or business of the attorney endorsed, nor the court in which the action was to be brought, stated. *Armstrong* v. *Bowes*, 12 C. P. (Ont.), 539. The place of abode or business of the attorney or agent is necessary if the notice is served by the attorney or agent, or the clerk of the attorney for him. A person who serves it as agent for the plaintiff, must endorse his name and place of abode, or business (*ib.*) and the notice must also be endorsed with the name and place of abode of the plaintiff. *Moran* v. *Palmer*, 13 C. P. (Ont.), 528.

The notice must declare the place of residence of the attorney. The subscription therefore of the attorney at the bottom of the notice, "A. B., Attorney for the said C. D., Simcoe, Talbot District," was held insufficient. *Bates* v. *Walsh*, 6 Q. B. (Ont.), 498; see also *Gillespie* v. *Wright*, 14 Q. B. (Ont.), 52.

Where the name and place of residence of the plaintiff's attorney were not endorsed on the notice but added inside at the foot of it, this was held sufficient. *Bross* v. *Huber*, 15 Q. B. (Ont.), 625.

The name and place of abode of the plaintiff's attorney need not be endorsed on the back of the notice; it is sufficient if it appears on any part of it. *Baxter* v. *Hallett*, Stephens Dig., N.B., 11. As on the face of it (*De Gondouin* v. *Lewis*, 10 A. & E. 117), if he describes his residence as of Birmingham generally, it will be sufficient (*Osborn* v. *Gough*, 3 B. & P., 551); but merely "given under my hand at Durham," was holden insufficient, for it was not descriptive at all of the attorney's place of abode. *Taylor* v. *Fenwick*, 7 T. R., 635.

A notice describing plaintiff's place of abode, as "of the Township of Garafraxa, in the County of Wellington, labourer," without giving the lot and concession, was held sufficient. *Neill* v. *McMillan*, 25 Q. B. (Ont.), 485.

A notice of action describing the plaintiff's residence, as of the Township of B., in the County of P., is sufficient. *McDonald* v. *Stuckey*, 31 Q. B. (Ont.), 577; see also, *Neill* v. *McMillan*, 25 Q. B. (Ont.), 485.

This notice may be served before the conviction, order or warrant complained of has been quashed, under the 4th section of the Act. *Haylock* v. *Sparke*, 22 L. J., M. C., 67.

A notice of action charging a Justice with an arrest and imprisonment, must state the time at which the grievance was committed, or otherwise it will be defective. *Sprung* v. *Anderson*, 23 C. P. (Ont.), 152.

A notice of action in trespass under "The Division Courts Act." Rev. Stats. (Ont.), chap. 47, s. 231, which is substantially the same as the Rev. Stat. (Ont.), chap. 73, was held insufficient for not stating the time and place of the alleged trespass. *Moore* v. *Gidley*, 32 Q. B. (Ont.), 233.

And it seems in an action against a Justice for arrest and imprisonment, the notice of action must allege a time and place. In an action against a Justice, the notice of action stated that the defendant assaulted plaintiff, imprisoned and kept him in prison for a long time, to wit, four days, and caused him to be illegally arrested, and gave him into the custody of a constable, and illegally committed and sent him in such custody to the gaol, at the Town of Lindsay, and caused him to be there confined for a long time. The notice was held insufficient, as omitting to state where and when the assault took place, and the evidence not being confined to the imprisonment at Lindsay. *Parkyn* v. *Staples*, 19 C. P. (Ont.), 240.

A notice of action to a person acting as a constable under the Con. Stats. L. C., chap. 101, stated the cause of action to the effect following: "For that you on the 20th day of December, 1864, unlawfully did apprehend and seize A. B., and unlawfully did keep him a prisoner for a long space of time, to wit, for the space of four days, and other wrongs to the said A. B. then did," it was held that this notice was defective in not shewing the place where the injury complained of was sustained. *Bettersworth* v. *Hough*, 16 L. C. R., 419.

The notice of action must contain a statement of the place where the trespass or injury was committed. *Kemble* v. *McGarry*, 6 O. S., 570. A notice of action against a magistrate must distinctly specify the place where the act complained of was done. *Madden* v. *Shewer*, 2 Q. B. (Ont.), 115.

The place where the plaintiff was imprisoned must be correctly stated. *Cronkhite* v. *Somerville*, 3 Q.B. (Ont.), 129. The notice stated a trespass on the 18th October and on divers other days. The goods were seized on that day, but returned and seized on the 18th of November and sold; the notice was held sufficient. *Oliphant* v. *Leslie*, 24 Q.B. (Ont.), 398.

The notice need not describe the form of action (*Sabin* v. *Debury*, 2 Camp., 196); but if it do, and state it incorrectly, the variance will be fatal. *Strickland* v. *Ward*, 7 T. R. 631 n.

A notice that the suit will be brought in the Court of Queen's Bench or Common Pleas is insufficient; the particular court intended must be specified. *Bross* v. *Huber*, 18 Q.B. (Ont.), 282; *Neville* v. *Corporation Ross*, 22 C.P. (Ont.), 487; see also *Armstrong* v. *Bowes*, 12 C.P. (Ont.), 539.

The forms prescribed by this statute must be strictly followed in the notice of action, and where the notice stated that the writ would be issued in one of the superior courts, but it was by mistake issued in the other court, it was held that the notice could not be amended, though section 49 of the Administration of Justice Act, 1873, provides that no proceeding at law or in equity shall be defeated by any formal objection, the objection not being of such a character as to be cured by this Act. *M'Crum* v. *Foley*, 6 P.R. (Ont.), 164; 10 C.L.J., N.S., 105.

It is no objection that the plaintiff declares by a different attorney from the one by whom the notice was given and process issued. *McKenzie* v. *Mewburn*, 6 O. S. 486.

Where a defendant after accepting service of an informal notice added, "and agree to accept the same as a sufficient notice of action to me under the statute," it was held that he could not afterwards rely on a defect in the notice. *Donaldson* v. *Haley*, 13 C.P. (Ont.), 87.

No particular addition or description of the magistrate need be given in the notice. *Haacke* v. *Adamson*, 14 C.P. (Ont.), 201.

It is not necessary to give notice of an action for a penalty against a Justice of the Peace for acting without proper property qualification ; a Justice acting without qualification is not entitled to such notice. *Crabb q.t.* v. *Longworth*, 4 C.P. (Ont.), 283.

Neither is notice of action necessary in an action for not returning a conviction. *Grant q.t.* v. *McFadden*, 11 C.P. (Ont.), 122.

11. In every such action the venue shall be laid in the County where the act complained of was committed, and in actions in County or Division Courts the action shall be brought in the County or Division within which the act complained of was committed or in which the defendant resides, and the defendant may plead the general issue, and give any special matter of defence, excuse or justification in evidence under such plea at the trial of the action.

12. No action shall be brought in any County or Division Court against a Justice of the Peace for anything done by him in the execution of his office if the Justice objects thereto ; and if within six days after being served with a notice of any such action, such Justice or his attorney or agent gives a written notice to the plaintiff in the intended action that he objects to being sued in such County or Division Court for such cause of action, no proceedings shall afterwards be had in such County or Division Court in any such action, but it shall not be necessary to give another notice of action in order to sue such Justice in any other Court.

13. In every such case after notice of action has been given as aforesaid, and before an action has been commenced, the Justice to whom such notice has been given may tender to the party complaining, or to his attorney or agent, such sum of money as he thinks fit as amends for the injury complained of in such notice ; and after the action has been commenced, and at any time before issue joined therein, such defendant, if he has not made a tender, or in addition to the tender, may pay into Court such sum of money as he thinks fit, and such tender and payment of money into Court, or either of them, may afterwards be given in evidence by the defendant at the trial under the general issue.

Where a Justice on receiving notice of action, makes a tender which is not paid into court, and the jury find the tender sufficient, the plaintiff is not entitled to have a verdict for the amount tendered; in other words, the tender without payment into court entitles the defendant to a verdict. *Gidney* v. *Dibblee*, 2 Pugsley, 388.

14. If the jury (or the Judge, if the case be tried without a jury) at the trial be of opinion that the plaintiff is not entitled to damages beyond the sum so tendered or paid into Court, they shall give a verdict for the defendant, and the plaintiff shall not be at liberty to elect to be nonsuited, and the sum of money, if any, so paid into Court, or so much thereof as is sufficient to pay or satisfy the defendant's costs in that behalf, shall thereupon be paid out of Court to him, and the residue, if any, shall be paid to the plaintiff.

15. In case money is paid into Court in any such action, and the plaintiff elects to accept the same in satisfaction of his damages in the action, he may obtain from any Judge of the Court in which the action has been brought, an order that the money shall be paid out of Court to him, and that the defendant shall pay him his costs to be taxed, and thereupon the said action shall be determined, and such order shall be a bar to any other action for the same cause.

16. If at the trial of any such action the plaintiff does not prove.

1. That the action was brought within the time hereinbefore limited in that behalf; and

2. That such notice as aforesaid was given one month before the action was commenced; and

3. The cause of action stated in such notice; and

4. That the cause of action arose in the County or place laid as venue in the margin of the declaration; and

5. (Where the plaintiff sues in a County or Division Court) that the cause of action arose within the County or United Counties for which such Court is holden; then and in any such case the plaintiff shall be nonsuited or a verdict shall be given for the defendant.

17. In case the plaintiff in any such action is entitled to recover, and he proves the levying or payment of any penalty or sum of money under any conviction or order as parcel of the damages he seeks to recover, or if he proves that he was imprisoned under such conviction or order and seeks to recover damages for such imprisonment, and it is proved that he was actually guilty of the offence of which he was so convicted, or that he was liable by

law to pay the sum he was so ordered to pay, and with respect to such imprisonment that he has undergone no greater punishment than that assigned by law for the offence of which he was so convicted, or for non-payment of the sum he was so ordered to pay, he shall not be entitled to recover the amount of such penalty or sum so levied or paid, or any sum beyond the sum of three cents as damages for such imprisonment, or any costs of suit whatsoever.

In New Brunswick the Rev. Stat. chap. 129, s. 11, provides that where the plaintiff shall be entitled to recover in any action against a Justice he shall not have a verdict for any damages beyond two pence, or any costs of suit, if it shall be proved that he was guilty of the offence of which he was convicted or was liable for the sum he was ordered to pay, and had undergone no greater punishment than that assigned by law.

The plaintiff having been convicted before defendants, two Justices of the Peace, of selling spirituous liquors without a license was fined a certain sum to be levied by distress, and if not paid within a limited time plaintiff to be imprisoned. At the expiration of the time limited for payment, defendants issued a warrant of commitment without previous issue of distress warrant. In an action against the Justices for false imprisonment, the court held that as the plaintiff was guilty of the offence of which she was convicted and her imprisonment did not exceed that assigned by law to the offence, the defendants were entitled to the protection of the statute. *Smith* v. *Simmons*, 2 Pugsley, 203.

This statute is substantially the same as the 17th section of the Rev. Stat. (Ont.), chap. 73. See *Campbell* v. *Flewelling*, 2 Pugsley, 403. But the statute will not apply if the Justice had no right to issue the warrant, and the plaintiff was not liable to pay the amount which by the warrant he was ordered to pay, and he has suffered a greater punishment than that assigned by law to the offence. *Campbell* v. *Flewelling, supra.*

This section of the statute is not confined to actions in which the Justices had jurisdiction. *Bross* v. *Haber*, 15 Q. B. (Ont.), 625. It extends as well to trespass as to case. *Haacke* v. *Adamson*, 14 C. P. (Ont.), 201.

The damages must be reduced where the defendant is proved

guilty of the offence of which he was convicted. *Haacke* v. *Adamson*, 14 C. P. (Ont.), 201.

The warrant of commitment directed the plaintiff to be kept at hard labour, which the Act under which the conviction took place does not authorize. The turnkey swore that the plaintiff "did no hard work in gaol." It was held, however, that this was not sufficient to show that he was not put to compulsory work, so as to bring the defendant within that part of the section which requires it to be proved that the defendant had undergone no greater punishment than that assigned by law to the offence. *Graham* v. *McArthur*, 25 Q. B. (Ont.), 478.

18. If the plaintiff in any such action recovers a verdict, or the defendant allows judgment to pass against him by default, the plaintiff shall be entitled to costs in the same manner as if this Act had not been passed.

19. If in any such case it is stated in the declaration, or in the summons and particulars if the plaintiff sues in the Division Court, that the Act complained of was done maliciously and without reasonable and probable cause, the plaintiff, if he recovers a verdict for any damages, or if the defendant allows judgment to pass against him by default, shall be entitled to his full costs of suit, to be taxed as between attorney and client; and in every action against a Justice of the Peace for anything done by him in the execution of his office, the defendant, if he obtains judgment upon verdict or otherwise, shall in all cases be entitled to his full costs in that behalf, to be taxed as between attorney and client.

20. So far as applicable, the whole of this Act shall apply for the protection of every officer and person mentioned in the first section hereof, for anything done in the execution of his office as therein expressed.

The privilege extended to Justices by the 4 & 5 Vic., chap. 26, as regards exemption from costs, were not cancelled by the latter Act, 14 & 15 Vic., chap. 54. *Finlay* v. *Raile*, 9 Q. B. (Ont.), 666.

Two actions were brought against a Justice for trespass and false imprisonment; on the 30th of August, 1851, a verdict for the plaintiff was found in one case of £2 10*s*., and in the other of 1s., it was held that the 14 & 15 Vic., chap. 54, applied, and that the plaintiff was entitled to his full costs in both suits. *Keely* v. *Raile*, 2 P.R. (Ont.), 155.

Where the plaintiff was restricted to only three cents damages he was held not to be entitled to any costs. It was held, also, that the 18th and 19th sections of the Con. Stats. U. C., chap. 126, taken together must be limited "to any such action" not provided for in section 17 of the same Act. It was held, also, that no one can have costs taxed to him who did not incur costs. *Haacke* v. *Adamson*, 10 U. C., L. J., 270.

When a magistrate commits a party for contempt, and on action brought for false imprisonment the plaintiff succeeds, he is entitled to full costs without a certificate. *Armour* v. *Boswell*, 6 O. S., 450.

SUMMARY OF THE CRIMINAL LAW OF CANADA.

ABANDONING CHILD.

(*See* CHILD.)

ABDUCTION.

The Statute 32 & 33 Vic., chap. 20, ss. 54, 55, embraces three classes of cases:—(1) Where a woman of any age, possessed of property, is from motives of lucre taken away or detained against her will, with intent to marry or carnally know her, or to cause her to be married or carnally known by any other person; (2) Where a woman under the age of twenty-one years is fraudulently allured out of the possession and against the will of her father, or of any other person having the lawful care or charge of her, with intent to marry or carnally know her, or to cause her to be married or carnally known by any other person; (3) Where a woman of any age is taken away and detained by force and against her will, with intent to marry or carnally know her, or to cause her to be married or carnally known by any other person.

It will be observed that the statute applies whether the prisoner's intention is to marry the woman himself, or to assist any other person to do so.

It would seem that it is necessary in the second case above put, that the woman should be possessed of property as in the first case, and in neither of these cases will the offender take any interest in such property.

The alleged wife is in all these cases a competent witness against the prisoner. *R* v. *Wakefield*, 1 Lew., 279.

In the second case it will be observed that the woman must be taken out of the possession of her father. This involves both a *taking* and also a *possession* by the father.

If the girl leaves without any inducement on the part of the defendant, and then goes to him, he is not within the statute. *R.* v. *Olifier*, 10 Cox, 402. Neither is he within the statute if it does not appear that he knew or had reason to believe that the girl was under the lawful care or charge of her father or mother, or any other person. *R.* v. *Hibbert*, L.R., 1 C.C.R., 184.

Of course mere absence for a temporary purpose, and with intention of returning, does not interrupt the possession of the father. It is no defence that the defendant did not know her to be under sixteen, or might suppose from her appearance that she was older, or even that he believed that he knew she was over that age. *R.* v. *Prince*, L. R., 2 C.C.R., 154. A taking by force is not necessary to constitute the offence. It is immaterial whether there be any corrupt motive, whether the girl consent, and whether the defendant be a male or female. *R.* v. *Hawley*, 1 F. & F., 648.

The expression, " taking out of the possession," means taking the girl to some place where the person in whose charge she is cannot exercise control over her, for some purpose inconsistent with the object of such control; a taking for a time only may amount to abduction. If the consent of the person from whose possession the girl is taken is obtained by fraud, the taking is deemed to be against the will of such person. *R.* v. *Prince*, L. R., 2 C.C.R,. 154.

An information under the 56th section of this statute which does not show that the unmarried girl is under sixteen years of age, and is taken out of the possession of and against the will of the father is insufficient. *Whittier* v. *Diblee*, 2 Pugsley, 243.

Under this 56th section, the girl must be in the posession of some person having the lawful care or charge of her, but if such exist, the consent of the girl to go away will not be a defence for the prisoner. A guardian is a person having the lawful care, &c., within the meaning of the statute, and it is not necessary to prove a strict guardianship. If the girl leave her guardian's house for a particular purpose with his sanction, and with the intention of returning, she does not cease to be in his possession within the meaning of the statute. There must be proof of the age of the girl, but the girl herself and her father or mother are competent to prove this. A certificate is not necessary, at all events where the prisoner undertakes to establish that the girl was not baptized. *R.* v. *Mondelet*, 21 L. C. J., 154.

ABORTION.

Under the 32 & 33 Vic., chap. 20, ss. 59, 60, three classes of persons may be guilty of crimes under this heading. The woman herself, the person who procures or supplies the drugs, &c., some other person.

For a woman being with child, with intent to procure her own miscarriage, to administer to herself any poison or other noxious drug, or to use any instrument or other means, *or* for any person to do the same with intent to procure the miscarriage of any woman, whether she be with child or not, is felony.

For any person to procure or supply poison or other noxious thing, or any instrument or other thing, knowing that the same is intended to be unlawfully used with intent to procure the miscarriage of a woman, is a misdemeanor.

Under the 40 Vic., chap. 28 administering poison, &c., with intent to commit murder, is felony.

If A procures poison and delivers it to B, both intending that B should take it for the purpose of procuring abortion, and B afterwards takes it with that intent in the absence of A, the latter may be convicted of causing it to be taken, under the 59th section of the 32 & 33 Vic., chap. 20. *R.* v. *Wilson*, 1 Dears. & B., 127.

The prisoner gave a woman savin and also directions how to take it. The woman took the savin accordingly. The prisoner also made up into pills a drug which the woman had obtained at the prisoner's request. After taking the savin and pills, the woman became and continued very ill until she was confined. It was held that this was a causing to be taken within the section. *R.* v. *Farron*, 1 Dears. & B., 164.

A woman became pregnant by the prisoner, and died from the effects of corrosive sublimate taken by her for the purpose of procuring abortion. The prisoner knowingly procured it for the deceased at her instigation, and under the influence of her threat of self-destruction if the means of procuring abortion were not supplied to her, it was held that the prisoner was not guilty of murder as an accessory before the fact. *R.* v. *Fretwell*, 9 Cox C. C., 152.

The thing supplied must be proved to be noxious, the supplying an innoxious drug, whatever may be the intent of the person supplying it, is not an offence against this section. *R.* v. *Isaacs*, 1 L. & C., 220.

Under section 60 of the Act, it is not necessary that the woman herself should intend to use the drug, or that any other person than the one who procured it should intend that it should be used. *R.* v. *Hillman*, 9 Cox C. C., 386.

ACCESSORIES.

(*See* Principals and Accessories.)

ACCOMPLICE.

A Justice has no power to make a promise of pardon, and it is his duty to commit an accomplice for trial, notwithstanding it is intended that he should give evidence for the prosecution.

Where the evidence would be too weak to justify a commitment, independent of the testimony of the accomplice, the proper course seems to be to take the deposition of the accomplice in the usual way, cautioning him at the same time that he is not bound to say anything which may criminate himself. In this case the accomplice would be bound over as a witness, and the circumstances explained to the Judge before the indictment against the prisoner is presented to the Grand Jury. Stone's Jus. Man., 48.

ADULTERATION OF FOOD, DRINK AND DRUGS.

The law on this subject is contained chiefly in the 37 Vic., chap. 8 (amended by the 40 Vic., chap. 13). Under this statute wilfully admixing, or ordering any other person to admix, with any article of food or drink, any deleterious or poisonous ingredient or material, to adulterate the same for sale, and wilfully admixing and ordering any other person to admix, any ingredient or material, with any drug, to adulterate the same for sale, subjects the offender, for the first offence, to a penalty of one hundred dollars, together with costs attending the conviction, and, for the second offence, the party is guilty of a misdemeanor, and is to be imprisoned for a period not exceeding six calendar months, with hard labour.

Where a person sold as butter a composition of butter, lard, dripping, tallow, palm oil and the fat of certain seeds, it was held that, unless the seller said that the butter was adulterated, he represented it to be butter and not anything else, and that no hardship was imposed on the seller by this construction, as he could easily ascertain whether the article was pure or not. *Fitzpatrick* v. *Kelly*, L. R., 8 Q. B., 337.

The appellant, a tea dealer, was convicted for selling as unadulterated, "green tea" which was adulterated. A person asked for two ounces of "green tea," at the appellant's shop, for which he paid 5½d., the shopman stating that he was authorized by his employers to guarantee all their green teas, of the value of 3s. per pound and upwards, as genuine green teas. On analysis the tea was proved to be painted, or faced with gypsum and Prussian blue, for the purpose of colouring it. The tea was sold in the same state in which it comes from abroad. The tea which is imported from China as green tea, and generally known as such in the tea trade, is painted and faced in this manner, but this practice is not known to the public. Pure green tea, though not known generally in the trade as "green tea" is imported from Japan. It was held that the conviction was right, under section 23 of the Act. *Roberts* v. *Egerton*, L. R., 9 Q. B., 494.

A person who sells mustard admixed with flour and turmeric, substances not injurious to health, declaring at the time of such sale that he did not sell the article as pure mustard, is not guilty of an offence under the 24th section, and it is not necessary in order to comply with this section, that he should declare the nature and proportion of the substances admixed. *Pope and Tearle*, L. R., 9 C. P. 499.

AFFRAY.

A fighting between two or more persons in some *public* place, to the terror of Her Majesty's subjects: for example, a prize fight. If it takes place in private, it will be an assault. It differs from a riot, inasmuch as there must be three persons to constitute the latter, and also in not being premeditated.

AGENTS, BANKERS, FACTORS, ATTORNEYS.

The 32 & 33 Vic., chap. 21, s. 76, relates to frauds by persons of this class. Although this statute uses the words "or other agent," they do not extend the meaning of the previous words, but only signify persons, the nature of whose occupation is such that chattels, valuable securities, &c., belonging to third persons would, in the usual course of their business, be entrusted to them. *R.* v. *Hynes*, 13 Q. B. (Ont.), 194; *R.* v. *Armstrong*, 20 Q. B. (Ont.), 245.

Under this section, there must be a direction in writing to apply the money in a specific manner. Where there is no such direction in writing, the prisoner cannot be convicted. *R.* v. *Cooper*, L. R., 2 C. C. R., 123.

The second branch of the section seems to apply to cases where the party deals with the securities without authority, and contrary to the purpose for which they were entrusted, and where the security, &c., is used for the purpose for which it is entrusted, the charge cannot be sustained, unless, perhaps, in a case where it is shewn that the prisoner at the time of receiving the security, intended to convert it to his own use. *R.* v. *Tatlock*, L. R., 2 Q. B. D., 157. See also on the construction of this section, *R.* v. *Christian*, L. R., 2 C. C. R., 94.

Misdemeanors under these sections are not triable at sessions. (32 & 33 Vic., chap. 21, s. 92); and if committed by a firm, &c., the person actually doing the act is alone liable. *Ib.* s. 91.

In regard to agency, a man is in general liable for what he authorizes another person to do. Thus where several persons combine for an unlawful purpose, any act by one of such persons in *prosecution* of such purposes renders all liable. *R.* v. *Curtley*, 27 Q. B. (Ont.), 613; *R.* v. *Slavin*, 17 C. P. (Ont.), 205.

See *post*, Indictable offences; also Principals and acessories.

So the owner of a shop is criminally liable for any unlawful act done therein in his absence, by a clerk or assistant; as for instance, for the sale of liquor without license by a female attendant. *R.* v. *King*, 20 C. P. (Ont.), 246.

AGGRESSIONS BY SUBJECTS OF FOREIGN STATES.

The 31 Vic., chap. 14, now protects the inhabitants of Canada against lawless aggressions from subjects of foreign states, at peace with Her Majesty. This Act was extended to Prince Edward Island by the 40 Vic., chap. 4; to the District of Keewatin, by the 39 Vic., chap. 21; to the North-West Territories by the 38 Vic., chap. 49, and to British Columbia by the 37 Vic., chap. 42. See also the 31 Vic., chap. 16, and 33 Vic., chap. 1.

The second section of the statute does not apply to a British subject, but only to a citizen or subject of any foreign state or country. See *R.* v. *McMahon*, 26 Q. B. (Ont.), 195.

The third section of the statute applies to the case of a British subject. *R.* v. *Lynch*, 26 Q. B. (Ont.), 208.

Where the prisoner is proved to have said he was an American citizen, and had been in the American army, and there is no evidence offered to contradict this, it is evidence against the prisoner as his own admissions and declarations of the country to which he belonged. *R.* v. *Slavin*, 17 C. P. (Ont.), 205.

Where a large body of armed men enter Canada, with intent to levy war, any person joining them *in any character*, though in itself peaceable, such as reporter merely, is equally liable with the others, for there is a common unfawful purpose, and any act in pursuance of it involves a share of the common guilt. *R.* v. *Lynch*, 26 Q. B. (Ont.), 208.

It is not necessary in order to render a party amenable to the statute, that he should actually have arms upon his person, it is quite sufficient that he is present and concerned with those who are armed for all who are present at the commission of the offence are principals, and are alike culpable in law. *R.* v. *Slavin*, 17 C. P. (Ont.), 205.

Under the fourth section of the Act, the offence in the case of a foreigner, and a subject is substantially different, In the case of a British subject, the Act in the second section requires proof.

not only of the *status* as such subject, but also of joining with foreigners in the commission of it. See *R.* v. *Magrath*, 26 Q. B. (Ont.), 385.

APOSTACY.

The Imperial Statute 9 & 10 Wm. III., chap. 32, s. 1, provides that if any one educated in or having made profession of the Christian religion, by writing, printing, teaching or advised speaking, maintains that there are more Gods than one, or denies the Christian religion to be true or the Holy Scripture to be of Divine authority, for the second offence, besides being incapable of bringing an action, or being guardian, executor, legatee or grantee, must suffer imprisonment for three years without bail. There shall be no prosecution for such words spoken, unless information of such words be given on oath before a Justice, within four days after they are spoken, and the prosecution be within three months after such information. The offender is to be discharged, if within four months after his first conviction he renounces his error.

APPRENTICE.

The Con. Stat. U. C., chap. 76, contained provisions respecting apprentices and minors. See Rev. Stat. (Ont.), chap. 135.

When the defendant, a Justice of the Peace, convicted one Q., an apprentice, for having absented himself from his master's service without leave, and adjudged that he should give sufficient security to make satisfaction to his master, according to the statute, and in default of such satisfaction to be imprisoned in the Common Gaol for two months unless the said satisfaction be sooner given. The conviction was quashed—first, because the articles of apprenticeship were not within the Act, for it appeared that the apprentice was a minor, and the articles were not executed by any one on his behalf, and secondly, because it could not be sustained under the 10th clause of the statute for two months' imprisonment, or under the 11th clause, because the satisfaction to be given was not ascertained, and as it was not ascertained, it amounted to an absolute imprisonment for two months, which was not authorized by the statute. *R. v. Robertson*, 11 Q. B. (Ont.), 621.

ARREST.

The Act respecting larceny and other similar offences, 32 & 33 Vic., chap. 21, s. 117, provides that any person found committing any offence punishable either upon indictment or upon summary conviction by virtue of this Act, may be immediately apprehended without a warrant by any person and forthwith taken together with the property if any on, or with respect to which the offence is committed, before some neighbouring Justice of the Peace to be dealt with according to law. So by the same section, the person to whom stolen property is offered may arrest the party offering it; see also 32 & 33 Vic., chap. 29, s. 3. By the Act respecting malicious injuries to property, (32 & 33 Vic., chap. 22, s. 69,) persons found committing any offence against the Act may in like manner be immediately apprehended without a warrant by any peace officer, or the owner of the property injured, or his servant. Similar provision is made by the 32 & 33 Vic., chap. 29, s. 2, and by section 4 any person may apprehend any other person found committing any indictable offence in the night; so by section 5 a constable or peace officer may without a warrant take into custody any person whom he finds lying or loitering in any highway, yard or other place during the night, and whom he has good cause to suspect of having committed or being about to commit any felony. By section 6 such person must be brought before a Justice of the Peace by noon of the following day.

Under the 33rd section of the 32 & 33 Vic., chap. 18, relating to coin, &c., any person may apprehend any other person found committing an indictable offence against the Act, and may convey or deliver him to some peace officer, in order to his being conveyed as soon as reasonably may be before a Justice of the Peace, to be dealt with according to law. Under the 32 & 33 Vic., chap. 20, s. 37, persons disturbing any assemblage of persons met for religious worship may be arrested on view by any peace officer present at such meeting, or by any other person thereto verbally authorized by any Justice of the Peace present thereat.

See further as to arrest, the Act for the better preservation of the peace in the vicinity of public works (32 & 33 Vic., chap. 24, s. 8); also the Act respecting certain offences relative to Her Majesty's army and navy (32 & 33 Vic., chap. 25, s. 7,) also the Act respecting cruelty to animals (32 & 33 Vic., chap. 27. s. 4,) and the Act respecting riots, (31 Vic., chap. 70, s. 4).

When it is intended to arrest an offender on the ground of his being "found committing" an offence against these Acts, the offender must be taken either in the act of committing the offence or on fresh pursuit. *Hanway* v. *Boultbee*, 1 M. & R., 15, but not on his return after committing the offence. *R.* v. *Phelps*, C. & M., 180. The words "found committing" mean either seeing the party actually committing the offence or pursuing him immediately and continuously after his committing of it. *R.* v. *Curran*, 3 C. & P., 397. Pursuit after an interval of three hours would not be a fresh pursuit. *Downing* v. *Capel*, L. R., 2 C. P., 461; *Leete* v. *Hart*, 37 L. J., C. P., 157. Immediately in the statute means after the commission of the offence, and not after its discovery. *Ib.*

Where a man is himself insulted by a person disturbing the peace in a public street, he may arrest the offender and take him to a peace officer to answer for a breach of the peace. *Forrester* v. *Clarke*, 3 Q. B. (Ont.), 151.

The fact that a party is violently assaulting the wife and child of another, is no legal justification for the latter, not being a peace officer, breaking into the house of the former in order to prevent the breach of the peace. *Rockwell* v. *Murray*, 6 Q. B. (Ont.), 412.

In *King* v. *Poe*, 15 L. T. N. S. 37, it was left undecided and in doubt whether a magistrate has a right to arrest a person for a misdemeanor committed in his view. Where there has been no breach of the peace, actual or apprehended, a magistrate has no right to detain a known person to answer a charge of misdemeanor verbally intimated to him, without a regular information before him in his capacity of magistrate that he may be able to judge whether it charges any offence to which the party ought to answer. *Caudle* v. *Ferguson*, 1 Q. B., 889.

Where a magistrate allows a prisoner to depart without examining into the charge against him with a direction to appear the next morning at the police office, and in the meantime on the ground that he was insulted by the prisoner when in custody before him the previous evening, gives verbal instructions to a constable to apprehend him and take him to the station-house or gaol, such imprisonment is illegal, and the magistrate cannot justify the arrest. *Powell* v. *Williamson*, 1 Q. B. (Ont.), 154.

Under the 1 Vic., chap. 21, it is illegal in a magistrate to cause the arrest of a party in the first instance, he must be first summoned before him. *Cronkhite* v. *Sommerville*, 3 Q. B. (Ont.), 129.

Where a defendant has been brought before one magistrate and bailed by him, although the statute may require the presence of three to convict the prisoner, a second arrest for the same charge by the same complainant before the time appointed for hearing is illegal. *King* v. *Orr*, 5 O. S. 724.

After the arrest of a person on suspicion of felony, a Justice of the Peace can only detain him a reasonable time for examination. *Ashley* v. *Dundas*, 5 O. S. 754.

ARSON.

This offence is regulated by the Act 32 & 33 Vic. chap. 22. It arises where a person unlawfully and maliciously sets fire to the house of another, or to any building described in the Act as the subject of arson. The setting fire must be to such an extent that some part of the house is actually burnt, and a bare intent or attempt to set fire to the house is not sufficient. Arch. Crim. Pldg., 509; see, however, section 12, *post*. The offence may also be committed when a party sets fire to a house whether it is then in his possession, or the possession of any other person, but in such case there must be an intent to injure or defraud some third person, as for instance when a man sets fire to his own house to defraud an Insurance Company. *R.* v. *Bryans*, 12 C.P. (Ont.), 161; 32 & 33 Vic., chap. 22, ss. 3 & 67. The burning must be malicious, but the malice need not be directed against the owner of the property. 32 & 33 Vic., chap. 22, s. 66. The burning must also be wilful and no negligence or mis-chance will amount to such a burning. 2 Russ Cr., 1025.

The 7th section of the 32 & 33 Vic., chap. 22, extends the

17

meaning of the term building. Under this section, the building need not necessarily be a completed or finished structure, it is sufficient if it is a connected and entire structure. *R.* v. *Manning*, L. R., 1 C. C. R., 338.

Under the 3rd section of the 32 & 33 Vic., chap. 22, the intent to injure or defraud is made a part of the crime, and must be proved at the trial. *R.* v. *Cronin*, 36 Q. B. (Ont.), 342.

This intention must be to injure or defraud some person who is not identified with the defendant. Therefore a married woman cannot be indicted for setting fire to the house of her husband with intent to injure him. *R.* v. *March*, 1 Mood. C. C., 182.

But it is not necessary to prove an intent to injure or defraud any particular person. It is sufficient to prove that the party accused did the act charged, with intent to injure or defraud, as the case may be. 32 & 33 Vic., chap. 22, s. 68.

The general rule that a party intends the natural consequences of his act must apply in arson as well as other cases. An "unoccupied" building may come within section 3 of the Statute, for if no one else is in occupation or possession of the building, the owner is in law in "possession." *R.* v. *Cronin*, 36 Q. B. (Ont.), 342.

An unfinished structure, intended to be used as a house, is not a house within the meaning of section 3 of this Act. *R.* v. *Edgell*, 11 Cox. C. C. 132.

Under section 8 of the statute, setting fire to goods in any building under such circumstances, that if the building were thereby set fire to, the offence would amount to felony, is felony. Under this section an intent to injure the owner of the goods is not sufficient, there must also be an intention to injure the owner of the building, and the act must be wilful and malicious as against him. *R.* v. *Child*, L. R., 1 C. C. R., 307.

The prisoner wilfully set fire to goods consisting of furniture and stock in trade, being in a house in his occupation, with intent to defraud an insurance company. The house was not set on fire or burnt, but he was held guilty of felony. *R.* v. *Lyons*, 8 Cox C. C., 84.

Throwing a light into a letter-box with the intention of burning the letters, but not the house, is not a felony within this section. *R.* v. *Batstone*, 10 Cox C. C., 20.

Under the 9th section, recklessly and negligently setting fire to forests, &c., is a misdemeanor, and by section 10 a magistrate may, when the offence is not serious, dispose of the matter summarily.

Under section 12 of the 32 & 23 Vic., chap. 22. unlawfully and maliciously attempting, by any overt act, to set fire to any building under such circumstances that if the same were thereby set fire to the offender would be guilty of felony, is felony.

The prisoner saturated a blanket with coal oil, and placed it so that if the flames were communicated to it the building would have caught fire. He then lighted a match and held it in his fingers till it was burning well, and then put it down towards the blanket and got it within an inch or two of the blanket when the match went out. The blaze did not touch the blanket, and the prisoner threw away the match and left without making any second attempt. No fire was actually communicated to the oil or blanket, it was held that these were overt acts immediately and directly tending to the execution of the principal crime, and that the prisoner was properly convicted under this section of an attempt at arson. *R.* v. *Goodman*, 22 C. P. (Ont.), 338.

Setting fire to a quantity of straw on a lory is not setting fire to a stack of straw within the meaning of the 21st section, the the straw being on its way to market, and it not appearing whether it was being removed to or from a stack. *R.* v. *Satchwell*, L. R., 2 C. C. R., 21.

ASSAULT AND BATTERY.

An assault is an attempt unlawfully to apply any, the least, actual force to the person of another, directly or indirectly. See *R.* v. *Shaw*, 23 Q. B. (Ont.), 619.

There need not be an actual touching of the person assaulted, but mere words never amount to an assault.

A battery is not necessarily a forcible striking with the hand, or stick or the like, but includes every touching or laying hold, however trifling, of another person, or his clothes in an angry, revengeful, rude, insolent or hostile manner, for example, jostling another out of the way. Thus, if a man strikes at another with a cane or fist, or throws a bottle at him, if he miss it is an assault, if he hit, it is a battery.

There can be no assault where the party consents to the act done. *R.* v. *Guthrie*, L. R., 1 C. C. R., 243; *R.* v. *Connolly*, 26 Q. B. (Ont.), 320.

Using insulting and abusive language to a person in his own office, and on the public street, and using the fist in a threatening and menacing manner to the face and head of a person, amounts to an assault. *R.* v. *Harmer*. 17 Q. B. (Ont.), 555.

A conductor on a train is not liable for an assault under the Con. Stats. Can., chap. 66, s. 106, in attempting to put a person off the cars who refuses, after being several times requested, to pay his proper fare. *R.* v. *Faneuf*, 5 L. C., J. 167. No doubt, however, if the conductor used more force than was necessary it would amount to an assault. Moderate correction of a servant, or scholar, by his master is not an assault; but wounding, kicking and tearing a person's clothes do not fall within the scope of moderate correction. *Mitchell* v. *Defries*, 2 Q. B. (Ont.), 430.

Chastisement unnecessary for the maintenance of school discipline, and out of proportion to the nature of the offence, and springing from motives of caprice, anger, or bad temper, cannot be justified by a schoolmaster. *Brisson* v. *Lafontaine*, 8 L. C. J., 173.

The offence of assault is a misdemeanor, and is so punishable. *R.* v. *Taylor*, L.R., 1 C.C.R., 194. The punishment usually inflicted is fine, imprisonment, and sureties to keep the peace; and the Court of Quarter Sessions has a general jurisdiction to fine and imprison for an assault. *Ovens* v. *Taylor*, 19 C.P. (Ont.), 49–52.

If on the hearing of a charge of assault evidence be given of a higher offence such as rape, the Justices may still convict of the common assault, provided they disbelieve the evidence as to the other point. *Ex parte Thompson*, 6 H. & N., 193; *Wilkinson* v. *Dutton*, 3 B. S., 821.

Where a child submits to an act, not knowing its nature, it is an assault; though if there were a positive will and consent exercised it would not be. The prisoner was indicted for indecently assaulting two boys, each of whom was eight years of age. It was proved that the prisoner did acts towards the boys which amounted to indecent assaults if they did not consent to them. The boys stated in evidence that they did not know what he was going to do to them when he did each of the acts in question. It appeared that the boys merely submitted to the acts, not knowing their nature, and it was held that the prisoner might be convicted of an assault. *R.* v. *Lock*, L.R., 2 C.C.R., 10.

It may be observed that indecent assaults fall within the provisions of the 32 & 33 Vic., chap. 29, s. 28, as amended by the 40 Vic., chap. 26.

The 32 & 33 Vic., chap. 20, s. 36, and following sections, govern the subject of assaults; various acts of assault are under this statute made misdemeanors. By the 32 & 33 Vic., chap. 29, s. 51, on a trial for any felony which includes an assault, there may be an acquittal of the felony and a conviction of the assault, if the evidence warrants such finding. But under this statute there cannot be a conviction of an assault, unless the assault is included in and forms parcel of the felony; and the assault must also be committed in attempting to commit the felony, and in pursuance of that object. *R.* v. *Dingman*, 22 Q.B. (Ont.), 283; *R.* v. *Cregan* 1 Hannay, 36; *R.* v. *Ganes*, 22 C. P. (Ont.), 185; *R.* v. *Smith*, 34 Q.B.(Ont.), 552. So on an indictment for shooting with a felonious intent, the prisoner if acquitted of the felony may be convicted of a common assault. To discharge a pistol loaded with powder and wadding at a person within such a distance that he might have been hit, is an assault. *R.* v. *Cronan*, 24 C.P. (Ont.), 106.

To support a charge of an assault on a constable in the execution of his duty, it is not necessary that the defendant should know that he was a constable then in the execution of his duty; it is sufficient that the constable should have been acting in the execution of his duty, and then been assaulted. *R.* v. *Forbes*, 10 Cox C. C., 362. If a constable sees an assault committed, he may, recently after that assault, and before all danger of further violence has ceased, apprehend the offender; and if in so doing he is resisted and assaulted, the person assaulting is liable to be convicted of assaulting a constable in the execution of his duty. *R. v. Light*, 7 Cox C.C., 389.

Where a police officer attempts an arrest, by virtue of a warrant, for any offence less than felony, as for instance, an offence punishable on summary conviction, the person resisting such arrest, and assaulting the officer in so doing, cannot be convicted of such assault, if the officer has not the warrant in his possession at the time of the arrest—a constable not being authorized to arrest for any offence less than felony, unless he has the warrant in his possession at the time. *Codd v. Cabe*, L. R., 1 Ex. D., 352.

A Justice of the Peace has no jurisdiction to try an assault summarily, unless it is given him by statute (*R. v. O'Leary*, 3 Pugsley, 264; *Re Switzer*, 9 U. C., L. J., 266); and he must strictly pursue the authority given, and in order to give him jurisdiction under the Statute of Canada, (32 & 33 Vic., chap. 20, s. 43) it is necessary that the complainant should request him to proceed summarily, and this request should be made at the time of the complaint, but the request need not appear on the face of the conviction. *Ib.* See also *R. v. Shaw*, 23 Q. B. (Ont.), 616.

Where the proceedings did not show whether such request was made or not, but it was proved that the complainant was present at the return of the summons, and gave evidence against defendant; if any "intendment" could be made it might be presumed complainant had made such request.

If a warrant of commitment, issued by a Justice of the Peace, is good on its face, and the magistrate had jurisdiction in the case, it is a justification to a constable to whom it is given to be executed, and a person resisting him is guilty of an assault. But a warrant good on its face, will not protect a Justice, if the warrant has no valid foundation, as if it is issued without any proper information being laid. *Appleton v. Lepper*, 20 C. P. (Ont.), 138. Where the warrant was based on a conviction for an unlawful assault, it was held not necessary, in order to make the warrant legal, and a justification to the constable that it should be stated in the conviction and warrant, that the complainant had requested the magistrate to proceed summarily.

A conviction for an unlawful assault may adjudge defendant to be imprisoned in the first instance, under section 43 of the 32 & 33 Vic., chap. 20. It is not necessary before a defendant convicted of an assault is imprisoned, that he should be served with a copy of the minutes of the conviction. *R.* v. *O'Leary*, 13 C.L.J., N. S., 133; 3 Pugsley, 264.

It is probable that the 32 & 33 Vic., chap. 20, s. 43, only applies to common assaults. At all events, the opinion of Mr. Justice Wilson, in reference to the Con. Stat. Can., chap. 91, s. 37, was that this statute only applied to common assaults; and the only substantial difference between the statutes is, that the 44th section of the consolidated statute spoke of a common assault. *Re McKinnon*, 2 U. C., L. J., N. S., 324.

A conviction by Justices under one statute, for what amounts to an assault, is a bar to a conviction under another statute for the same assault. This arises from the principles of the common law independently of any statutory enactment, and where the first conviction is by a competent jurisdiction, it matters not whether it is by a summary proceeding before Justices or by a trial before a jury. Thus in England where the appellant was summarily convicted before Justices under The Highway Act, 5 & 6 Wm. IV., chap 50, s. 78, of an assault in riding a horse against the respondent, it was held that the conviction was a bar to any proceedings under the section 42 of the English Act (24 & 25 Vic., chap. 100) corresponding to the above. *Wemyss and Hopkins*, L. R., 10 Q. B., 378.

A certificate of dismissal of a charge of assault will bar an action founded on the same facts, for tearing the plaintiff's clothes on the same occasion. *Julien* v. *King*, 17 L. C. R., 268.

A conviction for an assault on the wife, and a certificate under this section has been held in England to bar a civil action for damages by husband and wife in respect of the same assault, though the complaint before the magistrate was by the wife alone. *Masper* v. *Brown*, L. R., 1 C. P. D., 97.

Though a party is convicted of an assault on a charge of assault, under the 43rd section of the Act, and obtains a certificate under the 45th section, he may afterwards be indicted for manslaughter, should the party die from the effects of the assault. *R.* v. *Morris*, L. R., 1 C. C. R., 90. But a charge of assault and battery accompanied by a malicious cutting and wounding, so as to cause grievous bodily harm, would be barred by a certificate of acquittal of assault and battery on the same facts. *Re Conklin*, 31 Q. B. (Ont.), 165; so the conviction would bar an indictment for felonious stabbing (*R.* v. *Walker*, 2 M. & Rob., 446); or an assault with intent to commit a rape. *Re Thompson*, 6 H. & N., 193.

It has been held that a complaint under the 43rd section cannot be withdrawn by the complainant, even with the consent of the Justice. *Re Conklin*, 31 Q. B. (Ont.), 160. The contrary view is taken in Archbold's J. P., 85.

Under section 46, the Justice has a discretion to abstain from adjudicating, and he may exercise this discretion and abstain from adjudicating, though the defendant pleads guilty. *Re Conklin*, *supra*.

It would seem that the certificate under this section must be obtained from the convicting Justice on the first hearing of the case, and that it cannot be granted by the Sessions on quashing a conviction for an assault after an appeal to them. *Westbrook* v. *Calaghan*, 12 C. P. (Ont.), 616.

It is imperative on the Justice who has dismissed the cause on the grounds stated to grant this certificate if applied for, and he has no discretion to refuse it, and the certificate has been held to be properly granted after the lapse of seven days. *Hancock* v. *Somes*, 28 L. J., M. C., 278.

The word "forthwith" means a reasonable time, and five days, though not two months, will suffice, *ib.* *R.* v. *Robinson*, 12 A. & E., 672.

It seems, however' that the Justice is not bound to grant the certificate unless there is a hearing on the merits. *Re Conklin*, 31 Q. B. (Ont.), 160

It is probable that the form of certificate given in the schedule to the 32 & 33 Vic., chap. 31, *ante*, pp. 175-188, would apply to this case.

The following form is in use in England:—

Whereas A. B. of , in the County of , labourer, heretofore on the day of in the year of our Lord , came before me, one of Her Majesty's Justices of the Peace for the said County of , and complained to and informed me that C. D. of , in the County aforesaid, labourer, on at , did unlawfully assault and beat him, the said A. B., and whereas the said C. D. being duly summoned to answer the said charge, appeared before me, one of Her Majesty's Justices of the Peace for the County aforesaid, at , and the said A. B. also then and there attended before me for the purpose of proving the offence charged upon the said C. D. in and by the said complaint ; and I, the said Justice, do hereby certify that having heard the said case upon the merits and it manifestly appearing to me ["that the said offence was not proved" *or* "that the said C D. was lawfully justified in the committing of the assault and battery charged upon him in and by the said complaint," *or* " that the assault and battery proved was so trifling as not to merit any punishment,"] I thereupon then and there dismissed the said complaint.

Given under my hand, the of in the year of our Lord

E. F.

A conviction before a magistrate can only be proved by the production of the record of conviction, or an examined copy of it. Therefore, where a magistrate, in a case of common assault, ordered the accused to enter into recognizances and pay the fee, but did not order him to be imprisoned or to pay any fine, and an action having been subsequently brought, it was held that the above was not a conviction within the meaning of the 45th section, and was not a bar to the action, and also that the conviction, if any, was not proved. *Hartley* v. *Hindmarsh*, L. R., 1 C. P., 553.

Where an assault charged in an indictment, and that referred to in a certificate of dismissal, appear to have been on the same day, it is *prima facie* evidence that they are one and the same assault, and it is incumbent on the prosecutor to shew that a second assault occurred on the same day, if he alleges it.

The recital in the certificate of the fact of a complaint having been made, and of a summons having been issued, is sufficient evidence of those facts. *R.* v. *Westley*, 11 Cox C. C., 139.

On the hearing of a charge of assault, under the 43rd section, if it be shewn that a *bona fide* question as to the title to land is involved, the jurisdiction of the Justice is at once ousted by section 46, and the Justice cannot proceed to enquire into and determine by summary conviction, any excess of force alleged to have been used in the assertion of title. *R.* v. *Pearson* L. R., 5 Q. B., 237.

Where the title to lands is involved, the summary jurisdiction of the Justice is ousted; but to oust the jurisdiction, the claim of title must be on behalf of the defendant, or those through whom he claims, and the title of a third person cannot be set up. *Ex parte Cayen*, 17 L. C. J., 74. If the complaint can be decided, without deciding a question of interest in land, the Justices have jurisdiction. *R.* v. *Edwards*, 26 L. T., 257.

If in an action of trespass to land, tried before a Justice of the Peace, the defendant sets up title, and offers a deed in evidence, and the plaintiff also gives evidence of deeds and of a title arising by estoppel, on which the Justice undertakes to decide, the title is *bona fide* in question, and the Justice has no jurisdiction. *R.* v. *Harshman*, 1 Pugsley, 346.

The prisoner was charged with an assault with intent to commit murder, in that he had opened a railway switch with intent to cause a collision, whereby two trains did come into collision, causing a severe injury to a person in one of them. It was held that this was not an assault with intent to commit murder, within the meaning of the Extradition Treaty. *Re Lewis*, 6 P. R. (Ont.), 236; though it is a very grievous offence within the statute, 32 & 33 Vic., chap. 20, s. 31.

ATTEMPTS TO COMMIT OFFENCES.

(*See* INDICTABLE OFFENCES.)

ATTEMPTS TO MURDER.

The Statute 32 & 33 Vic., chap. 20, renders felonious various acts done with intent to commit murder. See sections 10 to 14. The 40 Vic., chap. 28, substituted a new section for the 10th section of this Act. Thus administering poison or other destructive thing (s. 10), destroying or damaging a building with gunpowder (s. 11), setting fire to any ship or vessel or any part thereof, or casting away or destroying any vessel (s. 12), or shooting at any person, or by drawing a trigger or in any other manner attempting to discharge at any person any kind of loaded arms (s. 13), or by any other means attempting to commit murder, is felony (s. 14.)

BAIL.

(*See ante, p.* 5.)

BANKRUPTCY.

(*See* INSOLVENCY.)

BARRATRY.

This is the offence of *frequently* inciting and stirring up suits and quarrels between Her Majesty's subjects, either at law or otherwise. The offence is a misdemeanor, punishable by fine and imprisonment. It is insufficient to prove a single act, inasmuch as it is of the essence of the offence that the offender should be a *common* barrator.

BETTING AND POOL SELLING.

The statute 40 Vic., chap. 31, which takes effect on the 1st of May, 1878, provides as follows:

1. In case any person uses or knowingly allows any part of any premises under his control to be used for the purpose of recording or registering any bet or wager, or selling any pool, or—

2. Keeps, exhibits or employs, or knowingly allows to be kept, exhibited or employed in any part of any premises under his control any device or apparatus for the purpose of recording or registering any bet or wager, or selling any pool; or—

3. Becomes the custodian or depositary of any money, property or valuable thing staked, wagered or pledged; or—

4. Records or registers any bet, or wager, or sells any pool—

Upon the result (*a*) of any political or municipal election, or (*b*) of any race, or (*c*) of any contest or trial of skill or endurance of man or beast;

Such person is guilty of a misdemeanor, and shall be liable to be imprisoned in any common gaol for any term less than one year, with or without hard labour, and to a fine not exceeding one thousand dollars.

In a prosecution under the English Act, 16 & 17 Vic., chap. 119, it was proved that the appellant occupied as tenant, a house with a piece of enclosed ground adjoining, used for cricket, foot-racing, and other games and sports. On the day named in the summons foot-racing took place on the grounds, to which persons were admitted on payment of sixpence. Within the grounds, but outside the space reserved for the runners, and amongst the spectators, some fifteen or twenty professional betters stood on chairs and stools in different spots, with books in their hands, calling out the odds on the various runners and betting with different persons, a man behind each of the professional betters recording the bets in a book, the persons betting paying one shilling each and receiving a ticket. The evidence satisfied the magistrates that the appellant knew of what was going on, and took no steps to prevent it, and that he might have prevented it if he had wished. It was held that he might be convicted of knowingly and wilfully permitting a place of which he was the occupier, to be used by certain persons for the purpose of betting with persons resorting thereto. *Haigh* v. *Sheffield*, L.R., 10 Q.B., 102; *Eastwood* v. *Miller*, L. R., 9 Q. B., 440, approved.

The English Act relating to betting houses, uses the words, "house, room, or other place." A tree in Hyde Park to which a man used to resort to bet, was held not a "place" under the Act. *Doggett* v. *Catterns*, 19 C.B., N.S., 765. But a temporary wooden structure erected during races, was held to be within this Act. *Shaw* v. *Morley*, L.R. 3 Ex., 137; so a field is a place within this Act, *Eastwood* v, *Miller*, 30 L.T. N.S., 716; so is any umbrella on a race-course. *Bowes* v. *Fenwick*, 30 L.T.N.S., 524; L.R., 9 C.P., 339.

Where an information charged defendant with having on the 5th October, and on divers other days and times between the said 5th October and the laying the information (16th November), kept a betting-house, a conviction for so using the house on the 8th

November was held good and valid. *Onley* v. *Gee*, 4 L.T., N.S. 338.

The offence of keeping a gambling-house comes within the provisions of the 32 & 33 Vic., chap. 29, s. 28, amended by the 40 Vic., chap. 26.

BIGAMY.

This offence consists in marrying a second time while the defendant has a former husband or wife still living. It is felony under the statute 32 & 33 Vic., chap. 20, s. 58, but the statute does not extend to a second marriage contracted elsewhere than in Canada by any other than a subject of Her Majesty resident in Canada,, and leaving the same with intent to commit the offence; or to any person marrying a second time whose husband or wife has been continually absent from such person for the space of seven years then last past, and was not known by such person to be living within that time; nor does it extend to any person who at the time of the second marriage was divorced from the first marriage, or to any person whose former marriage has been declared void by the sentence of any court of competent jurisdiction.

The first marriage must be valid. If it is *void*, bigamy cannot be committed, otherwise if it is *voidable* only. *R.* v. *Jacobs*, 1 Mood C. C., 140; see *Breakey* v. *Breakey*, 2 Q. B. (Ont.), 353. But it is not necessary that the second marriage should be valid and regular in all respects. *R.* v. *Brawn*, 1 C. & K., 144; *R.* v. *Allen*, L.R., 1 C.C.R., 367.

A *bona fide* belief by the prisoner at the time of the second marriage that her husband was then dead is no defence. *R.* v. *Gibbons*, 12 Cox, 237. The first wife is not admissible as a witness to prove that her marriage with the prisoner was invalid. (*R.* v. *Madden*, 14 Q. B. (Ont.), 588); and she cannot be allowed to give evidence either for or against the prisoner. *R.* v. *Bienvenu*, 15 L. C. J. 141. But after proof of the first marriage, the second wife may be a witness, for then it appears that she is not the legal wife of the prisoner. *R.* v. *Tubbee*, 1 P. R., (Ont.), 98.

There must also be proof that the husband or wife was alive at the date of the second marriage. *R.* v. *Lumley*, L. R., 1 C. C. R., 196; *R.* v. *Curgerwen*, L. R., 1 C. C. R., 1.

It has been held that where the prisoner relies on the first wife's lengthened absence, and his ignorance of her being alive, he must show enquiries made, and that he had reason to believe her dead, or at least could not ascertain where she was or that she was living, more especially where he has deserted her, and this notwithstanding that the first wife has married again. *R.* v. *Smith*, 14 Q. B. (Ont.), 565. It is conceived however that this case will not now apply. Under the statute the absence, unless for seven years, would not be a defence for the prisoner, and when there is continual absence for that time, the burden of proving that the prisoner knew that his wife was living within that time is upon the prosecution. *R.* v. *Curgerwen*, L. R., 1 C. C. R., 1.

After the expiration of the seven years the prisoner cannot be convicted, unless the prosecution prove that within such seven years the prisoner was aware of the existence of his first wife. If such evidence is not forthcoming, the prisoner may legally marry after the seven years have expired, though it is proved that his first wife is then living. See *R.* v. *Lumley*, L. R., 1 C. C. R., 198.

In a prosecution for bigamy where there is a foreign marriage, the foreign law must be strictly proved, and the marriage must be proved to be in accordance with that law. This is necessary, even where the Justices in their individual capacity know that the marriage has been celebrated with the formalities required by the foreign law. *R.* v. *Smith*, 14 Q. B. (Ont.), 565. This, however, is not necessary if the marriage is admitted by the defendant, and there are corroborating circumstances strengthening the admission. The testimony of the officiating clergyman, that he had a marriage license which was brought to him by one of the parties, that he duly returned the same, that all the forms of law were observed as required by the license, and that the marriage was performed according to the rights and ceremonies of his church, is sufficient proof of the license having been issued and returned, and of the marriage having been duly solemnized. *R.* v. *Allan*, 2 Oldright, 373.

It has been held that the admission of the first marriage by the prisoner, unsupported by other testimony, is sufficient to justify a conviction for bigamy, so far as proof of the first marriage is concerned. *R.* v. *Creamer*, 10 L. C. R., 404.

BRIBERY.

The 37 Vic., chap. 9, relates to the offence of bribery at elections. Under section 92, it is an offence to promise to pay a voter at an election his travelling expenses, conditionally on his coming and voting for a particular candidate, but a promise to pay a voter his travelling expenses without such a condition is legal. Where a letter desired an elector to come from H to C to vote at the latter place for a particular candidate, a postscript to the letter said: "Your travelling expenses will be paid," it was held that this was evidence of bribery by the writer of the letter. *Cooper* v. *Slade*, 6 E. & B., 447.

It was agreed between three candidates and their supporters that there should be a test ballot to determine who should stand at the election. R, one of the three, was at the head of the ballot, and ultimately elected M.P., but it appeared that his agents had given money to voters to vote for him at the test ballot without, however, making any stipulation as to their votes at the election. This was held to be bribery. *Brett* v. *Robinson*, L. R., 5 C. P., 503.

Under section 74, the offence of personation is complete upon the personator tendering the voting paper, although on being asked if he be the person whose name is signed to the voting paper, he answers "No," and the vote is accordingly rejected. A conviction for such offence need not set out the facts constituting the offence. *R.* v. *Hague*, 9 Cox C. C., 412.

BURGLARY.

This offence has been defined to be a breaking and entering the mansion-house of another in the night, with intent to commit some felony within the same, whether such felonious intent be executed or not. A statutory definition of the crime is contained in the 32 & 33 Vic., chap. 21, s. 50. "Whosoever enters the dwelling house of another with intent to commit any felony therein, or being in such dwelling-house commits any felony therein, and in either case breaks out of the said dwelling-house in the night, is guilty of burglary."

Section 1 of the same statute enacts, that: "For the purposes of this Act (and of course the offence of burglary), the night shall be deemed to commence at nine of the clock in the evening of each day, and to conclude at six of the clock in the morning of the next succeeding day, and the day shall include the remainder of the twenty-four hours."

To constitute a dwelling-house within the law of burglary, the house must either be the place where one is in the habit of residing, or some building between which and the dwelling-house there is a communication either immediate or by means of a covered and enclosed passage leading from one to the other, the two buildings being occupied in the same right. *R.* v. *Jenkins*, R. & R., 224. See s. 52 of the Act.

Under s. 54 of the Act, breaking into any building within the curtilage, although it is not a dwelling-house in the sense applicable to burglary as already explained, is felony where the party commits any felony, therein or where, being in such building, he commits any felony and then breaks out.

By s. 53, entering any dwelling-house in the night with intent to commit felony is felony, and by s. 57, where a breaking and entering are proved to have been made in the day time, and no breaking out appears to have been made in the night time, or when it is left doubtful whether such breaking and entering or breaking out took place in the day or night time, the prisoner may be acquitted of the burglary but may be convicted of felony under the preceding section of the statute, and a person charged with an offence, under the 56th section of the statute, cannot secure an acquittal by showing that the breaking and entering were such as to amount in law to burglary.

Housebreaking differs from burglary, in this, that the former may be committed by *day*, the latter by *night*. This offence consists in breaking and entering any dwelling-house, school-house, shop, warehouse, or counting house, with the intention of committing any felony therein, or being in such house committing any felony, and breaking out of the same.

Larceny in a dwelling-house is provided for by the 61st section of the Act. This crime differs from housebreaking, inasmuch as there need not be any breaking, nor any entry with a view to the commission of the larceny. The goods, however, must be under the protection of the house, and not in the personal care of the owner. If in such personal care, the prisoner would either be guilty of stealing from the person or robbery, if there were circumstances of violence, force, and putting in fear. In burglary, there need not be any actual larceny; it will suffice if there is an intent to commit a felony.

It will thus be seen that, in relation to the duties of Justices of the Peace, no extended enquiry into the technicalities of the aforesaid offences is necessary. The material question will be whether there is a felonious intention or a felonious act. If the offence is not burglary, it may be housebreaking; if not the latter offence, it may be larceny in a dwelling house; the various sections of the statute applying to almost all cases where either a felony has been committed, or there is an intention to commit the same.

So sacrilege is felony under the 49th section of the Act, so by section 59 of the Act, being armed by night with any dangerous or offensive weapon, with intent to break into any dwelling house, and commit any felony therein, or having in possession by night any burglar's implements, or having the face disguised with intent to commit felony, or being in any dwelling house with intent to commit felony, is a misdemeanor.

An attempt to commit a burglary may be established on proof of a breaking with intent to rob the house, although there be no proof of actual entry of any portion of prisoner's person. *R.* v. *Spanner*, 12 Cox C. C., 155.

Where a prisoner was indicted under the 53rd section, for breaking and entering a shop with intent to commit a felony, it was proved that he broke in the roof with intent to enter and steal, and was then disturbed; but there was no evidence that he ever entered the shop. It was held that he might be convicted of the misdemeanor of attempting to commit a felony. *R.* v. *Bain*, L. & C., 129.

An opening of a door in a shop under the same roof where the prisoner lived as a servant, for the purpose of committing a felony, is a breaking and entering. *R.* v. *Wenmouth*, 8 Cox C. C., 348.

18

Under the 59th section of this Act, proof of a general intent to break or enter any dwelling house is insufficient. It is necessary that a person should be proved to have the intent of breaking into or entering some particular building. *R.* v. *Jarrald*, 9 Cox C. C., 307.

CHAMPERTY.

(*See* MAINTENANCE.)

CHILD ABANDONING, STEALING, &C.

The 32 & 33 Vic., chap. 20, s. 26, enacts that whosoever unlawfully abandons or exposes any child, being under the age of two years, whereby the life of such child is endangered, or the health of such child has been, or is likely to be, permanently injured, is guilty of a misdemeanor. There cannot be an unlawful abandonment of a child under this section except by a person on whom the law casts the obligation of maintaining and protecting the child, and makes this a duty. A person who has the lawful custody and possession of the child, or the father who is legally bound to provide for it (see section 25 of this statute), may offend against the provisions of the statute. But strangers to the child, under no obligation to provide for it, do not come within the statute. *R.* v. *White*, L. R., 1 C. C. R., 311. If the abandonment, instead of merely injuring the health of the child, causes its death, the prisoner would, it seems, be guilty of murder or manslaughter according to the circumstances. *Ib.*, 314. Though a father has not the actual custody of his child, yet, as he is legally bound to provide for it, his abandonment and exposure of it brings him within the statute. *Ib.*, 311.

So the mother of a child, who has the actual custody of it, may come within the Act. The mother of a child, five weeks of age, packed it up in a hamper as a parcel, and sent it by railway, addressed to the place where its putative father was then living, giving directions to the clerk at the station to be very careful of the hamper and send it by the next train, but saying nothing as to its contents. The child reached its destination safely, but it was held that the mother had unlawfully abandoned and exposed the child. *R.* v. *Falkingham*, L. R., 1 C. C. R.. 222.

To create this offence at common law the abandonment must cause an injury to the health of the child. *R.* v. *Philpot*, 1 Dears., 179. An infant two and-a-half years old has been held not capable of appreciating correction. Therefore more violent punishment than a slight slap by the mother is not justifiable. *R.* v. *Griffin*, 11 Cox C. C., 402.

By the 32 & 33 Vic., chap. 20, s. 57, to unlawfully, either by force or fraud, lead, or take away, or decoy, or entice away, or detain a child, under the age of fourteen years, with intent to deprive the parent or other person having the lawful care or charge of the possession of the child, or with intent to steal any article upon or about the child, or with any such intent to receive or harbour any such child, knowing the same to have been so led away, is felony. But persons claiming any right to the possession of the child do not fall within the statute.

CHURCHES, WORSHIP IN, &C.

Under the 32 & 33 Vic., chap. 20, s. 36, obstructing or assaulting a clergyman or other minister in the discharge of his duties is a misdemeanor.

This section would only protect the clergyman when engaged in the performance of the acts therein mentioned, and not when performing other duties such as collecting alms. *Cope* v. *Barber*, L. R., 7 C.P., 393.

COINAGE OFFENCES.

Every description of offence relating to coin is now provided for by the 32 & 33 Vic., chap. 18, and by section 35 every offence made punishable on summary conviction may be prosecuted in the manner directed by the Act respecting the duties of Justices of the Peace out of sessions in relation to summary convictions and orders. 32 & 33 Vic., chap. 31.

This Act was extended to Prince Edward Island by the 40 Vic., chap. 4; to the District of Keewatin by the 39 Vic., chap. 21; to the North-West Territories by the 38 Vic., chap. 49; to British Columbia by the 37 Vic., chap. 42; and to the Province of Manitoba by the 34 Vic., chap. 14.

The mere possession of a large quantity of pieces of counterfeit coin of the same date and make, each being wrapped up in a separate piece of paper, affords evidence of a guilty knowledge and of an intention to utter under the eleventh section. *R.* v. *Jarvis*, 7 Cox C. C., 53.

Under the 12th section the prisoner cannot be convicted of felony without proof of the previous conviction, and when a prisoner is indicted for felony under this section, and the previous conviction is not proved, he cannot be convicted of the misdemeanor of uttering—the law not admitting of a conviction for misdemeanor on a charge of felony unless in cases expressly provided for by statute. *R.* v. *Thomas*, L. R., 2 C. C. R., 41.

It is a misdemeanor at common law to make or procure engraved dies with intent therewith to make a foreign coin, even though all the instruments necessary had not been obtained. *R.* v. *Roberts*, 7 Cox C. C., 39. But the possession of a mould for coining the obverse side of a half crown with other coining materials was deemed sufficient evidence to go to a jury on a charge of felony. *R.* v. *Weeks*, 8 Cox C. C., 455.

A galvanic battery is a machine within the 24th section. *R.* v. *Glover*, 9 Cox C. C., 282.

COMPOUNDING OFFENCES.

Merely to forbear to prosecute is no offence, there is wanting something else to constitute a crime, and this essential is the taking of some reward or advantage. But forbearing to prosecute a felon on account of some reward received is a misdemeanor. To corruptly take any reward for helping a person to property stolen or obtained, &c., by any felony or misdemeanor (unless all due diligence to bring the offender to trial has been used) is felony. See 32 & 33 Vic., chap. 21, s. 115. So an advertisement offering a reward for the return of stolen or lost property, using words purporting that no questions will be asked, or seizure or inquiry made after the person producing the property, or that return will be made to any pawnbroker or other person who has bought or made advances on such property, renders the advertiser, printer and publisher liable to forfeit two hundred and fifty dollars. See 32 &

33 Vic., chap. 21, s. 116. See also the 35 Vic., chap. 35, amending the latter Act.

Compounding misdemeanors seems strictly to be illegal, as impeding the course of public justice. Where the misdemeanor compounded is one which is injurious to the community generally, and not confined in its consequences to the prosecutor himself, its compromise is as illegal as the compromise of felony. *Dwight* v. *Ellsworth*, 9 Q. B. (Ont.), 540.

In general a prosecution can only be compromised by leave of the court. A prosecution, for selling liquor without license, cannot be compromised without leave of the court. *Re Fraser*, 1 U. C., L. J., N. S., 326.

The statute 18 Eliz., chap. 5, contains provisions against compounding informations on penal statutes. But this statute does not extend to penalties which are only recoverable by information before Justices. *R.* v. *Mason*, 17 C. P. (Ont.), 534.

Compounding a felony is the taking of some reward for forbearing to prosecute, or making some bargain by which something is to be done for not prosecuting—the staying of such prosecution being the subject, or the principal or special subject, of the arrangement. It is of no consequence whether a charge has been formally preferred before a magistrate or not, it is equally an offence to compound in such a case after an information has been laid. *Topence* v. *Martin*, 38 Q. B. (Ont.), 411.

It is essential to the validity of a conviction that the party charged should be convicted of a single, distinct, positive and definite charge, and a conviction in the alternative is bad. *R.* v. *Mabey*, 37 Q. B., (Ont.), 248. See *ante*, p. 127.

COMPULSION.

If a person committing a crime is not a free agent, and is subject to actual force at the time it is committed, he is excused; as if the person who does it is compelled by threats, by a superior force, instantly to kill him or to do him grievous bodily harm if he refuses; but threats of future injury, or the command of any one not the husband of the offender, do not excuse any offence. So necessity may, in some cases excuse, for instance A and B, swimming in the sea, after a shipwreck, get hold of a plank not large enough to support both. A pushes off B, who is drowned. This is not a crime. Stephen's Dig., 21-2.

CONCEALING THE BIRTH OF A CHILD.

The 32 & 33 Vic., chap, 20, s. 61, enacts, that if any woman is delivered of a child, every person, who by any secret disposition of the dead body of the said child, whether such child died before, at, or after its birth, endeavours to conceal the birth thereof, is guilty of a misdemeanor.

The denial of the birth only is not sufficient. There must be some act of disposal of the body after the child is dead. *R.* v. *Turner*, 8 C. & P., 755.

And in order to convict a woman of endeavouring to conceal the birth of her child, a dead body must be found and identified, as that of the child of which she is alleged to have been delivered. *R.* v. *Williams*, 11 Cox, 684.

The statute applies to persons other than the mother, as well as the mother herself.

The expression in the statute "delivered of a child," does not include delivery of a fœtus, which has not reached the period at which it might have been born alive. *R.* v. *Berriman*, 6 Cox C. C., 388; see *R.* v. *Colmer*, 9 Cox C. C., 506.

"Secret disposition" must depend upon the circumstances of each particular case, and the most complete exposure of the body might be a concealment, as for instance, if the body were placed in the middle of a moor in the winter, or on the top of a mountain, or in any other secluded place where it would not likely be found. *R.* v. *Brown*, L. R., 1 C. C. R., 244. But there is no doubt there must be some disposition of the body, which under the circumstances is likely to prevent its being found.

To come within the meaning of the term secret disposition, there must be a putting the child into some place where it is not likely to be found. *R.* v. *Sleep*, 9 Cox C. C., 559.

The section only applies to the concealment of the *dead* body of the child, and a woman who endeavours to conceal the birth of a child by depositing it while alive in the corner of a field, and leaving it to die there, cannot be convicted of concealing the birth. *R.* v *May*, 10 Cox C. C., 448.

CONSPIRACY.

Conspiracy is an agreement by two persons or more to do or cause to be done an unlawful act, or to prevent the doing of an act ordained under legal sanction by any means whatsoever, or to do or cause to be done an act, whether lawful or not, by means prohibited by penal law. *R.* v. *Roy*, 11 L. C. J., 93.

The gist of the offence is the combination, therefore the parties will be liable, though the conspiracy has not been actually carried into execution. *Ib.* *Horsman* v. *R.*, 16 Q. B. (Ont.), 543. But the combination must be something more than intention merely. See *Mulcahy* v. *R.*, L. R., 3 E. & I. App., 306-317-328. It is not necessary that the object should be unlawful, for when two or more persons fraudulently combine,the agreement may be criminal, although if the agreement were carried out no crime would be committed, but a civil wrong only inflicted on the party. *R.* v. *Warburton*, L. R., 1 C. C. R., 276.

It seems, however, necessary that either the object of the conspiracy should be unlawful, or if the object is not unlawful that the *means* used to attain that object should be unlawful, see *R.* v. *Roy*, 11 L. C. J., 93. See 32 & 33 Vic., chap. 20, s. 42, as to conspiracies to raise the rate of wages. Under the 32 & 33 Vic.,chap. 20, s. 3. A conspiracy to commit murder is a misdemeanor, and under the 31 Vic., chap. 71, a conspiracy to intimidate a Provincial Legislative body is a felony. From the very nature of conspiracy it must be between two persons at least, and one cannot be convicted unless indeed he is indicted with others, who may, however, be dead or unknown. A man and his wife cannot be indicted for conspiring alone, because they constitute one person in law. Arch., Cr. Pldg., 942.

Conspiracy is one of the offences within the provisions of the 32 & 33 Vic., chap. 29, s. 28, amended by the 40 Vic., chap. 26. The Justice, therefore, in committing for trial should be careful to bind over the prosecutor to prosecute and give evidence.

The conspiracy is complete as soon as the agreement is entered into. *Heymann* v. *R.*, L. R., 8 Q. B., 102. Persons aiding and abetting at a mock auction may be indicted for a conspiracy. *R.* v. *Lewis*, 11 Cox C. C., 404.

The directors of a joint stock bank knowing it to be in a state of insolvency, issued a balance sheet shewing a profit, and thereupon declared a dividend of six per cent. They also issued advertisements inviting the public to take shares upon the faith of these representations of the flourishing condition of the bank. They were held guilty of a conspiracy to defraud. *R.* v. *Brown*, 7 Cox C. C., 442.

Under the 32 & 33 Vic., chap. 21, s. 85, any director, manager, or public officer, or member of any body corporate or public company who makes, circulates or publishes any written statement or account which he knows to be false in any material particular, or with intent to deceive or defraud, is guilty of a misdemeanor.

It is an indictable offence where parties, by false pretences and fraudulent representations and lies, enter into a conspiracy together, by those means to raise the price of any vendible commodity. *R.* v. *Berenger*, 3 M. & S., 67. And where the object of the conspiracy was not merely to obtain a settling day and official quotation upon the Stock Exchange of the stock of a certain company, and so induce persons to believe that the company was duly formed and constituted, but also to induce persons to act on that belief and deal in the shares of the company, it was held indictable. *R.* v. *Aspinall*, L. R., 1 Q. B. D., 730. Affirmed in appeal, L. R., 2 Q. B., D., 48.

A prosecution is not maintainable against a person for conspiracy to do any act or to cause any act to be done for the purposes of a trade combination unless such act is an offence indictable by statute or is punishable under the Act, 35 Vic., chap. 31.

COPYRIGHT.

The 38 Vic., chap. 88, is the Act respecting Copyrights (see the Statutes of 1876, reserved Acts, also 38 & 39 Vic., chap. 53). Under section 12 of this Act photograph copies of engravings from pictures are equivalent to copies from the picture itself, and though a number of copies are sold together, the sale of each copy is a separate offence. *Ex parte Beal*, L. R., 3 Q. B., 387. See also *Graves* v. *Ashford*, L. R., 2 C. P., 410; *Bradbury* v. *Hotten*, L. R., 8 Ex., 1.

Various penalties are imposed by this Act on persons infringing copyright. The penalty for falsely pretending to have copyright is three hundred dollars (s. 17), and under section 24 if any person willfully make or cause to be made any false entry in the register books of the Minister of Agriculture, or shall wilfully produce or cause to be tendered in evidence any paper falsely purporting to be a copy of an entry in the said books, he shall be guilty of a misdemeanor.

CONTEMPT.

(*See* INTRODUCTORY CHAPTER.)

CRUELTY TO ANIMALS.

The 32 & 33 Vic., chap. 27, as amended by the 33 Vic., chap. 29, governs this offence. Whosoever wantonly, cruelly or unnecessarily beats, binds, illtreats, abuses or tortures any animal, &c., or whosoever driving any cattle or other animals is by negligence or ill usage in the driving thereof the means whereby any mischief, damage or injury is done by any such cattle or other animal, is liable, upon conviction before a Justice of the Peace, to a fine not exceeding ten dollars.

The prosecution is to be under the " Act respecting the duties of Justices of the Peace out of sessions in relation to summary convictions and orders." 32 & 33 Vic., chap. 31 ; see sec. 7.

This Act was extended to Prince Edward Island by the 40 Vic., chap. 4 ; to the North-West Territories by the 38 Vic., chap. 49 ; to British Columbia by the 37 Vic., chap. 42 ; and to the Province of Manitoba by the 34 Vic., chap. 14.

This statute interdicts unnecessary abuse, not for any lawful purpose, but whenever the purpose for which the act is done is to make the animal more serviceable for the use of man, the statute ought not to be held to apply. For instance, castration of horses or other animals is not prohibited. But cutting the combs of cocks in order to fit the birds for one or other of two purposes, cock-fighting, or winning prizes at exhibitions, is an offence within the Act. *Murphy* v. *Manning*, L. R., 2 Ex. D., 307.

The amendment introduced by the 33 Vic., chap. 29, prevents bull-baiting, cock-fighting, &c.

The 38 Vic., chap. 42, prevents cruelty to animals while in transit by railway or other means of conveyance within the Dominion of Canada. Under this statute, cattle on railways, vessels, &c., are not to be kept more than twenty-eight hours without unloading them for food, rest, &c. A penalty of $100 is imposed on any person knowingly and wilfully violating the provisions of this Act.

DESERTION, ENTICING TO.

(*See* DESERTION.)

DISORDERLY HOUSES.

(See Act 32 & 33 Vic., chap. 32 and notes thereon, *ante* p. 195.)

DRILL, ILLEGAL.

(*See* UNLAWFUL TRAINING, &c.)

DRIVING, WANTONLY AND FURIOUSLY.

The 32 & 33 Vic., chap. 20, s. 34, provides that whosoever having the charge of any carriage or vehicle, by wanton or furious driving or racing, or other wilful misconduct, or by wilful neglect, does, or causes to be done, any bodily harm to any person whatsoever, is guilty of a misdemeanor, and shall be liable to be imprisoned in any gaol or place of confinement other than a Penitentiary, for any term less than two years, with or without hard labour.

DRUNKENNESS.

Voluntary drunkenness will not exempt a person from criminal liability ; for instance, A, in a fit of voluntary drunkenness, shoots B dead, not knowing what he does. A's act is a crime. But involuntary drunkenness, and diseases caused by voluntary drunkenness may excuse ; for instance, A, under the influence of a drug fraudulently administered to him, shoots B dead, not knowing what he does. A's act is not a crime; or if A, in a fit of *delirium tremens*, caused by voluntary drunkenness, kills B, mistaking him for a wild animal, attacking A, A's act is not a crime. Stephen's Dig., 19.

A man cannot, when drunk in his own house, be forcibly removed therefrom, even at the request of his own family, unless his conduct is such as would constitute him a nuisance to the public, *i.e.*, by his creating a public disturbance. *R.* v. *Blakeley*, 6 P. R. (Ont.), 244.

ELECTIONS.

(*See* Bribery.)

EMBEZZLEMENT.

(*See* Larceny).

EMBRACERY.

This is an attempt to influence a jury, corruptly to give a verdict in favour of one side or party by promises, persuasions, entreaties, money, entertainments, and the like. The offence is a misdemeanor. A juryman himself may be guilty of this offence by corruptly endeavouring to bring over his fellows to his view. The offence is a misdemeanor, both in the person making the attempt, and also in those of the jury who consent.

There are certain other acts, interfering with the free administration of justice at a trial, which are considered as high misprisons and contempts, and are punishable by fine and imprisonment. Such are the following: Intimidating the parties or witnesses; endeavoring to dissuade a witness from giving evidence, though it be without success; advising a prisoner to stand mute; assaulting or threatening an opponent for suing him; a counsel or attorney for being employed against him; a juror for his verdict; a gaoler or other ministerial officer for what he does in discharge of his duty; for one of the Grand Jury to disclose to the prisoner the evidence against him.

ENTICING SOLDIERS OR SAILORS TO DESERT.

The 32 & 33 Vic., chap. 25, enacts that whosoever, not being enlisted in Her Majesty's service, by words or with money, or by any other means whatsoever, directly or indirectly, persuades or procures, or goes about or endeavours to persuade, prevail on or procure, any such soldier, sailor, &c , to desert, or conceals, receives, or assists a deserter, knowing him to be such, may be convicted in a summary manner before two Justices of the Peace. See form of information for this offence, *ante* p. 64.

This Act was extended to Prince Edward Island by the 40 Vic., chap. 4; to British Columbia by the 37 Vic., chap. 42, and to the Province of Manitoba by the 34 Vic., chap. 14.

ESCAPE.

An escape is where one who is arrested gains his liberty by his own act, or through the permission or negligence of others, before he is delivered by the course of the law. Where the liberation of the party is effected either by himself, or others, without force, it is more properly called an *escape*; where it is effected by the party himself, with force, it is called *prison breaking*; where it is effected by others, with force, it is commonly termed a *rescue*.

Under the 32 & 33 Vic., chap. 29, s. 84, whoever escapes from, or rescues, or aids in rescuing, any other person from lawful custody, or makes, or causes any breach of prison, if such offence does not amount to felony, is guilty of a misdemeanor. Under section 85, whosoever knowingly and unlawfully, under colour of any pretended authority, directly procures the discharge of any prisoner not entitled to be discharged, is guilty of a misdemeanor, and the person so discharged shall be held to have escaped. The Penitentiary Act of 1875, 38 Vic., chap. 44, makes further provisions in regard to escapes. An escape during conveyance to the penitentiary is felony, and prisoners escaping, or attempting to escape, therefrom are to have, on conviction, three years added to the term of their imprisonment. *Ib.*, s. 26. See also s. 27 as to breaking prison, or attempting to break out of the cell, &c. Under section 29, every person who rescues, or attempts to rescue, any prisoner, while being conveyed to any penitentiary, or while being imprisoned therein, or while passing to or from work, at or near any penitentiary, and every person who, by supplying arms, tools, or instruments of disguise, or otherwise in any manner aids any such prisoner in any escape, or attempt at escape, shall be guilty of felony.

Under section 30, keepers, &c., having the custody of any prisoner, and carelessly allowing him to escape, are guilty of a misdemeanor.

One W was brought before magistrates in the custody of the defendant, a constable, to answer a charge of misdemeanor, and after witnesses had been examined he was verbally remanded until the next day. Being then brought up again, and the examination concluded, the Justices decided to take bail, and send the case to the assizes. The prisoner said he could get bail if he had time to send for them, and the Justice verbally remanded him until the following day, telling the defendant to bring him up then to be committed or bailed. On that day the defendant negligently permitted him to escape, for which he was convicted. It was held that W was not in the custody of the defendant merely for the purpose of enabling him to procure bail, but under the original warrant; and the matter was still pending before the magistrates until finally disposed of by commitment to custody or discharge on bail, and that the conviction was proper. *R.* v. *Shuttleworth*, 22 Q.B. (Ont.), 372.

EVIDENCE.

The rules of evidence are in general the same in civil and criminal proceedings. *R.* v. *Atkinson*, 17 C.P. (Ont.), 304.

As a general rule when Justices are authorized by statute to hear and determine or examine witnesses, they have also the power to take the examinations on oath or solemn affirmation, as the case may be (see 32 & 33 Vic., chap. 31, s. 45); and in every case where an oath or affirmation is directed to be made before a Justice, he has full power and authority to administer the same, and to certify to its being made. 31 Vic., chap. 1, s. 7, sixteenthly.

In indictable cases the 32 & 33 Vic., chap. 30, s. 30, expressly empowers the Justice to administer an oath to a witness, and the same power is also given in the case of summary convictions. 32 & 33 Vic., chap. 31, s. 45. The oath is generally in the following form:—

"The evidence you shall give touching this information (*or* complaint, *or* the present charge, *or* the application, *or as the case may be*,) wherein is informant (*or* complainant, *or as the case may be*), and is defendant (*or as the case may be*), shall be the truth, the whole truth, and nothing but the truth, so help you God.

The New Testament should, during the administration of the oath, be held in the witness's right hand, and at its conclusion he should kiss it. Any Quaker or other person allowed by law to affirm instead of swearing in civil cases, or solemnly declaring that the taking of any oath is according to his religious belief unlawful, who is required to give evidence in any criminal case, shall instead of taking an oath in the usual form, be permitted to make his solemn affirmation or declaration, beginning with the words following, that is to say,—" I, A.B., do solemnly, sincerely, and truly declare and affirm;" which said affirmation or declaration shall be of the same force and effect as if such Quaker or other person as aforesaid had taken an oath in the usual form. 32 & 33 Vic,, chap. 29, s, 61.

The form of oath must be in every case such as the witness considers binding on his conscience according to his particular religious belief. A conviction for crime, or an interest in the result, does not render a witness incompetent. 32 & 33 Vic., chap. 29, ss. 62, 63. In some cases, however, the evidence of an interested witness must be corroborated.

By section 64 of the 32 & 33 Vic., chap. 29, a witness may be cross-examined as to previous statements made by him in writing, or reduced into writing, relative to the subject matter of the case, without such writing being shown to him; but if it is intended to contradict the witness by the writing, his attention must, before such contradictory proof can be given, be called to those parts of the writing which are to be used for the purpose of so contradicting him.

The 40 Vic., chap. 26, s. 5, provides that for the purposes of the above section, a deposition of a witness, purporting to have been taken before a Justice or Justices on the investigation of the charge, and to be signed by the witness and the Justice or Justices, returned to and produced from the custody of the proper officer, shall be *prima facie* presumed to have been signed by the witness.

The 32 & 33 Vic., chap. 29, s. 58, *et seq.*, contains other provisions as to witnesses and evidence which are not necessary to be given here.

Witnesses are allowed to speak of *facts* only, and the *opinions* of witnesses are not, as a general rule, admissible in evidence.

In order to secure impartial and truthful testimony, it is an establisbed rule that a witness should not, on examination-in-chief, be asked leading questions, *i.e.* questions in such form as to suggest the answers desired. On cross-examination, however, a witness may be asked leading questions, the witness not being favourable to the party cross-examining.

Where a prisoner calls witnesses as to character only, it is not usual to cross-examine them, though the strict right to do so exists. After the cross-examination, the party producing the witness has a right to re-examine him for the purpose of explaining any statements of the witness on cross-examination, but unless by permission of the court, there is no right on re-examination to go into new matter not tending to explain the cross-examination. The person producing the witness should therefore, on the examation-in-chief, ask all necessary questions.

A prisoner cannot, in the existing state of the law, give evidence for himself, nor can his wife be admitted as a witness for him. *R.* v. *Humphreys*, 9 Q. B. (Ont.), 337; *R.* v. *Madden*, 14 Q. B. (Ont.), 588.

The wife of any one of several prisoners jointly indicted, stands in the same position with respect to the admissibility of her evidence as her husband, and she cannot give evidence for either of the prisoners. *R.* v. *Thompson*, L. R., 1 C. C. R., 377.

But a married woman may give evidence in favour of a person who has committed a crime jointly with her husband, provided the husband is not on trial for the offence. *R.* v. *Thompson*, 2 Hannay, 71.

One witness is in general sufficient.

In treason, two witnesses are required (see 31 Vic., chap. 69, s. 6), and in perjury, if only one witness is produced, his evidence must be corroborated, In forgery also, the evidence of the person whose signature is forged must be corroborated. 32 & 33 Vic., chap. 19, s. 54.

It is usual to require that the testimony of an accomplice be corroborated as to the *identity* of the âccused, but not as to the *manner* in which the crime was committed.

The confession of a prisoner is only admissible when free and voluntary. Any inducement to confess held out to the prisoner by a person in authority, or any undue compulsion upon him, will be sufficient to exclude the confession. This rule is carried so far that if an oath is administered to the prisoner before taking his statement, under the 32 & 33 Vic., chap. 30, s. 31, the oath will be a sufficient constraint or compulsion to render his statement inadmissible. *R.* v. *Field*, 16 C. P. (Ont.), 98. But the deposition on oath of a witness is admissable against such witness, if he is afterwards charged with a crime (*ib.*); see also *R.* v. *Finkle*, 15 C. P. (Ont.), 453. *R.* v. *Coote*, L. R., 4 P. C. App., 599, excepting so much of them as consists of answers to questions to which he has objected, as tending to criminate him, but which he has been improperly compelled to answer. The exception depends upon the principle "*nemo tenetur seipsum accusare*," but does not apply to answers given without objection, which are to be deemed voluntary. *R.* v. *Coote*, *supra*.

A dying declaration is only admissible in evidence where the death of the deceased is the subject of the charge, and the circumstances of the death the subject of the dying declaration. There must also be an unqualified belief in the nearness of death, a belief, without hope, that the declarant is about to die, and the burden of proving the facts that render the declaration admissible is upon the prosecution. *R.* v. *Jenkins*, L. R., 1 C. C. R., 192.

As to the competency of witnesses, a child of any age, if capable of distinguishing between good and evil, may be admitted to give evidence. A child of six years of age was examined; on being interrogated by the Judge and making answers that there was a God, that people would be punished in hell who did not speak the truth, and that it was a sin to tell a falsehood under oath, although he stated he did not know what an oath was. *R.* v. *Berube*, 3 L. C. R., 212.

On a trial for murder, an Indian witness was offered, and on his examination by the Judge, it appeared that he had a full sense of the obligation to speak the truth, but he was not a Christian, and had no knowledge of any ceremony in use among his tribe binding a person to speak the truth or imprecating punishment upon himself, if he asserted what was false. It appeared also, that he and his tribe believed in a future state, and in a Supreme Being who created all things, and in a future state of reward and punishment according to their conduct in this life. He was then sworn in the ordinary way on the New Testament, and it was held that his evidence was admissible. If the witness had belonged to any nation or tribe that had in use among them any particular ceremony which was understood to bind them to speak the truth, however strange and fantastic the ceremony might be, it would have been indispensible that the witness should have been sworn according to such ceremony, because all should be done that can be done to touch the conscience of the witness according to his notions, however superstitious they may be. *R.* v. *Pah-mah-gay*, 20 Q. B. (Ont.), 195.

Under the 40 Vic., chap. 26, s. 3, on a prosecution for receiving stolen goods, evidence may be given at any stage of the proceedings, that there was found in the possession of such person other property, stolen within the preceding period of twelve months, and such evidence may be taken into consideration in proof of guilty knowledge.

So by s. 4, a conviction within five years preceding, involving fraud or dishonesty may be given in evidence for the same purpose, but three day's notice must be given of the intention to adduce such evidence.

On a charge of sending a threatening letter, other letters written by the prisoner, both before and after the one in question are admissible to explain its meaning.

On a charge of malicious shooting, if it be doubtful whether the shot was fired by accident or design, proof may be given that the prisoner at another time intentionally shot at the same person. *R.* v. *Voke*, R. & R., 531.

On a trial for endeavouring to obtain an advance from a pawnbroker upon a ring, by the false pretence that it is a diamond ring, evidence may be given that two days before the transaction in question, the prisoner had obtained an advance from a pawnbroker upon a chain which he represented to be a gold chain, but which was not so, and endeavoured to obtain from other pawnbrokers advances upon a ring which he represented to be a diamond ring, but which in the opinion of the witness was not so. *R.* v. *Francis*, L. R., 2 C. C. R., 128.

In trespass against a magistrate for false imprisonment, and seizing and selling goods and chattels where he suffers judgment by default, it is unnecessary for the plaintiff to prove that he gave notice of action or commenced his suit within six months. *Mills* v. *Monger*, 4 O. S. 383.

The admission by a constable sued in trespass with two Justices, that a paper produced at the trial was a copy of the warrant under which he committed the trespass, is not sufficient evidence as against the Justice to entitle the constable to claim an acquittal under the sixth section of the 24 Geo. 3, chap. 44. *Kalar* v. *Cornwall*, 8 Q. B. (Ont.), 168.

EXTORTION AND OTHER MISCONDUCT OF PUBLIC OFFICERS.

Every malfeasance or culpable non-feasance of an officer of Justice with relation to his office, is a misdemeanor punishable by fine or imprisonment or both. Forfeiture of his office, if profitable, will also generally ensue.

As to malfeasance—in cases of oppression and partiality the officers are clearly punishable, and not only when they act from corrupt motives, but even when this element is wanting if the act is clearly illegal, for example, if a magistrate commit in a case in which he has no jurisdiction.

Extortion in the more strict sense of the word, consists in an officer's unlawfully taking, by colour of his office, from any man any money or thing of value that is not due to him, or more than is due, or before it is due. This offence is of the degree of misdemeanor, and all persons concerned therein, if guilty at all, are principals. Two or more persons may be jointly guilty of extortion where they act together and concur in the demand. *R.* v. *Tisdale*, 20 Q. B. (Ont.), 273.

Where two persons sat together as magistrates, and one of them exacted a sum of money from a person charged before them with felony, the other not dissenting, it was held that they might be jointly convicted. *Ib.*

As to non-feasance. An officer is equally liable for neglect of his duty as for active misconduct. A refusal by any person to serve an office to which he has been duly appointed, and from which he has no ground of exemption, is an indictable offence. An indictment may be maintained against a Deputy Returning Officer at an election for refusing, on the requisition of the agent of one of the candidates to administer the oath to certain parties tendering themselves as voters. *R.* v. *Bennett*, 21 C. P. (Ont.), 238.

The 26 Geo. II., chap. 14, s. 2, gives an action to any person to recover a penalty of £20 against any one who demands a greater fee than that which is established.

In an action under 26 Geo. II., chap. 14. s. 2, to recover penalties against a clerk of Justices for taking a fee higher than that in the authorized table, the venue is local under 31 Eliz., chap. 5, s. 2, though the plaintiff happen to be the person grieved. *Lewis* v. *Davis*, L. R., 10 Ex., 86.

A person resisting a constable in executing an execution issued by a Justice of the Peace in the form K. in the schedule to the (N. B.) Rev. Stat., chap. 137, is liable to an indictment. *R.* v. *McDonald*, 4 Allen, 440. The fact that the defendant did not know that the person assaulted was a peace officer, or that he was acting in the execution of his duty, furnishes no defence. *R.* v. *Forbes*, 10 Cox., 362. It is sufficient that the constable was actually in the execution of his duties at the time of the assault.

EXTRADITION.

The 40 Vic., chap. 25, makes provision for the extradition of fugitive criminals. It has been recently held that this Act is not yet in force. *R.* v. *Williams*, unreported, Q.B.(Ont.), 11 January, 1878, Harrison, C. J. The 31 Vic., chap. 94, as amended by the 33 Vic., chap. 25, with the Imperial Act 33 & 34 Vic., chap. 52, must therefore still govern.

As, however, ordinary Justices of the Peace have not now the power to act in extradition cases, of course it is unnecessary to treat of the provisions of these Acts.

FALSE PERSONATION.

At common law false personation is punishable as a cheat or fraud, but certain particular cases are dealt with by statute.

Under "The Dominion Elections Act, 1874," 37 Vic., chap. 9, s. 74, a person shall for all purposes of the laws relating to Parliamentary elections be deemed to be guilty of the offence of personation, who at an election of a member of the House of Commons applies for a ballot paper in the name of some other person, whether such name be that of a person living or dead, or of a fictitious person, or who, having voted once at any such election, applies at the same election for a ballot paper in his own name ; and the offence of personation, or of aiding, abetting, counselling or procuring its commission is punishable by a fine not exceeding $200, and by imprisonment not exceeding six months. Under the 32 & 33 Vic., chap. 19, s. 6, personating the owner of certain stock, &c., and transferring or receiving, or endeavouring to transfer or receive the dividends is felony.

FALSE PRETENCES.

(*See* LARCENY.)

FIRE-ARMS, IMPROPER USE OF

The Statute of Canada, 40 Vic., chap. 30, provides that whosoever has upon his person a pistol or air-gun, without reasonable cause to fear an assault or other injury to his person, or his family or property, may be required to find sureties to keep the peace for a term of six months, and by section 2, whosoever, when arrested, either on a warrant issued against him for an offence or whilst committing an offence, has upon his person a pistol or an air-gun, is liable, upon conviction, to a fine of not less than twenty dollars. So by section 3, having a pistol or air-gun, with intent therewith, unlawfully and maliciously to do injury to any other person renders the person liable, on conviction, to a fine not less than fifty dollars.

Offences against the provisions of the Act must be prosecuted within one month, and are to be tried and dealt with in pursuance of the "Act respecting the prompt and summary administration of criminal justice in certain cases." See the 40 Vic., chap. 30, s. 5 ; see also 32 & 33 Vic,, chap. 20, ss. 74 and 76.

FISHERIES.

The 31 Vic., chap. 60, was passed for the regulation of fishing and the protection of fisheries.

This Act was amended by the 38 Vic., chap. 33. It was extended to British Columbia and Prince Edward Island by the 37 Vic., chap. 28.

FORCIBLE ENTRY OR DETAINER.

The violent taking or after unlawful taking, the violent keeping possession of lands and tenements with menaces, force and arms, and without the authority of the law. This offence is a misdemeanor at common law, and an indictment will lie for it if accompanied by such circumstances as amount to more than a bare trespass and constitute a public breach of the peace. *R.* v. *Wilson*, 8 T. R., 357. See, also, *R.* v. *Martin*, 10 L. C. R., 435.

The statutes 8 Hy. IV., chap. 9; 8 Hy. VI., chap. 9; 6 Hy. VIII., chap. 9, and 21 Jac. 1, chap. 15, as to forcible entries seem to be in force in this country. *Boulton* v. *Fitzgerald*, 1 Q. B. (Ont.), 343 ; *R.* v. *McGreavy*, 5 O. S., 620.

Under these statutes the party aggrieved by a forcible entry and detainer, or a forcible detainer, may proceed by complaint made to a local Justice of the Peace, who will summon a jury and call the defendant before him, and examine witnesses on both sides if offered, and have the matter tried by a jury. *Russell* v. *Loyd*, 14 L. C. R., 10.

A mere trespass will not support an indictment for forcible entry, there must be such force or show of force as is calculated to prevent any resistance. *R.* v. *Smyth*, 1 M. & Rob., 155.

The object of prosecutions for forcible entry is to repress high-handed efforts of parties to right themselves. *R.* v. *Connor*, 2 P. R. (Ont.), 140.

And a party may be guilty of forcible entry by violently and with force entering into that to which he has a legal title. *Newton* v. *Harland*, 1 M. & Gr., 644.

Where a person having the legal title to land is in actual possession of it, the attempt to eject him by force brings the person who makes it within the provisions of the statute against forcible entry. It will do so though the possession of the person having such legal title has only just commenced, though he may himself have obtained it by forcing open a lock, though his ejection has not been made by a "multitude" of men, nor attended with any great use of violence, and though the person who attempts to eject him may even set up a claim to the possession of the land. *Laws & Telford*, L. R., 1 Appeal Cases, 414.

This offence is now brought within the provisions of the 32 & 33 Vic., chap. 29, s. 28, which requires as a preliminary to the presentment or finding of an indictment by a grand jury, that the prosecutor or other person presenting the indictment should be bound by recognizance to prosecute or give evidence against the person accused of such offence. See 40 Vic., chap. 26, s. 2.

FOREIGN ENLISTMENT OFFENCES.

The Imperial Statute 33 & 34 Vic., chap. 90, governs offences of this character throughout the Dominion of Canada and the adjacent territorial waters.

It is to be found in the statutes of 1872. A warrant of commitment recited that M. was charged, on the oath of W., "For that he, M., was this day charged with enlisting men for the United States army, offering them $350 each as a bounty," without charging any offence with certainty, without stating that the men enlisted were subjects of Her Majesty, and without showing that W. was unauthorized by license of Her Majesty to enlist, was held bad. *Re Martin*, 10 U. C., L. J., 130.

FORGERY.

This offence is defined as the fraudulent making or alteration of a writing to the prejudice of another man's right. *Re Smith*, 4 P. R. (Ont.), 216. The offence is a misdemeanor at common law. It is now governed by the Statute 32 & 33 Vic., chap. 19, which makes it felony.

This Act was extended to Prince Edward Island by the 40 Vic., chap. 4; to the District of Keewatin by the 39 Vic., chap. 21; to the North-West Territories by the 38 Vic., chap. 49; to British Columbia by the 37 Vic., chap. 42; and to the Province of Manitoba by the 34 Vic., chap. 14.

The 31 Vic., chap. 71, relates to forgery in connection with Provincial Legislatures and their Acts.

Though the Statute 32 & 33 Vic, chap. 19, makes forgery a felony, yet cases not provided for by the statute may still be punished at common law. The 45th section of the statute provides that whosoever maliciously and for any purpose of fraud or deceit forges any document or thing written, printed or otherwise made capable of being read, is guilty of felony, and forging a document not expressly mentioned in the statute has been held criminal.

The prisoner at Woodstock, with intent to defraud, wrote out a telegraph message, having the heading and appearance of a telegraphic despatch of the Montreal Telegraph Co., and purporting to be sent by one, C., at Hamilton, to M,, at Woodstock, authorizing M. to furnish the prisoner with funds. This message was delivered to M. by a boy, as from the telegraph office, and upon the faith of it M. endorsed a draft for $85, drawn by the prisoner on C., on which the prisoner obtained the money. It was held that the prisoner was guilty of forgery. *R.* v. *Stewart*, 25 C. P. (Ont.), 440.

The instrument forged must have some apparent validity, that is, it must purport on the face of it to be good and valid for the purpose for which it is created, and not be illegal in its very frame, though it is immaterial whether if genuine it would be of validity or not. *R.* v. *Brown*, 3 Allen, 13; *R.* v. *Pateman*, R. & R., 445.

An instrument which is declared by law to be wholly void, is not the subject of forgery if on its face it affords evidence that it comes within the law declaring it void. *Taylor* v. *Golding*, 28 Q. B. (Ont.), 198, 203.

Forging or uttering in Canada a writing purporting to be a bank note issued by a banking company in the State of Maine, amounts to the crime of forgery, though it is not proved that the company had power by charter to issue notes of that description, it being shown that the note carried on its face the semblance of a bank note issued by a company in the State of Maine, and there being nothing in its frame to show it illegal. *R.* v. *Brown*, 3 Allen, 13. It is sufficient if the instrument is in such form as to deceive persons of ordinary observation. *R.* v. *Collicott*, R. & R., 212.

The forgery must be of some document or writing, therefore the painting an artist's name in the corner of a picture, in order to pass it off as an original picture by that artist, is not forgery. *R.* v. *Closs*, 21 L. J., M. C., 54.

As to the fabrication, it need not be of the whole instrument. Very frequently the only false statement is the use of a name to which the defendant is not entitled. It does not matter whether the name wrongly applied be a real or a fictitious one. *R.* v. *Lockett*, 1 Leach, 94. Even to make a mark in the name of another person with intent to defraud that person is forgery. *R.* v. *Dunn*, 1 Leach, 57. It is forgery within the meaning of the 32 & 33 Vic., chap. 19, s. 23, to make a deed fraudulently with a false date when the date is a material part of the deed, although the deed is in fact made and executed by and between the persons by and between whom it purports to be made and executed. *R.* v. *Ritson*, L. R., 1 C. C. R., 200.

Not only a fabrication but even an *alteration* however slight if material will constitute forgery. A person having an order for the delivery of wheat for the support of poor persons in a municipality is guilty of forgery, if with intent to defraud he materially alters the order so as to increase the quantity of wheat obtainable thereunder. *R.* v. *Campbell*, 18 Q. B. (Ont.), 416. Section 45 of the 32 & 33 Vic., chap. 19, provides that the wilful alteration for any purpose of fraud or deceit of any such document or thing, or of any document or thing the forging of which is made penal by the Act shall be held to be a forging thereof.

It is forgery to execute a deed in the name of and as representing another person, with intent to defraud, even though the prisoner has a power of attorney from such person, but fraudulently conceals the fact of his being only such attorney, and assumes to be principal. *R.* v. *Gould*, 20 C.P. (Ont.), 159.

It must be proved that the alleged forgery was intended to represent the handwriting of the person whose handwriting it appears to be, and is proved not to be, or that of a person who never existed. The person whose name is forged is a competent witness, but his evidence requires corroboration. 32 & 33 Vic. chap. 19, s. 54; *R.* v. *McDonald*, 31 Q. B. (Ont.), 337; *R.* v. *Giles*, 6 C.P. (Ont.), 84. Whether he be or be not called as a witness, the handwriting may be proved not to be his by any person acquainted with his handwriting, either from having seen him write, or from being in the habit of corresponding with him; and under the 32 & 33 Vic., chap. 29, s. 67, comparison of a disputed writing with any writing, proved to the satisfaction of the Court to be genuine, may be made by witnesses, and such writings and the evidence of witnesses respecting the same, may be submitted to the Court and jury as evidence of the genuineness or otherwise of the writing in dispute. The instrument must be made with intent to defraud, which is the chief ingredient of the offence. It is not, however, necessary to prove an intent to defraud, any particular person; it is sufficient to prove that the party accused did the act charged with intent to defraud. 32 & 33 Vic., chap. 19, s. 51. As there must be evidence of an intent to defraud the writing of a signature in sport without any intention to defraud or pass it off as genuine, is not a forgery. A man may draw a promissory note for any sum he pleases, and in favour of any person, and payable to him or to his order, or to bearer, and so long as it remains simply as *his own* promissory note, in his own possession, and charging no other person but himself with liability he may alter it at his own free will in all or any particulars. But when another person becomes interested in the note, or discounts it, or receives it in payment, it is then fraud and forgery to pass it off as containing the names of persons who have not in fact signed or endorsed it. See *R.* v. *Craig*, 7 C.P. (Ont.), 239; *R.* v. *Dunlop*, 15 Q. B. (Ont.), 119 It is the intent to deceive and defraud that the law considers criminal, but where this intent exists it is immaterial whether any person is actually defrauded by the forgery, or that any person should be in a situation to be defrauded by the act. *R.* v. *Nash*, 21 L. J. M. C., 147.

The offence of forgery is not triable at the Quarter Sessions. *R.* v. *McDonald*, 31 Q. B. (Ont.), 337; *R.* v. *Dunlop*, 15 Q. B. (Ont.), 118.

The offence of *uttering* the forged instrument is provided for by the 32 & 33 Vic., chap. 19, and made an offence of the same nature as the forgery itself. The words used in the statute are: "offers, utters, disposes of, or puts off, knowing the same to be forged, or altered," &c. A tender or attempt to pass off the instrument will be sufficient, and there need not be an acceptance by the other. It is an uttering if the forged instrument is used in any way, so as to get money or credit by it, or by means of it, though it is produced to the other party, not for his acceptance, but for some other purpose. *R.* v. *Ion*, 21 L. J., M. C., 166. Of course, the forged character of the instrument, and the intent to defraud must be proved, as in forgery. It will be also necessary to prove that the defendant *knew* the instrument to be forged, as for instance, by showing that he had in his possession other forged notes of the same kind.

The making on a glass plate, a positive impression of an undertaking of a foreign state, for the payment of money, by means of photography, without lawful authority or excuse, is a felony within the 19th section of the Act. *R.* v. *Rinaldi*, 9 Cox C. C., 391.

Procuring the engraving merely of the royal arms on a plate, in the same position as that in which it would be found on a note of a banking company in a complete state, a note of which company the prisoner had in his possession, comes within the meaning of this section, and the prisoner is rightly convicted of the offence. *R.* v. *Keith*, 6 Cox C. C., 533.

A guarantee is the subject of forgery within the 23d section though no consideration appear. *R.* v. *Cœlho*, 9 Cox C. C., 8. This includes post office orders. *R.* v. *Vanderstien*, 10 Cox C. C., 177.

A bill of exchange, without the drawer's signature, is not a bill of exchange within the 25th section. *R.* v. *Mopsey*, 11 Cox C C., 143.

A guarantee given on the appointment of an agent to an insurance company, against loss, &c., by negligence, or dishonesty of the agent, is an undertaking for payment of money within the 26th section, and the agent may be convicted of forging such a document. *R.* v. *Joyce*, 10 Cox C. C., 100.

An I. O. U. is an undertaking for the payment of money. *R.* v. *Chambers*, 12 Cox C. C., 109 ; L. R., 1 C. C. R., 341.

A "clearance," or certificate of payment of dues, given by the secretary of a friendly society, is not an acquittance, or receipt for money within this section. *R.* v. *French*, L. R., 1 C. C. R., 217.

A document in the following form :

"THORNTON, October, 1867.

"Received of the S. L. B. Soc'y, the sum of £417 13s., on account of my share, No. 8,071.

"£417 13s. pp. S. A.

"WM. KAY."

is a warrant, authority, or request, for the payment of money within this section. *R.* v. *Kay*, L. R., 1 C. C. R., 257.

An instrument in the following form :

"$3.50. "CARICK, April 10, 1863.

"John McLean, tailor, please give Mr. A. Steel to the amount of three dollars and fifty cents, and by so doing you will oblige me.

[Signed] ANGUS MCPHAIL."

is an order for the payment of money, and not a mere request. *R.* v. *Steel*, 13 C. P. (Ont.), 619.

But an instrument, as follows:

"RENFREW, June 13, 1860.

"*Mr. McKay:*

"SIR,—Would you be good enough as for to let me have the loan of $10 for one week or so, and send it by the bearer immediately, and much oblige your most humble servant,

"J. ALMIRAS, P. P."

is not an order for the payment of money. *R.* v. *Reopelle*, 20 Q. B. (Ont.), 260.

"*Mr. Warren:*

"Please let the bearer, Mrs. Tuke, have the amount of ten pounds, and you will oblige me.

"B. B. MITCHELL."

is an order for the payment of money and not a mere request. *R.* v. *Tuke*, 17 Q. B. (Ont.), 296.

FRAUDULENT MARKING OF MERCHANDIZE.

The 35 Vic., chap. 32, provides that every person who with intent to defraud, or enable another to defraud, any person, forges or counterfeits any trade mark, or applies, or causes or procures to be applied any trade mark to any chattel or article not being the production or merchandize of any person denoted or intended to be denoted by such trade mark, or not being the production or merchandize of any person whose trade mark is so forged or counterfeited, is guilty of a misdemeanor.

This Act repeals sections 30 and 31 of the Act respecting forgery, 32 & 33 Vic., chap. 19.

This Act was extended to Prince Edward Island by the 40 Vic., chap. 4.

GAMING AND GAMING HOUSES.

The law does not deem it within its province to punish such practices as gaming, unless either some fraud is resorted to or regular institutions are established for the purpose, so as to amount to a public nuisance.

The 40 Vic., chap. 32, makes provision for the prevention of gambling practices in certain public conveyances. Section 1 provides that "whosoever, in any railway car or steamboat used as a public conveyance for passengers, by means of the game commonly known as 'three card monte,' or of any other game of cards, dice, or other instrument of gambling, or by any device of like character, obtains from any other person any money, chattel, valuable security or property, shall be deemed guilty of the misdemeanor of having obtained the same unlawfully by false pretences, and shall be liable to be punished by imprisonment in any gaol or place of confinement for any term less than one year with or without hard labour, and with or without solitary confinement: and every person aiding, encouraging, advising or confederating with any person in the commission of the said offence, shall be deemed guilty thereof, and liable to be punished in like manner as a principal therein, and any attempt to commit such offence by actually engaging any person in any such game with intent to obtain money or other valuable thing from him, shall be a misdemeanor punishable in like manner as the offence itself.

The Act 38 Vic., chap. 41, is the general Act for suppressing gaming houses and to punish the keepers thereof. This statute was amended by the 40 Vic., chap. 33.

On report in writing by the chief constable, &c., that there are good grounds for believing that any house, room or place is kept or used as a common gaming house, the magistrate may, by order in writing, authorize the constable to enter or break open the doors of common gaming houses and seize all instruments, of gaming, moneys, &c., and take into custody all persons found therein.

The offence of keeping a gambling house comes within the provisions of the 32 & 33 Vic., chap 29, s. 28.

GAOLS.

The Act 40 Vic., chap. 37, provides for the safe custody of prisoners, in places where the common gaols become temporarily insecure.

The Lieutenant-Governor of any Province may by Proclamation, published in the *Gazette*, declare that the common gaol of any county is insecure, and name the gaol of any adjoining county as the gaol to which offenders within the first mentioned district may be committed or sentenced, and there after persons committed or sentenced shall be so committed, &c., to the gaol named in the Proclamation for that purpose. The trial of the prisoner may be in the county, or place in the gaol whereof he is confined.

Special provision is made for the case of treason, by the **31 Vic.**, chap. **74**.

HIGHWAYS.

(*See* NUISANCES.)

HOMICIDE.

(*See* MURDER.)

HUSBAND, NEGLECT OF, TO MAINTAIN HIS WIFE, &C.

(*See* VAGRANCY.)

IGNORANCE.

A mistake or ignorance of law is no defence for a party charged with a criminal act, but it may be ground for an application to the merciful consideration of the Government. *R.* v. *Madden*, 10 L. C. J., 344.

Ignorance or mistake of fact may in some cases be a defence, as for instance, if a man intending to kill a thief in his own house, kill one of his own family, he will be guilty of no offence. But if intending to do grievous bodily harm to A., he in the dark kill B., he will be guilty of murder, the exemption from liability proceeding on the assumption that the original intention was lawful. So a man is not liable for an accident which happens in the performance of a lawful act, with due caution. For example, A, properly pursuing his work as a bricklayer, lets fall a brick on B's head, and the latter dies in consequence of the injury, A will not be liable, but it would have been otherwise, had A at the time been engaged in some criminal act, or if he had not exercised proper skill or care.

INDECENT CONDUCT.

Every one commits a misdemeanor, who does any grossly indecent act, in any open and public place in the presence of more persons than one. *Elliot's case*, L. & C., 103 ; but it is uncertain whether such conduct in a public place amounts to a misdemeanor, if it is done when no one is present or in the presence of one person only.

A place is public if it is so situated that what passes there can be seen by any considerable number of persons, if they happen to look. *Webb's case*, 1 Den., 338 ; *Holme's case*, Dears. 207 ; *R.* v. *Orchard*, 3 Cox C. C., 248.

Thus the inside of a urinal open to the public, and by the side of a foot-path in Hyde Park, is a public place. *R.* v. *Harris*, L.R., 1 C. C. R., 288.

It is unlawful for men to bathe without any screen or covering so near to a public footway, frequented by females, that exposure of the person must necessarily occur, and they who so bathe are liable to an indictment for indecency. *R.* v. *Reed*, 12 Cox C. C., 1. It is not necessary that the exposure should be made in a place open to the public. If the act be done where a great number of persons may be offended by it, and several see it, it is sufficient. *R.* v. *Thallman*, 33 L. J., M. C., 58.

It must, however, be in sight of more than one person. *Webb's case*, 1 Den. C. C. R., 338.

Printing or publishing indecent or obscene books, prints or pictures is a misdemeanor at common law, and punishable with fine or imprisonment, or both (*R.* v. *Curl*, 2 Str., 788); and it is no defence that the object was not to corrupt. *R.* v. *Hicklin*, L. R., 3 Q.B., 360.

Keeping a booth on a public race course, for the purpose of showing an indecent exhibition, is an offence at common law. *R.* v. *Saunders*, L. R., 1 Q. B. D., 15.

INDIANS.

The Act 39 Vic., chap. 18, amends and consolidates the laws

respecting Indians. The provisions of this Act are too long to be inserted here.

INDICTABLE OFFENCES.

All treasons, felonies, and misdemeanors, misprisons of treason and felony, whether existing at common law or created by statute, are the subjects of indictment; so also are all attempts to commit any of these acts.

All crimes involve the elements of *will, criminal intention*, or *malice*. To make a person a criminal, the intention must be a state of mind forbidden by the law. For instance, a person innocently uttering a forged note, not intending to defraud, commits no crime; but if there is such intention the act is stamped with the character of crime. When the law expressly declares an act to be criminal, the question of intention or malice need not be considered. Malice is found not only in cases where the mind is actively or positively at fault, as where there is a deliberate design to defraud, but also where the mind is passively or negatively to blame—that is, where there is culpable or criminal inattention or negligence. It is usual to lay down that malice is either *express* or *in fact*, as where a person with a deliberate mind and formed design kills another; (2) *Implied* or *in law*, as where one wilfully poisons another, though no particular enmity can be proved, or where one gives a perfect stranger a blow likely to produce death. Here there is a wilful doing of a wrongful act without lawful excuse, and the intention is an inference of law resulting from the doing the act. The law infers that every man intends the necessary consequence of his own act. Malice in its ordinary sense of ill-will or malevolence, is not essential to a crime; malice in its legal signification of criminal intention is. For instance, legal malice may constitute homicide murder, though there may be an entire absence of ill-will; where there is ill-will or malevolence, homicide which would otherwise be manslaughter is constituted murder. Intention sometimes determines the criminality of an act. For instance, A takes a horse from the owner's stables without his consent. If he intend to fraudulently deprive the owner of the property, and appropriate the horse to himself, he is guilty of the crime of larceny; if he intend to use it for a time and then return it, without depriving the owner of his property therein, it will only be a trespass or civil injury.

A mere naked intention, however, is not criminally punishable. There must be some carrying out, or attempt to carry out, that intention into action. Thus although A makes up his mind to shoot B, and confesses this resolution, the law is powerless to deal with him; but directly he does anything in pursuance of that design he is within the grasp of the law.

If there be a present criminal intention, the prisoner is not exculpated because the results of the steps he takes to carry out that intention are other than those he anticipated or intended. For example, if A, intending to shoot B, shoot C, mistaking C for B, he is criminally liable; and if A shoots at B's poultry and by accident kills a man, if his intention was to steal the poultry he will be guilty of murder. See Harris' Crim. Law, 1, 2.

An *attempt* to commit a crime must be distinguished from an *intention* to commit it. Every attempt to commit a crime is itself an indictable misdemeanor at common law.

An attempt to commit a crime, whether the crime attempted be misdemeanor or felony, is a misdemeanor. *R.* v. *Connolly*, 26 Q.B. (Ont.), 322; *R.* v. *Goff*, 9 C.P. (Ont.), 438. So inciting another to commit a misdemeanor, as endeavouring to induce a person to take a false oath, is a misdemeanor. *R.* v. *Clement*, 26 Q.B. (Ont.), 297.

The act of attempting to commit a felony must be immediately and directly tending to the execution of the principal crime, and committed by the prisoner under such circumstances, that he has the power of carrying his intention into execution. *R.* v. *McCann*, 28 Q. B. (Ont.), 514.

It may be observed that the 32 & 33 Vic., chap. 29, s. 49, provides that a person charged with any felony or misdemeanor, may be convicted of an *attempt* to commit the same, and no person tried in this manner shall be liable to be afterwards prosecuted for committing or attempting to commit the felony or misdemeanor for which he was so tried. See *R.* v. *Webster*, 9 L. C. R., 196.

A disregard of or non-compliance with a positive command in

an Act of Parliament is indictable as a misdemeanor. *R.* v. *Toronto St. Ry. Co.*, 24 Q. B. (Ont.), 454.

By the 32 & 33 Vic., chap. 29, s. 50, although a felony appears on the facts given in evidence, a misdemeanor with which the party may be charged will not merge therein, and the party may still be convicted of *such* misdemeanor. But a party cannot, under this section, be convicted of any felony which may be disclosed in evidence, but only of *the misdemeanor* with which he is charged, if included in the felony proved. *R.* v. *Ewing*, 21 Q. B. (Ont.), 523.

Independently of some statutory authority, a person cannot, on an indictment for felony, be found guilty of a misdemeanor. *R.* v. *Thomas*, L. R., 2 C. C. R., 141.

An order made under a power given in a statute is the same thing, as if the statute enacted what the order directs or forbids, and disobedience of such order is a misdemeanor, for which an indictment will lie. *R.* v. *Walker*, L. R., 10 Q. B., 355.

When a person filling a public office, wilfully neglects or refuses to discharge the duties thereof, and there is no special remedy or punishment pointed out by the statute, an indictment will lie, as there would otherwise be no means of punishing the delinquent. *R.* v. *Bennett*, 21 C. P. (Ont.), 237.

The 31 Vic., chap. 71, s. 3, provides that any wilful contravention of any Act of the Legislature of any of the Provinces within Canada, which is not made an offence of some other kind, shall be a misdemeanor.

Under the 31 Vic., chap. 1, s. 7, twentiethly, any wilful contravention of any Act which is not made an offence of some other kind, shall be a misdemeanor, and punishable accordingly. But it seems that a mere non-feasance in no way criminal in itself, cannot be treated as a misdemeanor or any species of criminal offence, unless expressly declared to be such by competent Legislative authority. *R.* v. *Snider*, 23 C. P. (Ont.), 330-36.

INFANTS.

Under the age of seven, an infant cannot be convicted of felony (*Marsh* v. *Loader*, 14 C. B., N. S., 535), for until he reaches that age he is presumed to be incapable of crime, and this presumption cannot be rebutted by the clearest evidence of a mischievous discretion. Between seven and fourteen he is still *prima facie*, deemed by law to be incapable of crime; but this presumption may be rebutted by clear and strong evidence of such mischievous discretion. An infant under fourteen cannot, however, be convicted of rape as a principal, but he may as a principal, in the second degree.

INSANITY.

No act is a crime if the person who does it is at the time when it is done prevented either by defective mental powers or by any disease affecting his mind from knowing the nature and quality of his act, or from knowing that the act is wrong, or from controlling his own conduct, unless the absence of the power of control has been produced by his own default. But an act may be a crime, although the mind of the person who does it is affected by disease, if such disease does not in fact produce upon his mind one or other of the effects above mentioned in reference to that Act.

Every person is presumed to be sane, and to be responsible for his acts. The burden of proving that he is irresponsible is upon the accused person, but the jury may have regard to his appearance and behaviour in court. *R.* v. *Oxford*, 9 C. & P., 525; *R.* v. *Stokes*, 3 C. & K., 185; Stephens Dig., 17-18-19.

A person sodeficient in understanding as not to comprehend the proceedings on his trial, cannot be convicted of any offence, the trial must be stopped.

A deaf mute being tried for felony, was found guilty, but the jury found also that he was incapable of understanding, and did not understand the proceedings on the trial. It was held that he could not be convicted, but must be detained as a non-sane person during the Queen's pleasure. *R.* v. *Berry*, L. R., 1 Q. B., D., 447.

The 32 & 33 Vic., chap. 29, s. 99 and following sections relate to insane prisoners. The 105th section of this Act was amended by the 36 Vic., chap. 51.

In New Brunswick the 1 Rev. Stat., chap. 89, s. 1, enacts that "any person so disordered in his senses as to be dangerous when at large, may, on evidence of the fact, be apprehended and conveyed to the Provincial Lunatic Asylum on a warrant issued by any two Justices of any county." "Evidence" in this statute has been held to mean *viva voce* evidence, and the fact cannot be proved by affidavit. The evidence must also be given before the two Justices acting together, and it is not sufficient that an affidavit be made before one and shewn to the other. *McGuirk* v. *Richard*, 2 Pugsley, 240.

INSOLVENCY.

Under section 140 of the Insolvent Act of 1875 (38 Vic., chap. 16), certain acts done by an insolvent with intent to defraud or defeat the rights of his creditors, are declared to be misdemeanors. The last clause applies to pawning pledging or disposing of otherwise than in the ordinary way of his trade, any property, goods or effects the price of which remains unpaid by him during the three months preceding the insolvency. An insolvent may be guilty of an offence under this section, although the goods are not disposed of to his own use, but to satisfy creditors, and although the term of credit thereon has not expired at the time of the insolvency. *R.* v. *Kerr*, 26 C. P. (Ont.), 214.

LARCENY, EMBEZZLEMENT, AND OBTAINING BY FALSE PRETENCES.

The Act respecting larceny and other similar offences, is the 32 & 33 Vic., chap. 21. This Act was amended by the 35 Vic., chaps. 33 & 35; the 38 Vic., chap. 40; and the 40 Vic., chap. 29.

It was extended to Prince Edward Island by the 40 Vic., chap. 4; to the District of Keewatin by the 39 Vic., chap. 21; to the North-West Territories by the 38 Vic., chap. 49; to British Columbia by the 37 Vic., chap. 42; and to the Province of Manitoba by the 34 Vic., chap. 14.

Theft is the wrongfully obtaining possession of any movable thing which is the property of some other person, and of some value, with the fraudulent intent entirely to deprive him of such thing, and have or deal with it as the property of some person other than the owner. Cr. Law. Comrs., 3rd Report.

Independently of the provisions of the statute, 32 & 33 Vic., chap. 21, the goods taken must be *personal* goods, for none other can be the subject of larceny at common law. It is to be observed, however, that this statute specifies various subjects of larceny, which were not such at the common law. Sections 10 to 14 relate to the stealing of cattle and other animals. Sections 15 to 19 as to written instruments. It was held by the Court of Queen's Bench in Montreal (Dorion, C. J., and Sanborn, J., dissenting) that an unstamped promissory note is a valuable security, within the 15th section, and when the payee of such note stole it from the makers, and afterwards stamped and issued it, without right or authority, he was held properly convicted of larceny. *R.* v. *Scott*, 21 L. C., J., 225.

Sections 20 to 27 relate to the larceny of things attached or growing on land. These latter, at common law, could not be the subjects of larceny, as they were not *personal* goods.

Section 22 of 32 & 33 Vic., chap. 21, applies to the whole or any part of any tree *growing* and not cut down or made into cordwood. Under the 25th section it seems the offender must have *knowledge* of the possession, and, reading this section in connection with the others, it seems that, whatever trees, &c., are made the subject of larceny in the other sections are, if found in the possession, or on the premises of any one, to his knowledge, and without accounting for how he came by the same, to subject such person to a conviction for so having them. And that a tree, cut by the proprietor into cordwood, and taken away by some one after it has been made into cordwood, is, if stolen, a mere larceny of goods and chattels, and does not come within the 25th section of the Act, nor within the heading of these sections. Even if the section does apply to trees cut by the owner and lying on his land as he felled them, still it does not apply to cordwood, which is not "the whole or any part of any tree." *R.* v. *Caswell*, 33 Q. B. (Ont), 303.

Things attached to the land, and which are not embraced in these sections, are not the subjects of larceny, unless severed from the freehold, and unless between the time of severance and the taking, the property therein vests in the owner of the freehold. Where the severance and the taking are one continuous act, there can be no larceny. *R.* v. *Townley*, L. R., 1 C. C. R., 315.

Partridges hatched and reared by a common hen, while they remain with her, are the subjects of larceny (*R.* v. *Shickle*, L.R., 1 C. C. R., 158; and section 12 of this statute now applies to any bird ordinarily kept in a state of confinement, or for any domestic purpose.

Sections 28 to 37 of this statute relate to larceny from mines, or of ores or minerals.

At common law also, the taking must be of the goods of *another*. Therefore a man cannot steal his own goods, and husband and wife being one in law, they cannot steal each other's goods.

If any other person assists a married woman in dealing with things which belong to her husband in a manner which would amount to theft in the case of other persons, such dealing is not theft (*R.* v. *Avery*, Bell, 150), unless the person so assisting commits or intends to commit adultery with the woman (*R.* v. *Mutters*, L. & C., 511), in which case he, but not she, commits theft. But this exception does not apply to the case of an adulterer or person intending to commit adultery, who assists a married woman to carry away her own wearing apparel only from her husband. *R.* v. *Fitch*, D. & B., 187.

So also one joint tenant or tenant in common could not steal the goods which belonged to himself and the others jointly. Now, however, section 38 of the statute provides that, whosoever being a member of any co-partnership owing any money or other property, or being one of two or more beneficial owners of any money or other property, steals, embezzles, or unlawfully converts the same, or any part thereof, to his own use or that of any person other than the owner, shall be liable to be dealt with, tried, convicted and punished, as if he had not been or were not a member of such co-partnership, or one of such beneficial owners. It is to be observed, however, that the Court of Queen's Bench in Montreal has recently held that this statute is nugatory, and that a partner cannot be convicted under it either of larceny, embezzlement, or unlawful conversion. *R.* v. *Lowenbruck*, 18 L. C. J., 212.

There must also be an actual or constructive taking of the goods, as larceny involves a trespass. Where the owner by mistake gives the possession of the goods, but the defendant knew the mistake, and intended from the first to steal; this is a sufficient taking. *R.* v. *Middleton*, L. R., 2 C. C. R., 38.

There must also be a carrying away; but as the felony lies in the very first act of removing the property, the least removing of the thing taken from the place where it was before, with intent to steal, is a sufficient asportation. See *R.* v. *Townley*, L. R., 1 C. C. R., 319.

To constitute larceny, there must be a felonious intent to take the goods of another against his will, with intent to deprive the owner of his property therein. *R.* v. *McGrath*, L. R., 1 C. C. R., 210–11; See also, *R.* v. *Prince*, L. R., 1 C. C. R., 150; *R.* v. *Bailey*, L. R., 1 C. C. R., 347.

Returning the goods may be evidence to negative the felonious intent at the time of taking them, but it is no defence that the prisoner intended to return them when taken.

A finder of lost goods who converts them commits theft if at the time when he takes possession of them he intends to convert them, knowing who the owner is, or having reasonable grounds to believe that he can be found. Such conversion is not theft (*a*) if at the time when the finder takes possession of the goods he has not such knowledge or grounds of belief as aforesaid, although he acquires them after taking possession of the goods and before resolving to convert them; or (*b*) if he does not intend to convert the goods at the time when he takes possession of them, whether he has such knowledge or grounds of belief or not at any time. If the circumstances are such as to lead the finder reasonably to believe that the owner intended to abandon his property in the goods, the finder is not guilty of theft in converting them. See *R.* v. *Thurborn*, 1 Den., 387; *R.* v. *Glyde*, L. R., 1 C. C. R., 139.

If the thing taken and carried away is on the body or in the immediate presence of the person from whom it is taken, and if the taking is by actual violence, intentionally used to overcome or to prevent his resistance, or by threats of injury to his person, property or reputation, the offence is robbery. Robbery is in fact larceny, aggravated by circumstances of force, violence or putting in fear, and a party charged with robbery may be convicted of larceny, as the latter crime includes the former. *R.* v. *McGrath*, L. R., 1 C. C. R., 210-11.

For these reasons no sudden taking or snatching of property unawares from a person is sufficient to constitute robbery, unless some injury be done to the person or there be a previous struggle for the possession of the property, or some force used to obtain it, and the fear must precede the taking. Where there is no force or fear, and the property is taken suddenly, the offender is guilty of the offence of stealing from the person. Section 39 of the statute 32 & 33 Vic., chap. 21, provides for both the offences of robbery and stealing from the person. So by section 40 a person charged with robbery may be convicted of an assault with intent to rob, and by section 41 an assault with intent to rob is felony.

In robbery there must be a complete removal of the thing from the person of the party robbed—both a taking and a carrying away. An assault with intent to rob is distinguished from robbery in this that in the former there is no taking or carrying away, the purpose not being effected. A person charged with an assault with intent to rob cannot be convicted of a common assault. *R.* v. *Woodhall*, 12 Cox, 240.

If the possession of goods is lawfully obtained from the owner there can be no larceny, nor can there be any larceny if the property in the goods passes to the wrong doer. Where the owner *intends* to part with the property, though he may form such intention in consequence of some deceit or misrepresentation, there is no larceny, but there may be an obtaining by false pretences. But where the owner does not intend to part with the goods or money taken by the defendant, and the latter fraudulently gets possession of them, intending not to pay for them, he is guilty of larceny. Where the owner voluntarily parts with the possession intending to vest the property in the defendant, because he relies on the defendant's *promise* to pay for them, he cannot be convicted of larceny. *R.* v. *Bertles*, 13 C. P. (Ont.), 610.

If, however, the owner transfers the possession under a mistake and the prisoner, knowing the mistake, intends to steal, he is guilty of larceny. *R.* v. *Middleton*, L. R., 2 C. C. R., 38 ; *ante*, p. 311.

Where a servant is entrusted with his master's property with a general or absolute authority to act for his master in his business, and is induced by fraud to part with his master's property, the person who is guilty of the fraud, and so obtains the property, is guilty of obtaining it by false pretences and not of larceny; because to constitute larceny there must be a taking against the will of the owner, or of the owner's servant duly authorized to act generally for the owner. But where a servant has no such general or absolute authority from his master, but is merely entrusted with the possession of his goods for a special or limited purpose, and is tricked out of that possession by fraud, the person who is guilty of the fraud, and so obtains the property, is guilty of larceny, because the servant has no authority to part with the property in the goods except to fulfil the special purpose for which they were entrusted to him. *R.* v. *Prince*, L. R., 1 C. C. R., 150.

It is not to be inferred from the foregoing that the offender will entirely escape criminal liability. The 93rd section of this statute provides that a person indicted for the misdemeanor of obtaining money by false pretences shall not be entitled to an acquittal though it is proved that he obtained the property in such manner as to amount to larceny.

According to the common law, and as illustrative of the distinction between larceny and embezzlement, if a servant received money on account of his master and put in his pocket before it reached his master's custody (as if a clerk in a shop on receiving money from a customer put it into his pocket before putting it into the till), he could not be convicted of larceny, for the money was never in the master's possession, but if the servant placed it in the till, his afterwards taking it out of the till, with a felonious intent, would be larceny, and it is still larceny. *R.* v. *Hennessy*, 35 Q. B. (Ont.), 603.

Now, however, section 70 of the statute removes even this distinction. If a clerk, or servant, or person employed for the purpose or in the capacity of a clerk or servant, fraudulently embezzles any chattel, money or valuable security, delivered to, or received, or taken into possession by him for, or in the name, or on account of his master or employer, he shall be deemed to have feloniously stolen the same from his master or employer, although such chattel, money, or security was not received into the possession of such master or employer otherwise than by the actual possession of his clerk, servant, or the person so employed. This section, however, only applies to cases where the chattel, money or valuable security is received from third persons on account of the master, and not where it is received directly from the master. *R.* v. *Cummins*, 4 U. C., L. J., 182.

There may, however, be an embezzlement by a clerk or servant of money received *from* as well as money received *for* his master. The difference is that in the first case the offence is a larceny at common law, when not a mere breach of trust. Under section 70, however, of the 32 & 33 Vic., chap. 21, it is not necessary that the servant should receive the money by virtue of his employment. Therefore, though the servant receives the money without authority and without any duty to receive, he is still liable under this section. See Arch. Cr. Pldg., 453. But the money must be received "for, or in the name, or on the account, of the master or employer." *R.* v. *Cullum*, L. R., 2 C. C. R., 28. As to receiving "on account of the master" within the meaning of this section. See *R.* v. *Gale*, L. R., 2 Q. B. D., 141. So also by section 74, if it is proved that a person charged with embezzlement, took the property in question in such manner as to amount to larceny, he shall not, by reason thereof, be entitled to be acquitted, but may be convicted of the larceny; and so *vice versa*, a person charged with larceny may be convicted of embezzlement or fraudulent application or disposition. So also by the common law a bailee, or person lawfully acquiring the possession of property for some specific purpose, could not be convicted of larceny in respect of any subsequent felonious conversion, if his intention at the time of obtaining possession were innocent. See *Pease* v. *McAloon*, 1 Kerr, 116. Now, however, by section 3 of this Act, whosoever being a bailee of any chattel, money or valuable security, fraudulently takes or converts the same to his own use, or to the use of any person other than the owner thereof, although he do not break bulk or otherwise determine the bailment, is guilty of larceny, but the section is not to extend to any offence punishable on summary conviction, and finally by section 99 of 32 & 33 Vic., chap. 21, if upon the trial of any person for larceny it appears that the property taken was obtained by such person by fraud, under circumstances which do not amount to such taking as constitutes larceny, such person shall not by reason thereof be entitled to be acquitted; and he may be found guilty of obtaining the property by false pretences, with intent to defraud, if the evidence proves such to have been the case.

There can be no offence under sections 69 & 70 of the 32 & 33 Vic., chap. 21, unless the person who converts stands to the owner of the property converted in the relation of a clerk or servant or person employed in the capacity of a clerk or servant.

It is a question for a jury whether a person accused of embezzlement is a clerk or servant or not. See *R.* v. *Negus*, L. R., 2 C. C. R., 34. A clerk or servant is a person bound either by an express contract of service, or by conduct implying such a contract, to obey the orders and submit to the control of his master in the transaction of the business which it is his duty as such clerk or servant to transact. *Ib.; R.* v. *Tite*, L. & C., 33; *R.* v. *Foulkes*, L. R., 2 C. C. R., 152.

A man may be a clerk or servant (1) although he was appointed or elected to the employment in respect of which he is a clerk or servant by some other person than the master whose orders he is bound to obey. *McDonald's case*, L. & C., 85.

2. Although he is paid for his services by a commission or share in the profits of the business. *R.* v. *Carr*, R. & R., 198.

3. Although he is a member of any co-partnership, or is one of two or more beneficial owners of the property embezzled. 32 & 33 Vic., chap. 21, s. 38.

4. Although he is the clerk or servant of more masters than one. *R.* v. *Spencer*, R. & R., 299.

5. Although he acts as clerk or servant only occasionally, or only on the particular occasion on which his offence is committed. *R.* v. *Hughes*, Moo. C. C., 370.

But an agent or other person who undertakes to transact business for another without undertaking to obey his orders is not necessarily a servant, because he receives a salary, or because he has undertaken not to accept employment of a similar kind from any one else, or because he is under a duty, statutory or otherwise, to account for money or other property received by him. *R.* v. *Callahan*, 8 C. & P., 154; Stephen's Dig., 243-4.

The offence of embezzlement cannot be committed by the appropriation of property which does not belong to the master of the alleged offender, although such property may have been obtained by such alleged offender by the improper use of the property entrusted to him by his master, but property which does belong to the master of the offender may be embezzled, although the offender received it in an irregular way. *R.* v. *Cullum*, L.R., 2 C. C. R., 28; *R.* v. *Glover*, L. & C., 466. Under our statute the property must be delivered to or received or taken into possession by the servant for or in the name or on account of his master or employer. See *ante*, p. 314.

The inference that a prisoner has embezzled property by fraudulently converting it to his own use may be drawn from the fact that he has not paid the money or delivered the property in due course to the owner, or from the fact that he has not accounted for the money or other property which he has received, or from the fact that he has falsely accounted for it, or from the fact that he has absconded, or from the fact that upon the examination of his accounts there appeared to be a general deficiency unaccounted for; but none of these facts constitutes in itself the offence of embezzlement, nor is the fact that the alleged offender rendered a correct account of the money or other property entrusted to him inconsistent with his having embezzled it. Stephen's Dig., 248-9.

In order to support a charge of obtaining money by false pretences (*a*) there must be a pretence of an *existing* fact; (*b*) it must appear that the party defrauded has been induced to part with his money by the pretence; and (*c*) the pretence must be untrue. *R.* v. *Crab*, 11 Cox, 85.

The prisoner must represent some fact as existing which does not exist, and a mere *promise* by the prisoner as to future conduct will not render him liable, the prosecutor relying upon the promise rather than being deceived by the representation. *R.* v. *Bertles*, 13 C. P. (Ont.), 607.

Not only is it necessary that there be a false pretence of an existing fact, but the prosecutor must be induced to part with his money in consequence of the false pretence, it must be the motive operating on his mind and inducing him to part with his money, in other words the prosecutor must be deceived by the representation. *R.* v. *Gemmell*, 26 Q. B. (Ont.), 312 ; *R.* v. *Connor*, 14 C. P. (Ont.), 529. If it is false to his knowledge it does not come within the statute. *R.* v. *Mills*, 7 Cox C. C., 263. As to what is sufficient, see *R.* v. *Howarth*, 11 Cox C. C., 588.

The crime of obtaining goods by false pretences is complete, although at the time when the prisoner made the pretence and obtained the goods he intended to pay for them when it should be in his power to do so. *R.* v. *Naylor*, L. R., 1 C. C. R., 4.

A dog is not included in the term "chattels," and is not the subject of the misdemeanor of false pretences. *R.* v. *Robinson*, 8 Cox C. C., 115.

The property obtained need not necessarily be in existence at the time the pretence is made if its subsequent delivery is directly connected with the false pretence. *R.* v. *Martin*, L. R., 1 C. C. R., 56.

The word "obtain" in the 32 & 33 Vic., chap. 21, s. 93, does not mean obtain the loan of, but obtain the property in any chattel, and to constitute an obtaining by false pretences it is essential that there should be an intention to deprive the owner wholly of the property in the chattel, and an obtaining by false pretences the *use* of a chattel for a limited time only, without an intention to deprive the owner wholly of the chattel is not an obtaining by false pretences within this section. *R.* v. *Kilham*, L. R., 1 C. C. R , 261. But now section 94 of the Act provides that "Whosoever by any false pretence causes or procures any money to be paid, or any chattel or valuable security to be delivered to any other person for the use or benefit or on account of the person making such false pretence, or of any other person with intent to defraud, shall be deemed to have obtained such money, &c., within the meaning of the statute."

The expression "false pretence" in the statute means a false representation, made either by words, by writing or by conduct, that some fact exists or existed, and such a representation may amount to a false pretence although a person of common prudence might easily have detected its falsehood by enquiry, and although the existence of the alleged fact was in itself impossible.

But the expression "false pretence" does not, as we have already seen, include a promise as to future conduct, not intended to be kept unless such promise is based upon or implies an existing fact falsely alleged to exist, or such untrue commendation, or untrue depreciation of an article which is to be sold as is usual between sellers and buyers, unless such untrue commendation or depreciation is made by means of a definite false assertion as to some matter of fact capable of being positively determined. *R.* v. *Bernard*, 7 C. & P., 784; *R.* v. *Hazleton*, L. R., 2 C. C. R., 134.

Questions frequently arise as to whether giving a cheque on a bank, in which the drawer of the cheque has no funds, is an obtaining by false pretences. It seems clear that drawing a cheque on a bank, where the drawer has no *account*, would be a false pretence, but where the drawer has an account, the mere fact that there are no funds is not sufficient, there must also be evidence that the drawer intended to defraud and obtain goods or money on the cheque (see *R.* v. *Hazelton*, *supra*), and did not intend to pay it on presentation.

A misrepresentation of quantity is a sufficient false pretence to sustain an indictment. *R.* v. *Sherwood*, 7 Cox C. C., 270. So if a man is selling an article by weight, and falsely represents the weight to be greater than it is, and thereby obtains payment for a quantity greater than that delivered, he is indictable for obtaining money by false pretences. *R.* v. *Ridgway*, 3 F. & F., 838.

Where money has been obtained on a forged cheque knowingly, it does not amount to larceny, but to obtaining money by false pretences. *R.* v. *Prince*, L. R., 1 C. C. R., 150.

The false pretence may be by a letter written by the prisoner, as well as by express words. If the words of the letter fairly and reasonably contain a statement of a false pretence, the prisoner may be convicted. *R.* v. *Cooper*, L. R., 2. Q. B. D., 510.

On an indictment for obtaining money by false pretences it was proved that the prisoner, a travelling hawker, represented to the prosecutor's wife that he was a tea dealer from Leicester, and induced her to buy certain packages, which he stated to contain good tea, but three-fourths of the contents of which was not tea at all, but a mixture of substances unfit to drink, and deleterious to health. It was proved that the prisoner knew the real nature of the contents of the packages, and that he designedly, falsely pretended that it was good tea, with intent to defraud. It was held that the prisoner was guilty of obtaining money by false pretences. *R.* v. *Foster*, L. R., 2 Q. B. D., 301.

As to the distinctions between larceny and embezzlement, and the obtaining of money, &c., by false pretences, it is the essence of the offence of larceny, that the property be taken against the *will* of the owner. *R.* v. *Prince*, L. R., 1 C. C.R., 154.

The owner of the thing stolen has no intention to part with his property therein to the person taking it, although he may intend to part with the possession. If taken by the consent of the owner; for instance, if he *intends* to part with the property; no larceny will be committed.

In false pretences, the property is obtained with the consent of the owner, the latter intending to part with his property, but the intention is induced by fraud. It therefore necessarily differs from larceny in the fact, that the property in the chattel passes to the person obtaining it, and it may, though perhaps not necessarily, differ from larceny in this, that the owner is induced to voluntarily part with his property in consequence of some false pretence of an existing fact made by the person obtaining the chattel. But the crime of obtaining money by false pretences is similar to larceny in this, that in both offences there must be an intention to deprive the owner wholly of his property, in the chattel. See *R.* v. *Killham*, L. R., 1 C. C. R., 261.

Embezzlement consists in obtaining the lawful possession of goods, &c., without fraud or any false pretences, as upon a contract, or with the consent of the owner in the ordinary course of duty or employment, or independently of such employment, and subsequently converting the goods, with a felonious intent to deprive the owner of his property therein. It differs from larceny in this, that the possession of the goods, &c., is lawfully obtained in the first instance, without the ingredient of trespass, and the conversion takes place while the privity of contract exists between the parties.

Under 32 & 33 Vic., chap. 21, s. 121, persons stealing property in one part of the Dominion may be tried and punished in that part where they have the property, in the same manner as if they had actually stolen or taken or obtained it in that part.

So by section 112 bringing into Canada property stolen, embezzled, or unlawfully obtained in any other country in such manner as by the laws of Canada would be a felony or misdemeanor, shall be an offence of the same nature, and punishable in like manner as if the stealing, embezzling, converting or unlawfully obtaining such property had taken place in Canada. The prisoner being the agent of the American Express Company, in the State of Illinois, received a sum of money which had been collected by them for a customer, and put it into their safe, but made no entry in their books of its receipt as it was his duty to do, and afterwards absconded with it to Canada where he was arrested. The prisoner was held guilty of larceny, and properly convicted under section 112 of the statute, though there was nothing to show that the act of the prisoner was by the law of the State of Illinois larceny, and it seems that proof of this description is not required. *R.* v. *Hennessey,* 35 Q. B. (Ont.), 603. See also *ante*, p. 8.

The 113th section of the 32 & 33 Vic., chap. 21, provides that the owner of stolen property, prosecuting the thief to conviction, shall have restitution of his property.

Under this section the title acquired by the owner of the property dates from the conviction and has no relation back to the original fraud, and when the thief parts with the goods, when he has a good title, the owner cannot recover either the goods or their proceeds, if converted into cash. *Lindsey* v. *Cundy*, L. R., 1 Q. B., D., 348, though by section 1 of the Act, "property" includes anything acquired by the converson, or exchange, whether immediately or otherwise. This case was reversed in appeal, on the ground that the property had never passed from the original owner. S. C., L. R., 2 Q. B. D., 96.

LAWLESS AGGRESSIONS.

(*See* AGGRESSIONS.)

LIBEL AND INDICTABLE SLANDER.

A libel is a malicious defamation, made public either by printing, writing, signs, pictures, or the like, tending either to blacken the memory of one who is dead, or the reputation of one who is alive, by exposing him (or his memory) to public hatred, contempt or ridicule.

All words spoken of another, which impute to him the commission of a crime punishable by law are indictable; so all words spoken of another, which have the effect of excluding him from society, for example, to say he has the leprosy; so writing or publishing anything which renders another ridiculous, or contemptible is indictable, except it be within the fair limits of literary criticism. So words used of a man which impair or hurt his trade, or livelihood, as to call a physician a quack, are indictable. To make a writing a libel it must be published, though by publication is not necessarily meant in a newspaper, for communication to a single person, in a private letter, is a publication. No words spoken, however scurrilous, even though spoken personally to an individual, are the subject of an indictment, unless they directly tend to a breach of the peace; for example, by inciting to a challenge. We must here except words seditious, blasphemous, grossly immoral, or uttered to a magistrate while in the execution of his duty.

The publication of any obscene writing is unlawful and indictable, and it is no defence that the object of the party was laudable, for, in case of libel, the law presumes that the party intended what the libel was calculated to effect. *R.* v. *Hicklin*, L. R., 3 Q. B., 360.

Proceedings before magistrates, under the 32 & 33 Vic., chap.

31 " in relation to summary convictions and orders " are strictly of a judicial nature, and the place where such proceedings are held is an open court. The defendant, as well as the prosecutor, has a right to the assistance of an attorney and counsel, and to call what witnesses he pleases, and both parties, having been heard the trial and judgment may be lawfully made the subject of a printed report, if that report is impartial and correct. *Lewis* v. *Levy*, E. B. & E., 537. The same rule would apply to investigations by magistrates in the case of indictable offences, so long as the magistrate continues to sit in open court, but if he chooses to carry on the proceedings in private, as he may do under section 35 of the 32 & 33 Vic., chap. 30, then the publication of the proceedings would be unlawful.

A Justice of the Peace may issue his warrant to arrest a party charged with libel. *Butt* v. *Conant*, 1 B. & B., 548.

The 37 Vic., chap. 38, relates to the crime of libel. Under this statute, publishing, or threatening to publish, any libel with intent to extort money, is a misdemeanor, so, under section 2, maliciously publishing a defamatory libel, knowing the same to be false, is a misdemeanor.

This Act was extended to Prince Edward Island by the 40 Vic., chap. 4.

LOTTERIES.

The Con. Stat. Can., chap. 95, is the Act now in force respecting lotteries.

Under section 1, if any person makes, prints, advertises, or publishes any proposal, scheme or plan for advancing, lending, giving, selling, or in any way disposing of any property by lots, cards, tickets or any mode of chance whatever, or sells, barters, exchanges or otherwise disposes of, or offers for sale, barter or exchange any lot, card, ticket, or other means or device for advancing, lending, giving, selling or otherwise disposing of any property by lots, tickets or any mode of chance whatever, such person shall upon conviction thereof, upon the oath of any one or more credible witnesses, or upon confession thereof, forfeit the sum of twenty dollars for each and every such offence, together with costs, &c.

By the Imperial Act, 10 & 11 Wm. 3, chap. 17, all lotteries are declared to be public nuisances. The Imperial Act 12 Geo. 2nd, chap. 28, superseded the 10 & 11 Wm. 3, chap. 17, with respect to lotteries of horses, carriages and other personal chattels. *Clarke* v. *Donelly*, R. & J. Dig., 1619.

The Imperial Act, 12 Geo. 2nd, chap. 28, is in force in this country notwithstanding the Con. Stat. Can., chap. 95. *Cronyn* v. *Widder*, 16 Q. B. (Ont.), 356; *Corby* v. *McDaniel*, 16 Q. B., (Ont.) 378; *Marshall* v. *Platt*, 8 C. P. (Ont.), 189; 27 & 28 Vic., chap. 32.

When one hundred and forty-nine lots of land were sold by lottery, the person getting No. 1 ticket to have the first choice; it was held that this was a lottery, though it did not appear that there was any difference in the value of the lots. The lottery consisted in having a choice of the lots, and that choice was to be determined by chance. *Power* v. *Canniff*, 18 Q. B. (Ont.), 403.

A sale of land by lot in which there were two prizes was held to be within the 12 Geo. 2nd., chap. 28. *Marshall* v. *Platt*, 8 C. P. (Ont.), 189; see also *Lloyd* v. *Clark*, 11 C. P. (Ont.), 248.

An information to forfeit land sold by lottery, contrary to 12 Geo. 2nd, chap. 28, may be filed by a private individual, and need not be by the Attorney-General or any public officer. *Mewburn* v. *Street*, 21 Q. B. (Ont.), 498.

MAINTENANCE.

This is the officious intermeddling in a suit that in no way belongs to one by *maintaining* or assisting either party with money or otherwise to prosecute or defend it. It is a misdemeanor punishable by fine and imprisonment. Champerty is a species of maintenance. It is the unlawful maintenance of a suit in consideration of some bargain to have part of the thing in dispute or some profit out of it. See *Carr* v. *Tannahill*, 30 Q. B., (Ont.), 223; *Kerr* v. *Brunton*, 24 Q. B. (Ont.), 395. Champerty is punishable at Common Law. *Scott* v. *Henderson*, 2 Thomson, 116.

Acts of maintenance or champerty are justifiable when the

party has an interest in the thing in variance, and at the present day the court would be very loth to declare an act of this kind to be an offence criminally indictable, unless some corrupt motive were manifestly present, or there was danger of oppression or abuse *Allan* v. *McHeffey*, 1 Oldright, 121. From the decision in *Smyth* v. *McDonald*, 1 Oldright, 274, that the Crown must first eject the occupant before selling land of which it is not in possession, it would seem that the law as to champerty is binding on the Crown. A sharing in the profits derived from the success of the suit is essential to constitute champerty. *Hilton* v. *Woods*, L. R., 4 Eq., 432; *Hartley* v. *Russell*, 2 S. & St., 244.

MALICIOUS INJURIES.

The Act respecting malicious injuries to property, is the 32 & 33 Vic., chap. 22. This Act was amended by the 35 Vic., chap. 34, and by the 40 Vic., chap. 29. It was extended to Prince Edward Island by the 40 Vic., chap. 4; to the District of Keewatin by the 39 Vic., chap. 21; to the North-West Territories by the 38 Vic., chap. 49; to British Columbia by the 37 Vic., chap. 42; and to the Province of Manitoba by the 34 Vic., chap. 14.

Injuring or destroying private property is in general no crime, but a mere civil trespass, over which a magistrate has no jurisdiction unless by statute. *Powell* v. *Williamson*, 1 Q.B. (Ont.), 155.

The above statute renders various acts criminal if they are unlawful and malicious. Arson is one of the injuries provided for by the Act. This offence has been already treated of, see arson, *ante*, p. 257.

An apparatus for manufacturing potash, consisting of ovens, kettles, tubs, is not a machine or engine within the meaning of the 19th section of the Act, the cutting, breaking, or damaging of which is felonious. *R.* v. *Dogherty*, 2 L.C.R., 255.

Under this section it is not necessary that the damage done should be of a permanent kind. If the engine is rendered temporarily useless, it will be an offence within this section. Thus, plugging up the feed-pipe of a steam-engine, and displacing other parts of the engine so as to render it temporarily useless and cause an explosion unless removed, comes within the Act. *R.* v. *Fisher*, L.R., 1 C.C.R., 7.

A party acting under a *bona fide* claim of right cannot be found guilty of malice under section 29 of the 32 & 33 Vic., chap. 22; and where such right is set up the magistrate should satisfy himself that it is honestly claimed.

The defendant had buried a child in a graveyard, near the remains of his own father. The complainant had a parcel of ground which the sexton of the church had appropriated to his exclusive use, without any authority from the incumbent or churchwardens. The complainant subsequently extended his fence by the like consent of the sexton only, and enclosed more ground, so that the fence crossed diagonally over the grave of defendant's child Defendant remonstrated, but obtained no redress or a removal of the fence, and proceeded to remove it himself. In process of doing so he broke a marble pillar of complainant's fence, for which he was summoned before a magistrate, for "wilfully and maliciously" destroying a fence, under the 29th section of the Act. He was fined $5 over and above the sum of $10 for damages for the injury done, and $6.50 costs. From this conviction the defendant appealed to the General Sessions of the Peace. It was held that although the defendant was guilty of a trespass, for which he might be mulcted in damages in a civil action, he was not liable to a fine, and that acting under a claim of right the act was not necessarily malicious. *R.* v. *Bradshaw*, 38 Q. B. (Ont.), 564.

The 66th section does not dispense with proof of malice in cases of this kind. The 66th section read with the 29th, merely means that every punishment imposed by the 29th section, upon any person *maliciously* committing any offence in that section named, shall be enforced, whether the malice which constitutes the offence be conceived against the owner of the property in respect of which it shall be committed, or against any other person; but malice either against the owner or some one must be proved, or legitimately inferred from the facts in evidence, in order to constitute an offence punishable under the Act (*ib.*).

Where malice is essential the *bona fide* belief by the party that he had the right to do the act, is important as regards the intention.

If the party does the act unlawfully, not believing that he has any right to take the proceeding, that would be evidence from which malice could be inferred. *R.* v. *Elston*, 5 Allen, 2.

Where in a proceeding before two Justices, under 1 Rev. Stat. N. B., chap. 133, for wilfully cutting and carrying away timber off complainant's land, there is shown to be a *bona fide* question of title or boundaries, and the act was done under a *bona fide* claim of right, the wilfulness of the act is negatived, and the defendant should be discharged. *Ex parte Donovan*, 2 Pugsley, 389.

Section 40 of this Act enacts that whosoever by any unlawful act or by any wilful omission or neglect, obstructs, or causes to be obstructed any engine or carriage using any railway, or aids or assists therein, is guilty of a misdemeanor.

The prisoner unlawfully altered some railway signals at a railway station, from "all clear" to "danger" and "caution." The alteration caused a train which would have passed the station without slackening speed to slacken speed, and come nearly to a stand still. Another train going in the same direction, and on the same rails, was due at the station in half an hour; it was held that this was obstructing a train within the meaning of the above clause. *R.* v. *Hadfield*, L. R., 1 C. C. R., 253.

The Act is not limited to mere physical obstruction. The prisoner, who was not a servant of the railway company, stood on a railway between two lines of rails at a point between two stations. As a train was approaching, he held up his arms in the mode used by the inspectors of the line, when desirous of stopping a train between two stations. The prisoner knew that his doing so would probably induce the driver to stop or slacken speed, and his intention was to produce that effect. This, as the prisoner intended that it should, caused the driver to shut off steam and diminish speed, and led to a delay of four minutes. It was held that the prisoner had obstructed a train within the meaning of the statute. *R.* v. *Hardy*, L. R., 1 C. C. R., 278.

It was proved that the prisoner caused the death of a mare through injuries inflicted by his inserting the handle of a fork into her vagina, and pushing it into her body. There was no evidence that the prisoner was actuated by ill-will towards the owner of the mare, or spite towards the mare, or by any motive except the gratification of his own depraved taste. The jury found that the prisoner did not in fact intend to kill, maim, or wound the mare, but that he knew what he was doing would or might kill, maim, or wound the mare, and nevertheless did what he did recklessly, and not caring whether the mare was injured or not. It was held that there was sufficient malice, and that the prisoner might be convicted under section 45 of the Act. *R.* v. *Welch*, L. R., 1 Q. B. D., 23.

Under the 59th section, the Act must be wilfully done. If the damage is unintentional, there is no ground for inferring malice. The prisoner had been fighting with persons in the street, and threw a stone at them which struck a window, and did damage to an amount exceeding $20. The jury found that the prisoner threw the stone at the people he had been fighting with, intending to strike one or more of them, but not intending to break the window. It was held that there was no malice, either actual or constructive, in the breaking of the window, and that the prisoner could not be convicted. *R.* v. *Pembliton*, L. R., 2 C. C. R., 119.

The 59th section of this Act applies where the damage exceeds twenty dollars. The 60th section where the damage does not exceed this sum. Where a person having a public interest (as a Surveyor of highways in removing an obstruction to the highway) acts *bona fide* in the discharge of his duty, he cannot be convicted under this section of committing wilful and malicious damage. When such person acts in good faith, it must be taken that he acts under a fair and reasonable supposition, that he had a right to do the act complained of, and the Justices should not find otherwise. *Denny* v. *Thwaite*, L. R., 2 Ex. D., 21.

Under the 60th section, the conviction should clearly show whether the damage, injury, or spoil complained of is done to real or personal property, stating what property, and what is the amount which the Justice has ascertained to be reasonable compensation for such damage, injury or spoil.

A conviction charging that defendant, at a time and place named, wilfully and maliciously took and carried away the window sashes out of a building, owned by one C, against the form of the statute, &c., without alleging damage to any property, real or personal, and without finding damage to any amount, was held bad. *R.* v. *Caswell*, 20 C. P. (Ont.), 275.

MANSLAUGHTER.

(*See* MURDER ; *see also* INDICTABLE OFFENCES.)

MARRIED WOMEN.

In general if a crime be committed by a married woman in the presence of her husband the law presumes that she acted under his immediate coercion and excuses her from punishment; but if she commit an offence in the absence of her husband, even by his order or procurement, her coverture will be no defence. The presumption, however, that the wife acts under coercion may be rebutted, and if it appear that she was principally instrumental in the commission of the crime, acting voluntarily and not by restraint of her husband, although he was present and concurred, she will be guilty and liable to punishment. See *R.* v. *Cohen*, 11 Cox, 99. It appears also that the rule exempting the wife does not apply to treason, murder, manslaughter or robbery. *R.* v. *Manning*, 2 C. & K., 903; *R.* v. *Cruse*, 8 C. & P., 541. It applies, however, to theft, receiving stolen goods knowing them to be stolen, uttering counterfeit coin, and misdemeanors generally. In these latter cases to which the rule applies a wife committing the offence in the presence of her husband is excused unless it is shown affirmatively that she was not coerced.

MASTER AND SERVANT.

The law on this subject has been materially altered by "The Breaches of Contract Act, 1877," 40 Vic., chap. 35. The Con. Stats. U. C., chap. 75, ss. 4, 5, 7, 9, 10 & 11; the Con. Stats. Lower Canada, chap. 27, as amended by the 29 & 30 Vic., chap. 34; and section 3 of the 2 Wm. IV., chap. 26, in Prince Edward Island are repealed from and after the first day of May, 1878, in so far as a violation of any of the provisions of any of the said sections was criminal.

By section 2 of the 40 Vic., chap. 35, any person who wilfully and maliciously breaks any contract made by him, knowing or having probable cause to believe that the probable consequences of his so doing, either alone or in combination with others, will be to endanger human life, or to cause serious bodily injury, or to expose valuable property, whether real or personal, to destruction or serious injury, is on conviction liable to a fine not exceeding one hundred dollars, or to imprisonment for a term not exceeding three months, with or without hard labour. There are other provisions in the Act, and as to the mode of prosecution and the meaning of the term malice, see sections 4 & 5.

The 5 Eliz., chap. 4, is not in force in Ontario, but the 20 Geo. II., chap. 19, is, and under sections 3 and 4 jurisdiction is given to two or more Justices, and cannot be exercised by one, and the party cannot be arrested on the complaint but must be summoned. *Shea* v. *Choate*, 2 Q. B. (Ont.), 211.

MENACES AND THREATS.

By the 32 & 33 Vic., chap. 20, s. 15, whosoever maliciously sends, delivers, or utters, or directly or indirectly causes to be received, knowing the contents thereof, any letter or writing threatening to kill or murder any person, is guilty of felony.

See also the 32 & 33 Vic., chap. 21, ss. 43, 44, 45 & 46, also s. 47, as to inducing a person by violence or threats to execute deeds, &c., with intent to defraud; and also the 32 & 33 Vic., chap. 22, s. 58, as to sending letters threatening to burn or destroy houses, buildings, ships, agricultural produce, &c.

So by the 32 & 33 Vic., chap. 21, s. 46, threatening to accuse any person of an infamous crime, with intent to extort money, &c., is felony. The offence will be committed though the accusation was not intended to be made to a magistrate (*R.* v. *Robinson*, 2 Mood., 14); and though the valuable thing sought to be gained was the sale of a horse. *R.* v. *Redman*, 35 L. J., M. C., 89.

Under section 48 of the 32 & 33 Vic., chap. 21, it is immaterial whether the menaces or threats be of violence, injury, or accusation to be caused or made by the offender or by any other person.

So the threat need not be of an accusation against the person threatened; threatening a father with an accusation against the son is sufficient. *R.* v. *Redman*, L. R., 1 C. C. R., 12.

Under section 45 of this statute, as to letters threatening to accuse of crime, with intent to extort evidence of the truth of the accusation, will not be allowed in defence. *R.* v. *Cracknall*, 10 Cox C. C., 408.

The 32 & 33 Vic., chap. 21, s. 43, makes it felony to send, deliver, or utter, or directly or indirectly cause to be received, knowing the contents thereof, any letter or writing demanding of any person, with menaces and without any reasonable or probable cause, any property, chattel, money, valuable security or other valuable thing. The words "without any reasonable or probable cause" apply to the money demanded, and not to the accusation constituting the threat. *R.* v. *Mason*, 24 C. P. (Ont.), 58: *R.* v. *Gardiner*, 1 C. & P., 479; *R.* v. *Hamilton*, 1 C. & K., 212.

A mere request without a threat is no offence (*R.* v. *Robinson*, 2 East, P. C., 1111); nor is an offer to give information if money is sent (*R.* v. *Pickford*, 4 C. & P., 227); but a letter stating that an injury is intended and the writer will not interfere to prevent it unless money is sent, amounts to an offence. *R.* v. *Smith*, 1 Den. C. C., 510.

A demand for money by letter, threatening bodily violence, or to charge with adultery, is an offence under this section. *R.* v. *Chalmers*, 10 Cox C. C., 450.

The menace under section 44 of the 32 & 33 Vic., chap. 21, must be such as to influence a reasonable mind. *R.* v. *Walton*, L. & C., 288. It is immaterial that the person has no money at the time of the demand (*R.* v. *Edwards*, 6 C. & P., 515); and a conviction may take place though the money was paid. *R.* v. *Robertson*, L. & C., 483.

The menace must be of such a nature and extent as to unsettle the mind of the person on whom it operates, and take away from his acts that element of free voluntary action which alone constitutes consent. *R.* v. *Walton*, 9 Cox C. C., 268. If a policeman, professing to act under legal authority, threaten to imprison a person on a charge not amounting to an offence in law unless money be given him, and the person believe the policeman and give him money, the policeman may be indicted for the offence of demanding money with menaces with intent to steal, although the offence is completed, and he might also be indicted for stealing the money, *R.* v. *Robertson*, 10 Cox C. C., 9.

MILITARY AND NAVAL STORES.

The 32 & 33 Vic., chap. 26, was passed to secure the better protection of Her Majesty's military and naval stores.

This Act was extended to Prince Edward Island by the 40 Vic., chap. 4; to British Columbia by the 37 Vic., chap. 42; and to the Province of Manitoba by the 34 Vic., chap. 14.

The 33 Vic., chap. 31, protects the clothing and property of seamen in Her Majesty's Navy.

MISPRISION OF FELONY.

Misprision of felony is the concealment of some felony (other than treason) committed by another. There must be knowledge of the offence merely without any assent, for if a man assent he will either be a principal or an accessory. Thus one will be guilty of misprision who sees a felony committed and takes no steps to secure the apprehension of the offender. The offence is a misdemeanor punishable by fine and imprisonment.

MURDER AND MANSLAUGHTER.

Murder is unlawful homicide with malice aforethought. Manslaughter is unlawful homicide without malice aforethought.

Malice is a necessary ingredient in and the chief characteristic of the crime of murder. *Re Anderson,* 11 C. P. (Ont.), 62.

Malice in its legal sense means a wrongful act done intentionally without just cause or excuse. *McIntyre* v. *McBean,* 13 Q. B. (Ont.), 542 ; *Poitevin* v. *Morgan,* 10 L. C. J., 97.

On every charge of murder where the act of killing is proved against the prisoner, the law presumes the fact to have been founded in malice until the contrary appears. *R.* v. *McDowell,* 25

Q. B., (Ont.), 112; *R.* v. *Atkinson,* 17 C. P. (Ont.), 304. And the onus of rebutting this presumption by extracting facts on cross-examination or by direct testimony lies on the prisoner (*ib.*)

In order the better to understand the nature of these offences, the reader is referred to the chapter on indictable offences.

The homicide must be of some reasonable creature in being, but a child becomes such being when it has completely proceeded in a living state from the body of its mother, whether it has or has not breathed, and whether the navel string has or has not been divided. *R.* v. *Poulton,* 5 C. & P., 329; *R.* v. *Crutchley,* 7 C. & P., 814. And the killing of such a child is homicide, whether it is killed by injuries inflicted before, during or after birth.

To make a killing murder the death must follow within a year and a day after the stroke or other cause, for if the death is deferred for that length of time the law will presume that it arose from some other cause.

With reference to malice, it does not necessarily mean malevolence or ill-will towards the deceased, for perhaps the majority of murders are committed with a view to robbery. The malice necessary, therefore, in case of murder may be said to be a felonious design or intention in general.

Generally in cases of homicide the prisoner's act must directly and immediately occasion the death, but a person is deemed to have committed homicide, although his act is not the immediate or not the sole cause of death in the following cases: (1.) If he inflict a bodily injury on another which causes surgical or medical treatment, which causes death, the treatment must, however, be in good faith and with common knowledge and skill; (2.) If he inflicts a bodily injury on another which would not have caused death, if the injured person had submitted to proper surgical or medical treatment, or had observed proper precautions as to his mode of living; (3.) If by any act he hastens the death of a person suffering under any disease or injury, which apart from such act would have caused death.

Where a woman died in childbirth, in consequence of her mother's neglect to use ordinary diligence in procuring the assistance of a midwife, there being no proof that the mother had

.ny means of paying for the services of a midwife, it was held hat the mother could not, under the circumstances, be found ;uilty of manslaughter. *R.* v. *Shepherd*, 9 Cox C. C., 123.

Where, from conscientious religious conviction that God would ieal the sick, and not from any intention to avoid the perform-.nce of their duty, the parents of a sick child refuse to call in iedical assistance, though well able to do so, and the child conse-uently dies, it is not culpable homicide. *R.* v. *Wagstaffe*, 10 Jox C. C., 530. It is to be observed, however, that, under the 2 & 33 Vic., chap. 20, s. 25, whosoever being legally liable to rovide for any person necessary food, clothing, or lodging, wil-.lly and without lawful excuse, refuses or neglects to provide the ame, is guilty of a misdemeanor. See *post*, Vagrancy.

As to manslaughter by a parent neglecting to provide medical .id for his child, see *R.* v. *Downes*, L. R., 1 Q. B. D., 25.

Manslaughter is distinguished from murder in wanting the in-;redient of malice, and it may be generally stated that where the ircumstances negative the existence of malice, in the legal sense, .nd the killing is unlawful and felonious, it will be manslaughter.

The offences of murder and manslaughter are governed by the 2 & 33 Vic., chap. 20. The same statute also makes felony 'arious acts done with intent to commit murder, or, as they .re described, attempts at murder.

In proceeding before a magistrate to get a party charged with omicide committed, it is necessary that death should be expressly roved, for otherwise *non constat* that any offence has been com-nitted.

NUISANCE.

Common nuisances are such annoyances as are liable to affect ll persons who come within the range of their operation. Every ne who commits a common nuisance is guilty of a misdemeanor. There seems to be no authority for a Justice convicting a party ummarily of a nuisance, and fining for the offence (*Bross* v. *Huber*, 18 Q. B. (Ont.), 286), and though the obstruction of highway is a public nuisance, a conviction by a magistrate for uch obstruction and order to pay a continuing fine, until the removal of such obstruction, was held bad, as unwarranted by any Act of Parliament. *R.* v. *Huber*, 15 Q. B. (Ont.), 589.

To constitute a public nuisance, the thing complained of must be such as in its nature or its consequences is a nuisance, an injury or a damage to all persons who come within the sphere of its operation, though it may be in a greater or less degree. *Little* v. *Ince*, 3 C. P. (Ont.), 545; *R.* v. *Meyers*, 3 C. P. (Ont.), 333.

Throwing noxious matter into Lake Ontario, or any other public navigable water, is a public nuisance, and renders the party committing it liable to an indictment. *Watson* v. *Toronto G. & W. Co.*, 4 Q. B. (Ont.), 158. Obstructions to navigable rivers are public nuisances. *Brown* v. *Gugy*, 14 L. C. R., 213.

Disorderly houses are public nuisances, and it is not necessary that any disorderly conduct should be perceptible from the exterior of the house. *R.* v. *Rice*, L. R., 1 C. C. R., 21.

So the non-repair of a highway, or the obstruction thereof, is a nuisance, indictable at common law. *R.* v. *Paris*, 12 C. P. (Ont.), 450.

The proper remedy for a public nuisance is by indictment. *Small* v. *G. T. R. Co.*, 15 Q. B. (Ont.), 283.

The circumstance that the thing complained of furnishes on the whole a greater convenience to the public than it takes away, is no answer to an indictment for a nuisance. *R.* v. *Bruce*, 10 L. C. R., 117; *R.* v. *Ward*, 4 A. & E., 384.

A conviction for obstructing a highway is bad, unless it appears on the face of it that the place was a public highway. *R.* v. *Brittain*, 2 Kerr, 614.

OBSCENE BOOKS.

The sale of an obscene book is a misdemeanor, even although a good ulterior object is intended to be served thereby. *R.* v *Hicklin*, L.R., 3 Q.B., 360. The obtaining obscene prints and libels for the purpose of afterwards publishing and disseminating them, is an act done in commencing a misdemeanor, and therefore an indictable offence. *Dugdale* v. *R.*, 1 E. & B., 435.

PAWNBROKERS.

A conviction under the Pawnbrokers' Act (Con. Stat. Can., chap. 31), for neglecting to have a sign over the door, as directed by the 7th section, is not sustained by evidence of one transaction alone, or the penalty attaches only on persons "exercising the trade of ı pawnbroker:" as mentioned in the first section, and a single act of receiving or taking a pawn or pledge is not an exercising the rade or carrying on the business of a pawnbroker. *R.* v. *Andrews*, 25 Q. B. (Ont.), 196.

PEACE ON PUBLIC WORKS.

The 32 & 33 Vic., chap. 24, was passed to secure the better preervation of peace in the vicinity of public works. It was amended y the 33 Vic., chap. 28, and 38 Vic., chap. 38. It was extended o Prince Edward Island by the 40 Vic., chap. 4; to the District f Keewatin, by the 39 Vic., chap. 21; to the North West Terriories, by the 38 Vic., chap. 49; to British Columbia, by the 37 Vic., chap. 42, and to the Province of Manitoba, by the 34 Vic., hap. 14.

PERJURY AND SUBORNATION OF PERJURY.

The Act respecting perjury is the 32 & 33 Vic., chap. 23. This Act was extended by the 31 Vic., chap. 71, and it was amended by he 33 Vic., chap. 26. It was extended to Prince Edward Island y the 40 Vic., chap. 4; to the District of Keewatin, by the 39 Vic., chap. 21; to the North West Territories, by the 38 Vic., chap. 9; to British Columbia, by the 37 Vic., chap. 42, and to the Proince of Manitoba, by the 34 Vic., chap. 14.

Perjury is the crime committed by one, who, when a lawful oath ; administered to him in some proceeding in a court of justice f competent jurisdiction, swears wilfully, absolutely and falsely, n a matter *material* to the issue or point in question.

The offence is a misdemeanor under the 32 & 33 Vic., chap. 23, nd it is to be observed also that under the seventh section of this tatute, all evidence and proof is material whether given or made rally, or by or in any affidavit, affirmation, declaration, examination or deposition. Therefore a false affirmation of a Quaker or other person, who is by law authorized to make an affirmation or declaration in lieu of an oath, may amount to perjury as well as oral evidence in open court. *See* "The Interpretation Act," 31 Vic., chap. 1, s. 7, sixteenthly.

When an oath is administered without any authority, the person taking such oath cannot be convicted of perjury. *R.* v. *Martin*, 21 L. C. J., 156; *R.* v. *McIntosh*, 1 Hannay, 372. The person administering the oath must be exercising his jurisdiction at the time the oath is administered. *McAdam* v. *Weaver*, 2 Kerr, 176.

It is a well known rule that the testimony of a single witness is not sufficient to convict on a charge of perjury. Two witnesses at least must contradict what the accused has sworn, or, at any rate, one must so contradict, and other evidence must materially corroborate that contradiction.

Subornation of perjury is an offence in procuring a man to take a false oath, amounting to perjury, who actually takes such oath.

The offence of perjury consists in taking a false oath in a judicial proceeding, and whether the oath is taken in a judicial proceeding before a court at common law, or acting on a statute, it is equally an oath taken in a judicial proceeding, and punishable as perjury. *R.* v. *Castro*, L. R., 9 Q. B., 350.

Any oath or affirmation administered under the authority of any Act of the Provincial Legislatures, shall entail the same consequences, with respect to perjury, as if the oath were administered under the authority of an Act of the Parliament of Canada. 31 Vic., chap. 71, s. 4.

The 33 Vic., chap. 26, amends section 3 of the 32 & 33 Vic., chap. 23, in relation to perjury committed in any Province in respect of a document to be used in any other Province.

The swearing falsely by a voter at an election of aldermen or common councilmen for the City of Toronto, that he is the person described in the list of voters, not being made perjury by any express enactment, is not an oath upon which by the common law perjury can be assigned, not being in any judicial proceeding or anything tending to render effectual a judicial proceeding.

Thomas v. *Platt*, 1 Q. B. (Ont.), 217. This would probably now be perjury under the 32 & 33 Vic., chap. 23, s. 2.

Taking a false oath is not an offence in law unless it be in a judicial proceeding, or on some other lawful occasion on which it has been made an offence by law to swear falsely. *Hogle* v. *Hogle*, 16 Q. B. (Ont.), 520.

PERSON.

The Act respecting offences against the person, 32 & 33 Vic., chap. 20, was extended to Prince Edward Island by the 40 Vic., chap. 4; to the District of Keewatin by the 39 Vic., chap. 21; to the North-West Territories by the 38 Vic., chap. 49; to British Columbia by the 37 Vic., chap. 42, and to the Province of Manitoba by the 34 Vic., chap. 14.

PIRACY.

This offence at common law consists in committing those acts of robbery and depredation upon the high seas, which, if committed upon land, would have amounted to felony there.

The Imp. Stat. 12 & 13 Vic., chap. 96, extends to Canada, and makes provision for the trial of this offence. See also 32 & 33 Vic., chap. 29, s. 136. It may be observed that our Great Inland Lakes are, for the purposes of this offence, considered as the high seas, and our magistrates can take cognizance of piracy committed on the lakes, although in American waters, and in the same manner as if committed on the high seas. *R.* v. *Sharpe*, 5 P. R. (Ont.), 135.

POLICE.

The 31 Vic., chap. 73, authorizes the Governor in Council to appoint Commissioners of Police. Under section 2, such Commissioners may appoint police constables, and under section 3, disobedience of orders, neglect of duty, or any misconduct, as such police constable, entails, on conviction before a Justice of the Peace, a fine not exceeding forty dollars.

This Act was extended to Prince Edward Island by the 40 Vic., chap. 4; to the District of Keewatin by the 39 Vic., chap. 21;

to the North-West Territories by the 38 Vic., chap. 49; and to British Columbia by the 37 Vic., chap 42.

POST OFFICE.

The Act 38 Vic., chap. 7, amends and consolidates the law for the regulation of the postal service.

Under section 72, and the following sections, a large number of acts of different descriptions are made criminal, such as stealing post letters, opening post letter bags, stealing parcels, receiving post letters or post letter bags, unlawfully issuing money orders, forging postage stamps or money orders, stealing any mail key or mail lock, wilfully destroying matter sent by mail or parcel post, enclosing explosive substances in matter sent by post, enclosing a letter, &c., in any other mailable matter, removing postage stamps or marks thereon, with a fraudulent intent, abandoning, obstructing or wilfully delaying the mail, &c. (40 Vic., chap. 34), cutting or ripping a post letter bag, being drunk on duty as a mail carrier, refusing to allow the mail to pass through a toll-gate, detaining the mail at a ferry, &c., soliciting the commission of any act prohibited, mutilating the official books, hypothecating the postage stamps, posting immoral or obscene books.

Every principal in the second degree and every accessory before or after the fact is punishable, as a principal in the first degree. *Ib.* s. 72, s.-s. 29.

Under section 73, the embezzlement or unlawful use of money entrusted to him by an officer of, or connected with, the post office is felony.

Under section 75, wilfully or maliciously injuring any street letter box, &c., is a misdemeanor.

Under section 76, using or attempting to use postage stamps which have been used before, subjects the party to a penalty of not less than $10, and not exceeding $40.

Any indictable offence under the Act, may be dealt with either in the district or county where the offence is committed, or that in which the offender is apprehended or is in custody. *Ib.* s. 79.

PRACTICE.

As to filing an amended conviction, the practice in moving to quash a conviction is this: when the conviction is returned it is filed. Up to the time of return and filing, the Justice may amend the conviction; but after the filing of the papers no amendment can be made. By analogy to this practice, after notice of appeal is given, and the time for hearing the appeal has arrived, no amendment can be made to the conviction after the proceedings in appeal have been entered on before the court. *R.* v. *Smith*, 35 Q. B. (Ont.), 518; see *ante*, pp. 129–130.

After a conviction is returned to the court on a *certiorari*, there is no power of amendment. Where, therefore, two defendants were jointly convicted for keeping liquors for sale without a license, contrary to the Rev. Stat. (Ont.), chap. 181, s. 40, and a penalty awarded against them jointly, it was held that the court could not amend the conviction so as to make separate convictions against each defendant, with an award of a separate penalty. *R.* v. *Sutton*, 14 C.L.J., N.S., 17; see *ante*, 129.

A conviction for keeping a house of ill-fame on the 11th of October, and on other days and times before that day, was held sufficiently certain as to time, for the only offence charged by these words was keeping and maintaining a bawdy-house, or house of ill-fame; and the fact that they kept such a house on the 11th of October, and on other days and times before that, did not constitute a distinct offence against the parties upon each of those days. *R.* v. *Williams*, 37 Q.B. (Ont.), 540; *Onley* v. *Gee*, 7 Jur. N.S., 570

The information in this case described the parties as of the Township of East Whitby, and it had "County of Ontario" in the margin. It alleged that they had kept a house of ill-fame, but it did not in so many words allege that they did so in the Township of East Whitby, or in the County of Ontario. The evidence, however, showed that their place at which such house was kept was in East Whitby, in which the Justices had jurisdiction. This was held sufficient. *R.* v. *Williams*, *supra*, see 32 & 33 Vic., chap. 31, s. 21, *ante*, p. 113; *R.* v. *Cavanagh*, 27 C.P. (Ont.), 537.

This case sustains the position already taken, that the place need not be alleged in the body of the information when it is shown in the margin. See *ante*, pp. 23, 24, 60, 98.

A person was convicted of being drunk in a public street, contrary to law, and adjudged to pay a fine of $50 and costs, or to be imprisoned for six months at hard labour. There was power given by by-law 478 of the City of Toronto, to imprison an offender for the above offence; but in the warrant of commitment no reference whatever was made to the by-law. It was held that as there was no common law right to imprison any one for being drunk on a public street, and the by-law not being referred to, the conviction was bad. *Re Livingstone*, 6 P.R. (Ont.), 17.

PRINCIPALS AND ACCESSORIES.

The Act respecting accessories to, and abettors of, indictable offences, 31 Vic., chap. 72, was extended to Prince Edward Island by the 40 Vic., chap. 4; to the District of Keewatin by the 39 Vic., chap. 21; to the North-West Territories by the 38 Vic., chap. 49; and to British Columbia by the 37 Vic., chap. 42

In cases of forgery, the accessory or abettor may be dealt with, tried and punished in the county or place in which he is apprehended or is in custody, 32 & 33 Vic., chap. 19, s. 48. The same rule prevails in the case of offences under the Act, regulating the postal service. 38 Vic., chap. 7, s. 79, s.-s. 4.

The general definition of a principal in the first degree is one who is the actor, or actual perpetrator, of the crime. Principals in the second degree are those who were present aiding and abetting the commission of the crime. To constitute an aider or abettor, the party must be actually present, aiding or in some way assisting in the commission of the offence, or constructively present for the same purpose, that is, in such a convenient situation as readily to come to the assistance of the others, and with the intention of doing so should occasion require. *Ashley* v. *Dundas*, 5 O. S., 753; *R.* v. *Curtley*, 27 Q. B. (Ont.), 617.

On the general principle that a person is liable for what is done under his presumed authority (see *R.* v. *King*, 20 C. P., (Ont.), 248), where there is a combination to effect some unlawful purpose, each person is liable for every act of any of the others in prosecution of the common design. *Ib.* and see *R.* v. *Slavin*, 17 C. P. (Ont.), 205. A felonious act, committed by one person in prosecution of a common unlawful purpose, is the act of all, but where the original purpose is lawful, the person committing the act will alone be liable. A person authorizing the commission of a crime is liable for the act of his agent in the execution of his authority. The agent is also liable for the unlawful act, although he may have the express, or implied, authority of his principal for its commission. See *R.* v. *Brewster*, 8 C. P. (Ont.), 208.

An accessory before the fact is he who, being absent at the time of the felony committed, doth yet procure counsel, command, or abet another to commit a felony. An accessory after the fact is one who, knowing a felony to have been committed by another, receives, relieves, comforts, or assists the felon. It is only in felonies that there can be accessories, for in misdemeanors all are principals. See *R.* v. *Tisdale*, 20 Q. B. (Ont.), 273; *R.* v. *Campbell*, 18 Q. B. (Ont.), 417; *R.* v. *Benjamin*, 4 C. P. (Ont.), 189.

On this point the statute 31 Vic., chap. 72, s. 9, provides that aiders and abettors in misdemeanors may be tried and punished as principals. Those, therefore, who would be accessories in felonies are principals in misdemeanors. So also by the 32 & 33 Vic., chap. 31, s. 15, persons aiding or procuring, &c, the commission of any offence, which is punishable on summary conviction, are liable to be proceeded against and convicted for the same, either together with the principal offender or before or after his conviction and shall be liable to the same punishment as the principal. Ordinarily there can be no accessories before the fact in manslaughter, for the offence is sudden and unpremeditated, but there may be accessories after the fact.

The offence of accessory is distinguishable from that of a principal in the second degree: the latter must be actually or constructively present at the commission of the fact. But it is essential to constitute the offence of accessory that the party should be absent at the time the offence was committed.

Knowledge that a person intends to commit a crime and conduct connected with, and influenced by, such knowledge, is not enough to make the person who possesses such knowledge or so conducts himself an accessory before the fact to any such crime, unless he does something to encourage its commission actively. Thus, B and C agree to fight a prize fight for a sum of money. A knowing their intention acts as stakeholder. B and C fight, and C is killed. A is not present at the fight, and has no concern with it, except being stakeholder. Even if, in such a case there can be an accessory before the fact, A is not accessory before the fact to the manslaughter of C. *R.* v. *Taylor*, L. R., 2 C. C. R., 147.

If an accessory before the fact countermands the execution of the crime before it is executed, he ceases to be an accessory before the fact, if the principal had notice of the countermand before the execution of the crime, but not otherwise. Stephen's Dig., 29.

Every one is an accessory after the fact to felony, who knowing a felony to have been committed by another, receives, comforts, or assists him, in order to enable him to escape from punishment or rescues him from an arrest for the felony, or having him in custody for the felony intentionally and voluntarily suffers him to escape, or opposes his apprehension. Provided that a married woman who receives, comforts, or relieves her husband, knowing him to have committed a felony, does not thereby become an accessory after the fact. Stephens Dig., 31.

A person charged as accessory to murder may be convicted as accessory to manslaughter, if the principal is acquitted of the murder and found guilty of manslaughter. Where the principals commit a joint crime, the person harbouring them is guilty of a separate offence for each person whom he harbours. *R.* v. *Richards*, L.R., 2 Q.B.D. 311.

In the following imaginary cases examples of each of the four kinds of participation in a crime will be found. A incites B and C to murder a person. B enters the house and cuts the man's throat, while C waits outside to give warning in case any one should approach. B and C flee to D, who knowing the murder has been completed, lends horses to facilitate their escape. Here B is principal in the first degree, C in the second degree: A is accessory before the fact, D after the fact.

The Statute of Canada, 31 Vic., chap. 72, contains various provisions in reference to the trial and punishment of accessories and abettors of indictable offences. So much of the eighth section of this Act as relates to felonies not wholly committed in Canada, and to persons accessories to such felonies, was repealed by the 32 & 33 Vic., chap. 17, s. 2. Under the Act respecting malicious injuries to property, 32 & 33 Vic., chap. 22, s. 70, persons aiding, abetting, counselling, or procuring the commission of offences against that Act, are liable, on conviction before a Justice of the Peace, to the same punishment as a principal offender is by the Act made liable.

Every person aiding or abetting the commission of any offence punishable on summary conviction, may be proceeded against together with the principal, or before or after his conviction.

RAPE.

This offence has been defined to be the having unlawful and carnal knowledge of a woman by force and against her will. Where the woman consents to the connection, even though her consent is obtained by fraud, the act does not amount to rape. *R.* v. *Barrow*, L.R., 1 C.C.R., 156.

Thus having connection with a woman under circumstances which induce her to believe that the party is her husband, is not a rape. *R.* v. *Francis*, 13 Q.B. (Ont.), 116; *R.* v. *Barrett*, L.R, 2 C.C.R., 157. But in such case the party is liable to be indicted for an assault. *R.* v. *Barrow*, L.R., 1 C.C.R., 156.

As to the degree of force required, the woman must be quite overcome by force or terror; and there must be as much resistance on her part as is possible under the circumstances, so as to make the ravisher see and know that she is really resisting to the uttermost. *R.* v. *Fick*, 16 C.P. (Ont.), 379.

A husband cannot commit a rape upon his wife by carnally knowing her himself; neither can a boy under fourteen years of age, as he is presumed to be physically incapable of committing the offence; but both a husband and a boy under fourteen may be convicted as principals in the second degree, and may be punished for being present, aiding, and abetting.

With respect to the crime of rape and of unlawfully and carnally knowing and abusing infants under the age of ten or between the ages of ten and twelve years, carnal knowledge means penetration to any the slightest degree. The 32 & 33 Vic., chap. 20, s. 65, providing that it shall not be necessary to prove the actual emission of seed, but the carnal knowledge shall be deemed complete on proof of penetration only.

But a child under ten years of age cannot give consent to any criminal intercourse, so as to deprive that intercourse of criminality under the 32 and 33 Vic., chap. 20, s. 51, and a person may be convicted of *attempting* to have carnal knowledge of such child, even though she consent to the act done. *R.* v. *Beale*, L.R., 1 C.C.R., 10. But the consent in such case will render the attempt no assault. *R.* v. *Cockburn*, 3 Cox, 543; *R.* v. *Connolly*, 26 Q. B. (Ont.), 323. In the case of girls between the ages of ten and twelve, on a charge of assault with intent to carnally know, or indecent assault or common assault, consent is a defence (*ib.*).

Where the woman is an idiot or lunatic the mere proof of the act of connection will not warrant the case being left to the jury. There must be some evidence that it was without her consent, *e. g.*, that she was incapable of expressing consent or dissent, or from exercising any judgment upon the matter from imbecility of mind or defect of understanding, and if she gave her consent from animal instinct or passion it would not be a rape. *R.* v. *Connolly*, 26 Q. B. (Ont.), 317.

Where the woman is an idiot, incapable of expressing assent or dissent, a party who attempts to have connection with her without her consent, is guilty of an attempt at rape. If, however, from animal instinct she yields to the prisoner without resistance, or if the prisoner, from her state and condition, had reason to think that she was consenting, he ought to be acquitted whether in the case of rape or an attempt at rape. *R.* v. *Barrat*, L. R., 2 C. C. R., 81; *R.* v. *Connolly*, 26 Q. B. (Ont.), 317.

The prisoner professed to give medical and surgical advice for money. The prosecutrix, a girl of nineteen, consulted him with reference to illness from which she was suffering. He advised that a surgical operation should be performed, and under pretence of performing it, had carnal connection with the prosecutrix. She submitted to what was done, not with any intention that he should have carnal connection with her, but under the belief that he was merely treating her medically and performing a surgical operation, that belief being wilfully and fraudulently induced by the prisoner. It was held that the prisoner was guilty of rape. *R.* v. *Flattery*, L. R., 2 Q. B. D., 410; *R.* v. *Barrow*, L. R., 1 C. C. R., 156, questioned.

RECEIVING STOLEN GOODS.

The 32 & 33 Vic., chap. 21, s. 100, makes it felony for any person to receive goods which have been stolen, if he knows the same to have been feloniously stolen. There must be a theft of the goods, and this theft must be a crime, either at common law or by statute, before a party can be convicted of receiving under our statute. *R.* v. *Smith*, L. R., 1 C. C. R., 266. By section 104 of our statute where the original offence is a misdemeanor the offence of the receiver is made a misdemeanor also. And by section 106 receivers of property where the original offence is punishable on summary conviction are liable to punishment on conviction before a Justice of the Peace in the same manner as the original offender. Before there can be a criminal receipt of goods under this statute or at common law, the goods must be *stolen*, or at all events, the stealing, taking, extorting, embezzling or otherwise obtaining, must amount to a crime at common law or under the statute. For instance, if after goods are stolen, they get back into the possession of the owner so as to be no longer stolen goods, a subsequent receipt by the prisoner will not render him liable, the goods having lost the character of stolen goods. *R.* v. *Schmidt*, L. R., 1 C. C. R., 15.

So if the *exclusive* possession still remains in the thief, a conviction for receiving cannot be sustained. It is also necessary that the defendant should at the time of receiving the goods know that they were stolen. *R.* v. *Wiley*, 2 Den., 37.

Independently of the statute, receiving stolen goods knowing them to be such is a misdemeanor.

Sections 103 of the 32 & 33 Vic., chap. 21, extends to cases where upon an indictment for a joint receipt, it is proved that each of the prisoners separately received the whole of the stolen property at different times, the one receipt subsequent to the other, and it makes no difference whether the receipt was direct from the thief or from an intermediate person. There is no distinction between separate receipts of the whole and of part of the property, and under section 102 there is no distinction between separate receipts at the same time and separate receipts at different times. *R.* v. *Reardon*, L. R., 1 C. C. R,, 31.

It is clear that the goods the party is charged with receiving must be stolen goods. A wife, though she may have committed adultery, cannot steal her husband's goods, and therefore the adulterer receiving from her the goods which she has taken from her husband, cannot be found guilty of receiving stolen goods. *R.* v. *Kenny*, L. R., 2 Q. B. D., 307.

Manual possession or touch is unnecessary. In order to sustain a conviction for receiving stolen goods, it is sufficient if there be a control by the receiver over the goods. *R.* v. *Smith*, Dears., 494.

A person having a joint possession with the thief may be convicted as a receiver. *R.* v. *Hobson*, Dears., 400.

It makes no difference whether a receiver receives for the purpose of profit or advantage, or whether he does it to assist the thief. *R.* v. *Davis*, 6 C. & P., 177.

Belief, without actual knowledge, is sufficient to maintain an indictment for receiving goods, knowing them to have been stolen. *R.* v. *White*, 1 F. & F., 665.

A husband may be convicted of feloniously receiving property which his wife has stolen voluntarily, and without restraint on his part. *R.* v. *McCathey*, L. & C., 250.

Recent possession of stolen property is evidence, either that the person in possession stole the property, or that he received it, knowing it to be stolen. *R.* v. *Langmead*, L. & C. 427.

If A, in the absence of B, feloniously receives stolen property from the thief, and A subsequently delivers it to B, who knowingly receives it, both may be jointly indicted. *R* v. *Reardon*, L. R., 1 C. C. R., 31.

The late Act, 40 Vic., chap. 26, provides: That where proceeding are taken against any person for having received goods, knowing them to be stolen, or for having in his possession stolen property, evidence may be given at any stage of the proceedings that there was found in the possession of such person other property stolen within the preceding period of twelve months, and such evidence may be taken into consideration for the purpose of proving that such person knew the property to be stolen, which forms the subject of the proceedings taken against him: Provided, that not less than three days' notice, in writing, shall have been given to the person accused, that proof is intended to be given of such other property stolen within the preceding period of twelve months, having been found in his possession, and such notice shall specify the nature or description of such other property, and the person from whom the same was stolen. *Ib.* s. 3.

Where proceedings are taken against any person for having received goods, knowing them to be stolen, or for having in his possession stolen property, and evidence has been given that the stolen property has been found in his possession; then if such person has within five years immediately preceding, been convicted of any offence, involving fraud or dishonesty, evidence of such previous conviction may be given at any stage of the proceedings, and may be taken into consideration for the purpose of proving that the person accused knew the property which was proved to be in his possession to have been stolen: Provided, that not less than three days' notice, in writing, shall have been given to the person accused, that proof is intended to be given of such previous conviction; and it shall not be necessary for the purposes of this section to charge in the indictment the previous conviction of the person so accused. *Ib.* s. 4.

In committing for trial a receiver of stolen goods, the Justice would do well to remember that under 32 & 33 Vic., chap. 21, s. 105, the receiver, whether charged as an accessory after the fact to the felony, or with a substantive felony, or with a misdemeanor only, may be dealt with, indicted, tried and punished in any county, district or place in which he has or has had any such property in his possession, or in any place in which the principal offender may be tried.

RIOTS, ROUTS AND UNLAWFUL ASSEMBLIES.

The Act respecting riots (31 Vic., chap. 70), was extended to Prince Edward Island by the 40 Vic., chap. 4; to the District of Keewatin, by the 39 Vic., chap. 21; to the North West Territories, by the 38 Vic., chap. 49, and to British Columbia, by the 37 Vic., chap. 42.

A single person cannot be convicted of riot, in respect of any acts of his alone and independently of and not in concert with others.

A procession having been attacked by rioters the prisoner, one of the processionists, and in no way connected with the rioters, was proved, during the course of the attack, to have fired off a pistol on two occasions, first in the air and then at the rioters. So far as appeared from the evidence, the prisoner acted alone and not in connection with any one else. It was held that a conviction of the prisoner jointly with a number of others for riot could not be sustained. *R. v. Corcoran*, 26 C. P. (Ont.), 134.

The 32 & 33 Vic., chap. 22, ss. 15 & 16, prohibits the unlawfully and with force demolishing buildings by persons riotously and tumultuously assembled together to the disturbance of the public peace.

The Act respecting riots and riotous assemblies, 31 Vic., chap. 70, provides that if twelve or more persons are unlawfully assembled to the disturbance of the peace, and being required by proclamation by a Justice of the Peace to disperse, they then continue together for an hour after, they are guilty of felony.

An unlawful assembly is any meeting of three or more persons under such circumstances of alarm, either from the large numbers, the mode or time of the assembly, &c., as in the opinion of firm and rational men are likely to endanger the peace, there being no aggressive act actually done. *R. v. Vincent*, 9 C. & P., 91.

A rout is said to be the disturbance of the peace caused by those who after assembling together to do a thing, which if executed would amount to a riot, *proceed* to execute that act but do not actually execute it. It differs from a riot only in the circumstance that the enterprise is not actually executed.

A riot is a tumultuous disturbance of the peace by three or more persons assembling together of their own authority with an intent mutually to assist one another against any who oppose them in the execution of some enterprise of a *private* nature, and afterwards *actually executing* the same in a violent and turbulent manner to the terror of the people, and this whether the act intended be of itself lawful or unlawful.

The difference between a riot and an unlawful assembly is this: The former is a tumultuous meeting of persons upon some purpose which they *actually execute* with violence, and the latter is a mere assembly of persons upon a purpose, which if executed would make them rioters, but which they do not execute nor make any motion to execute. *R.* v. *Kelly*, 6 C. P. (Ont.), 372.

An example will more clearly show the difference between these three crimes: A hundred men armed with sticks meet together at night to consult about the destruction of a fence which their landlord has erected; this is an unlawful assembly. They march out together from the place of meeting in the direction of the fence; this amounts to a rout. They arrive at the fence, and, amid great confusion, violently pull it down, this is a riot.

To constitute a riot the object need not be unlawful if the acts are done in a manner calculated to inspire terror. But there must be an unlawful *assembling*, therefore a disturbance arising among people already met together will be a mere affray, unless, indeed, there be a deliberate forming into parties. The object must be of a local or private nature, otherwise, as if to redress a public grievance, it amounts to treason.

The gist of the offence is the *unlawful manner of proceeding*, that is with circumstances of force or violence. Therefore assembling for the purpose of an unlawful object, and actually executing it, is not a riot if it is done peaceably.

If a man knowingly does acts that are unlawful, the presumption of law is that he intends the natural consequences of these acts, and ignorance of the law will not excuse him.

To constitute an unlawful assembly, it is not necessary that the purpose for which the persons assembled together was to do an unlawful act; an intention to do a lawful act in a violent and turbulent manner is as much a breach of the law as if the intended act were illegal. It is the manner in which the act is intended to be done which constitutes the offence. *R.* v. *Mailloux*, 3 Pugsley, 493-513.

To constitute a riot, it is not necessary that the Riot Act, 31 Vic., chap. 70, should be read. Before the proclamation can be read, a riot must exist, and the effect of the proclamation will not change the character of the meeting, but will make those guilty of felony who do not disperse within one hour after the proclamation is read. *R.* v. *Furzey,* 6 C. & P., 81.

ROBBERY.

(*See* LARCENY.)

SESSIONS.

The Court of Quarter Sessions has not jurisdiction in cases of treason, murder or libel. 32 & 33 Vic., chap. 29, s. 12 ; 32 & 33 Vic., chap. 20, s. 1. The Court, however, has jurisdiction in the case of administering poison or wounding with intent to murder (40 Vic., chap. 28, s. 1), as it is not now punishable with death. But it has no jurisdiction in the case of rape. 32 & 33 Vic., chap. 20, s. 49. Under the 40 Vic., chap. 28, s. 2, the offence of unlawfully and carnally knowing and abusing a girl under the age of ten years, is punishable by imprisonment for life or for any term not less than five years, and may consequently be tried at the sessions.

It will be observed that under the 25 Edwd. III., chap. 2, s. 7, counterfeiting the Queen's money is treason, and this offence is therefore not triable at the sessions. 31 Vic., chap. 69, s. 4.

Bribery, personation or other corrupt practices in elections to the Dominion Parliament are not triable at the sessions. 37 Vic., chap. 9, s. 118.

Offences against the Act preventing lawless aggressions (31 Vic., Vic., chap. 14), are not triable at the sessions. *Ib.* s. 4.

The Court of Quarter Sessions does not possess any greater powers than are conferred on it by statute. It has, however, jurisdiction over offences attended with a breach of the peace. But forgery and perjury not being attended with a breach of the peace are not triable at the sessions. *R.* v. *McDonald*, 31 Q. B. (Ont.), 337-9; *R.* v. *Yarrington*, 1 Salk., 406; *R.* v. *Haynes*, R. & M., 298; *R.* v. *Higgins*, 2 East, 5; *Butt* v. *Conant*, 1 B. & B., 548; *Ex parte Bartlett*, 7 Jur. 649; *R.* v. *Dunlop*, 15 Q. B. (Ont.), 118; *R.* v. *Currie* 31 Q. B. (Ont.), 582.

Under 32 & 33 Vic., chap. 20, s. 48, the Sessions of the Peace cannot try the offences specified in sections 27, 28 and 29 of that Act. A similar provision is made by the 32 & 33 Vic., chap. 21, s. 92, as to certain offences under it.

The exceptions contained in these statutes, and the excepted cases of forgery and perjury, define as nearly as may be what the general jurisdiction of the Sessions of the Peace is. The unexcepted offences they may try. *R.* v. *McDonald, supra*, 239.

The offence of kidnapping, under the statute 32 & 33 Vic., chap 20, s. 69, may be tried at the Quarter Sessions. *Cornwall* v. *R.*, 33 Q. B. (Ont.), 106. The Sessions of the Peace have under their jurisdiction power to try all felonies and trespasses whatever (unless excepted by statute). A felony created since the passing of the statute 34 Ed. 3, chap. 1, which created Courts of Quarter Sessions, is within the jurisdiction of the sessions. But not an offence less than felony, and not being a breach of the peace unless expressly empowered to try it. *Ib.*, 116; *R.* v. *Buggs*, 4, Mod., 379.

The Courts of Quarter Sessions have power to try also all misdemeanors which are a breach of the peace, or have a tendency to provoke a breach of the peace, but not cases of perjury or forgery. *Ex parte Bartlett*, 7 Jur., 649.

A bench warrant issued at the Quarter Sessions, tested in open sessions, and signed by the Clerk of the Peace, was held not invalid for want of a seal. *Fraser* v. *Dickson*, 5 Q. B. (Ont.), 231. And a warrant of committment under the seal of the court or signature of the chairman is not necessary. *Ovens* v. *Taylor*, 19 C. P. (Ont.), 49.

Where a statute enables two Justices to do an act, the Justices sitting in Quarter Sessions may do the same act, for they are not the less Justices of the Peace, because they are sitting in court in that capacity. *Fraser* v. *Dickson*, 5 Q. B. (Ont.), 233. It would seem, however, that the chairman of the sessions cannot make any order of the court, except during the sessions, either regular or adjourned. *Re. Coleman*, 23 Q. B. (Ont.), 615. The sessions possess the same powers as the Superior Courts as to altering their judgments during the same sessions or term, and for that purpose the sessions is all looked upon as one day. *R.* v. *Fitzgerald*, 20 Q. B. (Ont.), 546; see also *McLean* and *McLean*, 9 U. C., L. J., 217.

SLANDER.

Slander is not cognizable before magistrates, except the words used directly tend to a breach of the peace, as if one man challenge another; in such case a party may be bound to the good behaviour, and even indicted. *R.* v. *Langley*, 2 Salk., 697-8; see Libel, *ante*, p. 321.

SMUGGLING.

Smuggling is the importing or exporting either (a) goods without paying the legal duties thereon, or (b) prohibited goods. The existing law on the subject is contained in the Statute of Canada, 40 Vic., chap. 10, s. 76, *et seq.* Under this enactment the offence is made a misdemeanor. An indictment will not lie under the 81st section of this Act, for the misdemeanor created by the 76th, for the former section does not declare that the parties offending, &c., shall be deemed guilty of the misdemeanor created by the 76th, and the clause cannot be extended to the creation of a new crime by implication. *R.* v. *Bathgate*, 13 L. C. J., 299.

SODOMY OR UNNATURAL OFFENCES.

The 32 & 33 Vic., chap. 20, s. 63, now governs these offences.

The proof is the same as in rape, with two exceptions. It is not necessary to prove the offence to have been committed without the consent of the person upon whom it was perpetrated. Both parties, if consenting, are equally guilty, but if one of the parties is a boy under the age of fourteen years, it is felony in the other only. By the 64th section of the Act, to attempt to commit the said crime, or to make an assault with intent to commit the same, or to make any indecent assault upon a male person, is a misdemeanor.

Sending a letter proposing the crime, is an attempt to incite. *R.* v. *Rainsford*, 31 L. T., N. S., 488.

SUICIDE.

The attempt to commit suicide, by a person of sane mind, is a misdemeanor at common law, being an attempt to commit a felony. It is not an attempt to commit murder, suicide having been held not to be murder. *R.* v. *Burgess*, L. & C., 254.

SUNDAY.

The words, "or other person whatsoever," in the Con. Stat. U. C., chap., 104, s. 1, Rev. Stat. (Ont.), chap. 189 are meant to include all persons, *ejusdem generis* with those previously mentioned, but not others (*Sandiman* v. *Breach*, 7 B. & C., 96), and they cannot be taken to include all persons doing anything whatever on a Sunday, but must be taken to apply to persons following some particular calling of the same description as those mentioned. *Hespeler* v. *Shaw*, 16 Q. B. (Ont.), 104; *R.* v. *Hynes*, 13 Q. B. (Ont.), 194.

The work prohibited is not confined to manual labour, and hence includes the sale of a horse. *Fennell* v. *Ridler*, 5 B. & C., 406. But the work must be in the ordinary calling of the party (*Smith* v. *Sparrow*, 4 Bing., 84); nor does it include all callings, as, for example, an attorney's work. *Peate* v. *Dickens*, 1 C. M. & R., 422.

This statute does not prohibit contracts being made on Sunday, such as a bill of exchange (*Begbie* v. *Levi*, 1 Car. & J., 180), or the hiring of a servant. *R.* v. *Whitnash*, 7 B. & C., 596.

Baking provisions for customers is a work of necessity (*R.* v. *Cox*, 2 Burr., 787); but baking rolls in the way of business is prohibited. *Cripps* v. *Durden*, Cowp., 640.

A person is liable under the Act for plying with his steamboat on Sunday between the City of Toronto and the Island, persons carried between those places not being "travellers" within the meaning of the exception in the first section. *R.* v. *Tinning,* 11 Q. B. (Ont.), 636.

Where snares were found set on a Sunday, with two dead birds in them, which had been set on the day before, it was held, first, that a "snare" is an engine within the 4th section of the Act, and, secondly, that although the defendant was not upon the land on a Sunday, he was liable to be convicted for using the snares on that day for the purpose of taking game. *Allen* v. *Thompson,* L. R., 5 Q. B., 336.

SURETIES FOR THE PEACE.

This is simply a recognizance entered into by a party with one or more sureties, or by the party alone (if his own recognizance be deemed sufficient), before a Justice of the Peace out of sessions, or before the Quarter Sessions, conditioned for his keeping the peace or being of good behaviour for a certain time. The authority to require it is given to Justices by their commission. Therefore, if a Justice of the Peace be satisfied upon oath that a party has reasonable ground to fear, either from the direct threats of another or from his acts or words, that such other person will inflict or cause to be inflicted upon him some personal injury, or that such person will burn his house or cause it to be burnt, the Justice is bound to cause this security to be given; and the same if the threats be used against the wife or child of the party. But this does not extend to a man's servants, for they may themselves apply for sureties of the peace against persons from whom they fear personal injury; nor does it extend to threats as to a man's goods, for it is not a case within the authority thus given. Nor does it authorize the Justice when the applicant acts from mere malice or vexation. *Butt* v. *Conant,* 1 B. & B., 548.

The complaint which the applicant is required to make states that "he doth not make this complaint against, nor require such sureties from the said A.B., from any malice or ill-will, but merely for the preservation of his person from injury," see *ante,* p. 190. On application being made for sureties of the peace by complaint to the Justice on oath, the Justice has to consider whether the facts stated show a reasonable ground for the party's fear of personal injury; and if there be any ambiguity in the threats, it is for the Justice to give them such a construction as he thinks right, and his decision in that respect will be final (*R.* v. *Tregarthen*, 5 B. & Ad., 678) if the oath on which the complaint was founded be sufficient to warrant it. *Re Dunn*, 12 A. & E., 599. The Justice cannot on such an application convict the party complained against of an assault. *R.* v. *Davey*, 20 L.J., M.C., 189. If he thinks that sureties ought to be given, and the party complained against be not present, he may issue his warrant to bring him before him. This warrant is executed in the same manner as any other warrant to apprehend a party. As soon as the party is apprehended and brought before the Justice, the complaint is read over to him, and he is asked if he have any cause to show why he should not give the required sureties.

The party complained of cannot be allowed to controvert the truth of the facts stated in the complaint. *R.* v. *Doherty*, 13 East, 171. All he is allowed to do is to show that the complaint is preferred from malice only (*R.* v. *Parnell*, 2 Burr., 806), or explain any parts of the complaint that may be ambiguous. *R.* v. *Bringloe*, 13 East, 174 *n.*

If the Justice order the sureties to be given, and the defendant either refuse to give them or cannot do so, the Justice should commit him. See form of commitment in default of sureties, *ante*, p. 191. The warrant of commitment must specify a time certain during which the party is to be imprisoned, otherwise it will be bad. *Prickett* v. *Gratrex*, 8 Q. B., 1020.

The Justice may bind the party over for a limited time or until the next Quarter Sessions. Where a Justice of the Peace bound a party over to keep the peace for two years, the court held that he did not exceed his authority. *Willis* v. *Bridger*, 2 B. & A., 278. The amount of the security required is entirely in the discretion of the Justice. *R.* v. *Holloway*, 2 Dowl., 525.

A final commitment for want of sureties to keep the peace must be in writing. *Lynden* v. *King*, 6 O.S., 566. Such commitment should show the date on which the words were alleged to have been spoken, and contain a statement to the effect that complainant is apprehensive of bodily fear. *Re Ross*, 3 P. R. (Ont.), 301.

In a commitment for want of finding sureties for the peace, it is not necessary to state that the Justice had information on oath, which would justify him in binding the prisoner to keep the peace. *Dawson* v. *Fraser*, 7 Q. B. (Ont.), 391.

Justices should be careful not to require sureties of the peace without sufficient grounds; for if they do so from error of judgment, though they have a general jurisdiction over the subject matter, they render themselves liable to an action. *Fullarton* v. *Switzer*, 13 Q.B. (Ont.), 575.

Under the Act respecting forgery (32 & 33 Vic., chap. 19, s. 58), whenever any person is convicted of a misdemeanor under the Act, the court may, if it thinks fit, in addition to or in lieu of any of the punishments by the Act authorized, fine the offender, and require him to enter into his own recognizance, and find sureties, both or either, for keeping the peace, and being of good behaviour, and the same course may be adopted in the case of felonies.

The same course may also be adopted under the Act respecting offences against the person (32 & 33 Vic., chap. 20, s. 77) in the case of any indictable misdemeanor punishable under the Act, or any felony punishable otherwise than with death. Under the Act respecting larceny and other similar offences (32 & 33 Vic., chap. 21), s. 122, and the Act respecting malicious injuries to property (32 & 33 Vic., chap. 22, s. 74), in the case of any indictable misdemeanor or felony punishable under these Acts. Under the Act respecting the trial and punishment of juvenile offenders (32 & 33 Vic., chap. 33, s. 4), when the Justices consider that it is not expedient to inflict any punishment they may require the party to find sureties for his good behaviour.

Under the 40 Vic., chap. 30, making provision against the improper use of firearms, any person having upon his person a pistol or air-gun, without reasonable cause to fear an assault or other injury to his person or his family or property, may be required to find sureties for keeping the peace for a term not exceeding six months.

TELEGRAPH COMPANIES.

The 32 & 33 Vic., chap. 22, s. 41, makes it a misdemeanor to unlawfully and maliciously cut, break, throw down, destroy, injure or remove any battery, machinery, wire, cable, post, or other matter or thing whatsoever, being part of or being used or employed in or about any electric or magnetic telegraph or in the working thereof.

The Con. Stat. Can., chap. 67, s. 16, which declares it a misdemeanor in any operator or employee of a telegraph company to divulge the contents of a private despatch, only protects the rights of each individual sender or receiver of a message against disclosures of facts which come to the knowledge of the operators in the course of their employment. *Leslie* v. *Hervey,* 15 L. C. J., 9.

THREATS.

(*See* MENACES.)

TRADE MARKS.

Under "an Act respecting trade marks and industrial designs," 31 Vic., chap. 55, s. 7, (extended to British Columbia and Prince Edward Island by the 40 Vic., chap. 5,) it is a misdemeanor for any person other than the person who has registered the trade mark, to mark any goods or any article of any description whatever, with any registered trade mark, or to use any marked package which has been used by the proprietor of such trade mark, or to knowingly sell or offer for sale any article marked with such trade mark with intent to deceive and to induce persons to believe that such article was manufactured, produced, compounded, packed or sold by the proprietor of such trade mark.

The 9th section of this Act was repealed by the 35 Vic., chap. 32.

The above cited Act was amended by the 39 Vic., chap. 35.

See also fraudulent marking of merchandize.

TRADE UNIONS OR COMBINATIONS.

(*See* VIOLENCE, THREATS, MOLESTATION.)

TREASON.

The 25 Edward 3, is still in force in regard to this crime. The 31 Vic., chap. 69, s. 1, providing that nothing therein contained shall lessen the force of or in any manner affect anything contained in the statute of 25 Edward 3.

Under this statute, " when a man doth compass or imagine the death of our Lord the King, or of our Lady his Queen, or of their eldest son and heir, or if a man do violate the King's companion or the King's eldest daughter unmarried, or the wife of the King's eldest son and heir, or if a man do levy war against our Lord the King in his realm or be adherent to the King's enemies in his realm, giving them aid or comfort in our realm or elsewhere, and thereof be probably (or proveably *provablement*) attainted of open deed by people of their condition :" " And if a man counterfeit the King's great or privy seal, or his money, and if a man bring false money into this realm, counterfeit to the money of England, as the money called Lushburg or other like to the said money of England, knowing the money to be false; to merchandize or make payment in deceit of our said Lord the King and his people ; and if a man slea the Chancellor, Treasurer, or the King's Justices of the one bench or the other, Justices in eyre or Justices of assize, and all other Justices assigned to hear and determine being in their places, doing their offices," he shall be guilty of treason.

The 31 Vic., chap. 69, as amended, and with the statute of 25 Edward 3, chap. 2, (Imp.,) s. 7, now govern the subject of treason. To compass, imagine, invent, devise, or intend the death or destruction, or any bodily harm tending to death or destruction, maim or wounding, imprisonment or restraint of our Sovereign Lady the Queen, her Heirs or Successors, by any overt act or deed, is treason, punishable with death.

The 31 Vic., chap. 69, was extended to Prince Edward Island by the 40 Vic., chap. 4; to the District of Keewatin by the 39 Vic. chap. 21 ; to the North-West Territories by the 38 Vic., chap. 49; and to British Columbia by the 37 Vic., chap. 42.

The words, "or without," in the second and fifth sections of the 31 Vic., chap. 69, were repealed by the 32 & 33 Vic., chap. 17.

Under the 31 Vic., chap. 74, persons in custody in any gaol on a charge of high treason or felony may, if the gaol be deemed unsafe, be removed to any other gaol, or any other County or District in the Province. The latter Act was extended to Prince Edward Island by the 40 Vic., chap. 4; to the District of Keewatin by the 39 Vic., chap. 21; to the North-West Territories by the 38 Vic.,chap. 49; and to British Columbia by the 37 Vic., chap. 42.

UNLAWFUL TRAINING TO THE USE OF ARMS.

The 31 Vic., chap. 15, prohibits all meetings and assemblies of persons for the purpose of training or drilling themselves, or of being trained or drilled to the use of arms, or for the purposes of practising military exercises, movements or evolutions, without lawful authority for so doing. Under section 2, such meetings may be dispersed by any Justice of the Peace, and persons attending them may be arrested and committed for trial, if not bailed. So also the arms or ammunition kept for any unlawful purpose may be seized and detained. And persons having the same in possession, or carrying the same may be arrested. *Ib.* s. 3.

This Act was extended to Prince Edward Island by the 40 Vic., chap. 4; to the District of Keewatin by the 39 Vic., chap. 21; to the North-West Territories by the 38 Vic.,chap. 49; and to British Columbia by the 37 Vic., chap. 42.

VAGRANCY.

The 32 & 33 Vic., chap. 28, as amended by the 37 Vic., chap. 43, contains the law in reference to idle and disorderly persons. The Act was extended to Prince Edward Island by the 40 Vic., chap. 4; to British Columbia, by the 37 Vic., chap. 42; and to the Province of Manitoba by the 34 Vic., chap. 14. Under that part of the statute which refers to all common prostitutes, or night walkers, wandering in the fields, public streets, or highways, lanes, or places of public meeting, or gathering of people not giving a satisfactory account of themselves, it is necessary that a conviction should shew a request made on the woman, at the time of her arrest, to give an account of herself, and that she did not give a satisfactory account, and that therefore the arrest was made. A conviction, in the words of the statute, " not giving a satisfactory account of herself," does not imply or shew such prior demand or request to give an account, and is therefore bad.

R. v. *Levecque,* 30 Q. B. (Ont.), 509. The reason of this is obvious, a common prostitute has a right to walk the streets for a lawful purpose, and it is only when asked to give an account of herself that the obligation to do so arises under the statute.

Under that part of the section which speaks of persons as vagrants who are able to work, and thereby maintain themselves and families an obligation to maintain must be made out. It is not madeout in the case of a wife who has left her husbandand is living in adultery. *R.* v. *Flinton,* 1 B. & Ad., 227. A man cannot be convicted, under this section, who offers to take back his wife, although her refusal to return is sufficiently grounded on his ill usage, such offer negativing the refusal to support as well before as after the offer. *Flannagan* v. *Bishop Wearmouth,* 8 E. & B., 451.

The wife is not a competent witness under this Act. *Reeve* v. *Wood,* 5 B. & S., 364.

Notwithstanding the provisions of the Acts relating to the separate property of a married woman, such woman who, deserted by her husband and having no means of maintaining her children, leaves them and neglects to provide for them cannot be convicted on that ground as a vagrant. *Peters* v. *Cowie,* L. R., 2 Q. B. D., 131.

If the husband refuse to maintain the wife because she has left him and has committed adultery, he cannot be convicted. *R.* v. *Flinton,* 1 B. & Ad., 227. But it is no defence that he is an industrious man and is constantly at work. *Carpenter* v. *Stanley,* 33 J. P., 38.

The 32 & 33 Vic., chap. 20, s. 25, provides that whosoever being legally liable, either as husband, parent, guardian or committee, master or mistress, nurse or otherwise, to provide for any person, as wife, child, ward, lunatic or idiot, apprentice or servant, infant or otherwise, necessary food, clothing or lodging, wilfully and without lawful excuse refuses or neglects to provide the same, is guilty of a misdemeanor. In the case of a wife prosecuting her husband for neglect to maintain under this section, it is necessary to prove that the defendant is the husband of the prosecutrix; that the wife was in need of food clothing or lodging; that the husband was able to provide the same but wilfully and without lawful excuse refused or neglected to do so. The wilful refusal or neglect to provide food, clothing or lodging without lawful excuse is what constitutes the offence. If it appears that the refusal or neglect instead of being wilful is attributable solely to want of ability; that the wife is better able to support herself than the husband is to support her; that she is in no need whatever of support and does not ask food or require it, that she is living with another man as his wife; or that without justification she absents herself from her husband's roof and without excuse refuses to return; in these and similar cases it would be absurd to convict the husband as a criminal, and it must be held that there is "lawful excuse" for what otherwise might be held wilful refusal or neglect. *R.* v. *Nasmith* (unreported), Q. B. (Ont.), 28 Dec., '77, Harrison, C. J.

A conviction by one Justice of the Peace under this Act is bad, and it is doubtful whether if the Justice were sitting for and at the request of a police magistrate the conviction would be good. *R.* v. *Claney*, 13 C. L. J., N. S., 41; 7 P. R. (Ont.), 35.

Under the second section of the statute the conviction must be before a Police Magistrate or two Justices of the Peace. Where there is a police magistrate it should appear that the person convicting is the police magistrate himself, or that he is acting for the police magistrate by reason of his illness, or absence or at his request. See Rev. Stat. (Ont), chap. 72, s. 6.

A conviction for keeping a house of ill-fame on the 11th of October and on other days and times before that day, was held sufficiently certain as to time. The information described the parties as of the Township of East Whitby, and had "County of Ontario" in the margin. It charged that they kept a house of ill-fame, but did not expressly allege that they did so in that township or county. The evidence, however, showed that the place at which such house was kept was in East Whitby, in which the Justices had jurisdiction, and this was held sufficient. *R.* v. *Williams*, 37 Q. B. (Ont.), 540.

With regard to the punishment which may be inflicted for vagrancy, the 37 Vic., chap. 43, extends the term of imprisonment to six months. The rule seems to be that where a statute imposes a new punishment for an offence the former punishment enacted by a previous statute for the same offence is abrogated; therefore in the present state of the law there can only be an imprisonment for six months according to the later statute, and there is no authority to make the sentence with hard labour, or to inflict a fine of fifty dollars, the later Act speaking of imprisonment only, and repealing the former as to the punishment. See *ex parte Williams*, 19 L. C. J., 120.

VIOLENCE, THREATS AND MOLESTATION.

The 35 Vic., chap. 31, amends the law in reference to the above offences. This Act was amended by the 38 Vic., chap. 39, and the latter Act was repealed by the 39 Vic., chap. 37.

The provisions of these Acts have been extended to Prince Edward Island by the 40 Vic., chap. 4.

Under the English Act, corresponding to section 3 of this Act, an appellant having been convicted appealed from the conviction, and gave due notice to the prosecutor and to the convicting Justices, and the Justices as well as the prosecutor were named respondents in the appeal, but the Justices did not appear. The Quarter Sessions quashed the conviction and ordered the respondents, or some or one of them, to pay the appellant's costs. It was held that the Sessions had no power to award costs against the convicting Justices. *R.* v. *Goodall*, L. R., 9 Q. B., 557.

It is perfectly legal for workmen to protect their interests by meeting or combining together, or forming unions in order to determine and stipulate with their employers the terms on which they will consent to work for them. But this right to combine must not be allowed to interfere with the right of those workmen who desire to keep aloof from the combination, to dispose of their labour with perfect freedom as they think fit. Nor must it interfere with the rights of the masters to have their contracts duly carried out. Infraction of such rights will bring the wrongdoer within the pale of the criminal law of conspiracy.

The law on this subject is principally contained in the Act 35 Vic., chap. 31, and the Act 39 Vic., chap. 37 amending it. Under the 2nd section of the 35 Vic., chap. 31, prosecutions are to be according to the provisions of the Act relating to the duties of Justices of the Peace out of sessions in relation to summary convictions and orders, 32 & 33 Vic., chap. 31. But under the 3rd section of the 39 Vic., chap. 37, the accused may on appearing before the magistrate, &c., declare that he objects to be tried for such offence by the magistrate, and thereupon the latter shall not proceed with such trial, but may deal with the case in all respects as if the accused were charged with an indictable offence, and not with an offence punishable on summary conviction. The accused therefore has the power to elect to have the case tried on indictment and not by a court of summary jurisdiction.

VOLUNTARY OATHS.

The Statute of Canada, 37 Vic., chap. 37, provides that it shall not be lawful for any Justice of the Peace or other person to administer, or cause or allow to be administered, or to receive or cause, or allow to be received, any oath, affidavit, or solemn affirmation touching any matter or thing whereof, such Justice or other person hath not jurisdiction or cognizance, by some law in force at the time being, or authorized or required by any such law: Provided always that nothing herein contained shall be construed to extend to any oath, affidavit, or solemn affirmation before any Justice in any matter or thing touching the preservation of the peace or the prosecution, trial or punishment of any offence, nor to any oath, affidavit or affirmation, which may be required or authorized by any law of the Dominion of Canada, or by any law of the Province wherein such oath, affidavit or affirmation is received or administered, or is to be used, nor to any oath, affidavit or affirmation, which may be required by the laws of any foreign country, to give validity to instruments in writing, designed to be used in such foreign countries respectively: And provided further, that it shall be lawful for any Judge, Justice of the Peace, Public Notary or other functionary, authorized by law to administer an oath to receive the solemn declaration of any person voluntarily making the same before him in the form of the schedule to this Act, annexed in attestation of the execution of any written deed or instrument or allegations of fact, or of any account rendered in writing, and if any such declaration be false or untrue in any material particular, the person making such false declaration shall be deemed guilty of a misdemeanor.

2. Any Justice of the Peace or other person administering or receiving, or causing or allowing to be received, or administered any oath, affidavit, or solemn affirmation, contrary to the provisions of this Act, shall be deemed guilty of a misdemeanor, and shall be liable to be imprisoned for any term not exceeding three months, or to a fine not exceeding fifty dollars, at the discretion of the Court.

SCHEDULE.

I. A. B., do solemnly declare that (*state the fact or facts declared to*), and I make this solemn declaration conscientiously believing the same to be true, and by virtue of the Act passed in the thirty-seventh year of Her Majesty's reign, intituled (*insert the title of this Act*).

This Act was extended to Prince Edward Island by the 40 Vic., chap. 4.

Prior to the passing of this Act, a magistrate taking an affidavit without authority, was guilty of a misdemeanor, and a criminal information would lie against him for so doing. *Jackson* v. *Kassel*, 26 Q. B. (Ont.), 346.

The provision of the 23 Vic., chap. 2, s. 28, that all affidavits required thereunder, may be taken before "any Justice of the Peace," does not empower a Justice of the Peace to administer the oath anywhere in the Province, it merely authorizes him to do so n the place where he acts as such Justice. *R* v. *Atkinson*, 17 C. P. (Ont.), 295.

WEIGHTS AND MEASURES.

The Acts respecting weights and measures are the 36 Vic., chap. 47, amended by 38 Vic., chap. 36, and by the 40 Vic., chap. 15. By section 34 as amended, the forfeitures and penalties if under $50 are recoverable before one Justice; if over $50, before two Justices, or any magistrate having the power of two such Justices. This

Act was extended to Prince Edward Island by the 39 Vic., chap. 25. Earthenware vessels unstamped, but ordinarily used as containing a certain quantity according to Imperial measure, are "measures;" and if found unjust are liable to be seized, and the dealer on whose premises they are found is liable to penalties under the 27th section of the Act, for having them in his possession. *Washington* v. *Young*, 5 Ex., 403; *R.* v. *Oulton*, 3 E. & E., 568. They are not deemed unjust if against the seller himself. *Booth* v. *Shadgett*, L.R., 8 Q.B., 352.

A weighing-machine which from its construction was liable to variation from atmospheric and other causes, and required to be adjusted before it was used, was held not incorrect upon examination within the meaning of the statute, if examined by the Inspector before it had been adjusted. *London & N. W. R. Co.* v. *Richards*, 2 B. & S., 326.

A railway company kept a weighing machine which for a fortnight had been so out of repair, that when anything was weighed by it the weight appeared to be 4 lbs. more than was really the weight. It was held that the company were liable to conviction for having in their possession a weighing-machine which on examination was found to be incorrect, or otherwise unjust. *Great W. R. Co.* v. *Bailie*, 5 B. & S., 928.

A shopkeeper made use of a pair of scales which had a hollow brass ball hanging upon the weigh end of the beam, constructed so as to allow shot to be placed in the interior, and easily removable from the beam by merely lifting it off. When the ball was removed and replaced after the shot with which it was partly filled had been taken out, it was found that the scales were unjust, and against the purchaser. It was held that there was evidence that these scales were weighing-machines which were incorrect or otherwise unjust. *Carr* v. *Stringer*, L.R., 3 Q.B., 433.

REVISED STATUTES OF ONTARIO.

CHAPTER 74.

An Act respecting Summary Convictions before Justices of the Peace.

HER MAJESTY, by and with the advice and consent of the Legislative Assembly of the Province of Ontario, enacts as follows:—

PROCEDURE BEFORE JUSTICES.

1. Where a penalty or punishment is imposed under the authority of any statute of the Province of Ontario, or of any other statute or law now or hereafter in force in Ontario, and relating to matters within the legislative authority of the Legislature of the said Province, and is recoverable before, or may be inflicted by, a Justice or Justices of the Peace, or a Police or Stipendiary Magistrate, the like proceedings and no other shall and may be had for recovering the penalty, compelling the attendance of the parties or witnesses, hearing the complaint and for the conduct of the Court, the taking and estreating of recognizances, and the infliction of the punishment, and otherwise in respect thereof; and the convicting Justice, Justices, or Police or Stipendiary Magistrate shall perform the like duties in respect thereto, and in respect of any conviction or order made by him or them by virtue of such statute, as, under the statutes of the Dominion of Canada then in force might be had and should be performed, if such penalty or punishment had been imposed by a statute of Canada, unless in any Act hereafter passed imposing such penalty or punishment it is otherwise declared.

See *R.* v. *Snider*, 23 C.P. (Ont.), 330.

(2) Nothing in this section contained shall confer upon any person who considers himself aggrieved by a conviction or order made by any Justice, Justices, or Police or Stipendiary Magistrate, the right of appealing to the General Sessions of the Peace, or shall affect procedure on appeals.

2. The Clerk of the Peace for the County shall be the proper officer to whom shall be transmitted convictions to be filed, and recognizances in respect of which proceedings require to be taken at the General Sessions of the Peace.

APPEALS TO GENERAL SESSIONS.

3. Any party who considers himself aggrieved by a conviction or order made by a Justice or Justices of the Peace, or by a Police or Stipendiary Magistrate under the authority of any statute now or hereafter in force in Ontario, and relating to matters within the legislative authority of the Legislature of Ontario, may, unless it is otherwise provided by the particular Act under which the conviction or order is made, appeal therefrom to the General Sessions of the Peace

A statute giving an appeal does not take away the right to a *certiorari*, and it seems that it would not have this effect, even if it provided that the decision of the Court appealed to should be final.

In the case of a conviction for an offence not being a crime, affirmed in appeal to the Sessions, the writ of *certiorari* is not taken away by this statute. *Re Bates*, 40 Q. B. (Ont.), 284; see also *ante*, p. 146.

Under the Con. Stats. U. C., chap. 114, no appeal lay to the Quarter Sessions, in the case of any conviction for a *crime*, the Act only applying to a conviction for any matter cognizable by a Justice of the Peace, and not being a crime. *Re Lucas*, 29 Q. B. (Ont.), 81; *Re Meyers*, 23 Q. B. (Ont.), 613.

Under this section the right of appeal from convictions or orders is limited to those made under any statute in force in Ontario relating to matters within the legislative authority of the Legislature of Ontario. As to the legislative authority of the Legislature of Ontario, see the British North America Act, 1867, sections 91 & 92; see also *R.* v. *Taylor*, 36 Q. B. (Ont.), 183; *R.* v. *Boardman*, 30 Q. B. (Ont.), 553.

4. In case an appeal lies to the Court of General Sessions of the Peace from a conviction or order made, as aforesaid, under the authority of a statute of the Legislature of Ontario, or other statute or law now or hereafter in force in the Province of Ontario, and relating to matters within the legislative authority of the said Legislature, the practice and proceedings on the appeal and preliminary thereto, and otherwise in respect thereof, shall be the same as the practice and proceedings under the statutes of the Dominion of Canada then in force, on an appeal to the General Sessions of the peace from a conviction before a Justice of the Peace, made under the authority of a statute of Canada; except that either of the parties to the appeal may call witnesses

and adduce evidence in addition to the witnesses called and evidence adduced at the original hearing.

The notice of appeal and the entry into recognizance, if required by statute as conditions precedent to the right of appeal, must be proved or admitted, whether it is intended to try or only to move to respite the hearing; for, until it is made to appear to the court that the appeal is duly lodged at the proper sessions as well as that due notice has been given and recognizance entered into where so required by the Act applicable to the appeal, jurisdiction to hear or adjourn will not attach. But a respondent may waive proof of appeal or admit it so as to make proof unnecessary.

A mere technical objection to entertaining the appeal will be waived by the respondent asking an adjournment, but an objection of substance as to the jurisdiction of the court cannot be so waived. *Re Myers*, 23 Q. B. (Ont.), 611. And if notice of appeal has not been given in time or the recognizance entered into or other matter required to be done before the appellant can proceed with his appeal, the objection could probably be taken at any time, for it would shew that the court had no jurisdiction to entertain the appeal. *R.* v. *Crouch*, 35 Q. B. (Ont.), 433-9. Where, however, notice of appeal was duly given and admitted by the respondent, and the recognizance also duly entered into and filed with the Clerk of the Peace, but on the appeal coming on for hearing, and after the jury were sworn, the respondent's counsel objected that there was no proof of the recognizance, but afterwards continued the case, and did not renew the objection at the close, it was held that the respondent's counsel had admitted that the necessary recognizance had been entered into. *Ib.*

Where a *rule nisi* for a *mandamus* to the sessions commanding them to hear an appeal, called upon the Court of Quarter Sessions in and for the united counties, &c., instead of the Justices of the Peace for the united counties, and the rule had been enlarged in the prior term, on objection to the rule on the above ground, it was replied that the enlargement waived the objection, and this seem to have been acquiesced in by counsel and by the court. *Re Justices, &c.*, 13 C. P. (Ont.), 159. In fact, it seems that in all cases formal and technical objections are waived by an enlargement. *R.* v. *Allen*, 5 P. R. (Ont.), 453-8.

Under the (Ont.) 32 Vic., chap. 32, s. 36, an appeal from a conviction for selling liquor without license was required to be tried by the Chairman of the Quarter Sesssions without a jury. *Re Brown*, 6 P. R. (Ont.), 1; 8 C. L. J., N. S., 81.

Under this section the court has a discretion to grant a jury, and if a jury is not demanded by either appellant or respondent the court will proceed to try it. See *ante*, p. 143-144.

The general principle of appeals is that judgment is to be rendered upon the same facts that were before the inferior tribunal. See *R.* v. *Justices, &c.*, 5 O. S., 74; s. c., 4 O. S., 340. And such is the law on appeals from convictions under the statutes of Canada. *Ante*, p. 143. But this section expressly provides for the admission of further evidence.

Under the Con. Stats. U. C., chap. 114, there was no power of adjournment. The appeal was required to be heard at the Court of Quarter Sessions, appealed to, for the Act provided that the court should at *such sessions* hear and determine the matter of such appeal. *Re McCumber*, 26 Q. B. (Ont.), 516.

Where, therefore, such court, after proof of entry and notice of the appeal, adjourned the further hearing by order until the next sittings, and then made an order quashing the conviction, the orders were quashed. *Ib.* So the costs of an appeal from a Justice's conviction as well as the appeal itself had to be determined at the sessions appealed to. *R.* v. *Murray*, 27 Q. B. (Ont.), 134.

Under this section, however, there is a power of adjournment, the practice being the same as on appeal to the General Sessions from a conviction before a Justice of the Peace, made under the authority of a statute of Canada. See *ante*, p. 138-142.

The court will not give costs on adjourning an appeal, unless the objection is made at the time of the adjournment. *Re McCumber*, 26 Q. B. (Ont.), 516.

It seems doubtful whether under the 32 & 33 Vic., chap. 31, s. 74, an order of sessions, simply ordering costs of an appeal to be paid without directing them to be paid to the Clerk of the Peace as required by the Act is regular. *Re Delaney* v. *Macnab*, 21 C. P. (Ont.), 563; see *ante*, p. 147.

5. If upon the trial at the General Sessions of the Peace of an appeal from a decision of a Justice of the Peace, upon any matter within the legislative authority of the Legislature of Ontario, it is proved upon the oath or affirmation of any credible witness, that a person whose deposition has been taken upon the original hearing, is dead, or is so ill as not to be able to travel, or is absent from Ontario, or if it is proved in like manner that after diligent inquiry, such person cannot be found to be served with a subpœna, and if it is also proved that such deposition was taken in presence of the person accused, and that he, his counsel or attorney, had a full opportunity of cross-examining the witness, and if the deposition purports to be signed by the Justice by or before whom the same purports to have been taken, it shall be received as evidence in the prosecution without further proof thereof, unless it is proved that the deposition was not in fact signed by the Justice purporting to have signed the same.

See *ante*, pp. 38-42.

6. Any appellant may abandon his appeal by giving the opposite party notice of his intention in writing six days before the Sessions appealed to; and thereupon the Justice, Justices or Police Magistrate may tax the additional costs, if any, of the respondent, and add the same to the original costs, and proceed on the original conviction, or order, in the same manner as if there had been no appeal thereon.

WHEN AMENDED ACTS OF CANADA TO APPLY.

7. If the Parliament of Canada amends any statute, the operation whereof is extended by virtue of this Act, no such amendment shall have any force in Ontario, by virtue of this Act, until after the termination of the Session of the Legislature of Ontario, held next after the passing of the amending statute.

CHAPTER 75.

An Act respecting the Procedure on Appeals to the Judge of a County Court from Summary Convictions.

Her Majesty, by and with the advice and consent of the Legislative Assembly of the Province of Ontario, enacts as follows: —

1. In the construction of this Act—

(1.) "Justice" or "Justice of the Peace," shall include two or more Justices of the Peace or a Stipendiary or Police Magistrate;

(2.) "Conviction" shall include an order made by a Justice of the Peace; and

(3.) "Person convicted" shall include any person against whom an order is made as aforesaid.

2. Wherever, by any statute now or hereafter in force relating to matters within the legislative authority of the Legislature of Ontario, an appeal is given to the Judge of the County Court without a jury, from a summary conviction, had or made before a Justice of the Peace, and no special provision is made therefor, such appeal shall be to the Judge of the County Court of the County in which the conviction is made, sitting in Chambers, and the proceedings thereon shall be as hereinafter provided.

3. In any of the following cases, namely:

Firstly. If the appeal is against any conviction whereby only a money penalty is imposed, then, in case the person convicted deposits with the convicting Justices the amount of the penalty and the costs, and a further sum of ten dollars, or with two sufficient sureties enters into a recognizance (Form 1) before a Justice of the Peace, in a sum double the amount of the penalty and the costs, conditioned duly to prosecute the appeal, and to abide by and perform the order of the Judge thereupon, and to pay such costs as he may order;

Secondly. If the appeal is against a conviction whereby imprisonment is imposed, then, in case the person convicted, with two sufficient sureties, enters into a recognizance (Form 2), before a Justice of the Peace in a sum not less than one hundred nor more than two hundred dollars, as the convicting Justice directs, and in double the amount of any penalty and costs which the person convicted has been ordered to pay, conditioned as aforesaid, and also containing the further condition that the person convicted will surrender himself if the conviction is affirmed;

Thirdly. If the person convicted is in custody for non-payment of a fine and costs, or in consequence of imprisonment being imposed as aforesaid, and fails to make the required deposit, or to enter into a recognizance, as hereinbefore provided, but deposits with the said Justice the sum of ten dollars,

the said Justice shall, at the request of the person convicted, made within five days after the date of the conviction, forthwith transmit to the Clerk of the County Court, by registered letter post-paid, all the proceedings and evidence; which said proceedings and evidence, with a duplicate of any order made by the Judge as hereinafter provided, shall immediately, after the matter has been finally disposed of by the Judge, be transmitted by the Clerk of the County Court, in manner aforesaid, to the Clerk of the Peace, to be by him kept with the records of convictions.

4. In any of the cases of the classes firstly and secondly above mentioned, the convicting Justice, upon the recognizance being given or the deposit made, as the case may require, shall stay all proceedings upon the conviction, and if the person convicted is in custody, the said Justice shall issue his warrant (Form 3) to liberate such person.

5. In any of the cases thirdly above mentioned, the person appealing shall remain in custody while the appeal is pending, unless he is in custody for non-payment of a fine or costs, in which case the convicting Justice shall order his liberation upon his depositing (in addition to the said sum of ten dollars) the amount for the non-payment of which he is in custody.

6. Within ten days after the date of the conviction, but not afterwards, unless it is made to appear to the Judge that the delay arose wholly from the default of the convicting Justice, the Judge of the County Court, if he is of opinion from the said evidence that the conviction may be erroneous, may grant a summons calling upon the County Crown Attorney and the prosecutor to show cause why the conviction should not be quashed;

(2.) Such summons shall not be granted in any case after the expiration of one month from the date of the conviction.

S, on the 9th of February, 1875, was convicted before Justices of an offence against the Act, for the sale of spirituous liquors (Ont.) 37 Vic., chap. 32. On the 27th he obtained a *certiorari* to the Justices to return the conviction into the Queen's Bench, which was not served until the 9th of July. In the meantime, on the 3rd of March, he procured a summons from the County Judge by way of appeal from the conviction under the Act, alleging as a ground for obtaining it so late that the delay arose wholly from the default of the Justices. He persisted in his appeal, notwithstanding the *certiorari*, but the Judge refused to adjudicate upon the merits, holding that it had not been made to appear to him that the delay arose wholly from the default of the convicting Justices, and therefore, that he had no jurisdiction, the summons not having been procured within ten days after the date of the conviction. On the 13th of September, the Justices returned to the *certiorari*, that before its delivery to them they had at the request of S, transmitted the conviction and papers to the County

Judge upon the appeal under the Act. See s. 3, thirdly. In November, S having procured the papers to be returned by the County Court clerk at Barrie, to the magistrate's clerk at Orillia, moved to quash the return to the *certiorari*, and for another writ, or for an attachment for not having returned the conviction in obedience to it, or for an order to return the conviction forthwith, or to amend the return by including the conviction therein. In support of this motion, it was urged that the magistrates wrongfully put it out of their power to return the writ by transmitting the papers to the clerk of the County Court when they must have known that the time for transmitting the papers had expired, and that the appeal was too late.

The application was refused, for S having procured the transmission of the papers for his own appeal, could not insist that it was wrong; it was apparent that he had abandoned the *certiorari* in order to carry on his appeal, and when he served the writ he knew that the Justices had not the papers to return.

The County Court Judge has jurisdiction to issue a summons in appeal at any time within one month, if it appears to him that the delay in transmitting the proceedings is wholly the default of the Justices, and the court expressed an opinion that the Justices could not properly have refused to transmit the papers, on the ground that the appeal was not made in time; that is within five days after the date of the conviction; but that on the recognizance being furnished, they should transmit them at least within the month, leaving it to the County Court Judge to decide as to the cause of delay. *R.* v. *Slaven*, 38 Q. B. (Ont.), 557.

The Revised Statutes contain a provision for the transmission, by the clerk of the County Court, of the proceedings and evidence, after the matter is finally disposed of, to the Clerk of the Peace. See section 3, thirdly. This provision was introduced since *R.* v. *Slaven*, *supra*, was decided.

7. Upon the return of the summons the Judge upon hearing the parties may either affirm or quash the conviction, or, if he thinks fit, may hear the evidence of such other witness or witnesses as may be produced before him, or the further evidence of any witness already examined, and may then make an order affirming, or amending and affirming, or quashing the conviction as he may think just, and may order the payment of costs and may fix the amount thereof.

8. Upon the production of the Judge's order affirming, or amending and affirming the conviction, the Justice who has made the conviction shall, if the case is one in which a recognizance has not been given, issue his warrant for payment of such further sum for costs as the sum deposited with him is insufficient to pay ; if the conviction is quashed, the Judge shall order a return of the money deposited, and shall have authority to order payment of such sum for costs as he may tax and allow, and unless the sum is paid by the complainant, the Justice shall issue his warrant to levy the costs.

9. If by the conviction it is adjudged that the person convicted should be be imprisoned, and the conviction is affirmed, or amended and affirmed, or the person convicted fails duly to prosecute the appeal, the Judge shall issue his warrant (Form 4) for the commitment to the proper gaol or other place of imprisonment of the person convicted, and unless such person, within one week thereafter, surrenders himself into the custody of the constable or other officer entrusted with the execution of the warrant, the condition of the recognizance shall be deemed broken, and the recognizance forfeited ; and upon proof of the default being made by affidavit of the officer or otherwise, the Judge may certify (Form 5) the default on the back of the recognizance, and shall thereupon transmit the recognizance to the Clerk of the Peace ;

(2.) Such recognizance shall be thereafter proceeded upon at the General Sessions of the Peace in the same manner as a recognizance taken upon an appeal to the Sessions from a summary conviction may be proceeded upon ; and the said certificate shall be deemed sufficient *prima facie* evidence of the default of the defendant ; but such proceedings shall not relieve the person convicted from undergoing the term of imprisonment to which he was sentenced ; and the warrant of the Judge issued in that behalf, or any new warrant issued by him, may be executed in any part of Ontario in the same manner and subject to the like conditions as a warrant of a Justice of the Peace for the apprehension of an offender.

10. If by the conviction only a money penalty is imposed, the Judge upon being satisfied by affidavit or otherwise that default has been made upon a recognizance given on an appeal in such a case, shall certify in like manner, as is provided in the preceding section, and similar proceedings shall thereupon be had in respect of such recognizance.

11. In case it is proved to the satisfaction of the Judge that the person convicted had previously served a portion of his term, the Judge shall only issue his warrant for the commitment of the defendant for the residue of the

term of imprisonment to which he was sentenced; the Judge may, if he thinks fit, transmit his said warrant to the convicting Justice in order that he may place the same in the hands of a constable for execution.

12. Any warrant issued under this Act may be directed in the same manner, and executed by the like officers, as a warrant of commitment upon a summary conviction made under a statute of the Parliament of Canada.

13. In all cases of appeal to a County Court Judge from any summary conviction had before any Justice, the Judge to whom such appeal is made shall hear and determine the charge or complaint on which such conviction has been had, upon the merits, notwithstanding any defect of form or otherwise in such conviction; and if the person charged or complained against is found guilty, the conviction shall be affirmed, and the Judge shall amend the same if necessary.

14. The Justice shall retain any moneys deposited with him as aforesaid for the period of six months, unless judgment is sooner given; and upon the judgment in appeal being given, or upon the expiration of six months from the day of the date of the conviction, the Justice shall pay over such moneys to the person or persons entitled thereto, in accordance with the judgment; and if the judgment in appeal is not delivered within six months from the day of the date of the conviction, the conviction shall stand, but the respondent shall not be entitled to any costs of the appeal; and in case imprisonment was adjudged by the conviction, the convicting justice shall, or any other justice may, issue his warrant for the commitment of the person convicted for any portion of the term which he has not served, and no further proceedings shall be taken on the appeal.

15. No conviction affirmed or amended and affirmed on appeal by the County Court Judge shall be quashed for want of form, or be removed by *certiorari* into any of Her Majesty's Superior Courts of Record, and no warrant or commitment shall be held void by reason of any defect therein, provided it is therein alleged that the party has been convicted, and there is a good and valid conviction to sustain the same.

See *ante* p. 146.

16. In all cases where it appears by the conviction that the person convicted has appeared and pleaded, and the merits have been tried, and that such person has not (in manner hereinbefore provided) appealed against the conviction where an appeal is allowed, or if appealed against, that the conviction has been affirmed, or amended and affirmed, such conviction shall not afterwards be set aside or vacated in consequence of any defect of form whatever, but the construction shall be such a fair and liberal construction as is agreeable to the justice of the case.

17. In all process and proceedings before the Judge of the County Court under this Act, the Judge shall, with reference to the matters herein contained, have all the powers which belong to or might be exercised by him in the County Court ; and all necessary process may be issued from the office of the Clerk of the County Court.

18. The several forms in the Schedule to this Act contained, varied to suit the case, or forms to the like effect, shall be deemed good, valid and sufficient in law.

SCHEDULE OF FORMS.

FORM 1.

(*Section* 3.)

RECOGNIZANCE TO TRY THE APPEAL; TO BE TAKEN ONLY WHERE A MONEY PENALTY IS IMPOSED.

Province of Ontario,
County of .

Be it remembered, that on , *A.B.*, of (*Labourer*) and *L.M.*, of (*Grocer*), and *O.P.*, of , (*Yeoman*), personally came before me (*or* us) undersigned one (*or* two) of Her Majesty's Justices of the Peace in and for the said County of , (*or* United Counties, *as the case may be*), and severally acknowledged themselves to owe to our Sovereign Lady the Queen the several sums following, that is to say, the said *A.B.* the sum of , and the said *L.M.* and *O.P.* the sum of each, of good and lawful money of Canada, to be made and levied of their several goods and chattels, lands and tenements, respectively, to the use of our said Lady the Queen, Her Heirs and successors, if he the *A.B.* shall fail in the condition hereunder written (*or* endorsed).

Taken and acknowledged the day and year first above mentioned at , before me (*or* us).

J. S.

Whereas the said *A. B.* was on the day of , A.D. , convicted before *C. D.* (and *E. F.*) one (*or* two) of Her Majesty's Justices of the Peace for the said County (*or* United Counties), for that (*stating the substance of the conviction*) :

And whoreas the said *A. B.* has undertaken to appeal against the said con-iction to the Judge of the County Court of the County of
ır United Counties of):

Now the condition of the above (*or* within) recognizance is such that if the ıid *A. B.* shall, within one month from the date of the said conviction, ob-ıin from the said Judge a summons calling upon the County Crown Attorney ıd the prosecutor to show cause why the said conviction should not be ıashed, and shall duly prosecute the said appeal, and shall abide by and ıly perform the order of the Judge to be made upon the trial of such ap-eal, and shall pay such costs as the said Judge shall order, then the said re-ɔgnizance to be void, and otherwise to remain in full force and virtue.

FORM 2.

(*Section* 3.)

ECOGNIZANCE TO TRY THE APPEAL; TO BE TAKEN WHERE IMPRISONMENT IS IMPOSED.

rovince of Ontario,
County of

Be it remembered that (*proceed as in Form* 1 *to the end, and add the fol-wing additional condition*) :—

And further, that if the said *A. B.*, in case the conviction is affirmed, or nended and affirmed, shall surrender himself into the custody of the con-able or other officer entrusted with the execution of the warrant, within ıe week after the Judge shall issue his warrant for the commitment of the ıid *A. B.*, then the said recognizance to be void, and otherwise to remain in ıll force and virtue.

FORM 3.

(*Section* 4.)

ARRANT OF DELIVERANCE WHERE DEFENDANT IS IN CUSTODY, AND ENTITLED TO BE LIBERATED.

rovince of Ontario,
County of

o the Keeper of the Common Gaol of the County of (*or* United Counties of, or to *E. F.*, the constable having in his custody *A. B.* hereinafter named, *or as the case may require*).

Whereas *A. B.* has before one (*or* two) of Her Majesty's Justices of the

Peace in and for the said County (*or* United Counties) of entered into his own recognizance and found sufficient sureties to prosecute before the Judge of the County Court of the County *or* United Counties (of , an appeal from a conviction had before me (*or* us) for that (*stating the substance of the conviction*), for which the said *A. B.* was committed to your custody :

These are therefore to command you, in Her Majesty's name, that if the said *A. B.* do remain in your custody for the said cause and for no other, you shall forthwith suffer him to go at large.

Given under my (*or* our) hand and seal (*or* hands and seals) this day of , in the year of our Lord , at , in the County (*or* United Counties) aforesaid.

J. S. { L.S. }

J. N. { L.S. }

FORM 4.

(*Section* 9.)

WARRANT OF THE JUDGE OF THE COUNTY COURT WHEN IMPRISONMENT ADJUDGED AND CONVICTION AFFIRMED.

Province of Ontario, }
County of }

To all or any of the Constables and other Peace Officers in the said County, and to the Keeper of the Common Gaol of the said County.

Whereas *A. B.*, late of (*labourer*), was on or about the day of convicted before J. S., one of Her Majesty's Justices of the Peace in and for the said County, for that (*stating the offence*), and it was thereby adjudged (*stating the judgment*): And whereas the said *A. B.* has appealed against the said conviction to me, *H. K.*, the Judge of the County Court of the said County of : and whereas, after hearing the said appeal, I, the said *H. K.*, have affirmed the said conviction (*or* have amended the said conviction as follows : *stating the amendment made*, and have affirmed the said conviction as so amended):

These are therefore to command you, the said Constables or Peace Officers, or any of you, to take the said *A. B.*, and him safely to convey to the Common Gaol at , and there to deliver him to the Keeper thereof, together with this warrant; And I do hereby command you, the said Keeper of the said Common Gaol, to receive the said *A. B.* into your custody in the said Common Gaol, there to imprison him (and to keep him at hard labour) for the space of , being the term (*or* being the portion yet unserved of the term) mentioned in the said conviction; and for your so doing this shall be your sufficient warrant.

Given under my hand and seal, this day of in the year of our Lord , at , in the County of

H. K. { L. S. }

FORM 5.

(*Section* 9.)

CERTIFICATE OF DEFAULT TO BE ENDORSED ON THE RECOGNIZANCE.

I hereby certify that the within-named *A. B.* has not surrendered himself (*stating according to the fact the default on account of which the recognizance is forfeited*) in accordance with the condition of the within recognizance, but therein has made default, by reason whereof the said recognizance is forfeited.

H. K.

CHAPTER 76.

An Act respecting Returns of Convictions and Fines by Justices of the Peace.

HER MAJESTY, by and with the advice and consent of the Legislative Assembly of the Province of Ontario, enacts as follows:—

1. Every Justice of the Peace before whom any trial or hearing is had, under any law giving jurisdiction in the premises, and who convicts and imposes any fine, forfeiture, penalty, or damages, shall make a return thereof and of the receipt and application by him of the money received from the person convicted, in writing under the hand of such Justice, quarterly, on or before the second Tuesday in each of the months of March, June, September and December in each year, to the Clerk of the Peace (and in the case of any

convictions before two or more Justices, such Justices, being present and joining therein, shall make an immediate return thereof), in the following form :—

RETURN of Convictions made by me *(or us, as the case may be)* from the day of , 18 , to the day of , of 18

Name of the Prosecutor.	Name of the Defendant.	Nature of the Charge.	Date of Conviction.	Name of Convicting Justice.	Amount of penalty, fine or damages.	Time when to be paid to said Justice.	Time when paid.	To whom paid over by said Justice, and when.	If not paid, why not, and general observations, if any.

A. B., Convicting Justice,

or

A. B. and C. D., Convicting Justices (*as the case may be*).

2. Every such return shall include all convictions and other matters mentioned in the preceding section, not included in some previous return, and also all cases wherein a fine or any part thereof has been paid since the last previous return ; and in the column for observations in every such case, shall be written the words "*Paid on case formerly returned;*" and such returns shall be filed by the Clerk of the Peace among the records of his office.

3. In case the Justice or Justices, before whom any such conviction takes place, or who receive any such moneys, neglect or refuse to make such return thereof, or in case any such Justice or Justices wilfully make a false, partial or incorrect return, such Justice or Justices so neglecting or refusing, or wilfully making such false, partial or incorrect return, shall forfeit and pay the sum of eighty dollars, together with full costs of suit, to be recovered by any person who sues for the same by action of debt (or informa-

tion) in any Court of Record in the Province, one moiety whereof shall be paid to the party suing, and the other moiety into the hands of the Treasurer of the Province, to and for the public uses of the Province.

4. All prosecutions for penalties arising under the provisions of the next preceding section shall be commenced within six months next after the cause of action accrues, and the same shall be tried in the County or place wherein such penalties have been incurred ; and if a verdict or judgment passes for the defendant, or the plaintiff becomes nonsuited or discontinues the action after issue joined, or if upon demurrer, or otherwise, judgment is given against the plaintiff, the defendant shall recover his full costs of suit as between attorney and client, and shall have the like remedy for the same as any defendant has by law in other cases.

5. The Clerk of the Peace of the County in which any such returns are made shall, within two weeks after the times hereby limited for the making of said returns, cause the same to be published in one public newspaper in the County, or if there is no such newspaper, then in a newspaper of an adjoining County, and shall also within the said period fix up in the Court House of the County, and also in a conspicuous place in the office of the Clerk of the Peace, for public inspection, a Schedule of the returns so made by the Justices ; and the same shall continue to be so fixed up and exhibited until the end of the next ensuing General Sessions of the Peace ; and for every Schedule so made and exhibited by the Clerk of the Peace, he shall be allowed in his accounts with the County the fee of four dollars, besides the expense of publication, all of which shall be paid by the Treasurer of the County.

6. All returns so received by the Clerks of the Peace shall be entered of record by them quarterly, in the same manner as formerly recorded at Quarter Sessions ; and the duties, liabilities, fees and emoluments of the Clerks of the Peace in respect thereof, shall continue the same as if such returns had been made to the Court of General Sessions, until otherwise varied by competent authority.

7. The Clerk of the Peace of each County, within twenty days after the end of each General Sessions of the Peace, shall transmit to the Treasurer of the Province a true copy of all such returns made within his County.

8. Nothing herein contained shall exonerate Justices of the Peace from duly returning to the General Sessions of the Peace of their respective Counties, any convictions, or records of convictions, which are by law required to be so returned.

CHAPTER 77.

An Act respecting the Fees of Justices of the Peace.

Her Majesty, by and with the advice and consent of the Legislative Assembly of the Province of Ontario, enacts as follows :—

1. The fees mentioned in Schedule A. to this Act, and no others, shall be and constitute the fees to be taken by Justices of the Peace, or by their Clerks, for the duties and services therein mentioned.

2. The costs to be charged in all cases of convictions, where the fees are not expressly prescribed by any statute, shall be those contained in Schedule B. to this Act.

3. This Act shall not authorize any claim being made by the Justices aforesaid, for fees of any description connected with cases above the degree of misdemeanor.

4. Any Justice or Justices wilfully receiving a larger amount of fees than by law are authorized to be received, shall forfeit and pay the sum of eighty dollars, together with full costs of suit, to be recovered by any person who sues for the same by action of debt or by information in any Court of Record in the Province, one moiety whereof shall be paid to the party suing, and the other moiety to the Treasurer of the Province, to and for the public uses of the Province.

SCHEDULE "A."

(*Section* 1.)

TABLE OF FEES TO BE TAKEN BY JUSTICES OF THE PEACE OR THEIR CLERKS IN THE CASES MENTIONED IN SECTION 1.

1. For an Information and Warrant for apprehension, or for an Information and Summons for assault, trespass, or other misdemeanor.. $0 50

2. For each copy of Summons to be served on defendant or defendants 10

3. For *a Subpœna (only one* Subpœna *on each side to be charged for in each case, which may contain any number of names,)* 10
(If the justice of the case requires it, additional Subpœnas shall be issued witho t charge.

4. For every Recognizance, (*only one to be charged in each case*) $25

5. For Information and Warrant for surety of the peace for good behaviour, (*to be paid by Complainant*)...................... 50

6. For Warrant of Commitment for default of surety to keep peace or good behaviour, (*to be paid by Complainant*)...... 50

SCHEDULE "B."

(*Section* 2.)

TABLE OF FEES TO BE TAKEN BY JUSTICES OF THE PEACE OR THEIR CLERKS I CASES OF CONVICTIONS WHERE FEES ARE NOT PRESCRIBED BY ANY OTHER STATUTE.

1. For Information and Warrant for apprehension, or for Information and Summons for service.......................... .... $0 50

2. For every copy of Summons to be served upon defendant or defendants.......................... 10

3. For every *Subpœna* to a witness (*only one* Subpœna *on each side to be charged for in each case, which may contain any number of names.*) 10 (*If the justice of the case requires it, additional* Subpœnas *shall be issued without charge.*)

4. For hearing and determining the case........................ 50

5. For Warrant to levy penalty 25

6. For making up every Record of Conviction where the same is ordered to be returned to the Sessions, or on *certiorari* 1 00

7. For copy of any other paper connected with any trial, and the minutes of the same if demanded—per folio of one hundred words 10

8. For every Bill of Costs, (*when demanded to be made out in detail.*)... 10

---

9. But in all cases which admit of a summary proceeding before a single Justice of the Peace, and wherein no higher penalty than twenty dollars can be imposed, there only shall be charged for the conviction not more than 50

And for the warrant to levy the penalty 25

10. And in all cases where persons are subpœnaed to give evidence before Justices of the Peace in cases of assault, trespass or misdemeanor, the witness shall be entitled, in the discretion of the Justice, to receive for every day's attendance, where the distance travelled in coming to and returning from such adjudication does not exceed ten miles $50

And for each mile above ten 05

CHAPTER 181.

An Act respecting the Sale of Fermented or Spirituous Liquors.

HER MAJESTY, by and with the advice and consent of the Legislative Assembly of the Province of Ontario, enacts as follows :—

1. This Act may be cited as "*The Liquor License Act.*"

INTERPRETATION.

2. In this Act the words and expressions following shall be construed as follows :—

(1.) "Liquors" or "Liquor" shall be construed to mean and comprehend all spirituous and malt liquors, and all combinations of liquors and drinks and drinkable liquids which are intoxicating.

(2.) "Tavern license" shall be construed to mean a license for selling, bartering or trafficking by retail in fermented, spirituous or other liquors, in quantities of less than one quart, which may be drunk in the inn, ale or beer-house, or other houses of public entertainment in which the same liquor is sold.

(3.) "Shop license" shall be construed to mean a license for selling, bartering or trafficking by retail in such liquors in shops, stores, or places other than inns, ale or beer houses, or other houses of public entertainment, in quantities of not less than three half-pints at any one time, to any one person, and at the time of sale to be wholly removed and taken away, in quantities not less than three half-pints at a time.

(4.) "License by wholesale" or "Wholesale license" shall be construed to mean a license for selling, bartering or trafficking, by wholesale only, in such liquors in warehouses, stores, shops, or places other than inns, ale or beer-houses, or other houses of public entertainment, in quantities not less than five gallons in each cask or vessel at any one time ; and in any case where such selling by wholesale is in respect of bottled ale, porter, beer, wine or other fermented or spirituous liquor, each such sale shall be in quantities not less than one dozen bottles of at least three half-pints each, or two dozen bottles of at least three-fourths of one pint each, at any one time.

REGULATIONS AND PROHIBITIONS.

37. All licenses shall be constantly and conspicuously exposed in the warehouses, shops or in the bar-room of taverns, inns, alehouses, beerhouses, or other places of public entertainment, and in the bar-saloon, or bar cabin of vessels, under a penalty of five dollars for every day's wilful or negligent omission so to do, to be recovered with costs from the merchant, shopkeeper or tavern, inn, alehouse or beerhouse-keeper, or keeper of any other place of public entertainment, or master, captain or owner of the vessel so making default.

38. Every person who keeps a tavern, or other place of public entertainment, in respect of which a tavern license has duly issued and is in force, shall exhibit over the door of such tavern, inn, alehouse, beerhouse, or other place of public entertainment, in large letters, the words "*Licensed to sell wine, beer, and other spirituous or fermented liquors,*" and in default thereof shall be liable to a penalty of five dollars, besides costs.

See as to this section, *R.* v. *Lennox,* 26 Q. B. (Ont.), 141.

39. No person shall sell by wholesale or retail any spirituous, fermented, or other manufactured liquors, without having first obtained a license under this Act, authorizing him so to do ; but this section shall not apply to sales under legal process, or for distress, or sales by Assignees in Insolvency.

As to the penalty for contravention of this or the 40th section of the Act, see s. 51.

If the prosecution is for selling without license the conviction should allege the sale to be without license. See *ex parte Woodhouse,* 3 L. C. R., 94 ; see schedule D, No. 3, also section 75 ; see however, *McCully* v. *McCay,* 3 Cochran, 82.

Section 25 of the (Ont.) 32 Vic., chap. 32, applied where there was no license ; s. 26 when there was a license to sell not less than a quart, but the party was without the license therefor, that is to sell the smaller quantity. *R.* v. *Firmin,* 33 Q. B. (Ont.), 523.

This section prevents any person selling without license, and s. 43 applies where the offender has a license but sells during prohibited hours.

2. No person unless duly licensed shall by any sign or notice hold himself out to the public that he is so licensed; and the use of any sign or notice for this purpose is hereby prohibited.

40. No person shall keep or have in any house, building, shop, eating-house, saloon, or house of public entertainment, or in any room or place whatsoever, any spirituous, fermented or other manufactured liquors for the purpose of selling, bartering or trading therein, unless duly licensed thereto, under the provisions of this Act.

Under this section, the offence is keeping liquors, &c., for the purpose of selling, bartering, or trading therein. As to the evidence necessary to prove that the liquors are kept for such purpose, see sections 80 & 96.

Two defendants cannot be jointly convicted under this section, and an award of one penalty jointly against them is erroneous. The offence does not arise from the joint act of the defendants, but from the personal and particular omission of each defendant to procure a license, and it is several in its nature; and when such defendants are jointly charged in an information, it is a violation of the provisions of the 32 & 33 Vic., chap. 31, s. 25, which requires every complaint to be for one matter only. See *ante*, p. 114–5; *R.* v. *Snider*, 23 C. P. (Ont.), 330.

Such a conviction of two defendants was therefore quashed on *certiorari*. *R.* v. *Sutton*, 14 C. L. J., N. S., 17.

A conviction for selling liquor without license, which did not state that the liquor was not supplied upon a requisition for medicinal purposes, was held bad under the (Ont.), 32 Vic., chap. 32, s. 23. *R.* v. *White*, 21 C. P. (Ont.), 354. See also *ex parte Clifford*, 3 Allen, 16; *Mills* and *Brown*, 9 U. C., L. J., 246.

In the case of *R.* v. *White*, *supra*, the exception was contained in the *enacting* clause of the statute, and it is not to be inferred from this decision that a conviction under this or the 39th section should negative the exceptions contained in sections 41 or 42, these exceptions being in different subsequent sections. See *ante*, p. 128.

A conviction under this section need not negative the exceptions contained in sections 41 and 42. *R.* v. *Breen*, 36 Q. B. (Ont.), 84. See *ante*, p. 128.

The form of conviction in the Schedule G applies in the case of a contravention of section 43 of the Act.

But where the proof must negative the circumstances of exception, the allegations in the instrument of conviction must do the same, otherwise the conclusion *contra formam statuti* will not remedy the defect. *R.* v. *Jukes*, 8 T. R., 542.

41. Sections thirty-nine and forty shall not prevent any brewer, distiller, or other persons duly licensed by the Government of Canada, for the manufacture of fermented, spirituous, or other liquors, from keeping, having or selling any liquor manufactured by him in any building wherein such manuture is carried on, provided such building forms no part of and does not communicate by any entrance with any shop or premises wherein any article authorized to be manufactured under such license is sold by retail, or wherein is kept any broken package of such articles.

2. Such brewer, distiller or other person is, however, further required to first obtain a license to sell by wholesale under this Act, the liquor so manufactured by him, when sold for consumption within this Province, under which license the said liquor may be sold by sample, or in original packages, in any Municipality, as well as in that in which it is manufactured; but no such sale shall be in quantities less than those prescribed in sub-section four of section two of this Act.

42. The said sections numbered thirty-nine and forty of this Act shall not prevent any chemist or druggist duly registered as such, under and by virtue of "*The Pharmacy Act*" (Rev. Stat. (Ont.), chap. 145), from keeping, having, or selling liquors for strictly medicinal purposes, and then only in packages of not more than twelve ounces at any one time, except under certificate from a registered medical practitioner; but it shall be the duty of such chemist or druggist to record in a book, to be open to the inspection of the License Commissioners or Inspector, every sale or other disposal by him of liquor, and such record shall show as to every such sale or disposal, the time when, the person to whom, the quantity sold, and the certificate, if any, of what medical practitioner, and in default of such sale or disposal being so placed on record, every such sale or disposal shall, *prima facie*, be held to be in contraventio of the provisions contained in the said thirty-ninth and fortieth sections of this Act.

A conviction of defendant, who was a registered druggist, for selling spirituous and intoxicating liquors by retail, to wit, one bottle of brandy to one O. S., at and for the price of $1.25, without having a license so to do as by law required, the said spirituous and intoxicating liquor being so sold for other than strictly medicinal purposes only, was held valid for the defendant was not as a druggist authorized to sell without license, and it was unnecessary for the prosecutor to show that he was not licensed, or to negative any exemptions or exceptions. *R.* v. *Denham*, 35 Q. B. (Ont.), 503; see the form Schedule D., No. 11; also section 85.

43. In all places where intoxicating liquors are, or may be, sold by wholesale or retail, no sale or other disposal of the said liquors shall take place therein, or on the premises thereof, or out of or from the same, to any person or persons whomsoever, from or after the hour of seven of the clock on Saturday night till six of the clock on Monday morning thereafter, and during any further time on the said days, and any hours or other days during which, by any statute in force in this Province, or by any by-law in force in the Municipality wherein such place or places may be situated, the same, or the bar-room or bar-rooms thereof, ought to be kept closed, save and except in cases where a requisition for medical purposes, signed by a licensed medical practitioner or by a Justice of the Peace, is produced by the vendee or his agent; nor shall any such liquor, whether sold or not, be permitted or allowed to be drunk in any such places during the time prohibited by this Act for the sale of the same, except by the occupant or some member of his family, or lodger in his house.

As to the evidence necessary in prosecutions under this section, see section 82.

As to the penalty for contravention of this section, see section 52 of the Act. The penalty is recoverable against the persons who are the proprietors or tenants, or agents in occupancy.

This section applies when the defendant has a license, but sells during the prohibited hours.

A conviction under this or the 44th section should show that the sale was not made on a requisition for medical purposes. See *R.* v. *White*, 21 C.P. (Ont.), 354; see the form of conviction in the Schedule G. If the conviction were for allowing the liquor to be drunk on the premises during the prohibited hours, it would be necessary to aver that such consumption was not by the occupant or some member of his family, or lodger in the house. See Schedule D., Nos. 5 & 6.

44. Where a license is issued under this Act to authorize the sale of liquors

upon any vessel navigating any river, lake, or water in this Province, no sale or other disposal of liquor shall take place thereon or therefrom, to be consumed by any person other than a passenger on the said vessel, whilst such vessel is at any port, pier, wharf, dock, mooring, or station ; nor shall any liquor, whether sold or not, be permitted or allowed to be consumed in or upon any vessel departing from and returning to the same port or wharf, dock, mooring, or station, within the time hereinafter in this section mentioned, by any person during the hours prohibited by the preceding section for sale of the same except for medical purposes, as provided in the preceding section.

2. In case any such sale or other disposal of liquor takes place, the said license shall *ipso facto*, be and become forfeited and absolutely void, and the captain or master in charge of such vessel, and the owner or person navigating the same, as well as the person actually selling or disposing of liquor contrary to this section, shall be severally and respectively liable to pay to the Crown, for the public uses of this Province, the sum of one hundred dollars ; and any person who sells or disposes of any liquor contrary to the provisions of this section, shall also be liable to the same penalty and punishment therefor as are hereinafter prescribed in the fifty-second section of this Act.

45. No person having a shop license to sell by retail, and no chemist or druggist, shall allow any liquors sold by him or in his possession, and for the sale of which a license is required, to be consumed within his shop, or within the building of which such shop forms part, or which communicates by any entrance with such shop, either by the purchaser thereof or by any other person not usually resident within such building, under the penalty, in money, imposed by the fifty-first section of this Act.

Under the 29 & 30 Vic., chap. 51, ss. 249 and 254, a person holding a shop license for the sale of liquor was punishable for an offence against law under the latter section, for selling liquors at his shop in quantities less than a quart. *R.* v. *Faulkner,* 26 Q.B. (Ont.), 529 ; 3 L.C.G., 185.

Now the holder of a shop license cannot sell in quantities less than three half-pints at any one time, to any one person. See section 2, s.-s. 3, *ante*, p. 384.

Under the (Ont.) 32 Vic., chap. 32, a license to sell spirituous liquors, whether by wholesale or retail, was necessary either in the case of a tavern or a shop ; and in the case of a shop it was not allowed to be consumed on the premises, or sold in quantities less than a quart. Therefore the sale of a bottle of gin without license was contrary to law. *R.* v. *Strachan*, 20 C.P. (Ont.), 182. In the information or conviction it is not necessary to state the quantity of liquor sold, except in the case of offences where the quantity is essential, and then it is sufficient to allege the sale of more or less than such quantity. See s. 74.

46. No person having a license to sell by wholesale shall allow any liquor sold by him, or in his possession for sale, and for the sale and disposal of which such license is required, to be consumed within his warehouse or shop, or within any building which forms part of or is appurtenant to, or which communicates by any entrance with any warehouse, shop, or other premises wherein any article to be sold or disposed of under such license is sold by retail, or wherein there are kept any broken packages of such articles.

Under a wholesale license the sale must be in quantities not less than five gallons in each cask or vessel at any one time; and of bottled ale, each sale must be in quantities not less than one dozen bottles, of at least three-half-pints each, or two dozen bottles of at least three-fourths of one pint each, at any one time. S. 2, s.-s. 4; *ante*, p. 384.

PENALTIES.

47. It shall not be lawful for the License Commissioners of any License District, or any of them, nor for any Inspector, either directly or indirectly, to receive, take, or have any money whatsoever, for any certificate, license, report, matter, or thing connected with or relating to any grant of any license other than the sum to be paid therefor as the duty under the provisions of this Act, or to receive, take, or have any note, security, or promise for the payment of any such money or any part thereof, from any person or persons whatsoever; and any person or persons guilty of, or concerned in, or party to any act, matter or thing contrary to the provisions of this section, or of sections ten and eleven, shall forfeit and pay to and for the use of Her Majesty a penalty of not less than fifty dollars, nor more than one hundred dollars, besides costs, for every such offence.

Under the old law, where licenses were granted by the councils, it was held that a reeve of a municipality was not liable to conviction for signing a certificate for a license, and delivering the same to the clerk with instructions not to hand it over to the applicant until the Inspector had reported in favour of the applicant. *R.* v. *Paton*, 35 Q.B. (Ont.), 442.

48. Any member of any Board of License Commissioners, or any Inspector, officer, or other person who, contrary to the provisions of this Act, knowingly issues, or causes or procures to be issued, a tavern or shop license, or a certificate therefor, shall, upon conviction thereof, for each offence pay a fine of not less than forty dollars, nor more than one hundred dollars, and in default of payment of such fine the offender or offenders may be imprisoned in the County Gaol of the County in which the conviction takes place, for a period not exceeding three calendar months.

49. If any officer of any Municipal Corporation is convicted of any offence under this Act, he shall, in addition to any other penalty to which he may be liable under this Act, thereby forfeit and vacate his office, and shall be disqualified to hold any office in any Municipality in this Province for two years thereafter.

50. If any member of any Municipal Council is convicted of any offence under this Act, he shall, in addition to any other penalty to which he may be liable under this Act, thereby forfeit and vacate his seat, and shall be ineligible to be elected to or to sit or vote in any Municipal Council for two years thereafter; and if any such person, after the forfeiture aforesaid, sits or votes in any Municipal Council, he shall incur a penalty of forty dollars for every day he so sits or votes.

51. Any person who sells or barters spirituous, fermented or manufactured liquors of any kind, or intoxicating liquors of any kind, without the license therefor by law required, or who otherwise violates any other provision of this Act, in respect of which violation no other punishment is prescribed. shall for the first offence, on conviction thereof, forfeit and pay a penalty of not less than twenty dollars besides costs, and not more than fifty dollars besides costs; and for the second offence, on conviction thereof, such person shall be imprisoned in the County Gaol of the County in which the offence was committed, to be kept at hard labour for a period not exceeding three calendar months.

The occupant of the house is the person liable to the penalty, under this section, though the sale is made by some other person who cannot be proved to have acted under or by the directions of such occupant. See section 83.

52. For punishment of offences against section forty-three of this Act, a penalty for the first offence against the provisions thereof, of not less than twenty dollars with costs or fifteen days' imprisonment with hard labour, in case of conviction, shall be recoverable from, and leviable against, the goods and chattels of the person or persons who are the proprietors in occupancy, or the tenants or agents in occupancy of the said place or places, who are

found by himself, herself, or themselves, or his, her, or their servants or agents, to have contravened the enactment in the said forty-third section, or any part thereof; for the second offence, a penalty against all such of not less than forty dollars with costs, or twenty days' imprisonment with hard labour; for a third offence, a penalty against all such of not less than one hundred dollars with costs, or fifty days' imprisonment with hard labour; and for a fourth or any after offence, a penalty against all such of not less than one nor more than three months' imprisonment with hard labour, in the Common Gaol of the County wherein such place or places are.

53. The Mayor or Police Magistrate of a Town or City, or the Reeve of a Township or Village, with any one Justice of the Peace, or any two Justices of the Peace having jurisdiction in the Township or Village, upon information to them, or one of them respectively, that any keeper of any inn, tavern, ale-house, beer-house, or other house of public entertainment, situate within their jurisdiction, sanctions or allows gambling or riotous or disorderly conduct in his tavern or house, may summon the keeper of such inn, tavern, ale or beer-house to answer the complaint, and may investigate the same summarily, and either dismiss the complaint with costs to be paid by the complainant or convict the keeper of having an improper or a riotous or disorderly house, as the case may be, and annul his license, or suspend the same for not more than sixty days, with or without costs, as in his or their discretion may seem just; and in case the keeper of any such inn, tavern, ale-house, beer-house or place of public entertainment, is convicted under this section, and his license annulled, he shall not be eligible to obtain a license for the period of two years thereafter, and shall also be liable to the penalties by the fifty-first section prescribed.

54. Any person licensed to sell wine, beer or spirituous liquors, or any keeper of the house, shop, room, or other place for the sale of liquors, who knowingly harbours or entertains any constable belonging to any police force, or suffers such person to abide or remain in his shop, room or other place during any part of the time appointed for his being on duty, unless for the purpose of quelling any disturbance, or restoring order, or otherwise in the execution of his duty, shall, for any of the offences aforesaid, be deprived of his license.

55. Any person who, having violated any of the provisions of this Act, compromises, compounds or settles, or offers or attempts to compromise, compound or settle the offence with any person or persons, with the view of preventing any complaint being made in respect thereof, or if a complaint has been made with a view of getting rid of such complaint, or of stopping or having the same dismissed for want of prosecution or otherwise, shall be guilty of an offence under this Act, and on conviction thereof shall be im-

prisoned at hard labour in the Common Gaol of the County in which the offence was committed for the period of three calendar months.

This section is within the powers of the Provincial Legislature, though under the British North America Act 1867, s. 91, No. 27, the right to legislate as to the criminal law, is vested in the Parliament of Canada. *R.* v. *Boardman*, 30 Q. B. (Ont.), 553. See s. 92, Nos. 9, 15, 16.

See on this section, *R.* v. *Mason*, 17 C. P. (Ont.), 534.

56. Every person who is concerned in, or is a party to, the compromise, composition or settlement mentioned in the next preceding section, shall be guilty of an offence under this Act, and on conviction thereof shall be imprisoned in the Common Gaol of the County in which the offence was committed, for the period of three calendar months.

57. Any person who, on any prosecution under this Act, tampers with a witness, either before or after he is summoned or appears as such witness on any trial or proceeding under this Act, or by the offer of money, or by threats, or in any other way, either directly or indirectly, induces or attempts to induce any such person to absent himself, or to swear falsely, shall be liable to a penalty of fifty dollars for each offence.

Penalties not to be Remitted.

58. No Police Magistrate or Justice or Justices of the Peace, License Commissioner or Inspector, or Municipal Council or Municipal officer, shall have any power or authority to remit, suspend or compromise any penalty or punishment inflicted under this Act.

Recovery of Penalties by Distress.

59. For the recovery of the penalties in money under this Act, and legal costs, upon and after conviction in cases not appealable, and in cases appealable where an appeal has not been perfected according to law, it shall be lawful for any Justice, Justices or Police Magistrate to issue a warrant of distress to any constable or peace officer, against the goods and chattels of the person or persons convicted; and in case no sufficient distress is found to satisfy the said conviction, then in cases not otherwise provided for by this Act, it shall be lawful for the said Justice, Justices or Police Magistrate to order that the person or persons so convicted be imprisoned in any Common Gaol or Gaol or Lock-up House, within the County in which such conviction was made, for any period not exceeding thirty days, unless the penalty and all costs are sooner paid.

PROSECUTIONS.

65. All informations or complaints for the prosecution of any offence against any of the provisions of this Act, shall be laid or made in writing (within thirty days after the commission of the offence, or after the cause of action arose, and not afterwards,) before any Justice of the Peace for the County or District in which the offence is alleged to have been committed, or in Cities and Towns where there is a Police Magistrate, before such Police Magistrate, but may be made without any oath or affirmation to the truth thereof, and the same may be according to the form of Schedule C. to this Act or to the like effect.

Under this section the information must shew that it is laid within thirty days after the commission of the offence, or after the cause of action arose. See *ante*, p. 99.

But the information need not contain an express allegation to this effect. If it appears on the face of the information this will suffice. Thus where a conviction on its face was dated on the 30th of April, and alleged the sale of liquor on the 12th of April in the same year, it was held no objection that the proceedings were not stated to have been begun within the twenty days from the offence limited by s. 259 of the 29 & 30 Vic., chap. 51, for the fact sufficiently appeared on the face of the conviction. *Reid* v. *McWhinnie*, 27 Q. B. (Ont.), 289.

Where, therefore, the information in the form given in "Schedule C.," shews the day of sale as in that form, and also the day of the laying of the information, this will be sufficient without any express allegation that the laying of the information is within the the thirty days ; provided, of course, that the fact is so.

The court would no doubt sustain an information which followed the form C. in the schedule. See s. 75 ; *R.* v. *Strachan*, 20 C. P. (Ont.), 182 ; *Reid* v. *McWhinnie*, 27 Q. B. (Ont.), 289.

Under the (Ont.) 32 Vic., chap. 32, it was not necessary that it should appear on the face of the conviction that the prosecution was commenced within twenty days of the commission of the offence. This latter point, however, depended upon the peculiar language of the Act, or rather upon the fact that the section of the Act containing the limitation, was entirely distinct from the section creating the offence and imposing the penalty—the latter being s. 22, and the former s. 25. The rule in such cases is that the limitation arising under a distinct clause is matter of defence and need not appear on the face of the conviction. *R.* v. *Strachan*, 20 C. P. (Ont.), 182; *Wray* v. *Toke*, 12 Q. B., 492.

The conviction was sustained on the above ground, and on the further ground that it substantially followed the form given in the statute, and therefore no further allegations were necessary. See *ante*, p. 127.

It has been held in the Province of Quebec that in a prosecution for selling liquor without license, the information need not be under oath. *Ex parte Cousine*, 7 L. C. J., 112; see also *R.* v. *McConnell*, 6 O. S., 629.

As the procedure in these prosecutions is governed by the Statute of Canada, 32 & 33 Vic., chap. 31 (see Rev. Stat. (Ont.), chap. 181, s. 68), the formalities already stated to be necessary on informations must be observed. See *ante*, p. 96.

66. Any person may be prosecutor or complainant in prosecutions under this Act.

This section expressly enables any person to prosecute under the Act. See *ante*, p. 96.

A Deputy Revenue Inspector may validly sign a plaint or information for selling liquors without a license. *Reynolds and Durnford*, 7 L. C. J., 228.

67. No License Commissioner or Inspector of Licenses, who is a Justice of the Peace, shall try or adjudicate upon any complaint for an infraction of any of the provisions of this Act committed within the limits of the License District for which he is a Commissioner or Inspector; but this section shall not be construed to apply to a Judge, or Junior Judge or Deputy Judge of a County.

68. All prosecutions for the punishment of any offence against any of the provisions of sections thirty-nine, forty, forty-three, forty-four, forty-five, forty-seven, fifty-one and fifty-three of this Act, or any section for the contravention of which a penalty or punishment is prescribed by section fifty-one, whether the prosecution is for the recovery of a penalty or for punishment by imprisonment, may take place before any two or more of Her Majesty's Justices of the Peace having jurisdiction in the County or District in which the offence is committed, or in Cities and Towns where there is a Police Magistrate, before the Police Magistrate of the City or Town, who shall have authority to hear and determine any case in which the offence is alleged to have been committed within the County (for judicial purposes) wherein such City or Town is situate, in a summary manner, according to the provisions and after the forms contained in and appended to the Act of Parliament of Canada, (32 & 33 Vic., chap. 31,) entitled "*An Act respecting the duties of Justices of the Peace out of Sessions, in relation to Summary Convictions and Orders*," which Act and the Acts already passed, or which may be hereafter passed, amending the same. shall be held to apply to all prosecutions and proceedings under this Act, so far as consistent with this Act.

This section requires that the prosecution be before two or more Justices having jurisdiction where the offence is committed, or where there is a Police Magistrate, before such Police Magistrate. As we have already seen, compliance with this provision is necessary ; *ante*, p. 155-6. Where the conviction is by one Justice only, it should either shew that such Justice is the Police Magistrate, or that he is acting for the Police Magistrate by reason of his illness or absence, or at his request. *R* v. *Clancey*, 7 P. R. (Ont.), 35 ; Rev. Stat. (Ont), chap. 72, s. 6. And the Justices must be present and acting together during the whole of the hearing and determination of the case ; *ante*, p. 157. But one Justice may receive the information and take all proceedings preliminary to the hearing ; *ante*, p. 155.

2. The Justices or Police Magistrate shall in all cases reduce to writing the evidence of the witnesses examined before them, or him, and shall read the same over to such witnesses, who shall sign the same.

See as to this clause, *R.* v. *Flannigan*, 32 Q. B., (Ont.), 593-9.

69. All prosecutions under this Act, other than those mentioned in section sixty-eight, whether for the recovery of a penalty or otherwise, may be brought and heard before any one or more of Her Majesty's Justices of the Peace in and for the County where the forfeiture took place, or the penalty was incurred, or the offence was committed or wrong done, and in Cities and Towns in which there is a Police Magistrate, before the Police Magistrate ; and the procedure shall be governed by *The Act respecting Summary Convictions before Justices of the Peace.*

The Act referred to is the Rev. Stat. (Ont.), chap. 74.

70. In all cases where the Board of License Commissioners in Cities passes

a resolution in pursuance of the powers conferred upon them by the fourth and fifth sections of this Act, and in and by any such resolution, penalties are imposed for the infraction thereof, such penalties may be recovered and enforced by summary proceedings before the Police Magistrate (if any,) or before any Justice of the Peace having jurisdiction, in the manner and to the extent that by-laws of Municipal Councils may be enforced under the authority of "*The Municipal Act*" (Rev. Stat. (Ont.), chap. 174,) and the convictions in such proceedings may be in the form set forth in section four hundred and seven of the said last mentioned Act.

APPEALS.

(In cases under Section 51.)

71. In all cases of prosecution for any offence against any of the provisions of this Act, for which any penalty or punishment is prescribed by the fifty-first section of this Act, the conviction or order of the said Justices or Police Magistrate, as the case may be, shall, except as hereinafter mentioned, be final and conclusive, and except as hereinafter mentioned, against such conviction or order there shall be no appeal to the Court of General Sessions of the Peace, or to any other Court.

(2) An appeal shall lie from a conviction for any offence for which a penalty or punishment is prescribed by the fifty-first section of this Act to the Judge of the County Court of the County in which the conviction is made, sitting in Chambers, without a jury, provided a notice in writing of such appeal is given to the prosecutor or complainant within five days after the date of the said conviction, subject to the following provisions.

(3) The person convicted, in case he is in custody, shall either remain in custody until the hearing of such appeal before the said Judge, or (where the penalty of imprisonment with or without hard labour is adjudged) shall enter into a recognizance with two sufficient sureties, in the sum of two hundred dollars each, before the convicting Justices or Police Magistrate, conditioned personally to appear before the said Judge, and to try such appeal and abide his judgment thereupon, and to pay such costs as he may order, and in case the appeal is against a conviction whereby only a penalty or sum of money is adjudged to be paid, the appellant may (although the order directs imprisonment in default of payment), instead of remaining in custody as aforesaid, give such recognizance as aforesaid, or may deposit, with the said Justices or Police Magistrate convicting, the amount of the penalty and costs, and a further sum of twenty-five dollars to answer the respondent's costs of appeal.

(4) Upon such recognizance being given or deposit made, the said Justices or Police Magistrate shall liberate such person if in custody, and shall forthwith deliver or transmit by registered letter post-paid, the depositions and

papers in the case, with the recognizance or deposit, as the case may be, to the Clerk of the County Court of the County wherein such conviction was had.

(5) The practice and procedure upon such appeal, and all the proceedings thereon, shall thenceforth be governed by *The Act respecting the Procedure on Appeals to the Judge of a County Court from Summary Convictions* (Rev. Stat. (Ont.), chap 75), so far as the same is not inconsistent with this Act.

In cases other than those under Section 51.

72. In all cases of prosecutions for any offence against any of the provisions of this Act, other than those for which any penalty or punishment is prescribed by the said fifty-first section, an appeal shall lie from any order or conviction, in the same manner and to the same extent as is provided in and by *The Act respecting Summary Convictions before Justices of the Peace.*

The Act referred to is the Rev. Stat. (Ont.), chap. 74.

PROCEDURE IN CASES WHERE PREVIOUS CONVICTION CHARGED.

73. The proceedings upon any information for committing an offence against any of the provisions of this Act, in case of a previous conviction or convictions being charged, shall be as follows :

(1) The Justices or Police Magistrate shall in the first instance inquire concerning such subsequent offence only, and if the accused be found guilty thereof, he shall then, and not before, be asked whether he was so previously convicted, as alleged in the information, and if he answers that he was so previously convicted, he may be sentenced accordingly ; but if he denies that he was so previously convicted, or stands mute of malice, or does not answer directly to such question, the Justices or Police Magistrate shall then inquire concerning such previous conviction or convictions.

(2) The number of such previous convictions shall be proveable by the production of a certificate under the hand of the convicting Justices or Police Magistrate, or of the Clerk of the Peace, without proof of his signature or official character, or by other satisfactory evidence.

(3) A conviction may in any case be had as for a first offence, notwithstanding that there may have been a prior conviction or convictions for the same or any other offence.

(4) Convictions for several offences may be made under this Act, although such offences may have been committed on the same day ; but the increased penalty or punishment hereinbefore imposed shall only be recoverable in the case of offences committed on different days ; and after information laid for a first offence.

(5) In the event of any conviction for any second or subsequent offence becoming void or defective, after the making thereof, by reason of any previous conviction being set aside, quashed, or otherwise rendered void, the Justices or Police Magistrate by whom such second or subsequent conviction was made, may by warrant under his or their hand summon the person convicted to appear at a time and a place to be named in such warrant, and may thereupon, upon proof of the due service of such warrant, if such person fails to appear, or on his appearance, amend such second or subsequent conviction, and adjudge such penalty or punishment as might have been adjudged had such previous conviction never existed, and such amended conviction shall thereupon be held valid to all intents and purposes, as if it had been made in the first instance.

(6) In case any person who has been convicted of a contravention of any provision of any of the sections of this Act, numbered thirty-nine, forty, forty-one, forty-two or forty-four, or any section for the contravention of which a penalty or punishment is prescribed by section fifty-one, if afterwards convicted of an offence against any provision of any of the said sections, such conviction shall be deemed a conviction for a second offence, within the meaning of section fifty-one, and may be dealt with and punished accordingly, although the two convictions may have been under different sections; and in case any such person is afterwards again convicted of a contravention of any provision of any of the said sections, whether similar or not to the previous offences, such conviction shall in like manner be deemed a conviction for a third offence, within the meaning of section fifty-one, and may be dealt with and punished accordingly.

F., was convicted on the 5th of February, before W. R., a Justice of the Peace, for that he did on Sunday, the 19th of January, sell and receive pay for intoxicating liquor at his hotel, and was fined $40 and costs, to be paid forthwith, and in default of distress, to be imprisoned for twenty days at hard labour.

On the 12th of February, F. was convicted before D. S., and J. L., two Justices of the Peace, for that he did "on Sunday, the 26th of January, sell and receive pay for intoxicating liquors," &c., "the same being the third offence," &c., and was fined $100 and costs, and in default of distress, to be imprisoned for fifty days.

A certificate of the first named conviction was before the magistrates on the second conviction. There was also evidence of the sale of liquor by defendant on three Sundays, but the information did not allege the previous offence. It was not shown whether defendant was licensed.

The Court held that the first conviction was bad, for it did not show whether it was for selling liquor without a license, or having a license for selling on Sunday, and if for selling without a license it was bad because it awarded imprisonment at hard labour, and if for selling on Sunday, then because it was not alleged to be a second offence. It was held also, that the second conviction was bad, because, if for selling without a license, the fine was beyond what the statute warranted, and if for selling on Sunday, it was not shown or charged that defendant was licensed; and because the information did not charge the two previous offences. *R.* v. *French,* 34 Q. B. (Ont.), 403.

FORM OF INFORMATIONS AND OTHER PROCEEDINGS—AMENDMENTS.

74. In describing the offences respecting the sale or other disposal of liquor, or the keeping, or the consumption of liquor in any information, summons, conviction, warrant, or proceeding under this Act, it shall be sufficient to state the sale, disposal, keeping, or consumption of liquor simply, without stating the name or kind of such liquor, or the price thereof, or any person to whom it was sold or disposed of, or by whom it was consumed; and it shall not be necessary to state the quantity of liquor so sold, disposed of, kept, or consumed, except in the case of offences where the quantity is essential, and then it shall be sufficient to allege the sale or disposal of more or less than such quantity.

It is not necessary, in a conviction for selling liquor without license, to mention the statute under which the conviction took place. *R.* v. *Strachan,* 20 C. P. (Ont.), 182.

Prior to the passing of this statute it was held that the person to whom the liquor was sold should have been named or described. *R.* v. *Cavanagh,* 27 C. P. (Ont.), 537.

Where no person is mentioned, and a subsequent charge is made, evidence outside the conviction would have to be resorted to, to prove the identity of the charge and the defendant. Similarity of name would not alone be sufficient, and where the name was wholly unknown, it would especially be a question of external evidence. All carefully drawn forms mention the name of some vendee, or if unknown, it is so stated. *R.* v. *Strachan,* 20 C. P. (Ont.), 182-7.

An information stated that defendant, "a licensed hotel keeper in the Town of Peterborough, did, on Sunday, the 2nd July, 1876, at the hotel occupied by him in the said town, dispose of intoxicating liquor to a person who had not a certificate therefor, &c.," and the conviction thereunder stated that the defendant was convicted "upon the information and complaint of J. Q, the above-named complainant, and another, before the undersigned," &c., "for that the said defendant," &c., in the words of the information. The court held that the person to whom the liquor was sold should have been named or described, but that such an objection, under 32 & 33 Vic., chap. 29, s. 32, which applies to informations, was only tenable on motion to quash the information when before the magistrate; that it sufficiently appeared that the hotel was a licensed hotel, at which liquor was allowed to be sold; that a sale "at" the hotel was equivalent to a sale "therein or on the premises thereof," and that it sufficiently appeared that the defendant was "the proprietor in occupancy, or tenant, or agent in occupancy." It was held also that the words "and another" could be treated as surplusage, it appearing in fact that J. Q. was the only complainant. *R.* v. *Cavanagh*, 27 C. P. (Ont.), 537.

A conviction for that one H., on "did keep his bar-room open, and allow parties to frequent and remain in the same, contrary to law," was held clearly bad as showing no offence; so a conviction for that the said "H" did sell wine, beer, and other spirituous or fermented liquors, to wit, "one glass of whiskey, contrary to law," not alleging that the sale was without license, was held bad for uncertainty, as not showing whether the offence was for selling without license, or during illegal hours. *R.* v. *Hoggard*, 30 Q. B. (Ont.), 152.

A conviction under 40 Geo. III., chap. 4, for selling liquor without license was quashed because the information stated that "the defendant was in the habit of selling spirituous liquor without license," without charging any specific offence, and not showing time nor place, nor that the liquors were sold by retail, and also because the conviction directed the defendant to pay the costs of the prosecution without specifying the amount. *R.* v. *Ferguson*, 3 O. S., 220. But it was no objection, under 29 & 30 Vic., chap. 51, s. 254, that the costs of conveying the defendant to gaol in the event of imprisonment were specified, *Reid* v. *McWhinnie*, 27 Q. B. (Ont.), 289. See *ante*, p. 133.

In *Reid* v. *McWhinnie*, 27 Q. B. (Ont.), 289, it was held sufficient to state the offence in the conviction as selling "a certain spirituous liquor called whiskey," though s. 254 of the 29 & 30 Vic., chap. 51, which created the offence, mentioned "intoxicating liquor of any kind," for intoxicating liquor and spirituous liquor were used in the Act as convertible terms, and in the Customs Act of the same session whiskey was recognised as a spirituous liquor. The offence alleged was selling "a certain quantity, to-wit, one pint." This was held sufficient without negativing that it was a sale in the original packages within the exemption in s. 252 of the Act, for it would be judicially noticed that a pint was less than five gallons or twelve bottles, which the packages must at least have contained. *Ib.*

The following conviction for selling spirituous liquors by retail contrary to law, namely:—"That A. B., of, &c., merchant and shopkeeper, did within the space of six calendar months, now last past, in the year aforesaid, at, &c., sell and vend a certain quality of spirituous liquors in less quantity than one quart, to wit, one pint, &c., without license for that purpose, previously obtained, contrary to the form of the statute in such case made and provided," was held bad in substance, in leaving it doubtful under which of the statutes, 40 Geo. III., chap. 4; 6 Wm. IV., chap. 2; 6 Geo. IV., chap. 4—and for what offence the conviction was made. *Wilson* v. *Graybiel*, 5 Q.B. (Ont.), 227.

Where a statute imposes a fine for the first offence, and the conviction is for a fine, it has been held not necessary to specify whether the conviction was for the first or second offence, as from the punishment awarded the court would imply the first offence. *R.* v. *Strachan*, 20 C. P, (Ont.), 182.

Where a particular act constitutes the offence, it is enough to describe it in the words of the Legislature, and a conviction under the (Ont.,) 32 Vic., chap. 32, alleging that the defendant sold spirituous liquors by retail without license, stating time and place was held sufficient without a statement of kind and quantity. *R.* v. *King*, 20 C. P. (Ont.), 246; *Re Donelly*, 20 C. P. (Ont.), 165; *ante*, p. 129.

A conviction for selling liquor without license is bad, if it do not specify the day on which the offence was committed. *R.* v. *French*, 2 Kerr, 121; see the form of conviction Schedule "G."

Where the jurisdiction of the Justice appeared on the conviction, the offence being alleged to have happened at the Town of Moncton, where it was heard and tried, and the conviction being in the form prescribed by the (N. B.,) Rev. Stat., chap. 138, and the place of sale spoken of at the trial appearing to be known to all parties, and no objection having been then made that it was not within the jurisdiction of the Justices, it was held that the jurisdiction sufficiently appeared, though it was not shown by positive evidence that the offence was committed within the limits of the Town of Moncton. *Ex parte Dunlop*, 3 Allen, 281.

A conviction under 28 Vic., chap. 22, for selling liquor without a license, omitted to state that defendant had been convicted of selling "by retail." It was held on appeal to the Quarter Sessions that the offence was not sufficiently stated in the conviction, and it was accordingly quashed. It was also held that the proper time for applying to amend the conviction under the 29 & 30 Vic., chap. 50, was at the time it was made, and that it could not afterwards be amended under the provisions of that Act. *Bird* v. *Brian*, 3 L. C. G., 60; see 32 & 33 Vic., chap. 31, s. 68.

In an appeal from a conviction for selling liquor contrary to chapter 22 of the (N. S.) Revised Statutes, the Court will allow the original summons to be amended. *Taylor* v. *Marshall*, 2 Thomson, 10.

75. The forms given in the Schedules to this Act, or any forms to the like effect, shall be sufficient in the cases thereby respectively provided for, and where no forms are prescribed by the Schedules new ones may be framed according to those appended to The Act of Canada 32 & 33 Vic., chap. 31, entitled "*An Act respecting the duties of Justices of the Peace out of Sessions in relation to Summary Convictions and Orders*," or *The Revised Statute respecting the Procedure on Appeals to the Judge of the County Court from Summary Convictions*, Rev. Stat. (Ont.), chap. 75, or any Acts amending the same respectively—such forms being made short and concise in the mode indicated in the Schedules to this Act which shall serve as guides so far as the particula case will allow.

A conviction following the forms given by the Act will be good Where a conviction awarded imprisonment in default of distress, and in that respect followed the form in the Act, it was held sufficient. *R. v. Strachan*, 20 C.P. (Ont.), 182; see also *Reid v. McWhinnie*, 27 Q. B. (Ont.), 289.

76. In the event of any variance between the information and evidence adduced in support thereof, the Justice, Justices or Police Magistrate may amend or alter such information, and may substitute for the offence charged therein, any other offence against the provisions of this Act; but if it appears that the defendant has been materially misled by such variance, the said Justice, Justices or Police Magistrate shall thereupon adjourn the hearing of the case to some future day, unless the defendant waives such adjournment.

77. No conviction or warrant enforcing the same or other process or proceeding under this Act shall be held insufficient or invalid by reason of any variance between the information or conviction, or by reason of any other defect in form or substance, provided it can be understood from such conviction, warrant, process or proceeding that the same was made for an offence against some provision of this Act, within the jurisdiction of the Justice, Justices, or Police Magistrate who made or signed the same, and provided there is evidence to prove such offence, and it can be understood from such conviction, warrant, or process, that the appropriate penalty or punishment for such offence was intended to be thereby adjudged.

(2) Upon any application to quash such conviction, or warrant enforcing the same, or other process or proceeding whether in appeal or upon *habeas corpus*, or by way of *certiorari* or otherwise, the Court or Judge to which such appeal is made or to which such application has been made upon *habeas corpus* or by way of *certiorari*, or otherwise, shall dispose of such appeal or application upon the merits, notwithstanding any such variance or defect as aforesaid, and in all cases where it appears that the merits have been tried, and that the conviction, warrant, process, or proceeding is sufficient and valid under this section or otherwise, such conviction, warrant, process, or proceeding shall be affirmed, or shall not be quashed (as the case may be), and such Court or Judge may, in any case, amend the same if necessary, and any conviction, warrant, process or proceeding so affirmed, or affirmed and amended, shall be enforced in the same manner as convictions affirmed on appeal, and the costs thereof shall be recoverable as if originally awarded.

See as to amendment of conviction, *ante*, p. 339.

EVIDENCE, &c.

78. In any prosecution or proceeding under this Act, in which proof is required respecting any license, a certificate under the hand of the License Inspector of the District shall be *prima facie* proof of the existence of a license, and of the person to whom the same was granted or transferred; and the production of such certificate shall be sufficient *prima facie* evidence of the facts therein stated and of the authority of the License Inspector, without any proof of his appointment or signature.

It seems that magistrates have not the right, where a formal existing license is produced, to go behind it for the purpose of enquiring, not into the simple issue is the defendant licensed or unlicensed, but whether certain preliminary requisites have or have not been complied with before the license produced had been given to the tavern-keeper. And the quashing of a by-law, under which a certificate has been granted, and license issued for the sale of spirituous liquors, does not nullify the license, and a conviction for selling liquor without license cannot therefore, under these circumstances, be supported. *R.* v. *Stafford*, 22 C. P. (Ont.), 177.

The Revised Statutes (Ont.), chap. 62, s. 9, provides, that on the trial of any proceeding, matter or question, under "The Liquor License Act," or on the trial of any proceeding, matter or question before any Justice or Justices of the Peace, Mayor or Police Magistrate, in any matter cognizable by such Justice or Justices, Mayor or Police Magistrate, *not being a crime*, the party opposing or defending, or the wife or husband of such person opposing or defending, shall be competent and compellable to give evidence in such proceeding, matter or question.

An information under the 43rd section of the Rev. Stat. (Ont.), chap. 181, for selling intoxicating liquors on a Sunday, is an information for a crime within the meaning of the said section of the Rev. Stat. (Ont.), chap. 62, and therefore the defendant cannot be compelled to give evidence against himself—the general policy of the law not compelling any man to criminate himself—where, therefore, in a prosecution for selling liquor on a Sunday, the defendant was compelled to give evidence which established the charge, and there was no other evidence, the conviction was quashed. *R.* v. *Roddy*, 41 Q. B. (Ont.), 291.

The court, in this case, expressed an opinion that, where the proceeding, although before Justices of the Peace, is not simply for the recovery of money payable to some individual informant, but for the punishment of an offence against social order, and where the punishment may be not only the imposition of a fine, but imprisonment, and that at hard labour, the offence, whether created or assumed to be created by the Dominion or Provincial Legislature, is looked upon as a crime, and the prosecution a criminal prosecution, so as to exclude the testimony of the accused, either for or against himself. *Ib.* 302.

79. Any resolution of the Board of License Commissioners passed under the fourth and fifth sections of this Act shall be sufficiently authenticated by being signed by the Chairman of the Board which passed the same; and a copy of any such resolution written or printed, and certified to be a true copy by any member of such Board, shall be deemed authentic, and be received in evidence in any Court of Justice without proof of any such signature, unless it is specially pleaded or alleged that the signature to any such original regulation has been forged.

80. Any house, shop, room, or other place in which are proved to exist a bar, counter, beer pumps, kegs, jars, decanters, tumblers, glasses, or any other appliances or preparations similar to those usually found in taverns and shops where spirituous or fermented liquors are accustomed to be sold or trafficked in, shall be deemed to be a place in which spirituous, fermented or other manufactured liquors are kept or had for the purpose of being sold, bartered or traded in, under the fortieth section of this Act, unless the contrary is proved by the defendant in any prosecution; and the occupant of such house, shop, room or other place shall be taken conclusively to be the person who has, or keeps therein, such liquors for sale, barter or traffic therein.

81. In proving the sale or disposal, gratuitous or otherwise, or consumption of liquor for the purpose of any proceeding relative to any offence under this Act, it shall not be necessary to show that any money actually passed, or any liquor was actually consumed, if the Justices, Police Magistrate, or Court hearing the case is or are satisfied that a transaction in the nature of a sale or other disposal actually took place, or that any consumption of liquor was about to take place; and proof of consumption or intended consumption of liquor on premises under license or in respect to which a license is required under this Act, by some person other than the occupier of said premises, shall be evidence that such liquor was sold to the person consuming or being about to consume or carrying away the same, as against the holder of the license or the occupant of the said premises.

82. In Cities, Towns and incorporated Villages, in all cases where any person or persons other than members of the family or household of the keeper of a licensed tavern or saloon, is or are found frequenting or present, or gas or other light is seen burning in the bar-room of such tavern or saloon, where liquor is trafficked in, at any time during which the sale or other disposal of liquors is prohibited by any provision of this Act, any such fact, when proved, shall be deemed and taken as *prima facie* evidence that a sale or other disposal of liquors by the keeper of such tavern or other place has taken place contrary to the provisions of the forty-third section of this Act; and such keeper may thereupon be convicted of an offence against said section, and shall, upon conviction, be subject to the punishment prescribed in and by the fifty-second section of this Act.

83. The occupant of any house, shop, room or other place in which any sale, barter or traffic of spirituous, fermented or manufactured liquors, or any matter, act or thing in contravention of any of the provisions of this Act, has taken place, shall be personally liable to the penalty and punishments prescribed in the fifty-first and fifty-second sections of this Act, as the case may be, notwithstanding such sale, barter or traffic be made by some other person, who cannot be proved to have so acted under or by the directions of such occupant, and proof of the fact of such sale, barter or traffic, or other act, matter or thing, by any person in the employ of such occupant, or who is suffered to be or remain in or upon the premises of such occupant, or to act in any way for such occupant, shall be conclusive evidence that such sale, barter or traffic, or other act, matter or thing, took place with the authority and by the direction of such occupant.

This section applies where the act complained of was done either by the occupant or by some other person. *R.* v. *Breen*, 36 Q. B. (Ont.), 84.

It seems that if the act of sale by the person other than the occupant, were an isolated act, and wholly unauthorized by him, and not in any way in the course of his business, but a thing done wholly by the unwarranted or wilful act of the subordinate, the occupant might escape personal liability. *R.* v. *King*, 20 C. P. (Ont.), 246.

The statute points at two distinct classes of offenders; first, those who sell liquor without a license, and second, those who, having such license, sell liquor within the prohibited hours. In the latter case, though the tavern may be the property of the defendant, unless he is in occupancy as proprietor or as tenant or agent, he is not liable, Thus, if the owner of a tavern, but not occupying it or carrying on the business, had gone into it and sold a glass of liquor, he would not be within the Act. So if a stranger, a mere trespasser, went into the tavern either in the absence of, or against the will of the actual tenant or occupant, and not in any way as the agent of the occupant, and sold liquor to another person, he would not be within the Act.

A conviction that one G. P., of, &c., inn-keeper, after the hour of seven in the evening, and before the hour of twelve o'clock of the night of Saturday, in and at his tavern, &c., being a place where intoxicating liquors were allowed to be sold by retail, did unlawfully sell and otherwise dispose of, and permit, and allow to be drunk, &c., one glassful of beer, &c., was held bad, as not necessarily bringing the defendant within the class of persons designated by the statute of Ontario, 32 Vic. chap. 32, s, 24, viz.:—"The person or persons who are proprietors in occupancy, or tenants or agents in occupancy of the said place or places," for the word "inn-keeper" only amounted to a mere description and not to an averment of his filling such character; and the words "in and at his tavern," did not necessarily mean the proprietor in occupancy, &c., to whom the license was granted, and who alone was liable, but would also include the owner or proprietor, even if he were not the occupant. *R.* v. *Parlee,* 23, C. P. (Ont.), 359.

84. In any prosecution under this Act for the sale or other disposal of liquor without the license required by law, it shall not be necessary that any witness should depose directly to the precise description of the liquor sold or bartered or the precise consideration therefor, or to the fact of the sale or other disposal having taken place with his participation or to his own personal and certain knowledge, but the Justices or Police Magistrate trying the case, so soon as it appear to them or him that the circumstances in evidence sufficiently establish the infraction of law complained of, shall put the defendant on his defence, and in default of his rebuttal of such evidence, shall convict him accordingly.

85. In any prosecution under this Act, whenever it appears that the defendant has done any act or been guilty of any omission in respect of which, were he not duly licensed, he would be liable to some penalty under this Act, it shall be incumbent upon the defendant to prove that he is duly licensed, and that he did the said act lawfully.

The general rule of law is that the burden of proof lies on the party who substantially asserts the affirmative, though he may not do so in form. But where any one is proceeded against for doing an act which he is not permitted to do, unless he has some special license or qualification in his favour, it is sufficient to charge this want of license or qualification against the party, and it is for him to prove his license or qualification affirmatively. *R.* v. *Turner*. 5 M. & S., 206.

Therefore, in a prosecution for selling liquor without licence, it is for the defendant to show his license, not for the informant to negative its existence. *Re Barrett*, 28 Q. B. (Ont.), 559 ; *ex parte Parks*, 3 Allen, 237.

(2) The production of a license which on its face purports to be duly issued, and which, were it duly issued, would be a lawful authority to the defendant for such act or omission, shall be *prima facie* evidence that the defendant is so entitled, and in all cases the signature to and upon any instrument purporting to be a valid license shall *prima facie* be taken to be genuine.

Witnesses.

86. In any prosecution under this Act the Justice, Justices or Police Magistrate trying the case may summon any person represented to him or them as a material witness in relation thereto ; and if such person refuses or neglects to attend pursuant to such summons, the Justice, Justices, or Police Magistrate may issue his or their warrant for the arrest of such person ; and he shall thereupon be brought before the Justice, Justices or Police Magistrate, and if he refuses to be sworn or to affirm, or to answer any questions touching the case, he may be committed to the Common Gaol of the County, there to remain until he consents to be sworn or to affirm, and to answer.

Under the former statute, the informer was a competent witness, being expressly made so by the statute. *R.* v. *Strachan*, 20 C. P. (Ont.), 182.

87. Any person summoned as a party to, or as a witness in, any proceeding under this Act, may, by the summons, be required to produce, at the time and place appointed for his attendance, all books and papers, accounts, deeds and other documents in his possession, custody or control, relating to any matter connected with the said proceeding, saving all just exceptions to such production ; and shall be liable to the same penalties for non-production of such books, papers or documents, as he would incur by refusal or neglect to attend, pursuant to such summons, or to be sworn or to answer any question touching the case.

95. Any officer, policeman or constable, or Inspector of Licenses may, for the purpose of preventing or detecting the violation of any of the provisions of this Act, which it is his duty to enforce, at any time enter into any and every part of any inn, tavern, or other house or place of public entertainment, shop, ware-

house, or other place wherein refreshments or liquors are sold, or reputed to be sold, whether under license or not, and may make searches in every part thereof, and of the premises connected therewith, as he may think necessary for the purpose aforesaid.

(2) Every person being therein, or having charge thereof, who refuses or fails to admit such officer, policeman or constable, or Inspector demanding to enter in pursuance of this section in the execution of his duty, or who obstructs or attempts to obstruct the entry of such officer, policeman, constable, or Inspector, or any such searches as aforesaid, shall be liable to the penalties and punishments prescribed by section fifty-one of this Act.

96. Any Justice of the Peace or Police Magistrate, if satisfied by information on the oath of any such officer, policeman, constable, or Inspector, that there is reasonable ground for belief that any spirituous or fermented liquor is being kept for sale or disposal contrary to the provisions of this Act in any unlicensed house or place within the jurisdiction of the Justice or Magistrate, may in his discretion grant a warrant under his hand, by virtue whereof it shall be lawful for the person named in such warrant at any time or times within ten days from the date thereof, to enter, and, if need be, by force, the place named in the warrant, and every part thereof, or of the premises connected therewith, and examine the same and search for liquor therein ; and for this purpose may, with such assistance as he deems expedient, break open any door, lock, or fastening of such premises, or any part thereof, or of any closet, cupboard, box, or other article likely to contain any such liquor ; and in the event of any liquor being so found unlawfully kept on the said premises, the occupant thereof shall, until the contrary is proved, be deemed to have kept such liquor for the purpose of sale, contrary to the provisions of the fortieth section of this Act.

97. It shall be the duty of every officer, policeman, constable, or Inspector of Licenses in each Municipality, to see that the several provisions of this Act are duly observed, and to proceed by information and otherwise prosecute for the punishment of any offence against the provisions of this Act ; and in case of wilful neglect or default in so doing in any case, such officer, policeman, constable, or Inspector shall incur a penalty of ten dollars for each and every such neglect and default.

SCHEDULE "C."

(*Section* 65 *and* 75.)

GENERAL FORM OF INFORMATION.

ONTARIO, County of York, To Wit : } THE INFORMATION of A.B., of the Township of York, in the County of York, License Inspector, laid before me, C.D., Police Magistrate in and for the City of Toronto, [*or* one of her Majesty's Justices of the Peace in and for the County of York], the day of , in the year of our Lord one thousand eight hundred and

The said informant says he is informed and believes that X.Y., on the day of , in the year of our Lord one thousand eight hundred and , at the Township of York, in the County of York, unlawfully did sell liquor without the license therefor by law required [*or as the case may be—See forms in Schedule D*].

A. B.

Laid and signed before me the day and year, and at the place first above-mentioned.
C. D.,
P.M. *or* J.P.

SCHEDULE D.

(*Section* 75.)

FORMS FOR DESCRIBING OFFENCES.

1. *Neglecting to keep license exposed.* (Section 37.)

"That X. Y. having a license by wholesale [*or* a shop, *or* a tavern, *or* a vessel license] on at unlawfully and wilfully (*or* negligently) omitted to expose the said license in his warehouse [*or* shop, *or* in the bar-room of his tavern, *or* in the bar-saloon, *or* bar-cabin of his vessel," *as the case may be*].

2. *Neglecting to exhibit notice of license.* (Section 38.)

"That X. Y. being the keeper of a tavern [*or* inn *or* house *or* place of public entertainment] in respect of which a tavern license has duly issued and is in force on at unlawfully did not exhibit over the door of such tavern [*or* inn, &c.,] in large letters the words 'Licensed to sell wine, beer, and other spirituous or fermented liquors,' as required by '*The Liquor License Act.*'"

3. *Sale without license.* (Section 39.)

"That X. Y., on the day of in the year of our Lord one thousand eight hundred and at in the County of unlawfully did sell liquor without the license therefor by law required."

4. *Keeping liquor without license.* (Section 40.)

"That X. Y. on at unlawfully did keep liquor for the purpose of sale, barter and traffic therein, without the license therefor by law required."

5. *Sale of liquor on licensed premises during prohibited hours.* Sections 43 and 52.

"That X. Y. on at in his premises [*or* on, *or* out of, *or* from, his premises] being a place where liquor may be sold, unlawfully did sell [*or* dispose of] liquor during the time prohibited by "*The Liquor License Act*" (*or* by by-law of the Municipal Council of or of the License Commissioners for the District of *or as the case may be*') for the sale of the same, without any requisition for medical purposes as required by said Act being produced by the vendee or his agent."

6. *Allowing liquor to be drunk on licensed premises during prohibited hours.* (Sections 43 and 52.)

"That X. Y. on at in his premises, being a place where liquor may be [*or* is] sold, by retail [*or* wholesale] unlawfully did allow [*or* permit] liquor to be drunk in such place during the time prohibited by "*The Liquor License Act*" for the sale of the same by a person other than the occupant, or some member of his family, or a lodger in his house."

7. *Sale of less than three half-pints under shop license.* (Section 2 (3).

"That X. Y. having a shop license on at unlawfully did sell liquor in less quantity than three half-pints."

8 *Sale under wholesale license in less than wholesale quantities.* (Sections 2 (4), and 41.

"That X. Y. having a license to sell by wholesale on at unlawfully did sell liquor in less quantity than five gallons [*or*, than one dozen bottles of three half-pints each, *or* than two dozen bottles of three-fourths of a pint each]."

9. *Allowing liquor to be consumed in shop.* (Section 45.)

"That X. Y. having a shop license on at unlawfully did allow liquor sold by him (*or* in his possession), and for the sale of which a license is required, to be consumed within his shop [or within the building of which his shop forms part, *or*, within a building which communicates by an entrance with his shop], by a purchaser of such liquor [*or*, by a person not usually resident within the building of which such shop forms a part]."

10. *Allowing liquor to be consumed on premises under wholesale license.* (Section 46.)

"That X. Y. having a license by wholesale, on at unlawfully did allow liquor sold by him [*or* in his possession for sale] and for the sale of which such license is required, to be consumed within his warehouse [*or* shop, *or* within a building which forms part of (*or* is appurtenant to *or* which communicates by an entrance with a warehouse or shop, *or* premises) wherein an article to be sold (*or* disposed of) under such license, is sold by retail)*or* wherein there is kept a broken package of an article for sale under such license)]."

11. *Illegal sale by druggists.* (Section 42.)

"That X. Y. being a chemist [*or* druggist] on at did unlawfully sell liquor for other than strictly medicinal purposes [*or* sell liquor in packages of more than twelve ounces at one time without a certificate from any registered medical practitioner, *or* sell liquor without recording the same], as required by "*The Liquor License Act.*"

12. *Illegal sale under vessel license.* (Section 44.)

"That X. Y. being authorized to sell liquor on a vessel called the '*Spartan*,' on at unlawfully did sell [*or* dispose of] liqnor to be consumed by a person other than a passenger on such vessel while in port [*or* unlawfully did allow liquor to be consumed on such vessel during the time prohibited by "*The Liquor License Act*," for the sale of the same without any requisition for medical purposes, as required by said Act]."

13. *Keeping a disorderly house.* (Section 53.)

"That X. Y. being the keeper of a tavern [*or* ale-house, *or* beer-house, *or* house of public entertainment], situate in the City [*or* Town, *or* Village, *or* Township], of in the County of on in his said tavern [*or* house] unlawfully did sanction [*or* allow] gambling, [*or* riotous, *or* disorderly conduct] in his said tavern [*or* house]."

14. *Harbouring Constables on duty.* (Section 54.)

"That X. Y. being licensed to sell liquor at on unlawfully and knowingly did harbour [*or* entertain *or* suffer to abide and remain on his premises] O. P., a constable belonging to a police force, during a part of the time appointed for his being on duty, and not for the purpose of quelling a disturbance or restoring order, or executing his duty."

15. *Compromising or compounding a prosecution.* (Section 55.)

"That X. Y. having violated a provision of '*The Liquor License Act*,' on at unlawfully did compromise [*or* compound, *or* settle, *or* offer, *or* attempt to compromise, compound *or* settle], the offence with A. B., with a view of preventing any complaint being made in respect thereof [*or* with the view of getting rid of *or* of stopping, *or* of having the complaint made in respect thereof dismissed, *as the case may be*]."

16. *Being concerned in compromising a prosecution.* (Section 56.)

"That X. Y. on at unlawfully was concerned in [*or* a party to] a compromise [*or* a composition, *or* a settlement] of an offence committed by O. P., against a provision of "*The Liquor License Act.*"

17. *Tampering with a witness.* (Section 57.)

"That X. Y. on a certain prosecution under '*The Liquor License Act,*' on at unlawfully did tamper with O. P., a witness in such prosecution before [*or* after] he was summoned [*or* appeared] as such witness on a trial [*or* proceeding] under the said Act, [*or* unlawfully did induce, *or* attempt to induce O. P., a witness in such prosecution, to absent himself *or* to swear falsely]."

18. *Refusing to admit policemen.* (Section 95.)

"That X. Y. on the at being in [*or* having charge of] the premises of O. P., being a place where liquor is sold [*or* reputed to be sold], unlawfully did refuse [*or* fail] to admit [*or* did obstruct *or* attempt to obstruct] E. F., an officer demanding to enter in the execution of his duty [*or* did obstruct *or* attempt to obstruct E. F., an officer making searches in said premises, and in the premises connected with such place]"

19. *Officer refusing to prosecute.* (Sections 94 and 97.)

"That X. Y. being a police officer [*or* constable, *or* Inspector of Licenses] in and for the Township of York, in the County of York, knowing that O. P. had on at committed an offence against a provision of '*The Liquor License Act,*' unlawfully and wilfully did and still does neglect to prosecute the said O. P., for his said offence."

SCHEDULE "E."

(*Section* 75.)

FORM OF INFORMATION FOR SECOND, THIRD, OR FOURTH OFFENCE.

ONTARIO,
County of York,
To Wit:

THE INFORMATION of A. B., of &c., License Inspector, laid before me C. D., Police Magistrate in and for the City of Toronto [*or* one of Her Majesty's Justices of the Peace in and for the County of York], the day of in the year of our Lord one thousand eight hundred and

The said Informant says he is informed and believes that X. Y. on at [*describe last offence*].

And further that the said X. Y. was previously, to wit: on the 15th day of December, A.D. 1876, at the City of Toronto, before C. D., Police Magistrate in and for the City of Toronto [*or* at the Township of York, in the County of York, before E. F. and G. H,, two of Her Majesty's Justices of the Peace for the County of York], duly convicted of having, on the 30th day of November, 1876, at the Village of Yorkville, in the County of York, unlawfuly sold liquor without the license therefor required by law [*or as the case may be*].

And further, that the said X. Y. was previously, to wit: on the 28th day of November, A.D. 1876, at the Township of Vaughan, in the County of York, before, &c., [*as in the preceding paragraph*], again duly convicted of having, on the 10th day of November, A.D. 1876, at the Township of Etobicoke, in the County of York, having a shop license, unlawfully allowed liquor to be consumed within a building which communicates by an entrance with his shop, by a person not usually a resident within the building of which such shop forms a part [*or as the case may be*].

And further, that the said X. Y. was previously, to wit: on the 30th day of October, A.D. 1876, at the Village of Newmarket, in the County of York, before, &c. (*see above*), again duly convicted of having, on the 25th day of September, A.D. 1876, at the Village of Yorkville, in the County of York (being in charge of the premises of O. P., a place where liquor was reputed to be sold), unlawfully failed to admit E. F., an officer demanding to enter in the execution of his duty.

And the Informant says the offence hereinbefore firstly charged against the said X. Y., in his fourth offence against '*The Liquor License Act.*'"

A. B.

Laid and signed before me the day and year, and at the place first above mentioned,
C. D.,
J. P.

SCHEDULE "F."

(*Section* 75.)

SUMMONS TO WITNESS.

ONTARIO,
County of York, } To J. K.,of the City of Toronto, in the County of York,
To Wit:

Whereas, information has been laid before me, C. D., one of Her Majesty's Justices of the Peace in and for the County of York, (*or* Police Magistrate for the City of Toronto,) that X. Y., being a druggist, on the 10th day of January, A.D. 187 , at the Township of Vaughan, in the County of York unlawfully did sell liquor for other than strictly medicinal purposes, and it has been made to appear to me that you are likely to give material evidence on behalf of the prosecutor in this behalf.

These are to require you, under pain of imprisonment in the Common Gaol, personally to be and appear on Tuesday, the sixteenth day of January, A.D. 187 , at ten o'clock in the forenoon, at the Town Hall, in the Village of Richmond Hill, before me or such Justice or Justices of the Peace as may then be there, to testify what you shall know in the premises [and also to bring with you and there and then to produce all and every invoices, day books, cash books or ledgers and receipts, promissory notes, or other security relating to the purchase or sale of liquor by the said X. Y., and all other books and papers, accounts, deeds, and other documents in your possession, custody or control, relating to any matter connected with the said prosecution].

Given under my hand and seal this 12th day of January, A.D. 187 , at the Village of Richmond Hill, in the County of York.

C. D ,
J. P. (L.S.)

SCHEDULE "G."

(*Section* 75.)

FORM OF CONVICTION FOR FIRST OFFENCE.

ONTARIO,
County of York,,
To-Wit:

BE IT REMEMBERED that on the sixth day of January, in the year of our Lord one thousand eight hundred and seventy-seven, at the City of Toronto, in the said County of York, X. Y. is convicted before me, C. D., Police Magistrate in and for the City of Toronto (*or* before us, E. F. and G H. two of Her Majesty's Justices of the Peace, in and for the said County), for that he the said X. Y., on the second day of January, in the year of our Lord one thousand eight hundred and seventy-seven, at the Township of York, in the said County, in his premises, being a place where liquor may be sold, unlawfully did sell liquor during the time prohibited by "*The Liquor License Act*" for the sale of the same, without any requisition for medicinal purposes as required by said Act, being produced by the vendee or his agent (*or as the case may be*), A. B. being the informant and I (*or* we) adjudge the said X. Y., for his said offence to forfeit and pay the sum of twenty dollars, to be paid and applied according to law, and also to pay to the said A. B. the sum of six dollars for his costs in this behalf, and if the said several sums be not paid forthwith, then* I (*or* we) order the said sums to be levied by distress and sale of the goods and chattels of the said X. Y., and in default of sufficient distress in that behalf* [*or where the issuing of a distress warrant would be ruinous to the defendant and his family, or it appears that he has no goods whereon to levy a distress, then instead of the words between the asterisks** say* " inasmuch as it has now been made to appear to me (*or* us) that the issuing of a warrant of distress in this behalf would be ruinous to the said X. Y. and his family," *or* " that the said X. Y. has no goods or chattels whereon to levy the said several sums by distress"], I (*or* we) adjudge the said X. Y. to be imprisoned in the Common Gaol for the County of York, at Toronto, in the said County, and there to be kept at hard labour for the space of *fifteen days*, unless the said sums and the costs and charges of conveying the said X. Y. to the said Common Gaol, shall be sooner paid.

Given under my hand and seal [*or* our hands and seals] the day and year first above mentioned, at the City of Toronto, in the County aforesaid.

C. D., (L.S.)
Police Magistrate,
or E.F.
J. P. (L.S.)
G.H.
J. P. (L. S.)

SCHEDULE " H."

(Section 75.)

FORM OF CONVICTION FOR A THIRD OFFENCE.

ONTARIO, County of York, To wit: } BE IT REMEMBERED that on the twenty-second day of January, in the year of our Lord one thousand eight hundred and seventy-seven, in the City of Toronto, in the said County, X. Y. is convicted before the undersigned C. D., Police Magistrate in and for the City of Toronto, in the said County, [*or* C. D. and E. F., two of Her Majesty's Justices of the Peace in and for the said County], for that he, the said X. Y., on the thirtieth day of December, in the year of our Lord one thousand eight hundred and seventy-six, at the City of Toronto [*or* Township of Scarboro], in said County (*as the case may be*), having violated a provision of " *The Liquor License Act*," unlawfully did attempt to settle the offence with A. B., with the view of having the complaint made in respect thereof dismissed. And it appearing to me [*or* us] that the said X. Y. was previously, to wit: on the 15th day of December, A.D. 1876, at the City of Toronto, before, &c., duly convicted of having, on the 30th day of November, A.D. 1876, at the Village of Yorkville, unlawfully sold liquor without the license therefor by law required. And it also appearing to me [*or* us] that the said X. Y. was previously, to wit, on the 28th day of November,

A.D. 1876, at the Township of Vaughan, before, &c., (*see above*) again duly convicted of having, on the 2nd day of November, A.D. 1876, at the Village of Markham (being the keeper of a tavern, situate in the said Village of Markham), unlawfully allowed gambling in his said tavern (*or as the case may be.*)

I [*or* we], adjudged the offence of said X. Y. hereinbefore firstly mentioned, to be his third offence against "*The Liquor License Act*," (A. B. being the informant) and I [*or* we], adjudged the said X. Y. for his said third offence to be imprisoned in the Common Gaol of the said County of York, at Toronto, in the said County of York, there to be kept at hard labour for the space of three calendar months (*or as the case may be*).

Given under my hand and seal [*or* our hands and seals] the day and year first above mentioned, at Toronto, in the County of York.

C. D. (L.S.)
or C. D. (L.S.)
E. F. (L.S.)

SCHEDULE "I."

(*Section* 75.)

WARRANT OF COMMITMENT FOR FIRST OFFENCE WHERE A PENALTY IS IMPOSED.

ONTARIO. County of York, To Wit: } To ALL or any of the Constables and other Peace Officers in the said County of York, and to the Keeper of the Common Gaol of the said County at Toronto, in the County of York.

Whereas, X. Y., late of the City of Toronto, in the said County, was on this day convicted before the undersigned, C. D., Police Magistrate in and for the City of Toronto [*or* C. D. and E. F., two of Her Majesty's Justices of the Peace in and for the City of Toronto *or* County of York, *as the case may be*], for that he, the said X. Y., on at unlawfully did sell liquor without the license therefor by law required (*state offence as in the conviction*), (A. B. being the informant), and it was thereby adjudged that the said X. Y., for his said offence, should forfeit and pay the sum of (*as in conviction*), and should pay to the said A. B. the sum of for his costs in that behalf.

And it was thereby further adjudged that if the said several sums should not be paid forthwith, the said X. Y. should be imprisoned in the Common Gaol of the said County at Toronto, in the said County of York, there to be kept at hard labour for the space of , unless the said several sums and the costs and charges of conveying the said X. Y. to the said Common Gaol should be sooner paid.

And whereas the said X. Y. has not paid the said several sums, or any part thereof, although the time for payment thereof has elapsed.

[*If a distress warrant issued and was returned, no goods, or not sufficient goods, say,* "And whereas, afterwards on the 15th day of January, A.D. 1877, I, the said Police Magistrate (*or* we, the said Justices), issued a warrant to the said Constables or Police Officers, or any of them, to levy the said several sums of and by distress and sale of the goods and chattels of the said X. Y.;

"And whereas it appears to me (*or* us) as well, by the return of the said warrant of distress by the constable who had the execution of the same as otherwise, that the said Constable has made diligent search for the goods and chattels of the said X. Y., but that no sufficient distress whereon to levy the said sums could be found."]

[*Or where the issuing of a distress warrant would be ruinous to the defendant and his family, or if it appears that he has no goods whereon to levy a distress, then, instead of the foregoing recitals of the issue and return of the distress warrant, &c., say:*

"And whereas it has been made to appear to me (*or* us), that the issuing of a warrant by distress in this behalf would be ruinous to the said X. Y. and his family," *or* "that the said X. Y. has no goods or chattels whereon to levy the said sums by distress" *as the case may be*].

These are therefore to command you, the said Constables or Peace Officers, or any one of you, to take the said X. Y., and him safely convey to the Common Gaol aforesaid, at Toronto, in the County of York, and there deliver him to the said Keeper thereof, together with this precept.

And I (*or* we) do hereby command you the said Keeper of the said Common Gaol to receive the said X. Y. into your custody in the said Common Gaol, there to imprison him and keep him at hard labour for the space of , unless the said several sums and all the costs and charges of the said distress, amounting to the sum of , and of the commitment and conveying of the said X. Y. to the said Common Gaol, amounting to the further sum of shall be sooner paid unto you the said Keeper, and for so doing this shall be your sufficient warrant.

Given under my hand and seal (*or* our hands and seals), this day of A.D. 187 , at Toronto, in the County of York.

C. D. (L. S.)
or C. D. (L. S.)
E. F. (L. S.)

SCHEDULE "J."

(*Section* 75.)

WARRANT OF COMMITMENT FOR SECOND (*or* THIRD) OFFENCE, WHERE PUNISHMENT IS BY IMPRISONMENT ONLY.

ONTARIO, County of York, To Wit: County of York. } TO ALL or any of the Constables and other Peace Officers in the said County of York, and to the Keeper of the Common Gaol of the said County, at Toronto, in the County of York.

Whereas X. Y., late of the of in the said County, was on this day convicted before the undersigned C. D. &c., (*or* C. D. and E. F., &c., *as in preceding form*), for that he, the said X. Y., on at (*state offence with previous convictions as set forth in the conviction for the second or third offence, or as the case may be, and then proceed thus*): "And it was thereby adjudged that the offence of the said X. Y., hereinbefore firstly mentioned, was his second (*or* third) offence against "*The Liquor License Act*" (A. B. being the informant). And it was thereby further adjudged that the said X. Y., for his second (*or* third) offence, should be imprisoned in the Common Gaol of the said County of York, at Toronto, in the said County of York, and there to be kept at hard labour for the space of three calendar months.

These are therefore to command you the said Constables, or any one of you, to take the said X. Y., and him safely convey to the said Common Gaol at Toronto, aforesaid, and there deliver him to the Keeper thereof, with this precept. And I (*or* we) do hereby command you, the said Keeper of the said Common Gaol to receive the said X. Y. into your custody in the said Common Gaol, there to imprison him and to keep him at hard labour for the space of three calendar months.

Given under my hand and seal (*or* our hands and seals), this day of A.D. 187 , at Toronto, in the said County of York.

C. D. (L. S.)
or C. D. (L. S.)
E. F. (L. S.)

INDEX.

A.

B.

D.

F.

L.

M.

PAGE.

N.

O.

S.

PAGE.

U.

V.

W.